———————— HARRY HUNTT RANSOM ————————

HARRY HUNTT RANSOM

Intellect in Motion

ALAN GRIBBEN

UNIVERSITY OF TEXAS PRESS
Austin

Requests for permission to reproduce material from this
work should be sent to:
Permissions
University of Texas Press
P.O. Box 7819
Austin, TX 78713-7819
www.utexas.edu/utpress/about/bpermission.html

⊗ The paper used in this book meets the minimum requirements of
ANSI/NISO Z39.48-1992 (R1997) (Permanence of Paper).

Library of Congress Cataloging-in-Publication Data

Gribben, Alan.
Harry Huntt Ransom : intellect in motion / Alan Gribben. — 1st ed.
p. cm.
Includes index.
ISBN 978-0-292-71704-6 (cloth : alk. paper)
1. Ransom, Harry Huntt, 1908– 2. Educators—United States—Biography.
3. University of Texas at Austin—Biography. 4. Harry Ransom Humanities
Research Center—History. I. Title.
LA2317.R265G75 2008
378.1'11—dc22
[B]
2008006949

For
Dr. Hans Mark
who wanted this story told
Dr. William S. Livingston
who saw it through
and the late Burton E. Grossman
Harry's friend

CONTENTS

PREFACE

Biographies, much like universities, invariably become collective enterprises, the products of many contributors. In this instance such collaboration was essential, for the biographer had glimpsed his subject only once—on an autumn morning in 1974 when the retired chancellor, walking in his carefully measured gait as he exited the Humanities Research Center, was reverently pointed out to a newly hired assistant professor of English. Thus the writer has substantially taken his impressions of his subject from information, memories, and anecdotes provided by individuals who knew Harry Huntt Ransom personally. Fortunately, too, Ransom set down vivid recollections from his early days in a sheaf of helpful notes, and he also left behind hundreds of speeches, essays, and interviews defining his views on the academy. Of equal importance, the University of Texas at Austin kept for official purposes and for posterity nearly all of his voluminous correspondence, clippings, and memoranda, stored on twenty feet of shelf space and in fifty-four file-cabinet drawers in the Center for American History. Another campus archive held additional records pertaining to his enhancement of the library collections. It became possible, then, owing to the preservation of these pieces of Ransom's story and the cooperative spirit of his acquaintances, to reconstruct a mosaic of his life and times.

In compiling the materials for *Harry Huntt Ransom: Intellect in Motion,* I contacted scores of University of Texas administrators, faculty, and alumni; approached numerous librarians; and turned up dozens of other sources by announcing my undertaking in several venues of publicity. Within a few weeks of notifying the UT campus in 1989 about my intention to embark on a biography about Ransom, I was repeatedly stopped in hallways and on sidewalks by people volunteering ideas, names, and encouragement; those familiar with Ransom sketched for me his distinguishing habits and character traits, which I wove through the following narrative. Clearly I benefited from the privilege of having a charismatic subject, someone whose name still retained enough resonance that former and present members of the academic community proved eager to assist his biographer. Furthermore, this biography possessed advantages that no subsequent book can repeat. Harry Ransom's widow, Hazel, gradually overcame her aversion to public disclosures sufficiently to answer many questions in a series of prearranged interviews. Much was established before her death in 1993. Then by coincidence a book dealer whom I met in Galveston donated several formerly lost love letters written by Hazel to Harry during the postwar years. Graves W. Landrum, as well, was an invaluable resource as a witness to much of what transpired during Ransom's administration and as a candid respondent to my inquiries. He died in 1995. Other members of Ransom's generation also passed from the scene during the eighteen-year gestation of this book, but not before I had recorded their versions of events in my interview notes.

The fundamental story I found to tell was exemplified by Professor Emeritus Carl J. Eckhardt (1901–1995), longtime Director of the Physical Plant, who arrived at the University of Texas in 1920 to teach mechanical engineering and served under fifteen university presidents. Of all these, Harry Ransom was his favorite. Eckhardt allowed me to examine the affectionate letters, several handwritten, that he received from Dr. Ransom over the years. He spoke of Harry Ransom's "very rare" qualities and of his way of "constantly giving of himself for the good of others." To Eckhardt, "he inspired by example the search for goals not ordinarily attainable." Another essential part of the Harry Ransom story was contained in the hundreds of letters that deluged Dr. Ransom's widow, Hazel, in 1976 when the state, national, and international press carried word of his death. These letters of condolence spelled out Dr. Ransom's achievements and kindnesses more evocatively than the newspaper and magazine editorials that lamented his demise.

His solicitous presence still hovers over, and sanctifies, celebratory events at the Main Campus. In a time when it is increasingly customary for faculty and staff members of public universities never to have spoken in person with upper-echelon administrators, nearly everyone on the Austin campus, whatever their station, seemingly had known and conversed with Harry Ransom and thus felt that he or she was in touch with the central administration and its goals. It can be said that Ransom managed to instill a team concept in the workplace before that managerial idea became conventionally accepted in the United States. Although all academic institutions experience the dynamics of crests and troughs in morale, for several crucial decades Harry Ransom fostered a climate that encouraged people to participate excitedly in translating abstract ideals into tangible results and united the university community—students, staff, faculty, administrators, regents, and alumni alike—in sharing a dream of what the University of Texas could be.

Writing about Harry Ransom's life ultimately gave this biographer an altered perspective on the evolution of the American university. It is profoundly illuminating to contemplate how a university is built, physically as well as academically. Such research teaches one not to take for granted any single feature on a modern-day campus. During the course of this project, time and again I realized how easy it is to forget that every building, monument, library, fountain, garden, award, department, program, institute—indeed, every appointment to the faculty, staff, or administration—hardly materializes accidentally. Those administrators, professors, and staff members who teach or work at the University of Texas are in effect custodians of a fragile and costly enterprise that thousands of dedicated people across the state and nation have labored and sacrificed to construct. Perhaps through a biography like *Harry Huntt Ransom: Intellect in Motion,* readers can appreciate the phenomenal changes the University of Texas underwent after Harry Ransom joined the English faculty in 1935. Surveying Dr. Ransom's academic career as student, instructor, professor, associate graduate dean, college dean, vice president, provost, president, chancellor, and chancellor emeritus, one marvels at his meteoric ascent through these position titles and the relative scarcity of detractors he left in his wake. Boldness in leadership and a rapid climb to lofty posts in a complex, sharply competitive organization would typically engender a lasting contingent of adversaries. Yet this biographer encountered almost unanimous praise for Ransom's personal qualities, while locating only a few critics of his record of achievement (and even these limited their objections to aspects of his management style).

Of course to the international community Harry Huntt Ransom was known primarily for another achievement altogether—his astounding feat of building, within a mere quarter of a century, a world-class library collection and two notable buildings in which to house it. New York publisher Alfred Knopf summed up this miracle succinctly in remarking that Ransom's archives "put Texas on the cultural map."[1] By the time that Ransom passed from the scene, the reputation of the rare books and manuscripts at the University of Texas rivaled or surpassed those of many libraries in Europe and the northeastern United States that had enjoyed a head start of literally centuries. Ransom had shrewdly challenged the pride of his fellow Texans by pointing out the progress made by other states' libraries, and he had likewise shamed them by showing that Texas students had to leave their home state for advanced study of literary and historical materials.

Undoubtedly Ransom's greatest breakthrough in this regard was his recognition that it would be in the area of twentieth-century works where his institution had the best chance of competing for yet-unclaimed manuscripts and books. He also pioneered the practice of going after all the literary artifacts of living (or recently deceased) authors. Working notes, manuscript drafts, proof sheets, corrected galleys, first editions, correspondence, personal libraries, even writers' desks and chairs—everything and anything connected with literary production (and eventually with photographic and cinematic endeavors as well) found their way into his chaotic receiving areas in the Main Building. "The Great Acquisitor," as Ransom came to be called in some circles, was often credited (and just as often blamed) for giving Modernist materials a soaring price value. Ransom's reliance on designated New York booksellers as his auction and purchasing agents was especially resented. Within three decades after his death, however, the Harry Ransom Humanities Research Center ranked as one of the most important collections in the United States, with its holdings, which had been augmented by subsequent directors, valued at something like a billion dollars. The drawing power of this scholar-magnet has become virtually incalculable in terms of prestige for the university, city, and state in which it is located. Ransom's foresight in amassing this huge collection proved to be genuinely visionary.

Nowadays there arises inevitably the issue of the biographer's point of view—preconceived versus inductive—in collecting, quoting, and construing multiple, frequently divergent statements. "Some biographers know before they begin just what they want to say and how to say it," observed Herbert Marder. Other writers progress "from phase to phase, as if through a labyrinth, guessing at meanings, stripping away concealments . . . , hoping without any assurance of success to arrive at 'the thing itself.'"[2] I conscientiously followed the latter process, prepared to honor what was original and commendable about Harry Ransom's career, but willing as well to register his trials and shortcomings. What has emerged qualifies as neither hagiography nor iconoclasm. Still, many literary theorists currently dispute the possibility of producing anything approaching an objective biography, regarding all works of history and biography as the prejudiced reflections of the writers' personal values and social conditioning and deconstructing the distinctions between the genres of fictional literature and biography. But I would still like to think, for my part, that *Harry Huntt Ransom: Intellect in Motion* is as straightforward and basically accurate as Ransom, who venerated reliable facts and praised direct forms of expression, might have wanted it to be.

His years of administration were not without dilemmas and conflict. This book recounts Ransom's patience with feisty librarian Fannie Ratchford, the challenge of the radical student protest movement of the 1960s, his reluctant suspensions of the Texas Student League for Responsible Sexual Freedom and the Students for a Democratic Society, his affectionate but occasionally tense relationship with the Chairman of the Board of Regents, Frank C. Erwin, Jr., and the abruptness of his resignation from the chancellorship in 1970. These and other difficulties that he confronted, along with sunnier periods of harmony and commendation, assume their places in this story. The occasional criticisms of his lapses in judgment and execution are also taken into account.

During Ransom's life and since his death, university officers and others have honored him with degrees, resolutions, plaques, paintings, and sculptures. There was a memorial reading of his poetry. Hazel H. Ransom edited several volumes of his writings. Only a full-length biography has been lacking in the commemorations of his life. Such a book is vital, not only to his memory, but also, because of the standards he set for students, teachers, and administrators, in order to calibrate our contemporary scale of academic values. Ransom's was a life utterly dedicated to higher education; his early years were merely a preparation for this career, World War II an obligatory interruption. At all times he conveyed a passionate, contagious enthusiasm for university life and the liberal arts; everywhere he impressed people with the intensity and sincerity of his commitment. Even Ransom's shortcomings have lessons to offer: his tendency to delegate assignments without supplementary procedures and immediate review, for instance, exhilarated many individuals even if it perplexed a few others. His brilliant reputation in the world of rare book and manuscript libraries added luster to his school's name but overshadowed his recognition as a gifted administrator. Ransom's leadership helped his university and indeed the entire Southern and Southwestern regions adapt to a new era of racial integration, decentralized instruction, and the ascendancy of science, and he revised the concepts of what a modern university could promise and accomplish. While doing so, he managed to turn his background in and predilection for the humanities into an advantage rather than a liability in his relationships with administrators, regents, alumni, legislators, and taxpayers. In truth, he ranks among such distinguished university presidents and chancellors as Robert Gordon Sproul and Clark Kerr of the University of California at Berkeley, James Perkins of Cornell University, Herman B Wells of Indiana University, Nathan Pusey of Harvard University, A. Bartlett Giamatti of Yale University, Franklin Murphy of the University of California at Los Angeles, and Robert M. Hutchins of the University of Chicago. Harry Huntt Ransom of the University of Texas, one of the most influential figures in American higher education in the twentieth century, succeeded in enlarging and enhancing to the point of greatness a state-supported university system and also established one of the world's premier libraries in a region formerly known for its ranches and oilfields rather than its academic resources.

Imaginative and energetic, Ransom seems aptly characterized by one of the phrases he himself coined to describe the dawning educational age he envisioned: "Intellect in motion."[3]

Alan Gribben

ACKNOWLEDGMENTS

Dr. Hans Mark, former secretary of the U.S. Air Force, deputy administrator of NASA, chancellor of the University of Texas System, and now holder of the John J. McKetta Centennial Energy Chair in Engineering at the University of Texas at Austin, conceived, facilitated, encouraged, critiqued, and publicized this work about Harry Huntt Ransom during the nearly two decades of its gradual progress. Dr. Mark's firm conviction that an institution of higher learning as illustrious as the University of Texas should possess a full-length biography of its best-known and most influential administrator never wavered.

Fortunately, the Chancellor's Council of the University of Texas System made funds available to enable the author to step away from his teaching duties so the project could make definite headway during its crucial early phase. The late Burton E. Grossman was particularly generous, and a book of this scope simply could not have been launched without his benefaction.

Irene Wong proved her editorial skills again and again when she helped the author whittle down a bulky 885-page manuscript that had valiantly endeavored to tell, within a biography of Harry Ransom, virtually the entire story of the University of Texas and an unabridged history of its libraries. No scholar could gain the blessing of a more skilled, if merciless, editor or a more devoted friend and spouse.

UT Senior Vice President William S. Livingston stepped forward in 2004, when the project had stalled for more than half a decade, gave the book a thorough reading, helped arrange for additional interviews with people who had known the Ransoms, and exhorted the author to push his revisions toward publication. Dr. Livingston also suggested the University of Texas Press as possessing the most logical imprimatur for this biography and helped the author make revisions that met the press's expectations. Dr. Livingston's improvements and advice made it possible for the manuscript to become a book.

Dr. Margaret Berry, the respected historian of the University of Texas, always shared her faith that the task was both worthwhile and possible; her opinions vastly upgraded several drafts of the manuscript. In addition, she assisted in the selection and identification of photographs for this book. Dr. Peter Flawn, himself a former president of the UT Austin campus who built impressively upon Ransom's achievements, made useful comments. Dr. Miguel Gonzalez-Gerth had suggestions about tone and style and furnished crucial supplementary materials. Henrietta Jacobsen, executive assistant to the chancellor since 1954, added countless details to the narrative.

Monty Jones, associate director of the Office of Public Affairs for the UT System, took on the daunting task of reading and digesting numerous boxes of materials in the Center for American History in 1989; his pioneering labors there enabled the author to outline an approach to that massive assemblage of Ransom-related papers. He also accompanied the author on two research trips.

The making of this book was so complex and time consuming that the author feels indebted to individuals who prompted, cajoled, and enthused at key junctures. Ernestine Wheelock, former editor of *Texas Alcalde,* sent relevant leads and cheered on the author. The late Dr. Clarence L. Cline was an infallible source of information about the English Department and the university; without his advice, this book would lack much of its authority. Amy Jo Long, former director of the UT News and Information Service (now the Office of Public Affairs), read selected chapters of the manuscript, sketched Ransom's habits, and provided files related to Ransom's administration. The late Graves Landrum, Ransom's longtime administrative associate, contributed numerous hours and candid insights in the early stages of the project. Mr. Landrum's illuminations were vital.

A number of people on the University of Texas at Austin campus took a special interest in this project; among these generous supporters were former UT President and Chancellor William H. Cunningham, Dr. Larry Carver, the late Dr. Kurth Sprague, the late Dr. F. Warren Roberts and his wife, Patricia, the late Dr. W. Rea Keast, Dr. David Farmer, Dr. Dave Oliphant, John Kirkpatrick, Harold Billings, the late Kathleen Gee, Ralph Elder, and of course Dr. Thomas F. Staley, Director of the Harry Ransom Humanities Research Center.

Indispensable services came from Paul J. Youngdale, Becky Boyer, Martha A. Boyd, Lynda B. Hester, Joyce G. Pole, Dorothy Rattey, Robert Shanley, Jean Townsend, Dana Hendrix Barnekow, Will Howard, Kevin B. Mac Donnell, Doug Weiskopf, Margaret Blackstone, Dr. Paula Marks, and Frieda J. Speck.

I am grateful to Joanna Hitchcock, Director, and the Faculty Advisory Committee of the University of Texas Press for recognizing the value of a biography about Harry Ransom, and for the guidance of the staff at the Press and Dr. Marianne Tatom Letts, Copyeditor.

For information about the Ransom family's association with Trinity Episcopal Church in Galveston, I am indebted to the Reverend John C. Donovan, Rector Emeritus.

During a visit to Sewanee, Tennessee, and the University of the South, I benefited from the hospitality of Tom G. Watson, Vice President for University Relations; Robert M. Ayres, Jr., Vice Chancellor and President Emeritus; the late Elizabeth N. Chitty, Associate Historiographer; the late Arthur Ben Chitty, Historiographer; Anne Armour, Archivist; and David Dearley, Director of the Jessie Ball duPont Library.

The multitude of respondents who provided information about Harry Ransom are only partially acknowledged in the endnotes documenting this biography. A great many other people were originally recognized and quoted somewhere in the seven earlier drafts of the book manuscript; their names lamentably fell victim to the necessity of paring down the narrative to a publishable size. Their aid is nonetheless appreciated, since the anecdotes that they related gave the author confidence in his interpretations of events and provided a larger structure within which he could frame the biography.

At the institution where I currently teach, Auburn University at Montgomery, I owe gratitude to Chancellor John G. Veres III, Vice Chancellor Janet S. Warren, former Chancellor Guinevera A. Nance, former School of Liberal Arts Dean Marion Michael, and administrative associate Mollie Folmar for lightening my workload.

Finally, to the many unspecified friends and well-wishers of Harry and Hazel Ransom and of the University of Texas who contacted or assisted me: thank you, most sincerely, for every favor.

LIST OF ABBREVIATIONS

CAH	*Center for American History, University of Texas at Austin*
HHR	*Harry Huntt Ransom*
HRC	*Humanities Research Center (before it was renamed in 1983)*
HRHRC	*Harry Ransom Humanities Research Center, University of Texas at Austin*
LBJ Library	*Lyndon Baines Johnson Library, University of Texas at Austin*
MS	*Manuscript*
PH	*Photocopy*
RBC	*Rare Books Collection (predecessor of the Humanities Research Center; renamed in 1958)*
TS	*Typescript*
USouth	*Archives and Special Collections, Jessie du Pont Library, University of the South, Sewanee, Tennessee*
UT	*University of Texas*

ABOUT THE AUTHOR

D̲r. Alan Gribben taught on the English faculty of the University of Texas at Austin from 1974 until 1991. Since then he has served as head of the Department of English and Philosophy at Auburn University at Montgomery, where he received a Distinguished Research Professorship in 1998, the Alumni Faculty Service Award in 2005, and the Dr. Guinevera A. Nance Alumni Professorship in 2006. Dr. Gribben has been named to the editorial boards of *American Literary Realism, Libraries & Culture,* and other journals. He is the author of a two-volume reference work, *Mark Twain's Library: A Reconstruction,* and has also edited and written other books and articles about Mark Twain's life, image, and reading. Dr. Gribben earned his doctorate degree from the University of California at Berkeley.

HARRY HUNTT RANSOM

ONE

BEGINNINGS

During the transforming decade of the 1960s, an energetic humanist named Harry Huntt Ransom assumed the highest administrative posts at the University of Texas at Austin, for a time even holding the offices of president and chancellor simultaneously. Improbable as this English professor's rise to such powerful positions had seemed, after he was profiled by numerous journalists as innovative and newsworthy, Ransom and his endeavors became known far beyond the broad borders of Texas. He led his state-supported institution onto the national scene as a consequential force in many areas of academe, including the sciences, engineering, liberal arts, political science, business, medicine, education, communication, and athletics. Ransom also took advantage of the university's oil-fueled surge of funds to establish and supervise a massive rare books and manuscript library that earned international distinction. His direct influence ended in 1970 when he stepped down abruptly from the chancellorship, but the momentum he had generated would prove lasting. His shaping guidance can still be detected in the vast and prominent institution with which his name was once synonymous.

Although Harry Huntt Ransom was born in Texas, spent nearly all his life in the state, and is listed among quintessential Texas figures, his family had deeper ties to North Carolina, and his personal affinities and friendships would frequently turn his eyes and thoughts toward his forebears' native state. Before settling in North Carolina, however, the paternal side of his family had first been prominent in Virginia. The Ransoms were descended in North America from one Peter Ransom (1615–1663), who came to Virginia as a landowner in 1652. James Ransom (1725–1785), an early settler in Gloucester County, Virginia, participated in the American Revolution, and his son James, born in 1744, served as a delegate in 1775 to a convention of the provincial assembly in New Bern, North Carolina. Robert Ransom, Sr. (1800–1865), was too elderly to take part in the American Civil

War, but his sons Robert Ransom, Jr. (1828–1892), and Matthew Whitaker Ransom (1826–1904), distinguished themselves in service for the Confederacy. Robert gained the rank of Major General, and Matthew, an attorney after the war, served as a United States Senator from 1872 until 1895 and was Minister to Mexico until 1897.[1]

Following the Civil War, Robert Ransom, Jr., who had married Mary E. Huntt in 1856, became a farmer and engineer in North Carolina.[2] A son was born to them in 1867. This first Harry Huntt Ransom spent much of his boyhood in and near Richmond, Virginia, and absorbed stories of the wartime exploits of his father and uncle. He attended private schools in Virginia and then enrolled as a sixteen-year-old freshman at Western Maryland College in Westminster, Maryland, for the 1883–1884 academic year. He left that school in 1886 before the spring term ended. A classmate named George S. Wills remembered him as "a brilliant student" but "erratic," partly because of a "lack of money."[3] Two years later Ransom graduated from the University of North Carolina at Chapel Hill with a degree in Greek. He then commenced an itinerant career as a teacher and school principal in North Carolina.

Despite the potentially helpful eminence of his relatives, Ransom elected to leave the region in 1891. His son would explain that the senior Ransom "came out to Texas to teach because the family was pretty well impoverished in North Carolina. . . . He was . . . a casualty of the post–Civil War period."[4] There was widespread migration from the American South to Texas during the 1890s. Perhaps Ransom had heard of the burgeoning prosperity and civic beauty of Galveston Island on the Texas coast. Galveston's population of more than 29,000 people, though being overtaken by nearby Houston, was still surpassed in size only by Dallas and San Antonio. A cosmopolitan mixture of seaport bustle and refined languor, it was a city of gas-lighted parks, broad esplanades, and attractive squares whose financial district, the Strand, was almost as important to the state of Texas as the cotton exported from the Galveston wharves.

For two years, beginning in 1891, the senior Harry Huntt Ransom taught grades seven and eight at the public Goliad School. In 1893 he was promoted to a vice principalship at the Bath Avenue School, but was obliged to add to his earnings by teaching at a night school for boys. During this period he married, in his mid-twenties, a woman named Annie Martin, about whom little is recorded. According to family tradition she was born in Alabama, her ancestry was aristocratic, and the wedding took place outside of Texas. The couple had a son, Robert Martin Ransom (born in 1895), and a daughter, Julia Clay Ransom (born in 1899).

On January 26, 1895, Ransom published a letter to the editor in the *Austin Statesman* exuding the self-confidence of a man who had adopted the state of Texas as his permanent home and felt qualified to address its legislature in the state capital's leading newspaper. Conceding that "we educators" are said to be "theoretical and encyclopedia laden, being devoid . . . of business-like propensities," he proceeded to argue on behalf of legislation enabling communities to issue bonds "for school purposes." He also advocated "local tax in towns and cities," because according to "the State Superintendent of Public Instruction the schools of our State have outgrown the State apportionment." The letter was signed, "Respectfully, Harry Huntt Ransom, Galveston, Texas."[5]

His financial situation improved somewhat in 1896, when he was selected as principal and teacher of Latin in the 5th District City High School. Then in 1898, at the age of thirty-one, he settled into a lengthy stint as principal of the new Ball High School, where he taught Greek, history, and political economy. One of Ransom's students from this period would provide an emphatic testimonial about his abilities many years later: "I had four years of Latin and four years of Greek" at Ball High School, wrote Mrs. H. E. Barnett, Jr. "He was a brilliant man, and I believe I learned more English from him than I did from my regular English teachers."[6]

But misfortune struck the family during the next decade, when Ransom's wife died (the date is unclear, but daughter Julia Clay was a young girl at the time). Few glimpses are available of the senior Ransom during those years, so a letter he wrote from Ball High School to James Stephen Hogg on August 12, 1904, is of interest. Hogg had been an effective anti-monopoly reformer who imposed regulations on insurance companies and railroads during his terms as state attorney general and governor in the preceding decades; later becoming an affluent attorney and investor, Hogg remained a potent force in the Democratic Party. Ransom predicted that "the time will come when the Texas Democracy will call on you again to lead it in the fight for reform of abuses as it did in the nineties." Indeed, "the blessings of our great state reforms are due to your wise influence and direction; and the people of Texas will forever hold you[r] name and memory in highest esteem and sacred reverence. . . . You are still the people's preference and the Cincinnatus of Texas Democracy."[7]

The public-spirited citizen who harbored these passionate political sentiments now found himself free to remarry. A Ransom family genealogy chart records his second marriage as occurring in 1905, though in the sometimes-unreliable *Thirteenth Census of the United States: 1910,* both Ransom and his new wife state that they had been married for only two years. Whatever the case, Ransom's bride was Marion Goodwin Cunningham, member of a pioneer Texas family; her father, North Carolina–born Harvey S. Cunningham, had been a merchant in Victoria, Texas. Her maternal grandfather, Sherman Goodwin (1814–1884), a noted physician, had moved to Victoria, Texas, from Burton, Ohio, in 1849. In 1951 Harry Huntt Ransom would extol his great-grandfather Goodwin as a pioneer representing "Texas at its enduring best" and quote Goodwin's observation that "to all who have nursed the dying sick it is clear that both transient and fatal illness can open understanding, sympathy, and self-knowledge."[8] The heritage of anecdotes about this physician ancestor, coupled with the medical-world experience of Ransom's mother—in combination with an awareness that his namesake on his father's side, Dr. Henry Huntt, had been a charter member of the Washington, D.C., Medical Association and a physician to seven U.S. Presidents[9]—would account for the younger Harry Huntt Ransom's early ambition "to grow up to be a doctor."[10] He also harbored a great admiration for Admiral Cary T. Grayson ("one of the heroes of my . . . youth"), the attending physician for President Woodrow Wilson.[11]

Marion Goodwin Cunningham, born in 1870, was three years younger than her husband. Educated at Hollins College in Roanoke, Virginia, she had served as a medical missionary (with administrative rather than nursing duties) in Louisville, Kentucky. Like Ransom, she had lost a first spouse. From her previous marriage to a Texas minister named Barron, she had one daughter, Jean Barron (erroneously listed in the 1910 census as Marian E. Barron), who had been born in 1892.

On November 22, 1908, this second marriage for both Ransoms produced its only child. A few weeks later the parents, devoutly Episcopalian, took the infant boy to the Trinity Episcopal Church, a Victorian Gothic Revival–style edifice decorated with a Louis Comfort Tiffany stained glass window and located at the intersection of two palm tree–lined streets. In the attached Eaton Chapel they christened their son Henry Huntt Ransom, a name gradually discarded in favor of "Harry."[12] In a photography session following the ceremony, the father held the baby beside the baptismal font. Afterward the couple returned to their home on Ball Avenue, also known as Avenue H.

Soon after Harry's birth, however, the Ransoms moved to a stick-styled residence on Broadway (or Avenue J) among close-ranked wood-frame edifices with large shutters and tall front stairs mounting to first floors that were six or eight feet above the street level. Galveston homes had taken these precautions since a calamitous hurricane on September 8, 1900, had inundated the bridges to the mainland, destroyed 3,000 homes, and killed 8,000 of the 38,000 citizens. Many years later the younger Harry Huntt Ransom would declare his intention someday "to complete a book-length narrative essay on the Flood, which . . . my father counted as the main adventure in his otherwise rather prosaic life."[13]

Here at 1803 Broadway the Ransom family was interviewed extensively for the 1910 census. The senior Ransom was "43 on last birthday." He owned his home, which had a mortgage. His wife was forty years old and was not employed. In addition to little "Henry Huntt Ransom" and his mother's daughter Jean, there was Julia C. Ransom, age ten, who "can read and write," and her brother Robert M. Ransom, age fifteen, "clerk in bank." The census also listed two African American servants: Mollie Hopes, age forty-five, single, who "cannot read or write," and a man named Hopes, first name omitted, thirty-six years old, a "barber in barbershop." He "*can* read and write." Young Harry's only recollection of Galveston would be a "sense of being held up to the light, a window with bright sunshine on the curtain."[14]

In 1912 the senior Ransom, yielding to the lure of a better job opportunity (Galveston's economy had been severely affected by the storm), moved to Houston, now a city of nearly 80,000, almost twice the size of Galveston. Already it had begun to benefit from the combination of pine and cypress timberlands, cotton, railroads, and (since 1904) oil production that would give it a bright economic future; in 1914 the completion of the Houston Ship Channel would overcome the city's remaining disadvantage of lying fifty miles up Buffalo Bayou. Finally a deepwater seaport, Houston would then double its population within a decade. There, in that booming coastal city, the senior Ransom spent four years teaching Greek, Latin, and other subjects at the large Houston Senior High School. He left that post in 1916 to head the Latin Department of the new, immense South End Junior High School, where he stayed for another year. Nearly half a century later, the younger Ransom would grant an interview in which he voiced impressions of his father during these years.

My first memory of my father is his running up and down the halls chanting one of the Homeric passages or another. He was a relatively small man, with fiery red hair and a temper that went with it. . . . He was . . . very much interested in . . . persons from other climes and other environments and other cultures. He was not the sort of pal-companion father but very affectionate and very attentive to my interests in ideas and language.[15]

FIGURE I.I
*Harry Huntt Ransom, Galveston, 1909. Born November 22, 1908, Harry Huntt
Ransom was christened "Henry" like his father. Both became known as "Harry."*
Harry Ransom Humanities Research Center, The University of Texas at Austin.

Soon after their move to Houston the Ransoms purchased a dark-brown
two-bedroom bungalow for $3,500 in a northern addition called Wood-
land Heights that was designed for upper-middle-class professional people.
The slight elevation of the area helped its drainage and prevented mosquito
infestations and outbreaks of the yellow fever that still plagued central

FIGURE I.2

*Ransom, "Goodbye to Galveston," 1912. After Ransom's father moved the family
from Galveston to Houston, he taught at Houston Senior High School. Ransom
retained one indistinct memory of his Galveston years: "Being held up to the light,
a window with bright sunshine on the curtain."* Harry Ransom Humanities
Research Center, The University of Texas at Austin.

Houston. Well-to-do people had erected mansion homes along a spacious esplanade designated as Heights Boulevard, but more modest homes like the Ransoms' were constructed on the streets intersecting those premier addresses. The Ransoms' lot was fifty by one hundred feet. Their living room had "built-in seats at the side, and is finished in the mission style. . . . The whole house is equipped with beautiful electric fixtures," promised an advertisement. A front and back porch added space to the one-story dwelling.[16] Little Harry found, "on first coming to 525 Woodland, the sense of the emptiness of the house," but he soon also knew "joy at discovering unused wooden blocks and chips left over from the construction." There were deed restrictions, of course, because Woodland Heights was intended only for white people. The residents had to do without paved streets until 1919. Bread deliveries were available, but people had to cross Bayou Bridge on a trolley to reach grocery stores nearer the downtown district. Inasmuch as Woodland Heights was at the edge of the city, some people kept cows in their yards, and the Ransoms adopted this rural custom themselves. "Our cow and how she got lost and was found," a grown-up Ransom would remind himself in jottings about these years.

Harry Ransom started his schooling at the Travis School Kindergarten, presided over by director Miss Madeline Darough and her assistant Miss Aileen Eads. The next year he began attending the adjacent two-story brick Travis School, whose principal was Frank M. Black. He later recalled the school's proximity to Bayou Bridge and remembered his favorite teacher at Travis—Miss Laura Taylor, "but the first one [whose name eluded him] was beautiful." He suffered a bout of measles and was "examined for tonsil[l]itis." School soon became his most vivid experience, with its spelling lessons ("knife and a fork and a bottle and a cork and that's the way you spell New York"), "the privilege of sharpening pencils," and "trips across the Bayou Bridge to the Licorice Shop after school."

Relatives came to visit, including his cousin Harvey from New Orleans and his uncle Seymour Ransom. Presumably his half-brother Robert, who had stayed behind in Galveston, rejoined the family occasionally. Half-sister Julia Clay now wore "middies," patterned after sailor uniforms, and Jean played the guitar. Harry retained a "vague memory of Jean's marriage to 'Brother George,'" and another "memory of Mother's crying at a letter from Jean." He remembered hearing of a man in the community who committed suicide, and of the burning of a nearby orphanage. He learned about a riot by black soldiers at their military camp in Houston; seventeen people were killed, and several of the rebellious soldiers were executed at Fort Sam Houston in San Antonio. Occasionally the family made excursions to the park and the zoo. In their yard his mother planted geraniums, ivy, red and yellow cannas, and sweet gum trees; everywhere in the neighborhood he saw crape myrtles, pomegranates, fig trees, and jasmine vines. Once he engaged in a territorial fistfight with some children who were cutting off "sucker" branches from the "sycamores on our side of the street." There was also "the misfortune at the shed, and a mark for life," he would recall. Young Harry had jumped from a loft onto a mound of hay that contained a pitchfork that pierced his foot, leaving a permanent scar.[17] Summer nights brought out legions of "fireflies." Among other diversions were "Dad's gifts: Tom Swift! Picture books." Also, "combing Mother's hair." He remembered the "street car to town" and "the girls killed by the train." The first funeral he ever attended, in the summer of 1917, "was a ghastly thing. Terrible lightning storm." More pleasantly, he joined in watermelon parties that made bearable the sultry Houston summers. Perhaps crucially, there was "Dad's reading" as well as (cryptically) "Dad's stroke."

And then, with the advent of the World War, the family was on the move again: Washington, D.C., and Valley Lee, Maryland, in the autumn of 1917, partly to see Jean and her husband, George Hurlbut. "I was in the third grade this year. I remember nothing of what we studied except *words*—spelling lists which contained words which would appall my college freshmen today," he later remarked. "I was interested in books and got several for Christmas. I was dissatisfied with them, but I don't remember why." However, he did remember "the effect of war—young men enlisting." The Hurlbut family strained the patience of nine-year-old Harry, who would harbor memories of "my hatred of Mr. Hur[l]but and fear of George. Consciousness that things are wrong." With contempt, he endured "'Brother George' (the ass) teaching me 'how to run.'"

When Harry Ransom senior obtained, through a friend, a federal governmental appointment to oversee improvements in educational programs on a Native American reservation, the Ransoms abruptly moved to Park Hill, Oklahoma. There, ten-year-old Harry would witness an incident in which "the Indian boy dies from eating too many cucumbers; the terrible funeral" and the games that included "Indian baseball. The Cherokee vs. Choctaw." Obscure notes he made later referred to "the rebellion against Dad: the hidden gun" as well as "the drive to the school" and "the 'government' men." There were new fears in this raw land: "The terror at lightning," "the trip to Tallequah," "the snake," "'storm cellar.'" The aggregate experience resembled for young Harry, he would subsequently say, that of being suddenly transplanted into a desert. During all of the winter, spring, and summer of 1918, according to notes he set down as an adult, "I learned no

Cherokee; I must not have come very close to the boys in the school." On the other hand, "this spring war became very real to me. Since our arrival, the whole talk had been 'government.' Battles were reported and discussed daily." Other types of knowledge were intruding, as well. At the age of ten he had an "awareness of sex for [the] first time in spring of 1918—i.e. in any real sense." And, sadly, "by the age of ten I had still not become conscious at first hand of *any* great literature, although I was a 'bright' student."

But this lament applied only to his formal school; many years later he described the advantages his father's personal library collection had afforded him:

> For a relatively poverty-stricken teacher in those days, he had a large library. He was a book collector in what . . . was for the family a hideously extravagant arrangement. My half brothers [*sic*] and half sisters were nearly grown when I became aware of books at all, so that the books around me were my father's books and their books. My father had no prissy or pedagogical notions about reading, he simply thought it would be a good idea for me to read things like translations of the *Iliad* because it was an exciting story, not because it was a classic. So I opened my eyes on books which I didn't understand, I'm sure, fairly early. . . . I learned to read long before I started school.[18]

Harry's mother kept a note that he wrote during this period, laboriously scrawled on ruled tablet paper: "Dear Daddy / I give you these suspenders to hold up your pants. You may run you may dance but these suspenders will hold till they are old, old, old. / With lots of love and good wishes / From Harry / To his Daddy / Merry Xmas."[19]

Then, just as restlessly, his father moved again—this time back to Houston. The senior Ransom taught school as before, but he was unable to find the kind of position he wanted, and his health had begun to decline. Domestic forces were close to dividing Harry's parents, even as cataclysmic world events tore at distant nations.

TWO

TEXAS, TENNESSEE, TRAVELS

During the last year of World War I, young Harry Ransom, back in Houston, saw much to remind him that battles still raged overseas. Allen School, where he was attending fourth grade, had a truck-garden to furnish increasingly scarce produce, and his schoolmates helped with collection drives to assemble balls of lead and tin foil. Soldiers walked about the streets of his neighborhood carrying swagger sticks. He went to see a showing of Charlie Chaplin's parody of trench warfare, *Shoulder Arms*. War songs were in the air that year, including the humorous "K-K-K-Katy," known as "The Stammering Song," with a line that he would always recall as "Katie—beautiful Katy."[1] He observed a German military helmet being displayed by its proud new possessor. The patriotic fervor of the time inspired him to an early venture in public speaking; he delivered a carefully rehearsed speech on behalf of the Red Cross at a civic function. A startling reminder of wartime activity occurred close at hand when a small training aircraft from Ellington Field crash-landed and struck a portion of Mrs. McPhillips's rooming house, where the Ransoms were living.

To Harry, the McPhillips's boardinghouse had considerable interest. Mrs. McPhillips had a daughter, and there were one or two children among the boarders, along with several teachers. The landlady kept rabbits in a pen in the backyard, and Harry often earned ten cents by helping her with chores. A repeated sight outside his house—a terribly "crippled" boy riding a little car—would haunt his dreams "for years." Harry, by contrast, finally acquired his own bicycle. In the summer of 1919, the Ransoms decamped to the Shermans' place—"a helluva neighborhood" marked by garages and highways for the proliferating automobiles.

That summer was Harry's last residence in Houston. His life was now changed by an event for which no one subsequently had a full explanation. In the fall of 1919, the elder Ransom moved to Galena, Maryland, and

FIGURE 2.1
Harry Ransom, fourth grade, Houston. Young Ransom remembered his elementary school years in Texas with fondness. Harry Ransom Humanities Research Center, The University of Texas at Austin.

Marion Ransom and young Harry, following a visit to Julia Clay Ransom and other relatives and friends in New Orleans, left for Sewanee, Tennessee. A year later, the senior Ransom relocated to Cambridge, Maryland, where he became the principal of Cambridge High School. Ransom family lore made him the victim of a progressively debilitating nervous disease.[2]

FIGURE 2.2

Harry Huntt Ransom, Sr., 1918 (?). In 1919, Harry Huntt Ransom, Sr., separated from his family and went to Cambridge, Maryland, where he became principal of Cambridge High School; young Ransom and his mother relocated to Sewanee, Tennessee. Nearly all contact between the parents appears to have ended at this time. Harry Ransom Humanities Research Center, The University of Texas at Austin.

Whether this separation was occasioned entirely by the father's health or not, Marion Ransom presumably had her son's future foremost in mind when she moved to Sewanee. Site of the University of the South, a prominent Episcopal college and seminary, Sewanee simultaneously beckoned to her deep religious concerns and her growing resolve that young Harry should have a better-than-average education. Harry remembered the train ride from Chattanooga and the sight of his first mountains. After a steep, 2,000-foot train ride up to the Sewanee station on the Cumberland Plateau, Harry and his mother were met by a Mr. Phillips, driving a hack. The Ransoms "stayed at the old Green place— . . . really Southern," and later moved into Palmetto Hall, a large frame building in which faculty families and students resided. Soon the Ransoms were taking their first walks through tiny Sewanee. Here Harry found a civic life vastly more condensed than that of sprawling Houston, and his eyes took in the University Supply Store, Riley's Stable, Brooks's Emporium, Ruef's Meat Market, the town laundry, and a small area of homes where the black residents congregated.[3]

Bucolic Sewanee, perched amid fragrant forests and noticeably cooler than near-sea-level Houston, was an exotic change for Harry. Winding roads and paths parted the sylvan setting here and there, and faculty members' and administrators' homes sat tucked into emerald backdrops. Dense stands of towering hardwoods and pines vied for supremacy and sunlight along every edge of the manicured portions of the 10,000-acre campus. When time hung heavy, Harry joined other children in fidgeting on the platform at the station in anticipation of the arrival of the next "Mountain Goat" train, on which visitors and residents ascended from the tiny town of Cowan. That winter the relocated mother and son had "Christmas and Dickens by the fire" at Palmetto Hall, and meals brought over in a covered basket by a woman from Magnolia Hall.

This Tennessee chapter in Ransom's life constituted a highly formative phase of his intellectual and personal development. In the nine years between 1919 and 1928, he would attend the Mary Dabney School, the Sewanee Military Academy, and the University of the South. One might say that these latter two schools, which promised to shape the characters of young Christian men who undertook study there, actually succeeded in producing in Harry Ransom the epitome of those qualities for which they were striving. He was extremely receptive to their teachings, and the social stimulation, structured atmosphere, and mental challenge of the schools happened to be ideal for his emotional needs and cerebral thirsts. The Mary Dabney School, conducted in a one-story wood-frame house with ornate gingerbread trim, was operated by a history professor's wife—Mrs. Alice Porter Ware.[4] Years later Ransom would marvel over the "absolutely unbelievable combination" of her faculty and wonder if "any child of eleven" was "*ever* thrown under guidance like this before." Most notably, Dr. Selby L. Ware (the university's history professor, with degrees from Oxford and Johns Hopkins universities), taught history to the children.

Marion Ransom wasted little time finding employment. In a report issued in 1920 by the Sewanee hospital, then known as Emerald-Hodgson Hospital, she was mentioned as the newly hired "Housekeeper." Beyond its purpose as a fifty-bed campus infirmary, three-story Emerald-Hodgson was a very important facility in the entire region, because in addition to serving its student patients it also was the only hospital between Chattanooga and Nashville that treated charity cases for inhabitants of the Tennessee mountains. Those admitted for treatment included farmers, miners, summer vacationers, and people known to be distillers and distributors of illegal liquor. More than once Harry Ransom remarked that he grew up in a hospital, and this was true; within a short while he and his mother were granted a room in the adjacent Emery Annex, a cramped one-story sandstone building. Their quarters were located between the obstetrical unit and the morgue of what he called "a wonderfully disorganized establishment."[5]

The crucial fact for Marion Ransom, and the reason she accepted the housekeeper appointment with alacrity, was that children of the hospital staff were entitled to almost-free admission and tuition at the University of the South and its preparatory school, Sewanee Military Academy. Sewanee Military Academy had been founded in 1868 as the Sewanee Grammar School but was converted into a military academy in 1908. The school stressed discipline, devotion, and camaraderie. "Prepares boys for College or University, and for life," promised one advertisement of the time.[6] In order to hasten Harry's qualification for the military academy, his mother consented in 1920 to the incredible expedient of "jumping" him from the fourth to the eighth grade, a step he later termed "a hideous mistake socially and psychologically," if perhaps "sensible scholastically."[7] Accordingly he joined the other young cadets, most of them boarding students, who dutifully rose at 6:15 A.M., donned gray military uniforms, marched outside in formation for reveille, returned to wash up, marched in formation to breakfast, attended chapel and classes interrupted by lunch, engaged in athletic contests and exercises, marched to retreat and dinner in formation, participated in study hall, enjoyed a brief period of free time, and turned in before taps at 10:30 P.M. High-achieving boys earned ribbons, medals, and swords.

FIGURE 2.3

Marion Ransom (in dark dress, on right) with nurses and staff at Emerald-Hodgson Hospital, Sewanee. Trained as a medical missionary, Marion Ransom had duties that were administrative rather than medical. Harry Ransom could later recall the names of all the hospital doctors, nurses, and staff members. Harry Ransom Humanities Research Center, The University of Texas at Austin.

Snapshots dating from these years show a boyish, slightly pudgy Ransom in an ill-fitting uniform. Occasional difficulties arose, partly because he was a "day student" living at the hospital—a considerable distance from the school. On October 5, 1923, for instance, Cadet Ransom wrote respectfully to the Commandant of Cadets to request the removal of a report that he was five minutes late for drill. "Not only is it almost impossible for me to get home, eat dinner, and return to the Post in the very short time allowed me between recall from classes and drill," he argued convincingly, "but the bugle time on this date was appreciably in advance of that of the [chimes from the] University; consequently, it was impossible for me to reach the Academy by assembly." Even when he made it to class for roll call, one of his officers would often remark, "Audible, but not visible." Cadet Ransom, being so much younger, was inevitably shorter and smaller than the boys on either side of him in the line.[8]

FIGURE 2.4

Ransom, Sewanee Military Academy, early 1920s. Ransom earned a sobriquet,
"The English wiz," during this period. Harry Ransom Humanities
Research Center, The University of Texas at Austin.

At the Sewanee Military Academy he encountered both a "curious democracy" and an "amazing snobbery." One cadet named Ramage, considerably taller than he, frequently shoved Ransom around whenever the officers were out of sight. Finally an indignant Ransom, having taken numerous provocations, mounted a tree stump and managed to knock out the bully.[9] A friend from those days would testify that "Harry . . . had a temper under his friendliness that many a kid around here learned to respect. He was what we call 'birchy'—easy to peel off and work with, but tough."[10] Ransom's greatest dread became athletic contests, due to his disadvantage in competing against much older boys. When the Sewanee Athletic Club scheduled track meets with opponents, "I could do nothing, so I was made 'manager' and allowed to wear a 'letter.'" At semester's end, though, he found in Palmetto Hall "a wonderful racket frame and later became an excellent tennis player from 1920 to about 1924." Nonetheless, in his freshman year at the Academy, Ransom noted later, he abandoned "team sports for good. I felt I was hopeless." An eye condition gave him the appearance of squinting; displaying boarding-school cruelty, Ransom's classmates casually conferred on him the nickname "Sleepy." Behind all of these tests of popularity and character loomed the momentous decision his mother had made to accelerate his progress by skipping four grades. Consequently, the first dance Harry was invited to attend in Sewanee ("God! What a trial!") proved damaging to his self-confidence. His second dance, held "at Cap'n Hickerson's," was the occasion of an eternally embarrassing faux pas: "My 'date' (the first and last) was Nancy Phillips. I never danced after that mortifying night when I *backed* Nancy through the folding doors."

For a youth who no longer had his father around, the effect of the special interest taken in him by Colonel DuVal G. Cravens, superintendent of the school, appeared lifesaving to Mrs. Ransom. Cravens had drawn upon his experiences at St. Albans in Virginia and the Carlisle Military Academy in reinvigorating the curriculum and recruiting capable instructors. Even more important, perhaps, he was the father of four boys, and he seemed to sense the vitalness of bestowing approbation and encouragement on his cadet charges. Mrs. Ransom wrote to Colonel Cravens with the gratitude of an anxious parent during Harry's second year at the Academy: "I find it difficult to choose words to express to you my appreciation of your kind interest in Harry. I came to Sewanee, hoping to find the Academy the best of all places in which to lay the foundation of that education and that training which are to fit my boy to be worthy of service to his fellows. My hope is realized. . . . I know this, Harry's heart is full of unswerving loyalty to you. And I would that every parent might feel gratitude as deep as mine for what you are making possible."[11]

Immersed in the atmosphere of Sewanee, Harry avidly subscribed to the charitable teachings of Episcopalianism. He sent a brief essay to *St. Andrew's Cross: A Church Magazine for Laymen,* a monthly periodical published in Philadelphia, and was pleased by the editor's positive reply of March 26, 1924. Fifteen years old, Harry had achieved his first publication, an inspirational message: "We know a man whose very name suggests service. He is a big-fisted fellow with a big smile. He appreciates a joke and knows how to tell one. When his friend needs help, he doesn't get tearful, he gets to work to help him. If a man is cold, he gives him a coat, not sympathy, and when he is hungry he feeds him. . . . He is a minister, not because he says prayers, but because he helps people understand Christ."[12]

By his junior year, when his class contained thirty-five boys, the bespectacled youth was referred to deferentially in the Academy yearbook as "the English wiz."[13] Soon he was earning his share and more of available school honors; in fact, before he graduated in 1924, the headmaster jokingly suggested that he might want to "bring a tray with you" to collect the medals due him at the ceremonies.[14] Among these honors would be the Willis Calhoun Medal and the National Society of Colonial Daughters Medal for his essay on the Rhodes Scholarships. "I wish to congratulate you on your brilliant achievement during your last year at the Academy," Colonel Cravens wrote with satisfaction in June 1924. "On the basis of these awards, we shall expect great things of you."[15]

A welcome letter arrived on June 26, 1924, from classics professor Henry M. Gass, who was serving the University of the South as the summer-term dean for its College of Arts and Sciences. A teacher whom Harry Ransom reverenced, Gass had been the academic headmaster at Sewanee Military Academy from 1912 until 1922. Now he wrote cheerily to his former pupil: "My dear Harry: I have before me your certificate of admission to the University of the South, and am glad to advise you that it is satisfactory for unconditional entrance to the B.A. course. I shall be glad for you to come into my office during the summer and talk over the question of your course[s] for next year."[16]

At the University of the South, Ransom entered a school that enrolled fewer than 400 young men. Forty percent of them were not Episcopalian, as Ransom was, though the school was supported substantially by the Southern Dioceses of the Episcopal Church. There were additionally eight graduate students and twenty-eight students in the School of Theology. The

Sewanee faculty in the mid-1920s consisted of twenty-six professors and eight student teaching assistants. The school had instituted varsity athletic teams in major sports during the 1890s, beginning with football in 1891. Chapel was held daily, 9:00 to 9:30 A.M., though it might last only ten or fifteen minutes.

Harry Ransom elected to join the Kappa Sigma social fraternity, the third of eight national fraternal chapters chartered at Sewanee. Kappa Sigma had its own two-story sandstone house on Alabama Avenue for social functions, but its initiates were required to live elsewhere. The activities in the house, judging from a student newspaper account in 1925, seem sedate. One Saturday evening the active members entertained their pledge class with games, food, and music. Each guest was given a dozen beans to use in the game of "Questions." Another game was "Spot the Ad"— advertisements cut from magazines were posted about the house, with their products' names scissored out to make identifications more difficult. The pledges then ate fried oysters and listened to Tom Moore at the piano and "Howse" play the saxophone.[17]

Almost from the beginning Ransom decided to major in English, Greek, and Latin—subjects to which his father had been drawn. His entire curriculum, in fact, was slanted toward traditional humanities topics.[18] Henry M. Gass, a professor who, like Ransom's father, taught Greek and Latin, possessed a teaching style that became for Ransom one of his "strongest bulwarks." A yearlong course in Dramatic Expression (Public Speaking 4) proved to be of value in helping him speak extemporaneously. In his English courses at the University of the South, he principally sat under the tutelage of Professors William S. Knickerbocker and T. [udor] Seymour Long. Long held a B.A. degree from Cornell University and was serving as secretary of the Sewanee chapter of the English-Speaking Union. A more substantial relationship developed between Harry Ransom and Knickerbocker, who held B.A. (1917), M.A. (1918), and Ph.D. (1925) degrees from Columbia University.[19] In a letter of November 29, 1934, Ransom paid tribute to Knickerbocker's teaching abilities: "One of the healthiest elements in my undergraduate work was your refusal to sugar your comments on what I wrote," Ransom declared, adding, "The other day I glanced through a reading list on which I had taken notes 'way back in the summer of 1927. Down every page I saw the refrain 'Knicky says read—' An amazing list, [Arnold's] Literature and Dogma, [Carlyle's] Past and Present, [Newman's] the Apologia, and all manner of essays on art, economics, and religion."[20] In a letter Ransom wrote to Knickerbocker after the professor left Sewanee, Ransom paid an even more flattering compliment: "This I must say. Never since 1928 have I known teaching more winey and nourishing to good sense than instruction you gave in Walsh Hall. I remember a summer class in particular: I learned reading then, to get through a book without flitting or crawling and to come out with ideas instead of catch-phrases or skimmed emotions. I owe you a great deal in my own teaching, because I still try to affect students as you affected me."[21]

Once more campus distinctions began to mount, in spite of the fact that young Ransom "worked at a miscellany of odd jobs, from washing the dishes in a hospital to office boy for the *Sewanee Review.*" A few of the former Sewanee Military Academy boys kiddingly tried to reapply his nickname "Sleepy," but as one of his peers, DuVal G. Cravens, Jr., a son of the superintendent, conceded more than sixty years later, "He was the envy of all of us, intellectually. He seemed to do everything with such ease."[22] Now his prior familiarity with Sewanee and his fellow students from the military academy began to be an advantage. At the conclusion of his first year, Ransom was honored by being chosen to write and deliver the message of the freshman class.

By his sophomore year, Ransom had already established himself as the reliable publicist for the popular football team and received a $200 contract as a sports reporter for the Associated Press. In clearly another early triumph, Ransom was promoted from a staff position to the editorship of the campus yearbook, *Cap and Gown.* Two departments of yearbook reporting were entirely his: "Athletics" and "Humor." For the latter's pages he authorized an editorial gag acknowledging the notoriety brought to Tennessee by the Scopes "Evolution" trial (whose verdict and aftermath, including William Jennings Bryan's reflections, Ransom covered in July 1925 as an Associated Press reporter for editor and newsman Brian Bell); the yearbook ran a spoofing picture of Ransom and his friends identified as a so-called "Evolution Society of the Mountains of Tennessee." The editor's essay, "While Presses Wait," exulted in 1926: "Well, we're out! . . . For the first time since Noah was professor of Navigation, the 'Cap and Gown' has something left over besides extra copies and bills." A facsimile of a suddenly elegant signature—"Harry H. Ransom"—concluded the preface.[23]

He had plenty else to do. He was press agent for the Glee Club, even if he was not listed among its tenors, baritones, and basses. By 1926 he was serving as president of the Southern Conference of Publicity Managers. Almost magnetically, too, Ransom was attracted to ideas about possible roles for higher education. On April 21, 1926, for example, the *Sewanee Purple* reported that "the Society of Neograph was entertained Friday night at a broiled-steak supper by its president, Mr. H. H. Ransom. After an open

FIGURE 2.5

Ransom, a University of the South sophomore, worked as a reporter for the Associated Press, 1925. Ransom covered the famous "Scopes Trial" in Dayton, Tennessee, for the Associated Press. Harry Ransom Humanities Research Center, The University of Texas at Austin.

session and the discussion of the modern trend of college affairs, . . . [six students] were elected to membership." In October 1926 Ransom was invited to join Alpha Phi Epsilon, an honorary literary fraternity established the previous year for upperclassmen who distinguished themselves in "some forensic line such as debating, oratory, or writing."[24] As a graduating senior during 1927–1928, he was Phi Beta Kappa, president of the Neograph society, president of the Pi Omega literary society, columnist for a three-year-old humor magazine, *The Mountain Goat,* manager of the Purple Masque Dramatic Club, contributing editor of the weekly student newspaper, member of the Scholarship Society, President of the College Editors of America, Pierpont Fellow-Elect in Literature, and a Rhodes Scholarship alternate.

A sobering check upon his spirits had occurred on November 1, 1926, when Harry Ransom's sixty-year-old father died in Cambridge, Maryland. The son thus lost a parent he had presumably not seen for seven years. Neither he nor his mother was able to attend the funeral services. The *Cambridge Daily Banner* reported in a front-page article that the elder Ransom had served as principal of Cambridge High School "for six years," that "much of the time since Prof. Ransom came to this city his health has been poor but few, even of his intimates, expected the illness which overtook him three weeks ago." The death certificate stated that the death resulted from "Aortic Regurgitation," with "Neurasthenia" as a "contributory" condition. Burial was scheduled to take place in Newton. Another front-page *Daily Banner* article of November 2, 1926, reported: "Funeral Services for the late Prof. Harry Huntt Ransom, who died at the hospital yesterday morning, were held at Christ Church last night at eight o'clock and were attended by a very large concourse of people."

Events in Sewanee, however, inspired and cheered a college student. The Lord Bishop of London included the Sewanee campus on his tour of the United States in 1926. The next year poet and critic John Crowe Ransom (1888–1974), a distant Ransom relative as well as a founding member of the Fugitives, spoke at an open meeting of the E.Q.B. Club on campus; the title of his paper was "The South, Old or New?" That was the year that Harry Ransom, as a scholastically distinguished member of the junior class, was permitted to join designated upperclassmen in the coveted "Order of the Gownsmen," earning the privilege of wearing a black Oxford gown to classes, chapel, and school functions. Along with an "Honor Code" system of conducting all academic examinations, this was one of the most cherished traditions at Sewanee.

Harry Ransom's undergraduate student career ended in a crescendo of glory. During the days preceding Commencement in June 1928, he and

FIGURE 2.6

Ransom with his mother, Sewanee, 1928 (?). Marion Ransom stayed behind in Sewanee after Ransom graduated from the University of the South in 1928 and was accepted into Yale University's graduate program in English. Harry Ransom Humanities Research Center, The University of Texas at Austin.

James Teague upheld the affirmative side in the annual debate between Pi Omega and Sigma Epsilon. The question debated was, "Resolved, that the United States should cease to protect by armed intervention the property of its citizens located on foreign soil." Upon deliberation, the judges gave the victory to Ransom's side. On Friday he again represented Pi Omega in winning both the medals for oratory and for the best essay. He spoke, prophetically, on "A Plea for a Cultural Education."[25] Then, on Tuesday at the 10 A.M. Commencement ceremony in the enormous All Saints' Chapel (built to resemble Exeter Cathedral in England), Harry Ransom as class valedictorian delivered a now-lost oration that the student newspaper said "held within its masterful phraseology the respect and love which Sewanee commands of all who have been sheltered by its walls." The degrees were then conferred. Six academic awards were bestowed on Ransom, in addition to his Phi Beta Kappa distinction: The Ruggles Wright Medal for French, the Jemison Medal for Debate, the Overton Lea, Jr., Medal for Oratory, the Inter-Society Prize for the Essay, the Kentucky Medal for Greek, and the Washington Medal for an Essay on the Constitution of the United States.

On February 20, 1928, Ransom had received notice of his acceptance into Yale University's graduate program in English.[26] Yet he also contemplated the idea of attending law school; a Tennessee judge and friend, Jesse B. Templeton, was urging Ransom to enter the legal profession. Nevertheless he found himself strongly drawn to the study of literature; he wished that he could find a way to combine these two interests. He additionally thought over several tempting invitations from Sewanee contacts he had made—through his work as yearbook editor, school publicist, and sports writer—to enter the field of journalism with the Associated Press or work on several Southern newspapers. A friend named Frank Smith, for example, wrote jauntily to his former classmate Harry ("Old Thing") to offer a job on the Montgomery, Alabama *Advertiser:* "In earnest about wanting a job down here? Can fix you up, if desired. . . . Probably be a reporter's job about 30 [dollars a week] most any time you want it. . . . It would be great to have you here. . . . The town is really delightful. Nobody in a hurry and nobody gives a damn what you do or how you do it. Most liberal I've heard of. . . . Everybody has a hell of a good time. And gals! Oh, my gosh."[27]

Whichever option he would choose, Ransom had accepted the fact that he must move on from Sewanee, whose locale could offer its graduates little to prolong their stay.

THREE

THE SCHOLAR

"I have been hearing about Harry and all his accomplishments. . . . Somebody said he was the smartest boy who ever left the Mountain," wrote an admirer in October 1928 to Mrs. Jesse B. Templeton of Winchester, Tennessee, who, along with her husband, was supplementing Ransom's Associated Press income to finance his studies.[1] The student they were assisting had already traveled by train to New Haven, where he found a larger and considerably more prominent English Department than Sewanee's. Nine professors, including the illustrious author, critic, and orator William Lyon Phelps (1865–1943), six associate professors, and eleven assistant professors constituted the English faculty of Yale University. Another difference was also evident: approximately one-third of the English graduate students were female, a number of them from women's colleges like Smith, Mount Holyoke, and Vassar. The course of study Harry pursued in the first year of his residence at Yale included a two-term seminar in "Goldsmith to Galsworthy" from the English Department chairman, Professor George Henry Nettleton, together with additional two-term courses in "Milton" from Associate Professor Frederick E. Pierce, "English Prose Fiction" from Professor Wilbur L. Cross, and "Carlyle and Matthew Arnold" from Professor Karl Young.

Ransom was simultaneously taking steps to gain admission to Harvard Law School, since an interdisciplinary program of study was beginning to take shape in his mind. He would recollect in 1960 that "when I went to Yale I went as a confused and undetermined major. I wasn't sure I wanted to go into English. I worked for the Associated Press for some time—I was a sports writer, but in those days, sports writers covered everything from football games to bootlegging trials—and I thought perhaps I might go into journalism."[2] The turning point was Ransom's discussions with Chauncey Brewster Tinker (1876–1963), an authority on Dr. Samuel Johnson and the eighteenth century who had taught English at Yale for more than a quarter of a century. "By his grace and lenience," Ransom recalled, "I was allowed to go to Harvard for an interim to look at the . . . whole history of the ownership of ideas and literary texts."[3] One of his recommenders for Harvard Law School pointed out that Ransom's achievements and plans were all the more unusual inasmuch as "I do not think he is yet twenty-one."[4]

During the summer of 1929, Ransom returned to Tennessee, passing the months with his benefactors, Judge and Mrs. Templeton. On August 7, 1929, he wrote to his mother about a teaching method he wanted to try in an upcoming guest lecture. The style of delivery he had in mind would eventually become his trademark and differed markedly from prevailing practices: "Tomorrow I lecture [at Sewanee] on Arnold. I am planning an informal talk, shall use no notes, shall try to tell them simply those things which seem to me to be necessary to a proper understanding of a difficult question. . . . Man can not expect to apply his doctrine to such a problem as the personality of God. It is as though a man took a drinking glass to see the stars, or poured red wine into a telescope."[5]

Within a few weeks Ransom was back in New Haven, living on Chapel Street. He enrolled under Professor Karl Young's supervision to write an M.A. thesis on "Carlyle and the Bible,"[6] but he also entered Harvard Law School.[7] By November 15, 1929, Ransom had moved to 125 High Street in Cambridge, Massachusetts. He was resolving his uncertainty about whether to study law or literature by devising a Yale doctoral dissertation topic that would enable him to do both at once.

He spent part of the summer of 1930 in Cambridge, and then made arrangements on July 28, 1930, to rent a section of land known as the Rhodes farm in Madison County, Missouri, from his half-sister Jean Barron Hurlbut.[8] Ransom wanted an inexpensive hideaway in which to begin drafting his dissertation proposal and mulling over his future prospects, and the fertile green meadows and woodlands of rural southeast Missouri, not far from the Mississippi River and the northwest corner of Tennessee, appeared inviting.

He did not stay in Missouri long, because, with Depression conditions worsening, he elected to do what many other graduate students were doing: interrupt his studies to earn a modest instructor's salary at one of the hundreds of state schools that were solving enrollment and budgeting problems by hiring temporary teachers. In his case, he chose to accept two years of employment (1930–1932) at the State Teachers College in Valley City, North Dakota. Owing to his extensive experience with the Associated Press, the duties assigned him by departmental chairman Susan McCoy consisted of instructing composition, speech, and journalism teacher-training courses

FIGURE 3.1

Ransom at Harvard University, 1929 (?). Ransom attended Harvard Law School but did not seek a degree there. His interest in law was reflected in his Yale doctoral dissertation, "The Theory of Literary Property, 1760–1775." Harry Ransom Humanities Research Center, The University of Texas at Austin.

along with directing the publication of the campus newspaper. Forming deep personal friendships would never be Ransom's forte, yet he enjoyed a large number of casual academic and civic acquaintances; his membership in the Kiwanis Club, for example, dated from this period.[9] During the long winters he wrote poetry and indulged his curiosity about the large Scandinavian community.

Ransom returned to his studies at Yale University in the autumn of 1932, pleased to be readmitted to a program of graduate courses that now restricted its number of admissions in English to 100 students.[10] This time the directory of graduate students published his hometown as Winchester, Tennessee, noted his M.A. degree ("Yale University 1930"), and gave his address as 51 Lake Place. He promptly enrolled in Associate Professor Menner's two-semester seminar in "Old English," Professor Brooke's two-semester seminar in "Shakespeare," and Professor Tinker's two-semester offering in "The Age of Johnson." Ransom would later say that he "got into teaching and stayed in it because of the influence of early teachers. . . . I liked the way a Greek teacher at Sewanee, famous only to the people he taught, lived; the way two lecturers at Harvard (Samuel Williston and James Landis) talked, teaching the same course but very differently; and the way C. B. Tinker at Yale (who limited one of his classes to three people) got at research and got other people into it."[11]

It was this latter professor, Chauncey Brewster Tinker, who ultimately directed Ransom's dissertation and most notably provided the model for many of Ransom's subsequent achievements. Tinker's early life, like Ransom's, had hardly been typical. Orphaned at the age of twelve, his mother having died when he was only three, he was reared by a stepmother. Though blinded in one eye as a child, he nonetheless earned three degrees at Yale and would teach there from 1903 until 1945. Students came to adore this confirmed bachelor, and his literature classes were celebrated. The author of several books on Samuel Johnson's famous biographer James Boswell, Professor Tinker managed to obtain a large and previously unresearched cache of Boswell papers for Yale, no small feat. Thereupon he undertook a decades-long campaign to promote donations of materials and money to the Yale University Library. He was instrumental in founding the Yale Library Associates in 1930 for that purpose, and he became the first Keeper of Rare Books in the Sterling Memorial Library at Yale. At the end of his teaching career he donated his substantial personal collection of English literature papers to his alma mater. He was also a religious intellectual, and an address he delivered in 1932, "Why I Am a Churchman," was reprinted in various periodicals.

The doctoral dissertation that Ransom undertook under Tinker's supervision, "The Theory of Literary Property, 1760–1775," seemed like an unconventional subject then (and certainly would be today) for an English graduate student to investigate. Ransom had discovered, and been fascinated by, the fact that the elemental concept of copyright law protecting literary works was a relatively recent development in English history—indeed, that the first effective statute dated only from the eighteenth century. Thus, in a decade when many students were immersing themselves either in formalistic studies of literature or heavily biographical examinations of literary history, Ransom investigated a sweeping legal development that had radically altered the relationships of authors, publishers, and readers.

Ransom advanced to the final stage of his candidacy on September 11, 1933, when he passed his German test (having taken the Latin and French examinations in 1928) and thus completed his language requirements. Like many young scholars of his generation, however, he would have to wait a number of years before he could claim the doctoral degree he sought. Financial need in 1933 drove him back to Valley City, North Dakota, to the State Teachers College where he had undertaken his first teaching assignment. That would be his last year of teaching in North Dakota.

The intricacies and puzzles of copyright legislation and interpretation would absorb him, off and on, for decades, but the more pressing need was a reliable teaching appointment. The summer of 1934 passed slowly for him in Winchester, Tennessee, where he once more resided with Judge Templeton and his wife. As August drew to a close, he received a welcome letter from an official of the State Agricultural College of Colorado at Fort Collins, offering him an appointment as "Instructor in English, at an annual salary of $1,600.00, on a nine months of service basis, from September 1, 1934."[12] The sum was more than fair for a teacher who still lacked the completed doctorate degree, and it would enable him to avoid resorting to further reliance on his Winchester friends, with whom he exchanged services in return for Judge Templeton's financial assistance. He sent an affirmative reply and took a train to Colorado, where his mother later joined him.

Ransom's courses again included composition and speech offerings, but this time someone else on the faculty instructed the journalism courses. Ransom designed experimental classes in remedial composition and was allowed to teach advanced courses in nineteenth-century British literature. At Fort Collins he met Joseph Jones, who had just finished his doctorate at Stanford and had also been looking for a job at this singularly bleak time. Jones left Colorado in midyear—with the permission and blessing of the department chairman, Dr. Alfred Westfall—to take a better offer

FIGURE 3.2

Ransom at Fort Collins, Colorado, 1934. Ransom had already taught at State Teachers College in Valley City, North Dakota, for two years before joining the faculty at the State Agricultural College of Colorado at Fort Collins in 1934. The next year he would teach English composition to engineering students at the University of Texas at Austin. Harry Ransom Humanities Research Center, The University of Texas at Austin.

from the University of Texas in Austin.[13] Meanwhile Ransom, oblivious to this first faint brush with his destiny, became better known in the Fort Collins community. An undated newspaper clipping records that Ransom was the speaker at the birthday luncheon of the Shakespeare Club. Seventeen women attended.[14] In another development, Ransom's former mentor William S. Knickerbocker, editor of the *Sewanee Review* since 1926, began to invite Harry's submissions to that journal. Sending two poems on November 29, 1934, Ransom wrote: "They are not fugitive and they are not 'Southern.' The writing grew out of an interest in Norwegian and Icelandic literature which I found first in Dakota."[15]

Ransom expressed contentment with his Fort Collins position. He assured an acquaintance on February 26, 1935, that "Colorado proves an exciting place in which to live, and my job is by way of being a lucky find."[16] On the other hand, as though in anticipation of a job search, he had joined the Modern Language Association on December 17, 1934, thereby making himself eligible to attend its conventions.[17] When an offer did come, from the largest university in his native state of Texas, it left much to be desired: the University of Texas was willing to hire him only as a three-fourths-time, non-tenure-track Instructor in English. Even so, the advantages of a better-endowed, better-known school with a more amply equipped library outweighed the obvious deficiencies of the job contract. When Joe Jones arrived back in Austin, Texas, after taking a summer 1935 honeymoon in Europe with his bride, Johanna, his Fort Collins friend Harry Ransom was nearly the first person he met. Ransom and his mother spent the first year in a rented apartment on East 23rd Street.

The university that Harry Ransom joined in 1935 was, as it would turn out, poised on the brink of explosive growth. Though it had enrolled fewer than 6,000 students in 1928, it now had over 8,000 students and by 1940 would register more than 10,000. The discovery of oil on West Texas lands owned by the university, signaled by an oil strike on May 28, 1923, when Santa Rita #1 blew in, had heralded a new era of dignified buildings erected in a modified Spanish Renaissance style. A new Main Building, replete with a spacious library, soaring tower of twenty-seven stories, chiming clock, and observation deck, was scheduled to open in 1937. Austin itself, a city with a population in 1935 of approximately 55,000, was centered south of the university, its business district descending gradually toward the Colorado River. A sense of gigantic potential was unmistakable in both the city and the university.

Ransom entered an academic department that was in transition; the era of older professors who had personally known a few of the founding faculty members of half a century earlier was giving way to a generation drawn from diverse backgrounds, graduate schools, and literary approaches. In 1935, however, it was still dominated by a collection of "Southern Gentlemen," epitomized by the stiffly formal Morgan Callaway, Jr., an Old English scholar from Georgia who had studied at Johns Hopkins.[18] Next in seniority was a kindly Virginian, Killis Campbell, an Edgar Allan Poe expert who was also a product of the Johns Hopkins graduate program. South Carolinian James B. Wharey, a John Bunyan scholar who had come to UT in 1912, taught a course on "The English Novel" and was widely appreciated for his wittiness and his encouragement of classroom debate.[19] South Carolinian Robert A. Law, a prominent Elizabethan scholar, taught the Shakespeare classes.

Reginald Harvey Griffith, a Chicago Ph.D. but a Southerner by upbringing, was the departmental chairman at Texas when Ransom arrived. Described by one of his former graduate students as "a scholar rather than an administrator," he reputedly "lived in the Eighteenth Century, the contemporary of Pope, Swift, Addison, and Steele. . . . To each student he assigned a year in the life of Pope and [they] were to record in detail on separate cards everything that Pope did on each day."[20] In addition to his chairman's duties, Griffith was the unofficial rare books librarian of an extensive collection acquired by the University of Texas in 1918.

The deaths of Callaway, toward the end of Ransom's first year at UT, in April 1936, and of Campbell, in 1937, along with the aging of the senior professors and an increasing enrollment in the graduate courses, necessitated additions to the tenure-track faculty. These included Rudolph Willard, a Yale Ph.D.; Theodore Hornberger, a Michigan graduate; and E. Bagby Atwood, a University of Virginia Ph.D. Ransom instinctively gravitated toward a Texas-born professor who would become better known to the nation at large than any of his contemporary colleagues—folklorist, historian, author, and raconteur J. Frank Dobie, a non-Ph.D. maverick academic (M.A., Columbia University, 1914) whom his colleague Daniel M. McKeithan described as "a cool, refreshing breeze" on campus. "Much academic scholarship," Dobie remarked, "was mere digging up of bones in one cemetery and burying them in another." McKeithan, who had arrived as a doctoral student at the University of Texas in 1928 after earning A.B. and M.A. degrees from the College of Charleston, testified that "Dobie's humor, good nature, and vitality were unsurpassed. His talk was at least as good as his writing." Along with his close friends the naturalist and folklorist Roy Bedichek and the historian Walter Prescott Webb, Dobie was putting Texas on the national literary map. For years Dobie would offer a course titled "Life and Literature of the Southwest" that students flocked to take in such numbers as to cause him to hire grading assistants.[21]

An additional means of meeting the pressure of the growing enrollment in English composition courses, besides bringing in temporary instructors like Harry Ransom from other schools, was the employment of graduate students as instructors. One of the most impressive instructors was Alice Lovelace Cooke, born in Jonesboro, Texas, who completed her Texas Ph.D. in 1933 by writing a dissertation on Walt Whitman. She would teach as an assistant professor at the University until 1958.[22] Annie S. Irvine, too, earned a Ph.D. from the department, teaching as she progressed. A chain-smoking, demanding, entertaining teacher, Irvine was the only one of the female instructors to rise to the rank of Associate Professor.[23] Among the graduate students who took their turn at teaching the basic courses were a significant number who subsequently made their mark elsewhere: Arlin Turner, Lewis Simpson, and Floyd Stovall, for instance, would distinguish themselves as Americanists. Another, Clarence L. Cline, became an eminent authority on Byron, Meredith, and other figures of the Romantic and Victorian periods and eventually chaired the UT English Department.

Ransom's generation of more recent arrivals included Edward G. Fletcher, a gregarious Harvard Ph.D.; the well-liked Michael Crow, a Chicago Ph.D., medievalist, and Chaucerian; the affable Robert Wilson, another Chicago medievalist, specializing in Malory and medieval romances; Ransom's friend Joseph Jones, who gained a reputation for studying English literature written outside the United States and British Isles; and the erudite Willis W. Pratt, whose doctorate was earned at Cornell in 1935 and who published on Romantic poets, particularly Byron and Shelley. Leo Hughes, an eighteenth-century specialist who came to UT in 1938, a few years after Ransom, held a University of Illinois doctorate.

Ransom comfortably took his place as a part-time member of this evolving English faculty. At first his office was in B Hall, built in 1890. Ransom had office 327, just around the corner from Joe Jones's office, and he conscientiously held office hours daily, Monday through Saturday, between 10 and 11 A.M.[24] In 1937, upon completion of the Main Building, his office was moved to the twenty-third floor of the Tower, affording a breathtaking vista of the city of Austin and its environs. His six-day conference hours continued. Hughes recalled that Harry Ransom's office door in the Tower was almost always open to students—more than anyone else's. "He simply *liked* people."[25]

Since early in the century there had been ongoing tension in the Department of English between those who recognized American literature as

FIGURE 3.3

The University of Texas, Austin, 1938 (?). Ransom kept office hours for students Monday through Saturday in his office on the twenty-third floor of the new Tower and later maintained several other offices there during his administrative career. The Prints and Photographs Collection, Center for American History, The University of Texas at Austin.

a legitimate field of study and those who did not. "There is *no such thing* as American Literature," Callaway had intoned more than once.[26] This was mainly a difference over respective visions of the discipline of English. But it was not long before Ransom got his first glimpse of the bruising academic politics of a department composed of strong-willed individuals, and although the issue was more directly over governance rather than literary values, the fallout would be all encompassing. In 1937 Professor Philip Graham, a scholar of Southern American literature who had earned his Ph.D. at Chicago a decade earlier, began what would prove to be a ten-year term as English Chair. During that time, with the approval of Dr. Hanson Tufts Parlin, an English professor who had assumed the deanship of the College of Arts and Sciences in 1928, Graham and his allies essentially staged a revolution, wresting all powers and responsibilities except budget-making from the departmental Budget Council, comprised only of full professors, and distributing them among the other voting members of the department. This was the most important event in the early history of the department, but, according to Clarence L. Cline and others, Ransom took no part in overthrowing the senior faculty. In the aftermath, however, his position was upgraded to that of a full-time assistant professor and Professor Graham assigned Ransom a junior-level Shakespeare course, formerly a monopoly of Professor Law; Ransom's charismatic teaching qualities soon made it an immensely popular course. Fortunately, Robert A. Law remained friendly with him. Yet the bitterness of the departmental struggle as a whole eventually seeped into other issues and caused divisions for many years.

Even before this acrimony, not everyone in the English Department had been fond of Dean Parlin, despite his having been a professor of English at the university before assuming an administrative post. But his stock was high among the undergraduate students. Margaret Cousins remembered feeling flattered when she was recommended for Dr. Parlin's "Advanced Composition" course, for which "A" students from various college departments were eligible. "Dr. Parlin was a man of middle height, compact in figure, with an aristocratic head, balding, and a squarish face and hooded eyes," she recorded. "He was always sleekly tailored, in excellent conservative clothes, and it was impossible to imagine him in any relaxed or recreational stance. . . . He did not, like most professors, stroll the campus or fraternize with the student body." A "brilliant lecturer," he had another side: "He had little contact with his students. . . . There was a coldness about him, and it was possible to emerge from a conference on a term paper in tears."[27]

Ransom himself, however, shortly had cause to feel grateful to the dean.

Parlin was picking out certain young instructors to work as advisers in the College of Arts and Sciences, and as one of those chosen, Ransom became what today would be termed an assistant dean. Willis Pratt, another appointee, said that Parlin asked them to help him out in the dean's office after their classes for three or four years. Dean Parlin spoke openly to them of wanting to get some "new blood" from northern universities into the English Department rather than allowing it to continue its hallowed tradition of recruiting mainly from Southern schools. Parlin pointed with satisfaction to the people whose careers he was promoting by inviting them to work with him in the College office: Willis Pratt, with a Ph.D. from Cornell; Thomas Cranfill, from Harvard; Oscar Maurer, Yale; Joseph Jones, Stanford; and Harry Ransom, who would earn his Yale Ph.D. in 1938.

It was Harry Ransom who often made arrangements at the dean's behest for dinners at local restaurants where the dean could meet with the younger faculty away from academic settings. A bachelor, Dean Parlin periodically dined with his student advisers at the Hoffbrau, a steakhouse on West Sixth Street, when he wished to show his appreciation to these instructors. Equally welcome were his invitational "picnics" for faculty and students, held in a grove of pecan and live oak trees across the Colorado River. It was a privilege for instructors to be invited and to watch for the arrival of Dean Parlin, who invariably rode to the site with the food caterer.[28]

Parlin and his young advisers invented, among other experiments, a new degree plan for selected undergraduates, a program called Plan II to differentiate it from the standard university curriculum and degree requirements. Writing a later evaluation of the program, Ransom noted that "Texas was the first state institution to launch such a degree" and acknowledged that "the original concept was Dean H. T. Parlin's," who laid the groundwork for it in "innumerable (and sometimes interminable) discussions with small groups—usually at a local Mexican restaurant." Ransom stressed as well the fact that "students were involved in the planning almost from the start."[29] In introducing Plan II in February 1935, Dean Parlin had explained that "the aim is to inform the student in regard to the world he lives in and to offer him an opportunity partly through courses and partly through guidance in reading to round out his humanity." The Plan II graduate will have developed "not so much an accumulation of information as a point of view."[30] For Ransom, who assisted in fine-tuning this program, the brainstorming, proposals, and announcements about Plan II could be called a defining experience.

H. T. Parlin would stay in office twenty-one years, a record to this date for that position. Perceiving the importance of town-gown relations, he served as president of the Austin Community Concerts for fifteen years following its formation in 1935, "helping change Austin from the cultural desert it might otherwise have been" (in Clarence L. Cline's phrase) by letting its citizens hear some of the world's greatest musicians, including José Iturbi and Yehudi Menuhin. Parlin, who had attended the University of Colorado and earned his doctorate at the University of Pennsylvania, remained as widely disliked as esteemed within the English Department. His personal aloofness from students and autocratic administrative style would be utterly foreign to Ransom's manner. Even so, as if providentially, Ransom had been granted a fortuitous opportunity to study a dedicated dean at close range. Ransom had likewise found a university sufficiently complex to challenge all his talents, with an Arts and Sciences College that trained him in the fundamentals of administration and students who were coming to relish his unusual teaching style.

THE TEACHER

ℓ

Very soon after his arrival at UT in 1935, Harry Ransom became known as an outstanding undergraduate classroom teacher, someone whose name was passed eagerly from student to student as one of the University of Texas professors a student should definitely try to "take." Virginia (McNutt) Stansbury enrolled in a freshman English course with him in 1937. Like many of the students, she was struggling with the finances of a university education during the Great Depression. The man who convened her English course that semester was heavyset and hardly muscular, she noticed, but his deliberate motions and articulate speech gave force to his presence. His glasses were a prominent feature of his face. He wore dark suits, as did most of the male English faculty members whom she passed in the hallways. (They were under an "unexpressed pressure" to wear a conventional coat and tie or preferably a suit, despite the lack of air-conditioning and the sometimes-sweltering central Texas climate.)[1] It became immediately apparent that Mr. Ransom could be enormously patient, and that he was as much interested in the "Raggedy Anns" (as she thought of herself) as in the affluent students. His office door was always open to any of his pupils, it seemed. Above all, she would recall the impression of him as a "very kind" man during their conversations. She found herself resisting a schoolgirl crush on this youthful-looking Harry Ransom. When she revealed to him that, inspired by the class readings, she was writing some poetry, he allowed her to assemble her poems into one of the required term papers. She felt surprised that the ambitions of a novice would be taken so seriously. The next year she had Dr. James B. Wharey for Victorian poetry; he held the class entranced with mesmerizing, theatrical readings of verse, but she found him much more formidable, with his mustache and vest, than the obliging young instructor she remembered from her first year.[2]

FIGURE 4.I

Harry Ransom as a young professor, 1938 (?). A popular and charismatic teacher, Ransom's inimitable style drew many enthusiastic students. His handwriting on the blackboard, always precise, shows that this class was studying poetry by Robert Burns and Robert Browning. Harry Ransom Humanities Research Center, The University of Texas at Austin.

Ransom himself attended (and received graduate course-credit for) Dr. Wharey's section of English 296, "John Bunyan," which met in the summer of 1936 in Room 327 of B Hall. A sheaf of Ransom's classroom notes survives, written neatly in ink in his rounded script on ruled paper. An inveterate doodler in the confines of meetings, he deftly decorated one page with a pen-and-ink cartoon sketch of an English cleric with an attached antenna-halo. Returning to Wharey's serious mood, Ransom listed Wharey's 1928 edition of Bunyan nearby in a diagram of all editions of the Puritan author.[3]

Ransom's own students were far more attentive in the classroom. Betty McMillan's mother wrote from Portland, Texas, on December 29, 1938: "Betty is not unmindful of the fact that she has a brilliantly outstanding instructor in her [first-year] English course. She has been loud in her praise of your consistent efforts in presenting your course. We appreciate you."[4] Within only a few years his riveting classroom style and supportive conference techniques were attaining legendary status. Clarice (Hollman) Neal remembers enrolling in the sophomore English course under Harry Ransom in the Spring 1938 semester. In this survey course, Ransom often read aloud passages from Keats, Byron, and Browning. His intonations and emphases in these oral renditions clarified and vivified formerly difficult poems. "We sat there spellbound," she would recall. Around these readings he wove a lecture of diverse ideas and evocative interpretations. "He could talk about anything and make it seem *interesting*," she decided. She had never cared for poetry before, but this instructor rescued the poems from dusty antiquity and made them germane to people's everyday experience. The majority of her class of thirty-some students were women, and she learned, to her relief, that virtually all of them shared, in varying degrees, her partiality for this charismatic teacher. They joked about why they were never cutting his class, and commented to each other after the meetings about his brilliance and his intensity.[5]

Margaret (Doggett) Crow, a resident with Clarice in the privately owned Scottish Rite Dormitory, took Ransom's British literature course a year later, in the Spring 1939 term. His readings of selected Robert Browning poems—"My Last Duchess," "Soliloquy of the Spanish Cloister," "Up at a Villa—Down in the City," "Andrea del Sarto"—were so memorable that Margaret almost regretted her decision to major in history. She would remain friends with Harry Ransom throughout his lifetime.[6]

Ray Past, who would be Ransom's first doctoral dissertation student, recalls that Harry became absolutely "a matinee idol—even in the mornings—and drew coeds in hordes." Past tells an anecdote as revealing about the academic scene then as about Ransom's popularity: "I remember once standing with Dr. Reginald Griffith (himself!) in the corridor outside a classroom in which Ransom was winding up a session of his undergraduate Browning course. Eventually the class ended, the door opened, and out started pouring an apparently endless stream of young women full of vim and noisy, a soprano chaos, heels tapping, arms filled with notebooks, intent on their own business and clearly enjoying it. I mean it was an *army* of them, but finally, finally the last one swung by. There was a moment's relative silence before Griffith turned to me and sighed, 'Oh well, maybe they'll pass it on to their sons.'"[7] In Ransom's view, by contrast, the female student merited just as much individual attention as he himself had enjoyed at the all-male Sewanee, and such lighthearted hallway banter was outside the bounds of his lexicon of jests.

Helen (Shudde) Hill considered it a wonderful "treat" that she was able to start off her freshman year in Ransom's Plan II English course in September 1938. He urged the class members to drop by during his daily morning office hours in Room 2309 in the Tower of the Main Building. From time to time after the course ended she passed Harry Ransom on the campus, and she noticed that part of his teaching ability was his aptitude with names; he invariably nodded and addressed her as "Helen."[8]

One of Helen Shudde's classmates in Harry Ransom's two-semester Plan II course during the 1938–1939 academic year was a vibrant woman, brown-eyed and brown-haired, who would have an enormous impact on the life and career of her instructor. Five-feet-two-inch Hazel Harrod had come to the University of Texas from the vicinity of Waco, Texas, where her family owned property in the villages of Harrodsville and Otto (the latter of which had been her birthplace, on August 25, 1920). A student she had dated in Waco had recommended a particular English instructor for her freshman course—she was to "get Harry Ransom." Shortly thereafter she was wandering around Gregory Gym trying to register for this section, "looking rather lost," when "a man came up to me and said, 'May I help you?' I told him I was looking for Dr. Ransom. 'I am he,' the man said."[9] She enrolled in the recommended course, and within a few months the thirty-year-old Ransom started to "drop by" the library where eighteen-year-old Hazel was studying and walk her back to Littlefield Dormitory. "The world's most naive freshman," Hazel would later call herself for not realizing—as perhaps he did not, either—the attachment that was forming. Only at the end of the year did she sense his feelings for her when, one night, he confided (using the pet name he had invented): "Hazie, I have an interesting job offer from California. . . . " "Oh, that sounds great," she replied, trying to seem

sophisticated and encouraging. "Why don't you take it?"[10] The hurt that
came across his face in the next moment was her first, sharp notification
that their lives and aspirations could become intertwined. In this studious,
guileless girl from central Texas, Harry Ransom finally found a combination of traits that enabled him to shed his usual reserve.

For Hazel Harrod there was the awkwardness of overhearing her classmates talk about the instructor who was showing *her* so much attention in
private. "He seems so sweet, and then he gives us 'C's,'" she remembered
one of her girlfriends complaining. In subsequent years Hazel took other
courses from him—enrolling in his "Victorian Poetry: Browning and Ros-
setti" class in the Spring 1941 semester and in his "Shakespeare's Selected
Plays" course in the Spring 1942 term. A story that entered campus folklore
recounted how Hazel wryly (if proudly) informed the Waco friend who
had recommended Harry Ransom as her English instructor, "Well, I *got*
Ransom!" "*He* meant for *English*," her friend Myra Wilson joshingly reminded.[11] Eventually their attraction to each other would raise a few eyebrows around the English Department, but by then the rumors seemed a
small price to pay for the happiness they found in each other's company.
Marriage struck the pair as inadvisable during the first years of their commitment; Hazel needed to finish her degree (and increasingly she thought
of attending graduate school afterward), her parents were very protective
of their only child, Ransom had only completed his Yale doctoral degree
in 1938 and still was uncertain of his next step forward, his mother needed
someone to attend to her and depended upon him for financial support,
and the effects of the Great Depression lingered heavily over the nation.
Like thousands of other couples who found themselves stuck between the
economic disaster of the 1930s and the worsening world political and military conditions of the 1940s, Hazel and Harry elected to postpone any immediate thoughts of marriage.

Ransom's many students noticed no outward, discernible change in their
mentor. Joseph W. McKnight of San Angelo, whose career as a law professor at Southern Methodist University lay many years ahead of him, entered
the University of Texas at the age of sixteen in the fall of 1941. His first
class was Harry Ransom's Plan II English course, which met on Mondays,
Wednesdays, and Fridays at 8 A.M. in Sutton Hall. He would recall:

> The quality of his preparation was not a topic that occurred to me at the
> time; I didn't know that professors needed to prepare their lessons. But,
> in retrospect, I know that he was extraordinarily well prepared for each
> class. His object was to stretch our minds and understanding as much as

he could. The book we used was an anthology of occidental literature. Aristophanes's play, *The Frogs,* came along at the first of the course, and Milton's poem, *Samson Agonistes,* came a bit later. During the second semester we read Thoreau's *Walden* and Hudson's *Green Mansions,* among other things.[12]

Another student in the same Plan II class was Margaret (Swett) Henson. Fifty years later she still possessed the textbooks from the course—having packed and unpacked them frequently in her travels to Bogota, Colombia, as well as Louisiana, Arkansas, and Texas. "Without them I would never have had 'The Frogs' or 'Agamemnon' or 'The Aeneid'. . . . I still drag them out when PBS presents something that rings a bell." Though she had grown up in a Chicago suburb, Margaret Swett had stepped off the train in Austin in 1941 as a seventeen-year-old determined to attend and succeed at the University of Texas. "Being an outsider from Illinois . . . was difficult in the very clannish atmosphere of UT in 1941—many were acquainted before coming." She recalled meeting Dr. Ransom and reading the Greek selections for his first classes. The textbook contents extended through Sir Gawain and the Green Knight, Chaucer, Pope, and Wordsworth to Hemingway ("The Killers"), Lardner ("The Haircut"), Joyce (*A Portrait of the Artist as a Young Man*), and Woolf (*Mrs. Dalloway*). Margaret Swett's first paper was a comparison of Clytemnestra and Lady Macbeth. "Nobody had ever praised my efforts before and I really had no driving force about writing. . . . While not one of HHR's brilliant students, I learned, I enjoyed, and like to think that his words of encouragement had a great influence on my lengthy and strange academic career."[13] She would go on to become a college teacher and an author of books on Texas history.

Some idea of Ransom's preparations can be gained from notes extant from his classroom readings and community talks. He cut from a textbook and pasted onto sheets of paper eight excerpts from five of Shakespeare's plays and poems; large, neatly printed headings in Ransom's hand reveal their dramatic nature: "DEATH OF OTHELLO," "DEATH OF HAMLET," "PARTING OF ROMEO AND JULIET," "PARTING OF CASSIUS AND BRUTUS," "SUCH STUFF AS DREAMS," "SONNET XXX," "MAN DELIGHTS NOT ME" (from *Hamlet*), and "DEATH OF ANTONY."[14] Robert Wilson recalled that when one prominent member of the English faculty visited Ransom's class, he emerged nonplussed and complained that he found Ransom merely praising Shakespeare's sonnets and getting the students to read them in his presence, "as though they would thereby explain themselves." Wilson thinks the baffled professor

FIGURE 4.2

Hazel Harrod, 1938. Ransom became smitten with Hazel's combination of naiveté and studiousness. He courted eighteen-year-old Harrod by dropping by the library and escorting her back to Littlefield Dormitory. They would not wed until 1951, although she was considered Ransom's girlfriend during the years he spent in the military. Harry Ransom Humanities Research Center, The University of Texas at Austin.

failed to understand that Ransom avoided on principle anything imply-ing that the teacher was somehow brighter than the author and instead adopted strategies "more appreciative than analytical."[15] The technique as-suredly worked for most of his student audience. Roger S. Plummer took Ransom's Shakespeare course in 1947. "He knew Shakespeare inside and out," Plummer wrote. "His lectures were fascinating. . . . [and] more like seminars. He was very articulate, quite patient—the extent of any reproof would be a good-natured jibe at a student who obviously had not prepared for the lesson."[16] Three years later William Christian Smith, Jr., enrolled in the same Shakespeare course and found the instructor to be "brilliant, charming, and effective." Before Ransom entered the amphitheater room to address his large class he would go over to a window and concentrate. If interrupted, he would say, "Excuse me, but I need to focus for a minute." Sometimes Ransom would join the same students for lunch at Victor's Ital-ian Restaurant on the Drag, listening attentively to their ideas.[17]

Other students, too, formed impressions of Ransom at this phase of his career. Frank C. Erwin, Jr., later a formidable figure in political and educa-tional circles in Texas, a man whose devoted if tumultuous association with the University of Texas would be linked with Ransom's leadership, took an English literature course from Ransom. "Early in that course he introduced us to the wonders and beauty of poetry by our study of a well-known poem by Yeats"—"The Lake Isle of Innisfree."[18] Erwin, a future UT regent, par-ticipated in campus politics, the Silver Spurs, the Inter-Fraternity Council, and the Texas chapter of Ransom's collegiate Kappa Sigma social fraternity; like Ransom, Erwin was a Phi Beta Kappa when he graduated in 1941.[19]

Chad Oliver met Ransom after World War II, in 1946, when Oliver, who would become a popular anthropology professor at the University of Texas at Austin and a successful writer of science fiction, arrived as a fresh-man from Crystal City, Texas, and found his way to the Plan II advising room on the second floor of the Main Building. A man in a blue suit sat there, a big stack of books and a pack of Kent cigarettes lying close at hand. He seemed almost melancholy until his face brightened at the sight of a student to advise. "He must have been terribly overworked in those days," reflected Oliver, "but he laid aside his books and papers and greeted me as though he had been waiting all his life to know someone like me. He spent nearly two hours helping me plan my curriculum and my life." At the end of this advising session, the man with the black horn-rimmed glasses gave him three or four books to take home to read. Oliver knew he had met a teacher whose classes he wanted to take. The papers Oliver later wrote for these courses came back meticulously and insightfully annotated. The evident outlay of time seemed suggestive to Oliver of the loving labor of a frustrated writer or editor. In visits to Ransom's office, Oliver often noticed volumes of William Faulkner's writings, and heard Ransom allude to *The Hamlet* and say how much he would like to write a novel like that. In sum, averred Oliver, "I remember a man who never pulled rank, a man who always seemed relaxed and friendly, a man who was never afraid of a new idea. I remember a man with sad eyes who smiled at a raw, new student and said: 'Hi. I'm Harry Ransom. Let's talk about you.'"[20]

In the years following World War II, Ransom would join in teaching the graduate offerings in the English Department, including Introduction to Bibliography. His version, recalled Redding Sugg, Jr., a graduate student in the late 1940s, emphasized the *making* of books, including the modern author's revising of a manuscript, the galley proofs, the page proofs.[21] Ray Past said that the course directed students into Ronald B. McKerrow's *Introduction to Bibliography for Literary Students* (1928)—a seminal study of the book as a physical and historical product—and Douglas L. McMurtrie's *The Book: The Story of Printing and Bookmaking* (1937), focusing on how books "are made, designed, printed, gathered, sewn, bound, distributed, sometimes forged. . . . I became interested in illustrated books. . . . A lot of (most?) professors in literature would scoff at such a topic, but it was the kind of thing that intrigued Dr. Harry."[22]

At Yale, Ransom had studied Robert Browning's poetry under the eminent Browning scholar William Clyde DeVane (1898–1965), and at UT, Ransom found satisfaction in developing his own graduate seminar on the poet, meeting the class in a book-lined room in the Rare Books Collection in the library. During a "torrid summer" in 1947, Redding Sugg, Jr., found his Browning instructor "always crisply turned out in starched white shirt and tie and seersucker, sporting the trademark heavy dark-rimmed glasses."[23] Ray Past enrolled in this course, and saw evidence of Ransom's "tenacious memory" at every meeting. "He was so beautifully organized— and yet I never remember seeing him use notes," Past recalled. "He would say something like, 'About this matter there are seven points we need to consider, . . . ' and he would put the spread fingers and thumb of one hand against those of the other and tap them lightly together, at about belt level. Sometimes if he was concentrating particularly intensely he would raise the forefingers to his pursed lips. . . . He would then proceed to discuss fascinatingly and articulately exactly seven points."[24] Graduate student Charles W. Hagelman, Jr., also took the Browning course around this period. It was an "exciting" experience, he remembered, because Ransom "had convictions about Browning's impact on the poetry of the nineteenth and twentieth centuries. The Victorians were already out of fashion, so this was a radical view, that Browning was a major voice and a significant influence on Eliot and others." Ransom insisted that Robert Browning's techniques were essentially "modern." As for the format of the class, the students "came to class and talked over whatever was on his mind." The prevailing school of New Criticism "was a box of sorts, and Harry Ransom's mind didn't fit within any such limitations. He preferred to open people's minds. He would have allowed his students to do New Critical papers, but he never taught it." He *did* urge students to investigate the recent directions in textual editing and criticism, however; about trends in that field he had few reservations. But the intimidating shadow of New Criticism, which insisted on viewing literary works apart from all biographical, historical, or bibliographical considerations, repelled rather than attracted him as a required gospel, Hagelman deduced.[25]

Despite these specific preoccupations, Ransom retained his loyalty to the Plan II program he had helped Parlin implement. Future novelist Shelby Hearon (B.A., 1953) characterized Plan II in the early fifties as "new, fresh, hard and taught by the finest teachers at The University. . . . My favorite course was my senior tutorial with Harry Ransom." Evidently Ransom's reading list had many permutations; in Hearon's case, "each week we read a different novel and wrote a paper on it, all faintly organized around the idea of identity. Ransom had just rediscovered Hamlin Garland, whose work I was allowed to think was awful. Just as I was allowed to argue that *Sons and Lovers* was not, except in a surface way, a mother-son story. I thought *A Portrait of the Artist as a Young Man* the best book I'd ever read."[26]

Wayne Rogers, back from military service, joined the Plan II program of courses in English, history, mathematics, biology or anthropology, and a foreign language. He once heard Harry Ransom say that all Plan II students should sign a contract to complete at least two years in the program in order to avoid the vacuum "brought on by the destruction of all their basic values in the freshman year." He first encountered Ransom in a course entitled "Victorian Prose," an advanced seminar for English majors and graduate students in which "extensive" readings from Carlyle, Mill, Newman, and others were "followed by a short, always stimulating lecture and a long, challenging guided discussion in class. Harry was a master of the Socratic method. There was a mid-term exam but the final grade was based on either an open book exam or a written paper on a subject of the student's choice." After class, Ransom sometimes joined the students for lunch in the Commons—the lower floor of the Texas Union, a sea of tables that could hold five hundred people—and encouraged their talk of literature and current politics. He never imposed his political views on them, but listened intently to theirs. "We didn't even know he had an opinion, he was so interested in what we had to say. He didn't condescend, but treated us like adults." Yet he always wore a suit and tie, in contrast to the khaki-clad, tie-less students around him. At five feet nine inches and 165 pounds, by Rogers's estimation, he was now often overshadowed in these discussions by the larger frames of the young men back home from their military service. He still wore his signature circular horn-rimmed glasses from his Sewanee days. He once told the students, "I can wait a thousand years for progress," yet at another juncture advised them, "Don't wait for change."

Rogers had reentered a postwar collegiate world seriously debating such utopian concepts as "One-World Government," "Complete Educational Reform," and "The Abolition of Corporations." He noticed that, "unlike many of his faculty peers, Harry Ransom was not a social reformer. He had little interest in the elitist political philosophies of his time, being too taken up by the intellectual life for its own sake to have time for changing the world. . . . Harry had an internal strength that enabled him to surmount such squabbling with equanimity and to do what he thought was important."[27]

For many English graduate students, Harry Ransom became more than just a friend and adviser; he was the magnet that held together their circle of supportive fellow students. F. Warren Roberts remembered meeting with Ransom for coffee on the Drag on Friday nights in 1947 with a group of students that included George O. Marshall, Jr. (later a chairman at the University of Georgia), and Warren French, destined to become a distinguished scholar of American literature. Roberts had to leave school for several years for active duty with the U.S. Navy, but when he returned to his studies the same informal custom prevailed. Marshall referred to that later bunch—F. Warren Roberts, Sydney Schiffer, Robert J. Barnes, Joseph Cohen, Thomas L. Watson, Charles W. Hagelman, Jr., and himself—as "Harry's boys," who gathered "every other Friday night during the spring of 1953. On each occasion a student would discuss his dissertation and then field queries from the rest of us."[28] The main thing, said Barnes, was that "he could lift your spirits."[29] One graduate student, Ray Past, sensed that portions of his Ph.D. oral examination went roughly, "but after I waited an eternity out in a hallway in the Tower, here came Dr. Harry with a smile and an outstretched hand, saying, 'Let's go where we can sit and have a cold beer.' . . . We talked about the future: What's next? And how should I set about it? Not once did he rain on my parade by referring to the bloodshed he had just come from." Past later learned that Ransom had in fact intervened on his behalf during the committee's deliberations.[30]

From his first freshman students in 1935 to his last doctoral student in 1957, Harry Ransom's teaching career at the University of Texas at Austin would span twenty-two years and encompass half of the Great Depression, all of World War II, and part of the Cold War. Looking back on those days in 1970, Ransom set down some reflections on the making of an effective teacher. This essay, "The Teacher," demanded high expectations for those "born to the classroom," though allowing for individual styles. "The difference should always be the capacity, the talent, the purpose of the individual teacher—and more important, the differing individual student." He envisioned the role of teachers as one of total commitment to a student's potential. However, the instructor should try to avoid being an "Icon Smasher" (a teacher who delights in "pleasures of intellectual destruction"), a "Faculty Friend" (who "persuades a student to compromise with incompetence because the struggle for knowledge makes him uncomfortable"), or an "Oddball" ("phonies and poseurs who use every conceivable means to attract attention and avoid the hard work of communicating knowledge"). The good teacher must accept certain sobering limitations. "Teachers can instill respect for facts but not intellectual curiosity. . . . We can only encourage, incite, elicit, and once in a lifetime inspire real talent, devotion to truth, opinion that leads to sound judgment, and the kind of intellectual courage that true education in the long run always requires." In reality, the ironic answer to the question "What do we teach?" must be "Not much and often not what we think we teach." Nevertheless, asserted Ransom, perhaps recalling his own mentors at Sewanee and Yale, "no superior teacher has any trouble recalling one of his superior teachers who changed his life at the instant and gave him the means of continuing that process of change as long as he continues learning."[31]

FIVE

THE BARE FACT OF WAR

Harry Ransom and his mother, Marion, attended All Saints' Chapel, an Episcopalian ministry for university students as well as longtime Austin families. Located near the UT campus at Whitis Avenue and 27th Street and built in 1899 of Texas limestone, the structure enshrined historically notable stained glass windows. Harry Huntt Ransom and Marion Goodwin Ransom formally transferred their active Episcopalian affiliation from Sewanee to this church on October 30, 1936. Elderly, unmarried Dr. William J. Battle, a native of North Carolina, professor of Latin and Greek, and former (1914–1916) UT president ad interim, functioned as Senior Warden of the Vestry, the governing body; Ransom served as one of his vestrymen in 1936 and 1937. Thereafter Battle attentively followed the new young instructor's career. At the time, about thirty university students belonged to the All Saints' congregation. One of them, Evelyn (Buzzo) Moorman, a freshman student from Houston, was impressed that the Ransoms were always in "regular attendance every single Sunday." He was a "gentle, protective, older-brother figure to me and to his students," she said. "He had an ivy-league look about him. All of us felt he was 'on our side' in the struggle to achieve our goals. He had somewhat of a 'Mr. Chips' personality." She lived in Littlefield Dormitory on 26th Street at the time, and the Ransoms lived on 23rd Street, so they would walk her home.[1]

In 1937 the Ransoms moved to another apartment. That year they also made a brief trip to Sewanee, the last time they would visit "the Mountain" together. Ransom looked up several of his teachers from the Mary Dabney grammar school, having lunch with Dr. Ware (history), visiting an "enfeebled" Miss Mae DuBose (math), and encountering Miss Lizzie Wadham (art) as she was "wandering in the cemetery."[2]

Marion Ransom, a petite, energetic woman, had pinned her gray hair into a simple bun. She projected an authoritative presence in her dark clothing. One day when Evelyn Buzzo and Ransom crossed paths on the way to the campus, he jokingly asked her if she had heard him and his mother quarreling. It seemed that they had "disagreed politically, and the discussion had become heated." He "mock-complained of her 'combativeness' and her 'strong opinions.'" Buzzo perceived a devoted, respectful, and "wonderful" friendship between the Ransoms. All the same, various observers agreed, he was not a mama's boy who bowed to her whims. Ransom's ambitions benefited by her advice rather than her dictates. She did not have any grand plans for him; it was Ransom who formed his goals.

Evelyn Buzzo's husband-to-be, Warren Moorman, had been a freshman student in Plan II in 1936–1937, and Harry Ransom, his faculty adviser, became friends with him as well. In Evelyn's junior year, Ransom hired her to collate and type notes that "he had jotted on all sorts of whatever paper" for his doctoral dissertation on the history of English copyright law. "It was a fascinating subject, about which his enthusiasm was contagious," she said. She helped prepare a draft of his dissertation in his office that year. As a consequence, she—situated like "a fly on the wall"—listened to Ransom converse with his students: "He counseled them academically and personally. Intensity . . . is the word that best describes Harry Ransom. Concern and *real* emotional commitment to the welfare and improvement of circumstances for everyone he knew were basic to his nature." Until Ransom earned his doctorate in 1938, she good-naturedly addressed him as *"Mr.* Ransom" instead of *"Dr.* Ransom."[3]

Without sacrificing any of this dedication to his courses and his students, Ransom was taking several steps to make his academic future more secure. For one thing, he placed several articles in scholarly journals. His essay analyzing an eighteenth-century dispute about copyright law— "From a Gentleman in Edinburgh, 1769: An Early Sidelight on Literary Property"—appeared in his former teacher William S. Knickerbocker's *Sewanee Review* in 1936,[4] and he followed this in a 1938 issue with an article titled "Riddle of the World: A Note on Pope and Pascal." "Both writers . . . were pitiable invalids," Ransom concluded in the latter essay. "As a writer each developed a swift, epigrammatical style; a summary mode of thought; a talent for emphasis, clarity, compression. Both writers were involved in heated controversy and both enjoyed it." Yet, he observed, "essential purposes differ: the aim of the one is to convert; the aim of the other is to instruct." He produced these critical commentaries within an eddy outside the intellectual currents flowing through the academy of the 1930s, just as he had, earlier in the decade, invented a doctoral dissertation topic that insulated him from the pressures of that generation of graduate scholarship.[5]

His copyright research yielded three of the four primarily factual essays he published in *Studies in English,* a UT journal: "The Rewards of Authorship in the Eighteenth Century,"[6] "Some Legal Elements in Elizabethan Plays,"[7] "The Date of the First Copyright Law,"[8] and "The Brownings in Paris."[9]

Although upon the completion of his degree Ransom had been advanced to the level of Assistant Professor for the 1938–1939 year, he increased his options on January 25, 1940, when he filed an official application for placement with the Fisk Teachers Agency of Chicago. Listing his present salary as $2,600, he stipulated that he would be unwilling to move unless the proffered salary was at least $3,400. He stressed the balance he had achieved in his professional duties and scholarly activities: "I have no desire simply to change positions. I am interested primarily in opportunities for teaching, but I am also concerned with the research. . . . If conditions were such that I could spend my summers in study and writing, I should be glad to devote the longer term exclusively to teaching. That arrangement would honestly represent my interests. I should make extraordinary efforts to qualify for a deanship or assistant deanship. . . . I have no prejudices concerning type of college, geographical location, or type of student." He added that "for the past year I have been a member of the Dean's Council of four members who have charge of advising students on problems concerning the College," and "for three years I have been an associate editor of the Texas Folk-Lore Publications. . . . My major undertaking in research is a history of copyright law in England and America. This work is well under way, most of last year having been spent in Europe and Harvard in gathering material for it."[10] Within the next few months, Ransom was approached by the Fisk Agency about applying for faculty positions at Carleton College, New Jersey State Teachers College, and Michigan State University.

The research trip abroad cited by Ransom had taken place in the summer and fall of 1939. He left the University of Texas in July, intending to spend a year in England completing his study of literary copyright laws. He and his mother arrived on a Sunday morning aboard the Cunard White Star Line R.M.S. *Mauritania,* the largest liner ever taken into the London Docks. Although "the countryside was unbelievably green and beautiful," in London itself he found the populace practicing blackouts.[11] A photographic memento of Ransom and his mother from this trip shows him walking in a dark suit and vest, fedora, and black-frame glasses; he holds a folded newspaper. Silver-haired Marion in wire spectacles accompanies him, attired in her matronly, somber clothing. In another picture, they stroll past storefronts in a crowded London Street.[12]

Ransom observed British drills and other preparations for the impend-

FIGURE 5.1
Marion Ransom aboard the White Star Line R.M.S. Mauritania, *en route to London,*
1939. Harry Ransom Humanities Research Center, The University of Texas at Austin.

ing conflict: "Big Ben was darkened," he noted. "Fruit in the markets were
dim shapes under the light of black hooded lamps." "Self-appointed booing
squadrons . . . assembled before lighted shops [during the blackouts] to express displeasure." "No crimes."[13] International events were not cooperating
with his scholarly agenda. A feverish effort to complete some work before
the specter of armed conflict should become a reality now drove Ransom.

> I went to work at the [British] Museum hard and fast, accomplishing
> more than I usually get do[ne] in six months. . . . Everybody, it seemed,
> from the Gov to the Covent Garden porters, set about quietly getting
> ready for war. There was something magnificent and something quite
> frightening about the whole thing, like watching a man topple off a high
> roof without being able to do anything but watch. Gas masks had been
> handed out long before, air-raid shelters had been ready since the previ-
> ous September, anti-aircraft batteries had been set up in all the parks.[14]

To Professors Robert A. Law and R. H. Griffith, Ransom wrote that he
"found British Museum authorities removing great cases of the valuable
manuscripts from under my nose, and other libraries largely closed." He
notified Griffith: "This week has provided a great change of England's

FIGURE 5.2
*Ransom and his mother on a London street, 1939. Ransom and his mother witnessed
the early days of World War II in England. He kept notes, wrote poems, and gave
interviews about their harrowing experiences.* Harry Ransom Humanities Research
Center, The University of Texas at Austin.

self-possession into magnificent courage. I make no sense of claims and counter-claims about munitions; but if spirit has anything to do with waging war, Hitler is sure of a sad wakening when he undertakes to fight Great Britain."[15]

On September 1, 1939, the new German terror of *blitzkrieg* invaded Poland and threatened to sweep across Europe. Great Britain and France declared war on September 3; the Soviets entered Poland a few days later. The Ransoms prepared for an inevitable departure from England. "We stayed until war was an actuality. The embassy then said to get out. . . . I decided to go to Eire. We left Euston on the most excited night of September. The Irish mail was crammed long before the starting whistle. Roughnecks were trying to break windows in order to get on the train. Mother and I had third class tickets; all the coaches were loaded; people were jostling each other in the corridors." At Holyhead that morning, Ransom was checked closely by the police, who had been alerted to stop Irish Republican Army departees for Ireland. They were searching for bombs. "My trench coat may have looked sinister, but . . . I explained that I was a badly scared English teacher from Austin, Texas, U.S.A. looking for nine lost pieces of baggage." En route to Ireland, "the boat was carrying three times its normal load. . . . The only accommodation left was straight chairs in the lounge." The Ransoms sailed over with "nervous women, crying babies, a dozen Irish laborers returning home." Arriving in Dun Laoghaire, they found that "a fine Irish rain was falling." They "could hear the . . . news vendors calling the Irish Press in Gaelic."[16]

One event that registered the escalation of hostilities jarringly was the sinking of the *Athenia* by a German submarine. Ransom's former student Margaret Doggett was aboard the ship on a student cruise with twenty other young women, and Ransom and his mother hastened to find her in Galway, Ireland, following her rescue.[17] "He had visions of bandage-swathed bodies lying on hospital beds, but to his great relief the co-eds were not only in the 'pink of condition' but 'painting the town red,'" a newspaper reported.[18] The harrowing ordeal of the *Athenia* passengers inspired a passage in a narrative sea poem that Ransom penned in later years:

> Well, that night it was the Athenia went down
> (Torpedo had struck her or she hit a mine),
> And dawn came on up over Galway; the town
> Was cursing the rain, standing in line,
> Getting word slowly and waiting for more,
> Watching the clock all the way round,

Scuffing the floor.
There was some talk, but there wasn't a sound
Of a dead-list until the day was fair done.
Then it came in. "NONE LOST." Not a one.[19]

Every news report now confirmed the inescapable realization that Ransom's effort to do research abroad had reached an end. After he completed a census of legal manuscripts at Trinity College in Dublin, Ransom and his mother boarded the S.S. *Iroquois,* "a small, coast-wise vessel making its first Atlantic trip and the last boat to leave Eire. After two days out, it ran into a storm, which lasted forty hours." Ransom later tried to make light of this perilous journey, claiming to a reporter that his mother had been "having the time of her life on the upper deck" as it ploughed through a rough sea. "I'm not sure I'm kin to her," he joked. "When I was scared to death by air raid signals, she was having a huge time. She wanted to stay in London and see what would happen. She thought the trip on the *Iroquois* was fun. The only thing she didn't like was English cabbage; and if she could have cooked it herself, I suppose she would have enjoyed that." The storm abated, but rumors that the United States had declared war on Germany filled the *Iroquois* passengers with anxiety. Then the ship's captain compounded their dread by warning that the boat might be attacked off the American coast. To their relief, fifteen hundred miles out, the *Iroquois* received an escort of U.S. destroyers and scouting airplanes. "Nothing more serious was encountered than two porpoises and a flotilla of tin cans, which one nervous passenger thought was a school of submarine periscopes," Ransom recalled.[20]

Ransom returned to Harvard to undertake what he could in the way of extending his previous research in the law and literary collections there. But his "year abroad" was now a futile hope, and he returned to Austin to resume his teaching in the Spring 1940 term.

During this period of upheaval and frustration, Ransom was taken with the notion of making a comparison of the rankings of academic libraries. The three pages of blue-ink notes in which he denoted these figures and relative positions represent the first overt indication of his interest in building up the University of Texas collection to a point of distinction. He calculated that in the years 1935–1936, Harvard, Yale, Columbia, Chicago, and Illinois led in the number of volumes on deposit in their libraries. Harvard's annual increase was 117,310; UT's was only 12,111. In fact, twenty-three academic libraries, especially the University of California at Berkeley, reported greater annual increases than did the University of Texas. According to his figures, "Texas ranks 15th among the states in library facilities for research," behind New York, Massachusetts, California, Ohio, Illinois, Pennsylvania, Connecticut, Missouri, Michigan, New Jersey, Minnesota, Wisconsin, Massachusetts, and Indiana. In terms of expenditures, Texas ranked 37th, followed only by Pennsylvania, Delaware, Florida, Louisiana, Georgia, Rhode Island, South Carolina, West Virginia, Arkansas, Alabama, and Mississippi."[21]

Robert Wilson remembered Harry Ransom's returning from his months of research in London, Dublin, and Cambridge with eyestrain, and his being relieved of certain responsibilities involving vision in exchange for advising hours. Part of Ransom's eyestrain may have resulted from supervising the microfilming of 6,000 frames of copyright records during his trip abroad.[22] Shortly thereafter, however, Ransom threw himself back into his work as associate editor of the Texas Folk-Lore Publications and its annual volume. Confessing to Dobie his growing sense of belonging to the state in which he was born and had spent his earliest years, Ransom received an affirming reply from Dobie on March 29, 1941:

> Dear Harry:
> I have just . . . reread your letter. It made things a little misty to me the other day. . . . Much—so very much—as I appreciate what you say that is personal to me, the relationship you so clearly and sincerely reveal between yourself and Texas moves me more. I am often hear[t]sick at seeing so many people supposed to nurture the mind and spirit of youth who bear no relation whatever to all the heritages that these youth have.
> "A man deserves a heath." That is a noble sentence, rich, deep and meaty. Harry, why don't we call this folk-lore book A MAN DESERVES A HEATH[?][23]

But the threesome—Dobie, Boatright, and Ransom—instead produced a collection entitled *Texian Stomping Grounds*. Harry Huntt Ransom wrote in his preface, "A Man Deserves a Heath": "Among the feelings that have moved men powerfully, none has been more universal than love of the earth. Consciously or unconsciously, silently or in defiant proclamations, men have always identified themselves with their native soil. With their own countryside, with their home rock, they have associated the forces of their lives. Young men, not always in vain, have died for this ideal of the land; poets have sung it and old men have celebrated it in story. It has made some men narrow, but it has made others heroic. Famed or nameless, each of us is moved by this feeling for the place of his growth. Every man deserves a native heath."[24]

His personal friendships with such eminent Texas figures as Dobie having matured, he modestly notified the University of the South of his own impending inclusion in *The Biographical Directory of American Scholars* (on the same Sewanee alumni questionnaire form he vaguely stated that his political affiliation "varies"). But however much Ransom may have begun to feel he belonged at the university, the spreading specter of global hostilities, disrupting and destroying lives in more and more nations, loomed over his own personal fate. The bombing of Pearl Harbor by Japan on December 7, 1941, took the United States into a war declared by Congress on the day following the attack.

Men now left the university to join the armed forces, and this attrition of male students and professors steadily shrank the student body and the faculty. From the English Department, Willis Pratt and Harry Ransom would join the Army Air Force (AAF). "Harry could have stayed at UT," said Sunshine "Sunny" (Neeley) Thurmond, but "he wanted to serve." Sunny Neeley was secretary to Albert P. Brogan, Dean of the Graduate School; Harry had taken Sunny to a few university functions and football games before he met Hazel Harrod.[25] Another friend of Ransom's, Frances "Sug" (Mueller) Danforth, who earned degrees in journalism and English, was also a friend of Neeley. Sug Mueller joined the staff of *Alcalde,* the alumni magazine with offices in the Texas Union. For 10 A.M. coffee breaks, Neeley, Ransom, and Mueller flipped coins to see who would pay for their five-cent cups of coffee.[26] But these lighthearted get-togethers abruptly lost out to the imminence of Ransom's departure. Marion Ransom gave her son a Bible as a parting gift, its flyleaf inscribed on the day he left home, "Presented to 'H.H.R.' by 'M.G.R.' July 25 1942."[27] That day Harry needed a ride to the Missouri-Pacific station on Third Street to report for military service, and Sug and Sunny borrowed a car and took him to catch his train.

Enlisting as a second lieutenant in the Air Corps, he sent a telegram from Florida to his concerned mother—"SWORN IN TODAY FEEL FINE KEEP WELL LOVE=HARRY"—on July 27, 1942, at 9 P.M.[28] He had begun six weeks of Officers Training School. A careening world had caught up with the trajectory of his scholarly career. On August 8, 1942, Ransom wrote from Miami on "Officers' Training School" letterhead stationery to his former classics teacher at Sewanee, Professor Henry M. Gass: "It seems a long road from Aristotle's *Ethics* to Miami Beach. I finished my doctorate at Yale in 1938. Since then I have been assistant professor in English and Counselor for the College at Texas. I was up for promotion this year, but the opportunity to join the Technical Training Command of the AAF was too good to turn down. . . . Only heaven knows, though, what

is to happen. Here all things are stripped down to the bare fact of war. . . .
Meanwhile the University of Texas promises great things."[29]

Ransom belonged to Squadron F, Class 42H in Miami. Another Texan,
Wilson Hudson, came to Florida and was assigned to Class 42I. Comparing notes, Hudson learned that he and Ransom had both been recruited by
Officer Gaylor "Red Dog" Johnson, a Rice graduate. Johnson had taken
Hudson away from his graduate studies at the University of Chicago cam-
pus.[30] UT colleague Willis Pratt also visited Ransom in Florida. Pratt had
laid aside his research on British Romantic poets to prepare books about
aircraft identification and prisoner of war information.[31] On November 5
at 4:10 P.M., Ransom sent a Western Union telegram to Mrs. Marion G.
Ransom, 1606 Congress: "Leave granted arrive late Saturday afternoon.
Love=Harry."[32] An undated newspaper clipping from this period reads:
"Lieutenant Harry Ransom, former professor of English at the University,
is in Austin awaiting Army orders. He has come from Washington, D.C.,
where he recently received his commission."[33] Very likely Ransom was in
Austin making arrangements to move his mother to Orlando, Florida,
where he would be stationed at the Army Air Force School of Applied Tactics between 1942 and 1944. He soon held the rank of Captain and was
classified as a Military Intelligence Officer, Grade 9300, whose duty in Orlando was to edit overseas intelligence reports for the Air Forces Tactical
Center and the Army-Navy Staff College.[34]

Hazel Harrod, meanwhile, completed her B.A. degree in 1942 and was
hired by the university to teach composition courses as she began work
for her M.A. degree in English (which she would receive in 1944). Separation from Hazel was definitely a trial, but Ransom believed that these
personal sacrifices were essential in wartime. He greatly admired a passage
from Winston Churchill's famous wartime address to Great Britain, delivered on December 5, 1942: "We are all of us defending a cause: the cause of
freedom and of justice, of the weak against the strong, law against violence,
mercy and tolerance against brutality and iron-bound tyranny."[35] Ransom's
commitment to this concept of patriotic duty found expression at the typewriter rather than with a weapon, and resulted in varied publications for
the United States Army Air Force. He authored *An Analysis of Troop-School
Courses in Use by the AAF* (1943), *AAF Intelligence Studies* (1943–1944), *Termi-
nology of Air Warfare* (1945), "Notes for an Epitaph: Rise and Fall of the
Luftwaffe" (1945), "Tactical Air Operations" (co-author, 1945), "The Veteran and Adult Education" (1945), "Educational Plans of 500,000 AAF Veterans" (1946), *Employment of Veterans* (1946), and "Historical Procedures in
the AAF" (1946).[36] More than five years of world conflict elapsed between

FIGURE 5.3

Ransom, Air Force School of Applied Tactics, Orlando, Florida, 1943. Classified as a Military Intelligence Officer, Ransom edited overseas reports for the Air Forces Tactical Center and the Army-Navy Staff College. Harry Ransom Humanities Research Center, The University of Texas at Austin.

Ransom's aborted research trip to Great Britain in 1939 and the surrender of Germany and Japan in 1945, after which American service personnel eagerly swarmed home to pick up their lives. Returning veterans would soon swell the university populations, and professors would be in demand. Whereas by 1945 the UT enrollment had dropped to 7,027, in 1947 it would leap to 17,260.

From 1944 to 1946, Ransom, by then a Public Relations Officer, served as Director of the Air Force Editorial Office in Washington, D.C. Among the perks was access to professional theater: in May 1946, for instance, he attended a performance of Michael Todd's production of *Hamlet* starring Maurice Evans.[37] Gerald Langford visited Ransom at the Pentagon Building that same month. Langford, a Ph.D. from the University of Virginia, was doing educational work for the Marine Corps Headquarters, also in Washington. He had applied for a professorship at UT, and Professor L. L. Click, Chairman of the English Budget Council and Assistant Dean of the College of Arts and Sciences, referred him to Harry Ransom at the Pentagon for an interview. Langford soon sat before an immense desk in Ransom's office amid plush surroundings. "He was a charmer," Langford remembered. Ransom told him about the department and Austin, "a quiet little inexpensive country town." The interview went well, and Langford quickly heard from Professor Click that he would be hired.[38]

Ransom himself would soon be discharged from the military. He had advanced from Second Lieutenant to First Lieutenant to Captain in the Army Air Force, and then had been promoted to Major. He was decorated with the Army Commendation Ribbon, the American Campaign Medal, and the World War II Victory Medal. His highest honor was the award of the Legion of Merit in 1947 as an officer of public relations, for contributing to the development and publication of *Air Force* magazine during the war.[39] He served as deputy director and later as editor of this official journal of the U.S. Army Air Force. Ransom would describe his stint with that periodical as working "at nearly everything from lieutenant-office boy jobs to the directorship."[40] On May 15, 1946, shortly before his discharge from military service, Major Ransom sent a three-page memorandum to his superior officer, Colonel Bowman, sketching the possibilities for a "peacetime journal" to supersede *Air Force*. Such a periodical "should put into the hands of officers and men a professional journal of military aviation—readable in style, attractive in format, reliable in content." He suggested that AAF personnel be encouraged to submit "articles, art, and comment" to the magazine (Ransom himself had anonymously contributed poems to *Air Force* during his editorship).[41] This urge of Ransom's to start up a heterogeneous journal of wide scope would manifest itself again during the next decade, in part because of his fondness for the unpredictable nature of the *Sewanee Review*.

Ransom's abilities had not gone unnoticed within the military. He was approached about taking a position with the Educational Services Division of the Air University at Maxwell Field in Montgomery, Alabama, which would formally open on September 3, 1946; its mission involved specialized education programs for career officers of the Army Air Force.[42] Ransom declined the job offer, choosing instead to return to his teaching position at the University of Texas, where the English Department promoted him to Associate Professor in 1946 and granted him tenure. On June 19, 1946, he went on terminal leave from the Army Air Force and was honorably discharged on October 16, 1946. Having arrived in Austin by July 4, four years after his enlistment, he corresponded regularly with Hazel Harrod, now openly considered Ransom's girlfriend in the department. She was temporarily living on the East Coast.

The first few weeks of moving back to Austin frustrated and exhausted Ransom. For one thing, Marion Ransom returned to Austin in a weakened condition. Early in 1943, she had been the victim of a pedestrian-automobile accident at an intersection on Main Street in Orlando, Florida, having been struck by a careless driver. Dismissed from the hospital after treatment for bruises, she suffered lingering effects from the injuries. Her son thereafter found himself responsible for her recurring medical expenses.[43] Moreover, owing to the influx of students back into the university, the housing situation in Austin had turned desperate. "Several hundred people have applied for [Beauford] Jester's place at the Normandie Arms (where the Ransoms had lived in 1940), assuming he'd be Governor and give it up," Ransom reported.[44] With his mother in declining health, Ransom moved their belongings "carton by carton" into a "dark, stuffy, and small" apartment on Speedway. Bouts of sinusitis, fatigue, and an incipient hiatal hernia plagued him. Ransom was still mourning the January 1945 deaths of his longtime friends Judge and Mrs. Templeton of Winchester, Tennessee, and felt exasperated that he could retrieve only some books and a few pieces of memorabilia from their estate. He had relied on an "old timer there whom I do trust," but she did not prove effective in representing his interests.[45]

Frazzled like many returning wartime veterans who had aggressively won a world war, Ransom experienced vexation and stress during this muggy summer of adjustment from military to civilian life. Everything had become a trial. "It is SO hot," he wrote to Hazel. "The refrigerator is busted and the road to the place is so bumpy that my Chevrolet busts a spring

FIGURE 5.4

Ransom, Washington, D.C., 1945. In 1947, Captain Ransom, as an officer of public relations, was awarded the Legion of Merit for contributing to the development and publication of Air Force *magazine during World War II.* Harry Ransom Humanities Research Center, The University of Texas at Austin.

every bounce. . . . I can find no storeroom for the furniture."[46] An English instructor at UT named Arthur H. Scouten encountered Ransom waiting for the Tower elevator during this miserable period of transition. "I was on my way out," Scouten would recall, "and shook hands with Harry, and said I was going to cross the street and eat supper. 'No,' said Harry, 'I'll take you to dinner; we'll eat in a Mexican restaurant.' For that we needed the car. When we walked up to the car, . . . he saw that he had locked himself out." Scouten suggested that they dine at one of the restaurants on Guadalupe Street while some garage people opened his car. But Ransom would not hear of rescinding his invitation and, to Scouten's astonishment, "just hauled off and hit the glass windshield on the left hand door. He just smashed it, with glass all over the place. He didn't use his fist," but rather "broke the glass on the door with the base of the palm of his right hand." In Scouten's words,

> I gaped at him, and the blood was running down all over his hand. He motioned for me to get in the car. When we reached the restaurant, he had blood on the seat, the wheel, his sleeves, and his hands. . . . He washed in the restroom, and the wife of the proprietor put some gauze on his hand and some adhesive, and we ate a Mexican dinner.

To Scouten the incident showed Ransom's "driving energy, just like Bobby Knight, the basketball coach at Indiana, or Lyndon Johnson,"[47] but this uncharacteristic impulsiveness more plausibly charted his discomfort and disorientation.

On top of everything else, Ransom was learning that the campus had not yet recovered its equilibrium from a divisive controversy of epochal proportions. In 1944 the Board of Regents had voted to fire President Homer Rainey for insubordination. Among other issues, the academic freedom of English professors to teach John Dos Passos's graphic novel *U.S.A.* in a required sophomore literature class and of economics professors to include political content in their courses had resulted in confrontations between faculty and students versus concerned regents and indignant citizens. Faculty voiced their right to academic freedom; the regents asserted their prerogative to take an interest in the curriculum. A number of prominent English professors resigned in protest in the aftermath of Rainey's firing, including Theodore Hornberger, Henry Nash Smith, Francis Mineka, and Herschel Baker. "I was away during the controversy . . . between the very conservative and the liberal groups here on this campus," Ransom told Joan Simpson Burns in 1967. "It was good fortune for me to be in the Air Force at that time."[48]

Correspondence between Hazel Harrod and Ransom was frequent during this period of his transition from the Army Air Force to the University of Texas. They had, coincidentally, exchanged places—she remained in Alexandria, Virginia (where she had moved to be nearer to him), after he had returned to Texas. To "Hazel darling," Ransom alluded to repercussions from the Rainey controversy, which he termed "so bad that I'm not even trying to learn the issues, much less take sides. . . . There are all kinds of gossip, much of it virulent." Repeatedly and tenderly he declared his love to Hazel: "I do want to share the sight of the hills, the first breeze at night, the first walk in the morning, the ring of poetry again, the chores in Shakespeare. . . . I miss you."[49] She was his "best philosopher, guide, and friend." He craved her counsel about his career choices: "I won't pretend not to worry about the university—it's that I need special advice about; other things I think I can judge clearly." He wondered about his further promotion possibilities at the university, even after an "eminently satisfactory" and "encouraging" conference with President T. S. Painter about Ransom's prospects at UT. "I'm constantly conscious of. . . . the beauty and the strength that you have brought into everything I've known and done for years," he wrote on August 16, 1946.[50] In Hazel Harrod's loving replies he was "Hal darling." She was solicitous and opinionated. Harrod mentioned the responsibilities of her summer job in Washington, D.C., while expressing a wish for a vacation. Their letters of 1946 discussed how long Harrod should continue teaching for the university before they married. Strict enforcement of nepotism rules prohibited any employment of two family members. Ransom's financial dilemmas included trying to buy a house on an associate professor's salary. Despite various hurdles, including "vicious double-dealing" real estate agents, Ransom finally purchased a house on Keasbey Street, at the northern edge of the Hyde Park district.[51]

Though now firmly ensconced in his department, Ransom nonetheless continued to strive. Wilson Hudson, who joined the UT English faculty in 1946, remembered that Ransom always stopped and chatted with him. One day, Ransom said, impatiently, "Wilson, do you know that we are *forty* years old, and if we don't do something in the next ten years, it will be too late." Hudson "knew he wasn't kidding."[52] Ransom regularly walked past Willis Pratt's adjoining office on his way home. Pratt recalls Harry's saying in a conversation that his mother used to tell him, "Keep going in a straight line and watch for a chance to rise."[53] As things transpired, he did not have to wait long after all for promotion to the final rank of full professor, although in a letter to Hazel he had worried about the "basically . . . unethical" overlooking of established UT scholars in the postwar rush to recruit "outside" figures. (Lewis Leary of Duke University, for one, was being considered.)[54] On April 27, 1947, Professor Click wrote to "Dear Dr. Ransom": "The Budget Council of the Department of English in recognition of your ability in research, efficiency in teaching, and aptitude for general usefulness to the institution, recommended that you be advanced to a professorship, effective September 17, 1947."[55]

Ransom's loyalties were tested on June 4, 1948, when the American College Bureau of Chicago wrote to ask if he would be interested in the presidency of Albany State College in New York. Mrs. Charles E. Goodell, president of the placement service, continued, "I have always thought you would be ready for one of the administrative positions and of course, I have always been watching your work. . . . For this type of position, deanship and presidency, I think you have so many of the qualifications that will help to increase our people's respect for education. This is my reason for writing you about these positions."[56] The Fisk Teachers Agency continued to send him inquiries about high administrative positions until 1948. Ransom considered and turned down each of the possibilities that presented themselves.

Part of Ransom's reluctance to relocate to another institution, whatever the inducements, stemmed from his mother's ill health. In April 1948, Marion Ransom entered Seton Hospital with a broken shoulder suffered in a fall. Marion, who had until now provided a stable home for him, could no longer care for herself very well. Ransom had unwisely sold the Keasbey house in 1948 and acquired a small house north of Austin off rural Braker Lane, wanting Marion to have the peace and privacy of a country setting, but to his dismay she soon became partially disabled. Consequently he worried about her using butane fuel and the hardships caused by their trucked-in water and its tin storage tank. (The water source had been misrepresented during the sale; a well on the property produced only sludge.) In August 1948, Marion's daughter, Mrs. Jean Barron Hurlbut, came from North Carolina to look after her mother. Hurlbut left in March 1949, and that winter the Ransoms moved back into town to an apartment on Lorrain Street in the Enfield area. In the spring of 1950, Ransom suffered a hiatal hernia (the "midriff trouble" that he had mentioned to Hazel as early as 1946) and entered Brackenridge Hospital for tests. Determinedly, Ransom tried to sell "Dead End"—the caustic name that he and Hazel assigned to the isolated Braker Lane house—but he and Marion had to move back to its rustic accommodations for another year.[57]

In June 1951 Ransom returned to University Avenue and rented the upper part of a house that had been divided up into a four-plex. Several months later, on August 11, 1951, encouraged by his chances at UT, forty-two-year-old Harry and thirty-year-old Hazel were married in a private ceremony at the Trinity Episcopal Church in Galveston where Harry had been christened in 1908. The couple spent their two-day honeymoon in the bridal suite of the Galvez Hotel.[58] Returning to Austin, they lived in an upstairs apartment adjacent to Marion's. For years Ransom also had to keep up the payments on the unwanted house in the country and even had to let someone live there almost rent-free in order to prevent break-ins and keep the wood painted against damage by the sun and wind. Nonetheless, after a year of renting in Austin for the threesome, Ransom was able to buy a two-story house and added on a bath, closet, and kitchenette for his mother.[59] There was no need to take into consideration the space needs of a larger family, because Ransom had known when he married Hazel that she had undergone a hysterectomy shortly after World War II. At that time he and Hazel's mother had conferred worriedly when a tumor (which turned out to be benign) was discovered. The impossibility of Hazel's bearing children made no difference in his feelings, he had assured her.[60]

A frail, eighty-three-year-old Marion finally succumbed to multiple health problems on August 31, 1953, following a year of painful illness. The next day, in a large morocco-bound copy of the Bible, Ransom recorded his mother's final words: "I want to stay with you. . . . Your Mother is all right. . . . I love you, love you. . . . Goodnight, precious boy—. . . . Knit to my soul I weave / Thy robe of immortality. . . . And, O God, especially bless Harry—" He responded in notes on the endpaper of the book: "Oh, God I pray that I may be like her and like the man she saw in me and like the man she hoped I might become." Marion Ransom's funeral took place at Trinity Episcopal Church in Victoria, Texas, on September 1. A newspaper reported that besides her son she was survived by two daughters, Mrs. Jean Barron of North Carolina and Mrs. Julia Darcy of New Orleans; two sisters, Mrs. C. McIntosh of Victoria and Mrs. Lydia Henning of New Orleans; and six grandchildren. The Reverend Paul H. Kratzig conducted the services, and burial was in Evergreen Cemetery.[61] Eleven people signed the visitors' register. The rector read four biblical verses at the service, including John 15:7: "If ye abide in me, and my words abide in you, ye shall ask what ye will, and it shall be done unto you," and I Corinthians 15:22: "For as in Adam all die, even so in Christ shall all be made alive."[62]

A few weeks later Ransom made a nostalgic visit to Tennessee, writing later to a friend: "Nearly everybody was away. Things have changed, of course, but a lot remains—including, of course, the beauty of the outlying places (which I suppose I remember more vividly than most sojourners there because I haunted them from the age of ten upwards). Most of all I missed people, and especially Major Gass. He and Mother died within a month of each other in August last summer; so I felt the gap there on the Mountain."[63] In 1960, Ransom would write simply to an acquaintance from his Sewanee years, "Mother died in 1953. She was, I think, the most gallant person I have ever known."[64]

SIX

CLIMBING THE
ADMINISTRATIVE LADDER

No longer a sanctuary for eighteen-to twenty-two-year-olds, the university now had to accommodate thousands of older, motivated, in-a-hurry military veterans in the same classrooms attended by intimidated high school graduates. These former soldiers made an impression on freshman Tom Jones, future lyricist of *The Fantasticks:* "You had to compete with them. . . . A lot of them had families, and they weren't kidding around. . . . And a lot of the professors were veterans, and they had been deprived of doing their thing for a number of years. And they came with a kind of wild enthusiasm. . . . There was this really febrile, burning thing going on."[1] Three years after having resumed his teaching and advising duties, Ransom filled out a Teaching Load Sheet in 1949 by adding up his student totals as 106—the heaviest student load except for Mody Boatright's 111.[2] The same year, he underlined a sentence on UT's policy regarding eligibility for retirement under the Teacher Retirement System of Texas. He wrote in the margin: "1935–1969" and "1965/1969," projecting his choice of retirement years if he stayed on at the University of Texas at Austin.[3]

Another foreign war erupted in June 1950, when North Korean Communists invaded South Korea and the United Nations and the United States began to send troops to defend South Korea. Ransom thought briefly of enlisting in the military again but decided against it because of his mother's poor health, his increasing responsibilities at the university, and the advice he got from a friend. On August 6, 1950, a former Army Air Force colleague responded to a letter from Ransom, urging him "to sit this one out. . . . I can see that it would be an inconvenience to the University for you to pull out in the middle of a term. . . . And then there is always the possibility that you won't have to go at all, in which case delay in signing up [for the reserves] would be all to the good. . . . I'm not yet convinced, Harry, that they will get so hard up for public relations officers that they will call up majors against their will. . . . If necessary, the University would request a deferment for you. . . . Put your present job up against one of writing or overseeing press releases, and see if you aren't persuaded that you are more useful to the country right where you are."[4]

Certainly the university *was* getting its money's worth out of this forty-two-year-old faculty member. At the undergraduate level, Ransom devised and taught a yearlong tutorial in Plan II, a "Great Issues" course that covered readings from Plato's *Republic* to Thomas Wolfe's *Look Homeward, Angel*. He assigned twenty-eight required books and recommended twenty-seven others. He taught variations of this course almost yearly from 1946 to 1957.[5] By 1950–1951, he was supervising sixteen master's students, seven active Ph.D. candidates, and twenty-three conference students in addition to his two- or three-course load, which added another forty to seventy students. His administrative work included Plan II conferences for Dean Parlin and half-time work in the graduate office for Dean Brogan.[6] In recognition of his abilities as a graduate adviser, on March 20, 1951, President T. S. Painter made Ransom the Assistant Dean of the Graduate School. Seventeen years after H. T. Parlin had first tapped him for special recognition and advising duties, Ransom was finally a part of the university administrative network. Newspaper photographs at this time show a bulkier but still boyish-looking Ransom, persistently wearing his trademark round tortoiseshell eyeglasses.

Students from this period were equally as enthusiastic about Ransom's teaching as their prewar predecessors, and his graduate students began to employ a term that soon caught on to describe the experience during his office conferences of becoming convinced that they were going to be successful; they referred delightedly to their having been "Ransomized."[7] George O. Marshall, Jr., remarked on the accessibility of the teacher Ransom even after he was appointed Associate Dean of the Graduate School in 1953: "In the middle of the afternoon he was nearly always available for coffee. As I waited in the outer office of the Graduate School I saw many a student drag in to confer with Dr. Ransom and come out with a renewed feeling of self-worth and a conviction that graduate study was worthwhile, after all. I heard one student say, as he walked out of Dr. Ransom's office, 'God bless that man!'"[8]

As Ransom entered the administrative levels, Amy Jo Long, formerly a reporter and assistant editor for *Fort Worth Press* and now employed by the UT News and Information Service, took note of the assistant dean of the Graduate School, whose background in reporting helped him estimate what would be newsworthy. Long agreed with Ransom that UT had too casually

FIGURE 6.1

Students at the University of Texas at Austin, 1958. Ransom made observations about every generation of students he encountered at UT—those of the Depression era, post–World War II, the fifties, and the Vietnam War period. Prints and Photographs Collection, Center for American History, The University of Texas at Austin.

been content to exist as an intellectual outpost, and early on she perceived that, with the state's expanding resources and a vision like Ransom's, UT might advance rapidly in prestige. Long and her officemates "followed his progress up the administrative ladder with great enthusiasm. He was quotable, energetic." Like many people, Long also admired his playful acrobatics with words; leaving the Main Building during a Christmas season in the 1950s, for instance, he whimsically wished her "an ineffable holiday."[9]

When Ransom was not teaching, advising, directing theses and dissertations, or conducting the business of the Graduate Faculty, he increasingly accepted invitations to make local, regional, and occasionally national speeches. For example, he spoke on "Texas, the Fact and Legend" for the Texas Day luncheon of the Standard Club in Austin,[10] described "Authors' Contracts before 1700"[11] to the English Institute at Columbia University, and reviewed "The Roots of Early Texas Biography" at meetings of the Daughters of the Republic of Texas in Austin and the Galveston Historical Society.[12] In addition, he made motivational speeches on the university campus: "The Place of the School of Social Work in Graduate Education" as a luncheon talk during an all-day conference sponsored by the School of Social Work;[13] a speech about grades for the Mortar Board Smarty Party;[14] and "Language Arts and the Teacher" to a convocation of education students and faculty members.[15] According to Hazel, Ransom generally preferred speaking situations where his role was well defined and where a handshake sufficed rather than a response to informal gestures such as hugging and back-slapping.[16]

William S. Livingston, a future vice president, dean of graduate studies, and acting president at UT Austin, found it almost miraculous how Ransom, in his mid-forties, suddenly developed into such an articulate spokesman. "He evolved into a charming, very verbal man," Livingston said. Though in public Ransom seldom resorted to jokes or what might be classified as outright humor, "he had a tremendous capacity to use words that carried verve, zing. What is more, he could make a speech that would mesmerize people at the Petroleum Club in Houston and deliver a variation of it just as effectively to goat ranchers meeting in Menard. He possessed an astounding capacity to adapt his style to different audiences." His hallmark became "the precise, emphatic use of words to express inspiring ideas. . . . He seldom raised his soft voice, but somehow it commanded attention. Forty-five minutes later you might not be able to recall exactly what he said, but you knew it had been riveting." Livingston admired another notable trait of Ransom's: he was immensely generous with his time. "He always had time to talk. If necessary, and it often was, he went *home* to write his speeches and do his complicated paperwork."[17]

Physics professor C. Paul Boner, an acoustics expert with a B.A. degree from UT and a Ph.D. from Harvard, replaced Hanson Tufts Parlin at the end of Parlin's twenty-one-year term as Dean of the College of Arts and Sciences. In 1954, however, Boner was promoted to the vice presidency for academic affairs. President Logan Wilson's elevation of Harry Huntt Ransom to the vacant deanship of the UT College of Arts and Sciences, effective October 1, 1954, marked the crucial turning point in Ransom's career. The appointment was lauded by those who had long touted his talents, but privately lamented by others who interpreted it as signaling the loss of an outstanding classroom instructor. A congratulatory letter from Professor Ralph B. Long lamented, "It's clear that you have a price to pay if you're to be Dean. I do hope the price can be kept relatively low, since I do think that what you are now doing is very, very important."[18] Nonetheless, many people would get the impression that Ransom's tenure as dean qualified as the most blissful period in the lives of both Harry and Hazel.

At last Ransom held a position in which he could begin to demonstrate the caliber of his concepts of education. Once installed as dean, he discovered another advantage of his new office: he had inherited the services of Mary Jane Hemperley and Frances Hellums Hudspeth, the latter the longtime executive assistant who had managed the records and staff for the previous deans. According to Winifred Vigness, a graduate student who worked under Frances Hudspeth's supervision in Dean Boner's office, Mrs. Hudspeth had been acquainted with Harry Ransom for more than a decade, and she worshipped him as a "young [though she herself was only a year older] shining light" who embodied her dreams for what UT could offer gifted students. Hudspeth, said Vigness, was "one of those people who makes it possible for others to be great," and she soon turned her personal devotion and considerable experience into assets for Ransom's administration. Intelligent, highly literate, and well-organized, Hudspeth assumed responsibilities far beyond her executive assistant status. Broad-faced, with light brown and gray hair bobbed short and parted to one side, she had a sandy complexion and pale blue eyes. She ran an office that exuded an atmosphere of warmth and personal attention to the undergraduates. Mrs. Hudspeth created "a welcome haven for youngsters just off Papa's ranch," and was "kind and gentle" in opening the doors of the university for Arts and Sciences students. She had a saying that Vigness heard her repeat whenever a staff member finished a report on time or anything else worked out

FIGURE 6.2

Gary Morrison, Frances Hudspeth, and Harry Ransom, 1954 (?). Mrs. Hudspeth is serving tea from a silver tea service, a gift to the library from Mrs. Miriam Lutcher Stark, a generous benefactor. As Ransom's executive assistant, Frances Hellums Hudspeth managed Ransom's office efficiently yet created an atmosphere of warmth and personal attention for the undergraduates. Harry Ransom Humanities Research Center, The University of Texas at Austin.

with prompter or better results than she anticipated: "Well, *that's* a lovely deed in this naughty world!"[19]

Mrs. Hudspeth, born in 1907 in Hico, Texas, had earned a bachelor's degree at UT in 1933, taught in rural schools near Hico, and instructed science classes in the Austin public school system between 1925 and 1940, until her employment by Dean Parlin. She had married a gifted teacher of chemistry in the Austin public schools, a UT graduate and World War II veteran, Jack C. Hudspeth. Early in their marriage, he contracted multiple sclerosis, a progressively debilitative disease of the nervous system that afflicted his brain and spinal cord and left him wheelchair-bound. The couple had no children and her husband's paralysis, pain, and misery made him so querulous ("difficult," she termed it) that her co-workers speculated it might have been almost a relief for her to grapple with problems at the office.

As dean, Ransom liked to meet newly recruited faculty members before approving their appointments, but he also interviewed established scholars on the campus. One of those who entered his office was Peter T. Flawn, a Yale Ph.D. hired eleven years earlier by the Department of Geology. Flawn, who would later become president of UT San Antonio and (in 1979) president of UT Austin, came to see Ransom about the directorship of the Bureau of Economic Geology. A cordial, gracious man greeted him from behind a desk. "You're very young for the job," remarked Ransom. "Well, Dr. Ransom," responded Flawn rather boldly, "You're very young for *your* job." To his relief, Ransom smiled jovially.[20]

Around this time, in the mid-1950s, Ransom changed his eyeglasses from circular lenses to a pair with rectangular black plastic frames. However, his telephone manner never altered throughout the rest of his days as an administrator. His secretary would answer first, and then he would come on the line in a low, soft-spoken voice. He always initiated the conversation by saying, "Mr. Ransom." Not "Dean" or any of his later titles. "*Mr.* Ransom."[21]

For a dean, his demeanor was warm and sometimes waggish. "What do you jackasses think you're doing over there?" he once kiddingly asked when calling his two professors of German, then bellowed with laughter when one of them answered, "Jackass speaking!" At a small reception in his honor at the Driskill Hotel, twenty faculty members presented him with a pen set. Picking up both pens, he joked, "I've always been wanting to write with both hands!" He became known for speaking with his department chairs as colleagues, not lower-ranking administrators.[22]

Still, the new dean, though often playful in manner, pushed himself hard. His habit of being in his office by 6 or 6:30 A.M. and his late, late dinnertimes were well known. When he made trips to New York City to conduct university business (or, eventually, to inspect book collections), he chose to travel by train. He never really enjoyed driving an automobile, and Hazel often did their in-town driving. Once in the city, Ransom sometimes contacted former student Patricia Billfaldt, who was living there: "He was always loaded down with a briefcase and a heavy dictating machine because he said that traveling on a train was the only way he could catch up with his correspondence," she recalled.[23] In the next decades he would, though, along with most Americans, dispense with rail travel and use the airlines.

As Ransom's non-teaching activities for the university increased, his published scholarship diminished, replaced in part by editorial essays, but he continued to write. He contributed papers at conferences (seven in 1956), made numerous speeches (fifteen official speeches in 1958),[24] and composed poetry, which constituted another body of his writings in itself. In January 1954, Ransom completed his research on copyright laws at the Library of Congress, and in July 1956 the University of Texas Press published his 145-page book, *The First Copyright Statute: An Essay on an Act for the Encouragement of Learning, 1710*. Its dedication page read simply "For Hazel." In the preface, he discussed the "historic" fact of "the first copyright law enacted by the English Parliament" in 1710: "Never before had a national law-making body drawn up a systematic statement of the conditions under which literary property might be owned" (x). A "calendar" listed developments following William Caxton's introduction of printing into England in 1476, itemizing every effort of authors, publishers, and booksellers to control their property, and the endeavors of entities within the government and the church to arbitrate the disputes and regulate this new industry. Taking into account Ransom's abstract topic—"the legal history of the communication of ideas in England"—the clarity, conciseness, and animation of this history were commendable.[25]

Ransom's expertise in copyright law benefited Professor Gerald Langford in 1956. Langford had written a biography of O. Henry, the famous short-story writer who lived for several years in Austin. After the book was accepted for publication, Langford discovered that the California attorney who was executor of the O. Henry estate, which controlled the copyright, had elected to "throw a wrench in the works." Ransom devoted a great deal of time to solving this problem; according to Langford, he jumped right into the case, negotiating directly with the lawyer. In the process he shrewdly used as a bargaining chip with the attorney the granting of access to the extensive UT Rare Books Collection on law. As the situation progressed, Ransom would often stop by Langford's office, put a foot up on a chair, and talk confidentially and reassuringly about copyright issues and the resolution of Langford's woes. Macmillan Company would publish Langford's *Alias O. Henry: A Biography of William Sidney Porter* in April 1957.[26]

Ransom's College of Arts and Sciences bulged with 5,500 students, almost one-third of the student body, and 600 faculty members, approximately one-half of the university teaching faculty. Ransom kept track of the hiring of twenty-two departments, concerned with enhancing their national standing. The Anthropology, Chemistry, English, Geography, Geology, History, and Zoology departments gained faculty in 1955–1956, but he noted that Bacteriology, Botany, Journalism, Mathematics, Physics, Romance Languages, and Speech "made no significant new additions."[27] The dean confronted a daunting shortage of funds to motivate and reward his existing faculty. As Ransom confided to a friend from his early teaching days, now at Columbia University: "For a university with the second largest endowment in the country, we sometimes operate like a North Dakota teachers college in the days of [Governor William] Langer."[28]

Then, in January 1955, Ransom became one of three newly elected faculty representatives on the University Development Board. The university's Board of Regents and the Ex-Students' Association each appointed five members to this development board; Ransom would have a six-year term.[29] William D. Blunk, another appointee, would serve as its director. Blunk was destined to earn Ransom's trust and professional friendship over the next decade and a half. In late 1955, Dean Ransom proposed to the Board the creation of an Arts and Sciences Foundation, very likely the first of its kind in the United States, in order "to stimulate and focus interest in teaching and research programs which are basic to higher education in Texas."[30] While establishing foundations within the university was not entirely novel, having been done for other purposes with the Geology Foundation, the Fine Arts Foundation, and the Pharmaceutical Foundation, this was a first venture for the liberal arts, the largest academic unit of the university. "I realize that there are members of the General Faculty who believe that the College has mainly a service function to perform, and I gladly support the notion of that service function. I believe, however, that . . . an unusually active—indeed a revolutionary—campaign is essential in spreading the word of the needs of Arts and Sciences in this state," wrote Ransom in a 1956 report to President Logan Wilson and Vice President C. Paul Boner.[31]

To underwrite this drive for excellence, the new Arts and Sciences Foundation would seek donations for campus conferences, visiting lectureships, supplementation of junior faculty salaries, assistance to faculty research projects, and travel expenses for faculty attending scholarly meetings. The foundation would be made up of "one hundred leading citizens—chosen from a list of one thousand."[32]

After two years of planning with members of the Arts and Sciences faculty, and with partial funding from the recently approved Arts and Sciences Foundation, Ransom launched a much-publicized "Program in Criticism" in the spring of 1956.[33] The program would prove stimulating to the UT faculty, he thought; would break down the cultural isolation of landlocked Austin, hundreds of miles from other state borders in any direction; and (perhaps even more important) would introduce prominent writers and critics to its local amenities and add the city to the national lecture-circuits for leading academics and literati. The first speakers arriving in spring 1956 were Milton scholar Kester Svendsen of the University of Oklahoma, Hazard Adams of Cornell University, Elder Olson of the University of Chicago (a practitioner of the Chicago School of literary criticism), W. K. Wimsatt, Jr., of Yale University, Cleanth Brooks of Yale University (billed as "a leading theorist of the school of New Criticism"), and Philip Wheelwright and William Arrowsmith of the University of California at Riverside. Other luminaries followed, including W. H. Auden of Oxford, Allen Ludden of WCBS in New York, T. S. Eliot (reading his poetry), and Northrop Frye of the University of Toronto. Overall, the harvest of the visits to Texas by these and other distinguished figures was good publicity for the university nationwide, which is what Ransom had hoped would happen. The distinction of this literary engagement (and the handsome—for the 1950s—honorarium of between $500 and $1,000) lured dozens upon dozens of scholars and creative writers to Austin, if only for a day. Moreover, the yearly ritual of selecting speakers also functioned like a job-market search, with a number of the visitors eventually becoming affiliated with the university.

A few prima donnas expected more veneration than they received, but most were surprised and pleased with the cultural and academic scene they encountered in Texas. On December 25, 1957, for instance, Henri Peyre, author of *The Contemporary French Novel* (1955) and Sterling Professor and Chair of the French Department at Yale, wrote glowingly to Ransom about his impressions: "I found my visit to Austin extremely profitable (for I learned much about your University, and about literature, and about the critical fervor of the young men you have assembled there) and [the visit was] very enjoyable and cordial. The morale of your young faculty members is unusually high, and their grateful admiration for you very striking. . . . I believe that. . . . those young scholars will be able to achieve much to place the University of Texas in the front rank of those which develop the humanities."[34] Many other guests would similarly remark on the favorable impression Ransom's younger scholars made on them.

All of those chosen by Ransom to manage this speakers series in its second year, 1957, were assistant professors: William Handy, Frederick Eckman, James Colvert, Charles P. Swiggart, Edwin T. Bowden, Roger W. Shattuck, and Hazard Adams (who himself had been an invited speaker the previous year, before joining the UT faculty). This active pursuit of younger faculty occurred not only in the liberal arts but in the sciences as well. Ransom would poll his departments and ask for lists of up-and-coming professors in each field, then try to hire them at salaries sometimes higher than the East and West Coast universities offered. He now had the ability to use discretionary funds from the Arts and Sciences Foundation for "salary supplementation," research money, and moving costs. In a series of memorandums, Ransom emphasized the importation of junior faculty and the underwriting of their research as a long-range strategy to confer eminence upon the university. An informal association of Ransom's colleagues (mostly newer, high-profile professors hired by Ransom) brashly proclaimed themselves "Harry's Boys." They seemed to represent to the campus those tapped by Ransom to be the core and ideal of fresh intellectual activity. This favoritism predictably caused a certain degree of resentment among the senior faculty, who felt that they had served the university loyally and well and were being ignored, while less experienced professors from predominantly Ivy League schools were being hired at salaries and with perquisites comparable to or exceeding theirs. Salaries increased only slightly for the general faculty while Ransom forged ahead in his recruiting efforts to build a nationally known faculty.

In Ransom's eyes, Assistant Professor William ("Bill") Handy, a proponent of New Criticism, the regnant school of literary theory committed to explications of the inner qualities of literary works, embodied the passionate energy behind that movement. Handy had earned his doctorate at the University of Oklahoma rather than from an Ivy League school (and had worked as an insurance salesman and served in the Army Air Force), and he acted as a lively foil to Ransom's habitual reserve. In fact, the informal Handy seemed downright nonchalant around Dean Ransom. In a letter of reference for Handy, Ransom observed, "If he has faults, they are mainly the result of enthusiasm, ebullience, and over-confidence about the importance of the humanities and English studies in general. Since I share these faults with him, I suppose I am inclined to discount them."[35]

At various times, the loosely networked group of "Harry's Boys" included Roger Shattuck of Romance Languages, Donald L. Weismann of Art History, John Silber of Philosophy, Winfred P. Lehmann of Linguistics, William Arrowsmith of Classics, and William Handy, Hazard Adams, and Charles Swiggart of English. They received reduced teaching loads, coveted University Research Grants, the sympathetic ear of a high-ranking administrator, the honor of being associated with the ongoing "Program in Criticism," and the envy of the campus. As an example of how Ransom recruited, Roger Shattuck recalled what happened after the chair of the UT Romance Languages Department made him an offer during the Modern Language Association meeting in Chicago: "A telegram arrived about as follows: 'Very interested in having you at University of Texas. H. H. Ransom.' The only Ransom I knew was John Crowe. I couldn't clear up the mystery until I paid my own way to visit Austin. That was the first time I was 'Ransomized,' as we used to say later—i.e., yielded to his smooth visionary talk and enigmatic smile. He spoke of putting together a bright young group to rival the Ivy League."[36] Among the special "University Professors" Ransom appointed was D. S. Carne-Ross, formerly with the BBC, who set up a literary translation center and co-founded *Arion,* a journal of the classics and humanities. Occasionally Ransom's rapid-fire hirings created awkward situations in academic protocol, as when he impulsively brought aboard a professor broadly specializing in Latin American Studies without first checking with anyone in the relevant departments.[37]

The potential recruits were not invariably receptive, and not everyone who came to Texas automatically became a member of the inner circle of "Harry's Boys" or enjoyed those privileges. A perplexed William Burford wrote to Ransom on September 23, 1958, after conferring with UT English Department Chairman Mody Boatright: "I had never known until now the situation in the English Department, since all my communications had been with you. . . . Probably I should have gone into the business of what courses I would teach more thoroughly, yet it never crossed my mind that I would be loaded down with freshman English. It is not that I object to teaching freshmen; on the contrary, the prospect of all the very different minds of these young men and women beginning their serious education is very exciting to me. I chose this kind of teaching rather than at a college such as Haverford, yet I must say my idea of what to expect here was largely formed by your description of the Plan II program and the Honors system you spoke of. I feel prepared and suited to do this kind of teaching, and

trust that I may soon do so."[38] Burford's initial bafflement was not an isolated case. Henrietta Jacobsen would confirm that in the later 1950s Ransom might meet someone in an airport, talk to him, and offer him a job on
the spot—with no résumé ever seen. The recruit would sell his house, move
his family, and turn up at UT business manager Graves Landrum's desk
asking for an office and a parking space. Ransom expected Landrum, Jacobsen, and other staff members to straighten things out—"and we always
did," said Jacobsen.[39]

Shattuck and Silber, by contrast, were given the prerogative of redesign-
ing the curriculum for Ransom's cherished Plan II program. They reveled in
the freedom of constituting a two-member committee and delivered what
they felt was a "brilliant" revision. "Your report has the engaging touch of
the totally impossible," responded Ransom, though he nevertheless imple-
mented much of it.[40]

Ransom routinely filed a summary for Vice President C. Paul Boner
about his extended trips on behalf of the university. His memorandum of
a trip to Washington, New York, and Princeton (January 8–22, 1955), for
instance, listed nine conferences. At the American Association of Colleges
meeting in Washington, D.C., he heard an address by President Milton S.
Eisenhower of Pennsylvania State College (later University). Following the
Conference of the Hazen Foundation in Washington, D.C., where deseg-
regation trends were analyzed by presidents and deans from several dozen
schools, including the University of North Carolina, Southern Methodist
University, and Yale, he concluded that "Texas is in an infinitely *better* situation here than any other southern institution."[41]

Those discussions were timely. A decade earlier, on May 16, 1946, African American Heman Sweatt had filed suit to be admitted to the heretofore
white UT School of Law. Sweatt was finally admitted in 1950, and though
he did not complete work for the degree, nonetheless his enrollment constituted the first of a series of breakthroughs in the "separate but equal"
racially segregated facilities for UT graduate schools. A charged political atmosphere kept black undergraduates out of the university until the historic
U.S. Supreme Court decision of *Brown v. the Topeka Board of Education* in
1954. In 1956, President Logan Wilson, acting on the recommendation of
the Board of Regents, issued an order to integrate the university racially,
forever changing student and alumni constituencies and ending racial exclusivity. Virtually all of these developments were peaceful in nature, yet
nevertheless tension-filled for those involved. In the fall of 1956, UT accepted 104 blacks: 30 freshmen, 55 graduate students, and 19 transfer students. In the largest sense, the battle for integration had been won. Blacks

FIGURE 6.3

Heman Sweatt in registration line for School of Law, 1950. Sweatt's lawsuit in 1946 successfully challenged the racially "separate but equal" facilities for UT graduate schools. Prints and Photographs Collection, Center for American History, The University of Texas at Austin.

FIGURE 6.4

Student demonstration for admission to Texas medical schools, date unknown. Student sign reads "As Texans, we want to study medicine in our home state not in Tennessee." In 1956, following the U.S. Supreme Court decision in Brown v. *the Topeka Board of Education (1954), President Logan Wilson, acting in concert with the Board of Regents, issued an order to integrate the university racially. It would take nearly another decade to achieve the goal of ending racial exclusivity in housing and hiring, but it occurred "without troops, marshals, violence, or bloodshed," Regent W. W. Heath took pride in pointing out.* Prints and Photographs Collection, Center for American History, The University of Texas at Austin.

were hereafter able to attend university functions without discrimination in admission or seating.[42]

Unexpectedly, C. Paul Boner, suffering health problems, resigned from the position of vice president for academic affairs to return to his Physics Department research. President Logan Wilson thereupon announced that on September 1, 1957, Harry Ransom would become the next vice president and provost for the Main University. He would be allowed to take Frances Hudspeth with him as he ascended to these new responsibilities. By now Mrs. Hudspeth had taken to calling Ransom "Bub," and he often addressed her as "Colonel" as a mark of deference, since his military rank had only been that of Major. (The quippish William Arrowsmith had taken to calling them both, privately, "Harry Hudspeth.")[43] Frequently putting in fifteen-hour days, she and Ransom had already become known campus-wide as a formidably efficient team. His assuming the position of vice president and provost in 1957 meant that he would function as the chief administrative officer of the Main University under Wilson, who presided over both the Main University and the UT System, which now included two medical schools (one in Galveston and one in Dallas), the M. D. Anderson Hospital for Cancer Research in Houston, the School of Public Health in Houston, and Texas Western College (in 1967 renamed the University of Texas at El Paso).[44] John Alton Burdine inherited Ransom's College of Arts and Sciences, serving as its dean until 1966.

As fortunate as Ransom was to have gained the skilled assistance of Frances Hudspeth when he assumed the dean's office and to have now obtained access to the astute and attractive Henrietta Jacobsen, who was attached to the president's office, he was equally blessed with the resourceful services of Graves W. Landrum, business manager of the Main University. Landrum, who reported to the new vice president and provost daily, said he gave "110 percent" of his energies simply because of Ransom's often-proclaimed trust in Landrum's abilities. Standing six feet four inches tall, with blondish hair, blue eyes, and metal frame glasses, Landrum had a low-key, deliberate manner that contrasted sharply with the more erudite style of the shorter, more urbane Harry Huntt Ransom. Even so, Landrum found that he "could communicate with Harry on any subject." Ransom recognized in Landrum a very talented individual who possessed in abundance what Ransom cheerfully admitted he himself lacked—a keen business acumen. Not considering himself "an arithmetic man," Ransom sometimes joked that he depended on Landrum's skill with bottom-line numbers to "keep him out of jail."[45]

A graduate of Abilene High School who had lived in various parts of Texas, Landrum had majored in business at the university in 1932, but left in 1935 and worked for nine years in the private sector. When he applied to the university for employment in December 1944, he was hired as a senior accountant in the office of the auditor. He and his wife, Marzee, reared a son who, like his father, attended UT Austin, and the Landrums' loyalty to the university, already staunch, was thus strengthened. Landrum would long recall the sight of his superior, "Dr. Ransom" (as Landrum invariably addressed him), walking across campus in the 1950s: he oftentimes carried an umbrella, and he never strode looking down; he was always gazing upward.[46]

But if Ransom was a definitely visible figure on the Main University campus during this period, it was President Logan Wilson who should be applauded for putting UT on a sounder financial footing. For one thing, he supported the creation of the Texas Commission on Higher Education, which lobbied the legislature for revenues. Under his guidance, UT increased the yield of the total Permanent University Fund portfolio in 1958–1959 from 2.78% the previous year to 3.04%[47] Graves Landrum, for one, gave Wilson full credit for promoting the university's initial drive toward the pursuit of excellence. To Landrum and the university community, these two UT officers presented a study in contrasts of style: Ransom came up from the ranks of the Main University, ran a "student-oriented" office, and had a reputation for being approachable, whereas Wilson, though effective, tended to give the appearance of being preoccupied, aloof, and all too resigned to the regents' will.

It was true, for that matter, that the Board of Regents had recruited Wilson as an experienced and (they hoped) rather pliable administrator to replace T. S. Painter, who had accepted the acting presidency (1944–1946) after Homer Rainey's firing, and then taken the presidency (1946–1952). (An acting president, James Clay Dolley, had filled the office until Wilson accepted the post in 1954.) Wilson, a native Texan from Huntsville, had received M.A. and Ph.D. degrees from Harvard University. He had taught sociology and served as an administrator at various schools, including the University of Kentucky, Newcomb College of Tulane University, and the University of North Carolina. During Wilson's term of eight years, he managed among other things to lift the censure of the university by the American Association of University Professors (AAUP) over the Rainey controversy.[48] Now Wilson and Ransom, unencumbered by this blot against their institution's name, could plan an expansion of its system, a building program for the Main University, the achievement of national rankings, and the establishment of a nationally respected library collection.

Letters of congratulations about Ransom's promotion poured into his office. W. Gordon Whaley, a professor of cellular biology who would become Dean of the Graduate School in 1958, prophesied: "This institution is now at a point where the right kind of efforts, as reflecting both much wisdom and some very courageous measures, could well see it achieve what Chicago did, or what Princeton did, when a strikingly similar kind of determination prevailed in the minds of a handful of people." Whaley soberly added, however, that "the task ahead involves selling to a public something that it probably will not understand and most likely will resent. . . . [and] selling to the faculty a level of attainment that much of that faculty cannot achieve. . . . The effort is not going to be a popular one [and will bring] some most awkward circumstances and some sharp and unpleasant criticism."[49] Ransom replied with guarded optimism, "I think that you are quite right and there will be serious problems along with our best chances for progress. I am completely sure that these problems can be met sensibly only by concerted effort. I intend to do everything I can to keep the communication channels clear." Ransom thanked Whaley for his friendship, support, and wisdom: "Without this kind of backing, I would much prefer to take to the academic woods and the quiet streams of copyright."[50] History professor Joe B. Frantz wrote with delight: "The appointment came as no surprise, as members of the history department, as well as other colleagues, had long since elected you over coffee. . . . It's axiomatic that no one loves an administrator, but the faculty whom I know are willing to make an exception in your case. . . . Our only regrets in this promotion are losing you from the classroom and from the Arts and Sciences office."[51]

In 1956, in anticipation of the university's seventy-fifth anniversary of its founding, Dr. Merton M. Minter, chairman of the Board of Regents, appointed Rex G. Baker as chairman of an epochal "Committee of 75," consisting of numerous prominent Texans. Baker, one of the co-founders of Humble Oil (later Exxon), determinedly organized the committee members into sub-committees that commenced a reassessment and definition of the university's mission. The importance of this group in the history of the university cannot be overstated. Ransom's own inclinations about higher education at the university influenced the vision proposed by the Committee of 75, and he in turn would articulate to the public this emerging blueprint for the university. Ransom's optimistically phrased "Sense of Mission" statement to the Committee of 75 dovetailed with an unexpected, world-changing event: on October 4, 1957, the Soviet Union launched its astonishing satellite, *Sputnik* I. As it circled the earth, the widely watched *Sputnik* challenged a long-perceived American superiority in science. Shocked and incensed that the Communist-led Soviet Union could demonstrate this technical capability, the U.S. Congress and state legislators made education from grade school to college an overnight national priority. Ransom's mission statement became in effect a direct answer to *Sputnik*.[52]

The grand ceremony celebrating the "75th Birthday Convocation" of the university took place on January 10, 1958, on the steps of the Main Building. An Associated Press photographer captured the event, showing black-robed professors, ringed by a crisp military guard, surrounding a podium. A solemn bearer of the mace stood in front of the U.S. and Texas flags. Ransom, sporting a crew cut, delivered one of his highly popular speeches, with references to *Sputnik,* praise for the individual student, and exhortations about "hard nose" mathematics and "hard-nose" language instruction. The most-quoted phrase from Ransom's address was "In an age preoccupied with outer space, no space is so important to education as the area which lies between the human ears."[53] About 1,000 people commemorated the anniversary by marching in the processional leading up to the steps of the Main Building.[54]

The tall, stately Logan Wilson was proving to be percipient and articulate. In a 1959 speech, "Roads to Realization," delivered at the first-anniversary meeting of the Committee of 75, President Logan Wilson frankly stated: "An average of 10 million dollars a year. This is the size of the gap which must be closed by private gifts and bequests to UT, if it is to become one of the 10 top universities in the country. . . . Private funds for UT spell the difference between merely above-average opportunity and truly excellent opportunity for those whom the University serves. UT will educate more than 100,000 Texas youth in the next decade."[55] The timing of this plea was propitious. New economic growth in Texas followed the national demand for Texas's natural resources of oil and natural gas. As a state historian observed, "The [Texas] petrochemical industry . . . produced 80 percent of the total U.S. output. . . . One immediate effect was to enrich thousands of landowners across the state. By 1955, almost $500,000,000 was paid annually to farmers, ranchers, and other landholders in rentals, royalties, and bonuses."[56]

Wilson had an able ally as vice president and provost. Ransom, immersed in the daily life of the Main University, could assist the regents in persuading Texans that they had a proprietary interest in an improved university. In Ransom's lifetime he would convince various people to make donations and gifts to the university totaling an estimated $30,000,000.[57] Future (1975–1981) Regent Tom Law, son of the one-time chairman of the English Department Robert Law, characterized Ransom as a "Renaissance Man"—he read widely, he wrote poetry, he phrased his thoughts succinctly, yet he was equally comfortable with regents, students, alumni, faculty, and donors, whether they hailed from small Texas towns or metropolitan East Coast cities.[58]

The pace of Hazel and Harry Ransom's lives now intensified. His friends noted that he was smoking more (as did his executive assistant, Frances Hudspeth). For that matter, most academics of the era seemed to smoke, and Hazel took up the habit, too. In an effort to preserve a modicum of privacy and uninterrupted leisure, in 1957 they purchased the 200-acre Bar-C-Bar Ranch on picturesque Little Onion Creek, near the tiny town of

Dripping Springs, twenty miles southwest of Austin. (They traded in the detested "Dead End" house as a down payment and began thirty-two years of mortgage installments.) There was some arable land near the creek, but otherwise native live oak and "cedar" (juniper) dominated the landscape. Hazel and "Hal" (as she still called Ransom) never made use of the small limestone rock ranch house, built in the nineteenth century, for university functions. This was to be their retreat. It had no telephone, and its very location was a mystery to virtually all of Ransom's associates. Harry and Hazel often walked the rocky paths that crisscrossed their land, he in old clothes rather than denim jeans, finding tranquility in the views of deer, wild turkey, blackberry vines, and glimpses of red bud, wild plum, pecan, walnut, and elm trees. The temperature was often ten degrees cooler than the climate in Austin, which sweltered in mid- and late summer. They sometimes drove over to Senator Lyndon Baines Johnson's ranch, just an hour away on the Pedernales River.

At the beginning of 1958, a preoccupied Ransom reluctantly accepted the necessity of leaving behind any and all of his teaching responsibilities; he additionally resigned from several doctoral dissertation committees and began turning down further requests to direct dissertations. Yet Ransom never lost sight of the credo that "the University is about students, and students are our deepest concern. In the administrative work, I often miss the classroom," he averred, and he would periodically make time for former students or advise students referred to him by friends.[59]

He became known for watching out for his faculty, too—especially the younger ones. In the summer of 1959, shortly after Gerhard J. Fonken came to UT to teach chemistry, he got a lesson in the breadth and depth of Ransom's concern. Fonken had arrived with little in his pockets, and an expected paycheck failed to appear. He had no way to cover rent or food bills. His department chairman suggested that Fonken call the vice president and provost, Harry Ransom. Dubious, Fonken spoke to Ransom's secretary and then, to Fonken's surprise, Ransom himself came on the line, listened patiently and cordially, and soon thereafter arranged for the entire paycheck to be delivered to Fonken's office. He had contacted the Payroll Office and directed that a paycheck be made outside the usual schedule. What struck Fonken was Ransom's commitment to assist an individual so new on the scene. "An instructor paid less than $5,000 was *that* important to him."[60]

With funding from the Carnegie Corporation plus private donations from the Clark Foundation of Dallas and the Hogg Foundation for Mental Health in Austin, Ransom was now able to promote "Departmental Honors

Programs" in Geology, Germanic Languages, Government, History, and Philosophy, as well as to bolster Plan II and establish an innovative "Junior Fellows" program, which chose twenty-five students from the top 10 percent of the entering first-year students for individual assignments and tutoring.[61] By now, UT was the largest university in the South and Southwest, enrolling 18,000 students. Assessing this growth, Ransom became aware that "the average student" might get lost at UT as "a mere statistic."[62] With the unanimous approval of the Board of Regents, he therefore established a Testing and Counseling Center "designed to advise students who come to the University with uncertain plans and prospects. I doubt that any other institution in Texas, or anywhere else," he noted, "is giving more emphasis to the opportunities to get an education."[63] The new center included individual career counseling, reading improvement programs, admissions testing, placement testing, and test scoring.[64]

What would be heralded as "the Ransom years" were commencing, in conjunction with the state's financial boom, the coming national focus on Texas politicians, and the renewed mission of the university. As Mrs. Hudspeth wrote excitedly to D. H. Lawrence scholar F. Warren Roberts during his sojourn in Italy in 1958: "You will find this place a veritable ant hill of activity. Mr. Ransom is the most perfect human catalyst I've ever known. It is amazing how potent an effect he has already had in this institution."[65]

SEVEN

THE RARE BOOKS COLLECTION

O**f all Harry Ransom's accomplish-
ments, the unlikely emergence at the University of Texas at Austin of a
renowned, world-class library center for rare books and manuscripts—
despite its remoteness in location from the heavily endowed and long-
established Harvard, Princeton, and Yale universities and its habitual willingness to trail behind momentum-gaining schools like the University of
California at Berkeley, the University of California at Los Angeles, the
University of Michigan, and the University of Illinois—became the phenomenon most deservedly and lastingly attached to his name. By the 1950s
nearly all state universities in the United States had resignedly accepted
the inevitable lead that the older, better-endowed universities had built up
in the acquisition of rare library materials, and had settled down to the
more mundane task of assembling broad general collections of academic
publications. Ransom, by contrast, operated on the assumption that even
a university library started in 1883 might, with vigorous support from administrators, regents, legislators, and private benefactors, still aspire in the
mid-twentieth century to enter the elite group of institutions with superior
rare book and manuscript collections. To his way of thinking, this crown-
ing if costly glory would attract ambitious faculty members and students
and, inevitably, national and international visitors. Such a bold move would
overcome advantages of East or West Coast prestige or Upper Midwest af-
fluence that the top dozen American universities enjoyed without much
challenge from other parts of the country.

Ransom's sense of timing about this ambition proved to be fortunate;
the boom in the oil exploration and production industry that had begun
enriching Texas corporations and citizens was diversifying an economic
structure long dependent upon ranching. But the road to a world-class library wound to its destination by a highly indirect route, and he drew his
inspirations for the concept from a variety of sources. One of these was a

nineteenth-century Swedish American book collector named Swante Palm (1815–1899), who had settled in early-day Austin. Ransom had paid tribute to Palm in a lecture at a meeting of the Texas State Historical Association in 1949, extolling Palm as a pioneer in library development in the state.[1] When Palm died in 1899, he left behind a tangible legacy of his lifelong interests: 10,000 books (3,000 of them Scandinavian) from his personal library, willed to the infant University of Texas. The gift increased its library holdings by 60 percent, and some of the volumes ultimately formed part of its Rare Books Collection. Ransom invoked Palm's name at every opportunity to celebrate the origins of intellectual life in Texas history. To a collector and former Texan, A. W. Yeats of Halifax, Nova Scotia, he wrote on May 21, 1956: "I was reminded by your letter of the amazing center which Swante Palm built here in 1855. . . . I think that on this sort of vision will depend the future cultivation of the state."[2] To the Secretary of the Committee on Publications for the American-Scandinavian Foundation in New York City, Ransom wrote on September 18, 1956: "We are doing our best to revive the original plan for expanding the Palm Library here. . . . Although Texas has a good deal of wealth, much of it is untutored in philanthropy."[3]

The majority of Palm's books had been worn out by students, exactly as he had intended, but by the time Harry Ransom entered the university administration, those volumes still valuable for scholarly purposes had entered the Rare Books Collection and were shelved under the watchful eye of its librarian, Fannie Ratchford. It was she who obligingly arranged a program in honor of Swante Palm on December 1, 1950, in the Miriam Lutcher Stark Library.[4] Harry Ransom's awareness of the immediate needs and potential greatness of the University of Texas Library stemmed very directly from his friendly relationship with this woman whose contributions have been insufficiently recognized, Fannie Elizabeth Ratchford (1887–1974), the longtime curator of rare books and director of research in rare book bibliography at the University of Texas.[5] The manner in which she presided over her staff, patrons, and facilities had gradually given her the stature of a university institution in her own right. When Fannie Ratchford came to work at the University Library in 1919, relatively few of its approximately 125,000 volumes could have been considered rare items, whereas forty years later the general collection totaled more than a million books and included a sizable group of rare items. She had been employed during the terms of four successive librarians: John E. Goodwin, Ernest W. Winkler, Donald Coney (who left in 1945 to become the librarian at the University of California at Berkeley), and Alexander Moffit. At first she was a library assistant, then a librarian (1927–1948), then the Rare Books Librarian. Ratchford had grown up in Paint Rock, a small town in West Texas, as the third daughter of nine children in the strongly Presbyterian family of a Civil War Confederate major whose ancestors had, like Ransom's, originally settled in Virginia and the Carolinas. Before attending the University of Texas in 1905 and 1906, Ratchford had taught school in rural and urban Texas districts. In 1919, at the age of thirty-two, she finally completed her B.A. requirements and then joined the UT Library staff so that she could remain in Austin to care for her mother.

Her job offer from the Rare Books Collection curator Dr. Reginald H. Griffith was really a form of graduate fellowship, because it enabled her to complete work on a master's degree in history in 1921. Professor Griffith, a scholar of Alexander Pope's works, was born in 1873 in North Carolina, received a Ph.D. in English from the University of Chicago, and retired from teaching English at UT in 1944. It was often remarked that his slender build and white beard gave him a resemblance to George Bernard Shaw. Instrumental in the founding of the University of Texas Press in 1950, Griffith had guided so many students during their research in rare library materials that after his retirement from the library in 1951, most people continued to regard him as the unofficial curator. But as Miss Ratchford (the only appellation by which she was known) increased her knowledge of the materials and showed an aptitude in developing policies for their use, he yielded authority to her.[6]

By the time that Ransom had achieved his ranks of associate (1946) and full (1947) professor, Miss Ratchford had become a truly formidable figure in the Library System. As the Wrenn Librarian, she presided over a fourth-floor domain specially designed and constructed in the Main Building, completed in 1937, to house a prize collection purchased in 1918 and augmented by further acquisitions thereafter. She was a slender woman with large and luminous eyes over a prominent nose. By the 1950s, she had salt-and-pepper hair. Miss Ratchford always served hot or iced tea, morning and afternoon, so that the scholars as well as her student assistants would feel no need to leave the rooms.[7] Each ceremony lasted twenty minutes. People visiting other collections in the library would often drop by for this ritual refreshment. Harry Ransom was a frequent guest at these tea gatherings, where Miss Ratchford employed a silver service donated by a generous benefactor, Mrs. Miriam Lutcher Stark. Sometimes sandwiches and cookies were added, and birthdays could occasion elaborate treats.[8]

Miss Ratchford had very definite ideas about who was qualified to share these teas or indeed to utilize the rare books. Only "serious" scholars and sponsored students were eligible. She was so protective toward her materials that she even refused to accept any of the regular Main Library cataloguers on her premises. No one ever walked out her door without being checked, including her own relatives.[9] To the students who worked for her, she was a figure of awe, someone from another period who had remained loyal to West Texas, the Presbyterian Church, and the Confederacy. Even her faculty favorites sometimes referred to her as the "kindly ogress."[10] She was so close-lipped about people's research that at one point she kept two UT English scholars ignorant of the fact that for years they had been working on essentially the same project (a Romantic poet) in contiguous rooms. However, a young Harold Billings, destined to become the director of General Libraries at UT, "respected Fannie Ratchford deeply," detected a "humanity" that compensated for her small frame and "rumors of occasional incivilities," and felt gratitude that she overlooked his junior rank when teatime arrived.[11]

Her own scholarship was extensive. She wrote articles on Swinburne, Byron, Pope, Scott, Tennyson, and other literary figures, but it was her research on Charlotte Brontë, particularly the connecting of creative patterns among numerous tiny manuscript booklets written in a minuscule hand— explicated by Ratchford in *The Brontës' Web of Childhood* (1941)—that fully established her scholarly credentials.[12] Ratchford's other major area of discovery involved the greatest University of Texas Library acquisition preceding Harry Ransom's era. John H. Wrenn, a Chicago broker and banker, had assembled a superb collection of nearly 6,000 rare books and manuscripts, many of them acquired with the help of the London bibliographer, collector, and editor Thomas J. Wise. After the unfailing UT benefactor Major George W. Littlefield (prompted by Dr. Griffith) personally donated the sum of $225,000, half the estimated value of Wrenn's collection, the university was able to obtain these books in 1918. Four thousand additional volumes, the Aitken collection, also assembled by Wrenn and his family, arrived in 1921 to complement the holdings.[13] But in 1934 John Carter and Graham Pollard shocked the book world by announcing that perhaps as many as fifty forgeries could be attributed to Wise, including an edition of Elizabeth Barrett Browning's *Sonnets from the Portuguese*.[14] The Wrenn and Aitken libraries together, it turned out, contained an almost complete set of those near-perfect forgeries. Although Wise initially protested his innocence, he soon lapsed into a silence that lasted until his death in 1937,[15] and the evidence grew to be overwhelming.[16] Fannie Ratchford's scholarly interest was piqued, and she herself published a series of articles and editions that documented Wise's brilliant if unethical workmanship and explained how his manipulations went undetected even by learned book dealers and collectors.[17]

In 1925 another notable gift had considerably enlarged the University of Texas Library holdings. Mrs. Miriam Lutcher Stark of Orange, Texas, wife of a former member of the Board of Regents and mother of the then-chairman of the Board, made a gift of nearly 8,000 volumes and several hundred manuscripts, including Lord Byron's "Ode to Napoleon" and fragments of his *Don Juan*. Subsequent gifts from the Starks brought the total to 10,000 volumes. Miriam Lutcher Stark's collection also contained manuscript documents of Hernando Cortés, Álvar Núñez Cabeza de Vaca, Queen Elizabeth, Oliver Cromwell, and Thomas Jefferson, as well as Shakespeare folios and Charles Dickens manuscripts. A Bible carried aboard the *Mayflower* especially attracted public attention.[18] These acquisitions strengthened Fannie Ratchford's hand in negotiating with the planners of the new Main Building about adequate space for the Rare Books Collection. Accordingly, in 1937 the collection took its place on the front side of the fourth floor in three large and sumptuously furnished rooms designated respectively for the Wrenn, Aitken, and Stark libraries that flanked an exhibition room (decades later, these would be converted by remodeling into the president's office). The Stark Library was displayed in a room decorated with gold trim, marble columns, brass doors, and a vaulted ceiling.[19]

Still, the responsibilities of this endeavor and Ratchford's concern about its future were beginning to take a toll. A young man she had been grooming to take over the "RBC," as the Rare Books Collection was increasingly called, was killed in Germany while serving with Patton's Army in November 1944, shortly after his graduation from UT. Walter M. Manly III had been one of her most promising student assistants, a leader in campus service organizations and the University Presbyterian Church, a member of Phi Beta Kappa, and practically like an adopted son to her in certain respects. Ratchford never quite got over this tragedy, which she commemorated by establishing a fund in Manly's memory to finance the publication of books sponsored by the Rare Books Collection, such as a book on Byron by Professor Willis Pratt.[20] Yet, looking toward the future as early as 1949, Ratchford was viewing Ransom as her possible successor. On May 9, she revealed to Regents Chairman Dudley K. Woodward, whose office was in Dallas: "I am beginning to see Dr. Ransom as the solution to the situation which is troubling me—a supplement to Dr. Griffith while Dr. Griffith is with us, and his successor when he goes; then my successor. In him the English Department and Rare Books Collection will be joined in a natural and peaceful manner."[21] Harry Ransom, for his part, began to think along the same lines about her successor in the RBC, since she would turn seventy and presumably retire in 1956. Ransom would write a letter to

FIGURE 7.1
*Fannie Elizabeth Ratchford, Rare Books Collection Librarian, Aikens Room, 1940 (?).
Ratchford's contributions to library development at UT were significant. When she retired
in 1957, Ransom was named the Director of the Rare Books Collection, a nucleus that he
would expand into the collections of the Humanities Research Center.* Harry Ransom
Humanities Research Center, The University of Texas at Austin.

Vice President C. P. Boner on December 7, 1955, containing a key proposal:
"Beginning September 1957, I hope that in addition to my duties as dean of
the College—assuming that I may be reappointed to that position—I may
undertake the Directorship of the Rare Books Collection." His stated reasons included two of special note: "I have been constantly associated with
the developmental program in the RBC since 1935, and am still active in it,"
and "I think Miss Ratchford would not be opposed to this arrangement."[22]

An untitled document dating from 1947 reflected Ratchford's chronic
frustration with the monies at her disposal and the university's recognition
of her worth. Noting that the Rare Books Collection had expanded to a
collection of approximately 40,000 volumes, Ratchford's unsigned memorandum argued that her salary had risen through twenty-eight years of ser-

vice from $1,200 (as an assistant in the Wrenn Library) only to $3,700. As the memorandum states, "upward of 30,000–40,000 persons, Texans and out-of-state visitors, schoolchildren and great scholars, pass through the rooms yearly, all receiving the impression of refinement, scholarship, and friendliness, as distinguishing characteristics of the institution."[23]

She also prepared a summary in 1948 for the benefit of the Committee on Rare Book Collections, chaired by Professor D. T. Starnes, on which professors Leo Hughes and Harry Ransom served. Throughout that year the committee issued a series of recommendations, measuring the RBC against comparable library units at Harvard, Yale, and the Universities of Michigan, Illinois, and California. Whereas the RBC had only $750 annually at its disposal for acquisitions, the committee recommended to the Library Committee that "a sum not less than $25,000" be allocated for such purposes. To elevate Fannie Ratchford's status, the report suggested that the RBC be "headed by the present Wrenn Librarian as a professor with membership in the General Faculty."[24] Marginal notes on a follow-up memorandum, sympathetic to Ratchford's position, were in Ransom's handwriting.[25] On a number of occasions Ratchford wrote directly to the Board of Regents to raise issues, sidestepping both the librarian and president. Thus, as Ransom entered upon his period of direct involvement with the RBC, that is, the Rare Books Collection, he encountered several historic tendencies that he would emulate, including a collection designated by three distinctive initials (just as the Humanities Research Center would later be known as the "HRC"), a publication program, lavish furnishings, independence from the Main Library, and a scholar-director capable of appealing to the regents on behalf of special projects and needs.

Conflicts simmered beneath the surface, however. English professor Richmond P. Bond (1899–1979), a noted textual bibliographer at the University of North Carolina, visited the Austin campus in 1957 as a consultant at Harry Ransom's request and sent back candid assessments of its personalities. (Bond, born in Mississippi and educated at Vanderbilt and Harvard, had served with the Pacific Fleet in World War II. He and Ransom shared an affinity for eighteenth-century British literature—Bond was an expert in mock-heroic poetry, among other things—and they would be lifelong friends.) Bond reached the conclusion that "Miss Ratchford is a problem plus. I tried to emphasize with her the lure of her further researches and the advantages of real retirement, but her gust [sic] for power and her pro-pro-feminism may win priority. It is quite doubtful whether she has been good for Rare Books in her contentment to sit tight on the collections and to play her own personal prejudices and proprietary instincts."[26] Indeed, to arriving new faculty and their spouses whom Ransom began attracting from elite academic programs to the University of Texas in the 1950s, "Miss Ratchford" and her elegant silver tea service seemed like quaint but annoying anachronisms.[27] F. Warren Roberts was shocked in October 1954 when Ratchford, habitually unreceptive to the writings of modern authors, denied him permission to hold a reception in the Stark Library for the widow of D. H. Lawrence. Frieda had consented to visit UT only after receiving from Ransom "a very nice letter, a simple one that one can understand. I don't like complicated things." But when Ratchford previewed the tape of a BBC interview that Frieda intended to play for the audience, she became adamant that the contents were unsuitable for her hallowed domain. Roberts was obliged to host the event at his home on West Avenue, where Frieda sat beside J. Frank Dobie and talked about Lawrence to an admiring group of teachers and graduate students.[28] Ann Bowden, who arrived in 1956 and would inherit many of Ratchford's duties, found her vindictive and secretive and reluctant to allow any African Americans to view the collections. On this latter point, Ratchford had sought the counsel of President T. S. Painter two years before Heman Sweatt's lawsuit to enter the university's Law School was settled by the Supreme Court. In an April 22, 1948, letter reflecting her segregationist views as well as the prejudices of an era when racial accommodations on campus were few, she related to President Painter the details of three recent visits to the RBC by African Americans seeking to use the materials. "I replied that RBC is not open to colored readers, but if they will come some afternoon at five, I will make the books available to them. . . . May I have your advice at your early convenience?"[29]

Professor Reginald H. Griffith retired from the library staff in 1951, but continued to play a role as an advocate of the Rare Books Collection. On January 27, 1954, President T. S. Painter's successor, Logan Wilson, raised a prophetic possibility in answer to Griffith's plea for greater storage and display space for RBC: "My idea is that we might erect a combination museum and art building on the southwest corner of the campus, near the Music School. Several floors of the building could be designed and set aside for galleries."[30] The following spring, on May 18, 1954, Fannie Ratchford appealed to Wilson, now acting chancellor following James P. Hart's resignation, asserting, "It has long been evident to me that there is no place in the University administration as it is now set up for an efficiently functioning and growing research library in the Humanities."[31] Ransom's own comments likewise became bolder. In a memorandum of May 31, 1954, to the

Arts and Sciences Dean, C. Paul Boner, Ransom pointed out that, unlike "Harvard, UCLA, Columbia, Yale, Michigan," at UT "we do not follow any normal organization or program for rare books." Alarmingly, "we are not keeping up even with Texas competitors (for comparison, note Rice, SMU, Houston, TCU)." Appealing to a Texan sensitivity about the state's national image, Ransom added that the eminent librarian and bookman Lawrence Clark Powell of UCLA "was on campus last week, alternately overwhelmed by our possibilities and horrified at our omissions."[32] On December 7, 1956, a discouraged Ratchford lamented that "any solution we hit upon now is but another patch sewed upon the clownish motley we wear. This crisis, coming so near the end of my long tenure, with no orderly succession prepared for, brings me to a point of desperation I have not known in any of the innumerable previous crises."[33]

Earlier that year, Lewis Hanke, professor of history and director of the Latin American Institute, issued an influential memorandum addressed to Graduate School Dean A. P. Brogan about the "Library Collections and Facilities at the University of Texas." It is difficult to establish how substantially Harry Ransom contributed to this document, whose language at points remarkably resembles his own; in any event, its contents happened to coincide exactly with his own concerns and views, and Ransom immediately utilized it as a lever to move his agenda forward. Noting that the UT Library had "recently passed the million mark" in book acquisitions, Professor Hanke observed nonetheless that Harvard University possessed more than six times that number of volumes. The crucial fact is that "a direct connection exists between the size and importance of a university and its library." Moreover, "a superior collection of books attracts an outstanding research faculty which practices good teaching." There were certain propitious signs at UT, Hanke added. "No university library in the great expanse from Duke University in North Carolina to the University of California comes very close to our 1,000,000-plus collection, and one must go as far north as the University of Illinois to find a larger one." A compelling argument emerged: "To develop a university worthy of the state, extraordinary library facilities must be provided because our students are so far distant from the great concentration of libraries in Chicago and the East Coast." His conclusion accorded with Ransom's opinion: "No 'University of the first class' will ever be achieved without a 'library of the first class.'"[34] Ransom commented to Brogan, "I can't conceive of any sane man's disapproving of any point in the memorandum," and seized the moment to introduce Brogan to a new concept: "I am particularly concerned at the moment . . .

with the establishment of an open-shelf undergraduate library." Meanwhile, "I will take on as a duty assignment the directorship of the Rare Books Collections."[35]

Throughout the summer, fall, and winter of 1956, Ransom, though not yet named the official RBC librarian, would pursue an elusive quarry, the Carl H. Pforzheimer Library in New York City, which Ransom described to President Logan Wilson as "the finest collection of single great pieces now in private hands. Its copy of this . . . Gutenberg Bible [printed 1450–1455] alone would make it a cynosure of the scholarly world. . . . If it were sold, its price would certainly be in the millions."[36] Ransom never had the personal satisfaction of reeling in this prize, though, according to Ann Bowden, "he always had Gutenberg on his mind."[37] Carl H. Pforzheimer (1879–1957), a prominent investment banker, philanthropist, and book collector, had assembled a truly amazing collection of first and important editions of influential authors published between 1475 and 1700, as well as manuscripts, journals, letters, and memorabilia. Among the treasures, for example, were various quarto and folio editions of Shakespeare, extreme rarities of Christopher Marlowe, and a work by John Milton containing the author's annotations. Ransom's efforts, frustrating to him at this juncture, would nonetheless have long-term results. In 1978 this very Gutenberg Bible, one of the few surviving copies of the first notable book printed with movable type, would finally be purchased by the University of Texas. Major portions of the Pforzheimer Library would later leave New York City for Austin in 1986.[38]

At the same time he was attempting to snare the contents of the Pforzheimer Library for his university, Ransom inaugurated a public relations campaign of impressive magnitude in support of an expanded library program. His kick-off address on December 8, 1956, received extensive attention throughout the state. Speaking to the prestigious Texas Philosophical Society in the Commodore Perry Hotel (at a meeting presided over by the Austin attorney and former UT chancellor James P. Hart), he questioned, "Why should Texas not establish here in the capital city . . . a center for the collection of knowledge, a 'central' for the diffusion of information? . . . The great urban, regional, and national centers for the collection of knowledge in London, Paris, Dublin, and Edinburgh were begun on an almost pitiable fraction of what this state could spend. . . . Most important of all, young Texans who now are persuaded to leave the state for collections elsewhere might be persuaded by such a research center to stay; and some who have left might be persuaded to come back." Pressing this point, he wondered, "who can be placid to find that an eastern school—not Texas—

is the place where scholars study two or three outstanding collections of early Texas history?" Introducing one of the salient concepts he would gain credit for promoting, Ransom informed his listeners, including the attending members of the press, that "wherever there was a frontier in America there was a counter-frontier . . . to put this man in communication with the immemorial tradition of his kind and thereby to secure to his descendants the benefits of the free mind."[39] A clarion call to action had been sounded, a new UT priority announced.[40]

EIGHT

THE TEXAS QUARTERLY

In the second year of Ransom's vice presidency and provostship, he inaugurated a new journal, the *Texas Quarterly*, as a key component in his campaign to bring national recognition to his institution. Ransom explained to Professor Richmond Bond of the University of North Carolina that *Texas Quarterly* formed one part of a "four-sided" strategy; as for the other three, "the Arts and Sciences Foundation will be the active developmental and policy group, the Friends of the Library will be the means of keeping touch with the alumni and donors, [and] . . . the Rare Books Collection will be turned into an active research organization instead of a wing of the library" (CAH).

As early as 1949, Ransom had recommended to the Office of the President that "we consider the establishment of a general quarterly designed for a much wider audience than that of any publication . . . issued by the University." On January 16, 1957, Dean Ransom pressed this idea again in a memorandum to President Logan Wilson and Vice President for Academic Affairs C. Paul Boner: "This quarterly, located for editorial and managerial purposes in the humanities, would look across the fields of the arts and the sciences. It would not merely imitate the YALE REVIEW or the VIRGINIA QUARTERLY or any other similar magazine. . . . Its firm purpose would be an integrated representation of the arts and sciences. . . . It would come out of Texas but would not be 'Texan' or draw exclusively on Texas writers" (CAH). But to Frank Wardlaw, director of the University of Texas Press, he wrote on February 25, 1957: "The more I consider the *Quarterly*, the surer I am that mere importation of internationally significant (intellectual, critical, artistic) pieces will not do by themselves. There must be a Texas touch—else why not leave the whole business to Yale or Oxford?" (CAH). This "Texas touch" turned out to be something as whimsical as a sketch of a girl standing beside an armadillo and holding a large magnolia blossom, which he selected for an early cover.[1]

When the first issue of *Texas Quarterly* appeared in February 1958, others were scheduled for publication in May, August, and November. Annual subscriptions were four dollars. Large in format ($9\frac{3}{4}'' \times 6\frac{3}{4}''$) and thick (240 pages), with a bronze-colored front cover reproducing a manuscript by Lord Byron, the lavishly illustrated premiere issue listed the forty-nine-year-old Ransom as "Editor," Frances H. Hudspeth as "Administrative Assistant," and associate English professor Thomas M. Cranfill as chairman of an editorial committee consisting of Hazard Adams, Edwin T. Bowden, James B. Colvert, Frederick Eckman, William J. Handy, David Hayman, Roger W. Shattuck, and Charles P. Swiggart ("nearly all under the age of 35," noted one newspaper reporter).[2] The contents included pieces on literature, architecture, psychology, physics, chemistry, labor and management, politics, travel, exploration, and anthropology.

An insert in the second issue (designated as Spring 1958) reported that *"the entire edition"* of the February number of *The Texas Quarterly* "was exhausted within ten days of publication" and implored readers to return any copies of that issue "which you do not intend to keep permanently" so that orders from individuals and libraries could be filled. This second issue included an essay by Ransom on "Teaching and Research," an article by UT historian Walter Prescott Webb about the American South, literary historian Louis D. Rubin, Jr.'s, assessment of novelists' treatments of the Civil War, UT historian Otis Singletary's view of "The Contemporary South," union leader Walter Reuther's defense of organized labor and collective bargaining, an article on the mathematical formulation for water waves, Hans Beacham's evocative photographs of impoverished East Sixth Street in Austin, and literary contributions by Robert Graves and Samuel Beckett. The editorial policy had now been established: a mixture of work by UT faculty from both the arts and the sciences, combined with contributions by distinguished "outside" writers. And there would be a lead-off editorial column in a section titled "Arts and Sciences" by Harry H. Ransom on whatever topic occurred to him at the time.

The *UT Record* explained that Ransom's new publication, "designed as an arts and sciences review," shows "how to cross lines and jump chasms that often separate academic disciplines." It quoted Ransom to the effect that *Texas Quarterly* attempts "to put in print the liveliest comment obtainable on issues of serious consequence to intelligent readers."[3] But the implementation of this formula required Ransom to take a stronger hand in the editing process than he originally intended. An impatient memorandum to the *Quarterly* staff, dated September 1, 1958, revised the editorial committee's functions: *"Staff organization has been confused. The editor made* an honest effort to get 'participation' by a group of unlike-minded people on the faculty. The result was dissension. . . . Beginning with the fourth issue, the editor takes complete responsibility for the magazine. Members of the faculty interested in working with *TQ* will act *in an advisory capacity only.* . . . Less literary criticism, and less fiction-for-the-sake-of-getting-some-fiction will appear after November. For this reason, it may be that Texas should establish the 'literary magazine' some members of the committee keep insisting *TQ* should be."[4] To UT professor Roger Shattuck, who was studying in Aix-en-Provence, France, he confided: "The organization of the *Quarterly* worries me. In brief, I think that the experiments last year were largely failures. . . . From now on," Ransom vowed, "the editorial plans and decisions of *TQ* will be centralized. I may get out an increasingly fuzzy periodical, but at least the fuzziness would not be bought at the cost of valuable younger faculty time and at a wasteful rate for departments and in pain of unpleasantness and misunderstanding with people."[5]

Edwin T. Bowden recalled this shift in Ransom's feelings about the committee he had created. The *Texas Quarterly* meetings of 1957 and 1958 took place in the Tower, Bowden said. Ransom often asked the secretaries—usually Mrs. Margarette Carlson or Miss Magdalena Benavides—to bring in some coffee.[6] There was a big ashtray on the table. Ransom was then a somewhat chunky man of average height with wide shoulders; usually he was attired in a dark pinstripe or business suit, rarely a sports jacket, and never a sports shirt. Despite his bulkiness, he was athletic enough to dash up two flights of stairs when he was in a hurry. His thick-rimmed glasses added to his appearance of solidness. He was an impressive, even imposing figure physically, listening intently, his expression broken with a fleeting grin of recognition at something said.

Eventually, according to Bowden, Ransom made it clear at a *TQ* committee meeting that he had concluded the members "were not imaginative enough, not intellectually probing." After that, the committee "became little more than a rubber stamp. He never dissolved that board; it just never had much role after the first two or three issues. Subsequently Ransom made the decisions and picked the contents by himself." Bowden surmised that Ransom's sense of disappointment partly stemmed from the fact that he had rather daringly "cut himself off from the English Department by hiring all of these bright young 'outside' people—endeavoring to build a 'new' department, journal, library, and University."[7] And now many of them seemed preoccupied with their own careerist ambitions, setting aside little time for the journal project and frequently speaking negatively of each others' efforts. Another problem was that the effort to reward members of the editorial committee with supplemental salaries had been stymied, Ransom explained, by "legal advice and . . . financial authorities of the University," who objected to "double compensation for faculty members."[8]

Ransom's decision to edit the publication almost single-handedly (William B. Todd's word for it would be "autocratically") swamped him with details. If there were any managerial failings in this reluctance to delegate the editorial responsibilities, there were also offsetting and tangible compensations for the university deriving from the journal itself. The local *Austin American-Statesman* quoted a University of Texas Press production employee: "We just haven't been able to keep up with the orders. It's amazing. You know this isn't the kind of thing to appeal to just everybody. Some of this stuff you gotta read three times to really get it."[9] In fact, as a public relations tool, nothing could have been more attention-getting at the time than *Texas Quarterly*. Ransom had caught and harnessed the mood of his native state and its desire to prove its new cosmopolitanism. Part commentary, part scholarship, part literary magazine with poetry and fiction, part photographic essay, part regional booster, part international sampler, the journal was difficult to categorize, and Ransom liked that aspect of it. Moreover, the success of *Texas Quarterly*, whose circulation reached 3,200 by its fourth issue, meant that the former office-boy for *Sewanee Review* finally had his own outlet for editorial commentary. Plaudits came from every direction. The *Dallas News* compared it favorably with other "scholarly literary magazines" such as *Yale Review*, *Sewanee Review*, and *Southwest Review*, heralding it as "a welcome addition in a field of limited but challenging publications that should never be ignored."[10]

Volume 2 of *Texas Quarterly* the next year named James Boggs, William Burford, Joe B. Frantz, James Meriwether, F. Warren Roberts, William B. Todd, and A. Leslie Wilson as "Contributing Editors" (the former editorial committee having evaporated). The cover of the Winter 1959 issue was adorned with a photograph of the sumptuous Wrenn Library in the Main Building, in effect advertising UT's book collections. Sometimes there were special thematic issues in the early years—the Spring 1959 issue explored the topic of Mexico. Freelance photographer Hans Beacham's striking photographs often adorned the pages of *Texas Quarterly*, ranging from glimpses of rugged peasant life in Mexico to his portrait of T. S. Eliot profiled against a stone exterior on the UT campus. For a special issue devoted to Britain (Winter 1960), Ransom traced British-Texas connections that included "early ranchers from England and Scotland" and "delight in words, conversation in the pub, tall tales at the fire."

Eventually the pretense of any editorial group faded away entirely; the

FIGURE 8.1

Graves W. Landrum, Harding Lawrence, Regent W. W. Heath, and Professor Donald Weismann, with the November 1965 issue of Texas Quarterly. Texas Quarterly, *begun in 1958 and edited by Ransom, showcased Texas as an emerging intellectual frontier. The journal featured a regional "Texas touch" as it aimed to combine the disparate academic disciplines of the arts and the sciences. Landrum, business manager of the Main University, reported to Ransom daily. He had joined Ransom's staff in 1957 when Ransom became vice president and provost.* Harry Ransom Humanities Research Center, The University of Texas at Austin.

Autumn 1962 issue, for example, identified Harry H. Ransom as the editor and credited Kim Taylor and F. Warren Roberts as "Associate Editors." The indispensable Frances H. Hudspeth, who handled the details of manuscripts and deadlines, had become the "Managing Editor." Clarence L. Cline, Gerald Langford, and William Burford were merely designated as "Advisory Editors for this issue," which contained articles on D. H. Lawrence, W. B. Yeats, Mark Twain, and miscellaneous other subjects. By then, Ransom sometimes led off the issue with a speech he had delivered or an occasional piece he had prepared; this issue published his thoughts on "Education During the Scientific Revolution," in which he acknowledged the vast alteration in human experience represented by the exploration of outer space. One discernible result of this monumental shift, he wrote, was the demise of "the false comforts of earlier American education" that had assumed knowledge "came in tidy packages, usually labeled with the name of an academic department like English or chemistry." More encompassing approaches to academic disciplines were emerging: "linguistics, biochemistry, biophysics." He predicted the rapid end of the era when "every college or university could be an intellectual realm in itself. . . . Today, very few universities and colleges can 'go it alone' intellectually; tomorrow none will be able to do so."

Ransom would keep in his personal library a cherished copy of the initial issue of *Texas Quarterly*—his most soul-satisfying concern in 1958.

NINE

THE RARE BOOKS COLLECTION
AND THE ACADEMIC CENTER

Soon after Miss Ratchford obtained a Guggenheim Memorial Foundation Fellowship for Research (her third) to spend a year examining the forgeries of Thomas J. Wise, she made plans to leave on the *Ryndam* for England on August 13, 1957.[1] Harry Ransom had written in her support to the Guggenheim Foundation, testifying to her "eminence as a creative scholar."[2] Subsequently he had added a letter describing Miss Ratchford as "an amazing combination of intellectual humility with great intellectual courage."[3] On June 21, 1957, Dean Ransom diplomatically recommended that Fannie Ratchford "be named Director Emeritus, Research in Rare Book Bibliography, beginning September 15. This suggestion in no way erases Miss Ratchford's long service. . . . It does, however, emphasize her academic advisory status, and its future significance in allowing academic departments access to her advice." Miss Ratchford's watch was ending, and she was handing over her cherished collection to the only person she thoroughly trusted. Harry Ransom finally would have control of a part of the university that he considered essential to its national stature.[4]

During the same year in which Harry Ransom realized his goal of inheriting the Rare Books Collection, an immense decision of another kind confronted him. Ancestral ties were strengthening an offer of the chancellorship at the University of North Carolina. On January 28, 1957, having returned from a visit to its campus, Ransom pondered in a letter to University of North Carolina President William Friday the possibility of relocating, "including sentiments about an ancient family connection with North Carolina and my pleasures in a happy day at Chapel Hill." He turned from these reveries to a series of reflections: "I have some deep convictions about the function of a state university," he began. For example, "I think the wistful distinction between 'state institu[t]ions' . . . and 'privately endowed institutions' is nonsense. I went to nothing but 'private' institutions as a student; I have taught in nothing but public institutions—a teachers college, an agricultural and mechanical college, and a state university. I see no difference except false distinctions and the tendency of very prejudiced people to look down their noses at public education."

In a summary of his administrative credo, he emphasized that "I am deeply—almost passionately—interested in the printed word. I think that great libraries are something great universities cannot do without. I think no library is great unless it is active and growing. . . . I think the work of university presses, importance of learned periodicals, the role of books, pamphlets, public lectures must be emphasized." Regarding his philosophy of faculty governance, he asserted, "I believe in the faculty-directed policy of education. I should not care to work for a program which I could not justify to a faculty so clearly that it would gain almost unanimous support. . . . I believe in educational change, today and tomorrow. I might well disturb people who think everything is fine as it is."[5]

Yet ultimately the North Carolina inducements were not quite enough. "For the time being I feel that I am committed to the University of Texas," he explained to President Friday. "To leave here this September would be to walk out on the expectations of others, as distinguished from my own expectations."[6] He confided to an Austin acquaintance, "I had a long and difficult bout with myself. . . . I suppose my roots in Texas are deeper than such roots usually go."[7] Professor Richmond Bond of the North Carolina English Department addressed a letter of March 3, 1957, to the "Best-Chancellor-We'll-Never-Have," noting as a humorous postscript that "Billy [Friday] wrote me that half the citizens of Texas were on their knees beseeching HHR not to leave and that half of those hadn't been in a church in thirty years," and then adding: "P.P.S. I do hope you got many and large concessions out of L. W. [Logan Wilson] for yourself and your projects."[8]

One reason that Ransom had seemed qualified to be named the new UT Vice President and Provost (an office he would assume on September 1, 1957) was that as dean of the College of Arts and Sciences he had conceived and established the Arts and Sciences Foundation. Now he undertook the founding of a similar organization to protect and enhance the rare book collections: the Friends of the Library set out to raise an initial $500,000 for a general endowment fund, as well as to put together one million dollars for the purchase and endowment of the vaunted Parsons Library in New Orleans. J. P. Bryan of the University Board of Regents had undertaken negotiations with the owner of that library, and in 1958 would lay claim to the collection for a promised total of $390,000, with the donors paying their pledged shares through 1960.[9] The materials gathered by Parsons (1878–1962), an attorney, scholar, and historian, would double the size of UT's Rare Books Collection, adding 40,000 books and 10,000 manuscripts along with works of art. Ransom dedicated himself to winning converts for these and subsequent library projects with a campaign of personal letter-writing and visits that would continue for more than a decade. The volume of his correspondence, especially in light of the fact that he was responsible for increasingly complex administrative assignments at a school that had grown to enroll 14,000 students and (as Ransom mentioned to one library sponsor in 1957) "may expect to double in size within the next twenty years," was simply staggering. Over and above his normal duties, nearly every day Ransom devoted two or three letters, and sometimes as many as eight or ten, to the nurturing of his favorite library projects. These were, moreover, detailed, individualized, compelling pieces of writing; each gave the impression of originality, of having been composed solely for that particular person.

In addition, printed fliers and brochures were necessary for mailing to prospective donors. On February 12, 1957, Ransom sent potential contributor Ellen Garwood a draft of a brochure describing the need for enhancing "the University library research center in Austin, which belongs to the people of the whole state," soliciting Garwood's suggestions. Because "top scholars are leaving Texas," and "many others . . . refuse to come—because the resources for study are not here," Ransom's brochure announced "the reestablishment of the Friends of the Texas Library, originally organized under E. L. DeGolyer." Everette Lee DeGolyer (1886–1956), a wealthy and world-renowned petroleum geologist and geophysicist, had died in Dallas on December 14. In 1946 DeGolyer had donated his collection of first and rare editions of modern American and British writers to UT and his history of science collection to the University of Oklahoma. "Just now our first goal will be collection," Ransom explained to Garwood, but added (as he invariably did), "for use—research and creative writing." Next would follow "an actual 'center' at the University," and then, "publication and the encouragement of publication."[10]

As its first task, the Friends were asked to support the acquisition of the incomparable Parsons Collection, which contained early archives related to the Louisiana territory and certain documents touching on Texas history. There were also more than one hundred incunabula (books printed before 1501), an impressive theatrical collection, the John Milton family Bible and early Bible editions, travel literature, histories of printing, early editions of Dante and other classics, and ancient materials ranging from Babylonian clay tablets to Egyptian papyri. Government professor William S. Livingston

FIGURE 9.1

*Ransom at his typewriter, 1961. A fast typist, Ransom would often draft a letter
of congratulations or condolence by typewriter, then copy it by hand for a more
personal touch.* Harry Huntt Ransom Scrapbook, 1961–1962, Center
for American History, The University of Texas at Austin.

happened to walk by the Main Building in 1958 as these treasures were being unloaded from a truck. Mrs. Hudspeth waved this tall man over and
showed him a small black stone she was holding in some tissue paper. She
pointed to its markings and exclaimed delightedly, "These are the earliest
human writings known to exist!"[11]

Coincidentally, a little earlier (in 1956) had occurred an immense bibliographic event, unfortunate for the University of Texas but fortuitous in
its publicity value, which Ransom seized upon so effectually that it turned
around his state's thinking about library resources. New Jersey oilman
Thomas Streeter had amassed an incredibly broad collection of Texana,
and in October 1956, after circulating news of its availability, he granted
Yale University an option to purchase the materials. The sale, for a reported
$300,000, was finalized and announced in February 1957. An outcry arose
at once in Texas as the extent of the loss of this opportunity registered with
the press and the public. Streeter himself exacerbated the controversy by

writing to the editor of the *Austin American-Statesman* and testifying that "at no time before that [Yale] contract was made had there been any suggestion by any of the Texas libraries of the slightest interest in acquiring the collection. If the educational leaders of Texas wish to acquire valuable material for their institutions it would seem that they ought to make a point of informing the many wealthy and public-spirited individuals of Texas of the existence of such material." Hulon W. Black, director of the UT Development Board that was establishing the Arts and Sciences Foundation, advised that "the Streeter experience may well serve as an example of what can happen if we don't begin early enough to raise money." Harry Ransom, recognizing that UT had the state's attention while people absorbed the shock of this forfeiture, took the occasion to announce "plans for a million-dollar Library Research Center in Austin. . . . that would provide a statewide 'locating service' for scholarly and creative purposes." Newspaper reporter Anita Brewer promptly characterized Ransom as possessing "the philosophy of a man who intends to get something done," and quoted his resolve that "the loss of the Streeter collection will make us all more vigilant, so invaluable collections will not be lost to us again."[12]

The Streeter calamity became a staple in Ransom's letters to prospective donors. For example, on September 10, 1957, Ransom lamented to Will L. Clayton, who with his daughter, Ellen, and her husband, Judge W. St. John Garwood, eventually pledged $75,000 to Ransom's plans, about "the purchase of the Streeter Collection by Yale University. . . . While all of us are delighted that a great educational institution in the East thus established a center of Texas studies, we are not able to say glibly, 'Let any Texas student who wants to study unique Texas materials go to Yale.'"[13] In a memorandum to President Logan Wilson, Ransom had listed the Streeter Collection as one of the regrettable "losses to Texas in recent months," along with "the [Bernard] De Voto Collection, and the Lawrence Collection." "I cannot resist adding," he reminded President Wilson, "that since 1917—when Texas began to lead all state universities in research collection—we have steadily declined (so that now Kansas, Illinois, Indiana, and Duke have passed us). . . . Library-philanthropy is not highly developed in Texas."[14]

UT English professor and future (1984–1990) department chairman W. O. S. Sutherland would say later that he, like many other faculty members, admired Ransom "because of his vision. . . . He was always living in the future." In Sutherland's view it was Ransom who "started the practice of seeking private funding for a public university, on the model of Yale or Princeton." Sutherland would remember seeing Ransom waiting for someone near the Main Building and seemingly being unable to stop his perpetual motion, jumping up and down slightly on his toes. With the same energy, said Sutherland, Ransom usually made decisions rapidly and was impatient with slow, bureaucratic procedures for doing things. What Mody Boatright and Clarence Cline did for the English Department, Sutherland said, Harry Ransom accomplished for the entire university.[15]

In a television interview in 1957 conducted by the Texas Book Club, Ransom tried to dispel the public's usual impression of "rare books as museum pieces. Some of them are. . . . But the real significance of research collections in Texas lies in the vitality they add to modern study." Ransom's prepared script alluded to T. S. Eliot's letter about *The Waste Land* and informed viewers that the Arts and Sciences College "hopes to present Eliot as one of its lecturers next year." He outlined a broader definition of "rare books" that would include "newspapers, pictures, and manuscripts that are very hard to come by," and stressed how "essential" these items are "to the work of young students, scholars, and creative writers."[16] At every such opportunity Ransom promoted his idea of the intrinsic usefulness of academic research. When Bud Mims interviewed him for a *Daily Texan* article on his rise to vice president and provost, Mims reported that this "active man of short, stocky stature" who "speaks in short, choppy phrases, his eyes squinting in thought," prophesied a "'period' when The University of Texas will ascend to a firm position among the top universities in the country."[17]

From Fannie Ratchford arrived long, chatty letters from Collingham Road in London addressed to "Dear Folks" as she passed along travel sights and rare book gossip. Ransom replied to her literary miscellanea in a lengthy letter on January 2, 1958, catching her up about "the near certainty of our acquiring the Woodward-Ruth Collection of [Francis] Bacon, a remarkable collection from Sir Arthur Conan Doyle's library, the likelihood that we will acquire the Bachmann Collection of English Literature, [and] the present motion in the Administration to ask the Regents to make a one hundred thousand dollar down payment on the Parsons Library." He lamented the death of Dr. Reginald H. Griffith of the English Department, "which marked an era for all of us." Among other developments, "we have added to the faculty, with the specific idea of part-time assignment to the Rare Books Collection, two very notable younger men. The first is Dr. William Todd, who is the second man in the Houghton Library (Bill Jackson was not at all happy at his choosing Texas over Harvard)." The second was "Dr. James Meriwether, who has specialized in Southern literature at Princeton and is responsible for several of their most remarkable rare book exhibitions. Todd will work, of course, primarily as descriptive bibliographer and as expert in the eighteenth century. Meriwether will be in the more recent period."[18] Ratchford replied that Dr. Griffith's death left her with "a haunting sense of incompleteness, that after spending two-thirds of my life under his direction, I should not be with him when the great transition came. . . . I wish he might have seen the Griffith Foundation in full operation. . . . I think you gave him the greatest earthly reward of his life." She went on to praise Ransom's purchases and report on her own discoveries; her research had revealed that the plays in the Wrenn Library at UT, dating from 1600 to 1660, were daring forgeries. Portions of them, in fact, consisted of leaves stolen from copies in the British Museum. "Notwithstanding all I knew of Wise's rascality, I am shocked at what I am learning of his practices. He was a man without conscience, who thought only of getting what he wanted, which was prestige and power through his library. He cared no more for books in themselves than for smoked out cigar butts."[19] Ransom wrote back elatedly a few days later to say that he had raised a quarter of a million dollars toward the Parsons Library purchase. Plus, "we are now sure of acquiring the Dannay Library," and he headily speculated that its contents might "stimulate a more popular sort of creative writing."[20]

Ransom's successful wooing of William B. Todd to an associate professorship in the English Department affords a snapshot of his recruiting method—personal meetings, urgent and energetic letters, tantalizingly flexible offers. On December 2, 1957, Ransom had vowed to Jack Stillinger of Cambridge, Massachusetts, that "we are going to do everything but lay the Tower on its side and run the Colorado River dry to get Bill Todd."[21] Eight days later he wrote to thank the Todds for allowing him to visit them ("the highlight of this trip"). Inviting Todd to join the UT faculty, Ransom promised Todd that he could teach Ransom's former offering—Research Methods and Bibliography. In the library, "your responsibility to me would be principally the development of the eighteenth-century collection of literature. . . . You will be given complete freedom to develop as a scholar in your own right or as a teacher of scholars and a director of research programs. I think it is not a mere Texas boast to conclude by saying that this is a good opportunity."[22]

Todd later recalled that much of the hiring of himself and others took place over the telephone; Ransom seemed too inundated with work to write them each time a query arose. To Todd, the process was an example of what the UT faculty, too, now meant by "Ransomizing," a veritable form of mesmerizing. The candidate came away with a euphoric glow, feeling as though the whole university depended on his choice—and sometimes he or she realized only later that no definite answers had been given to various questions. Upon his arrival at UT, for example, Todd found that his duties had never been precisely defined. He visited the Rare Books Collection and wandered around the premises. He found the collection was strong up to about 1750; after that, virtually nothing. When he mentioned the fact to Ransom, he seemed thunderstruck. Ransom had always assumed that Reginald H. Griffith was taking care of that literary period, but now grasped the fact that Griffith cared for little beyond Alexander Pope's death in 1744. Todd promptly ordered a copy of the first edition of Fielding's great novel *Tom Jones* (1749), the first move toward filling in an incredible gap in the collection.

Todd judged that Ransom was not fond of the cautious attitudes of most librarians. "He told me numerous times that he liked me because I didn't act like a librarian," Todd said, speculating that this impatience with library boards and staff may have sharpened his later determination to keep the eventual Research Center staff separate from the University Library. One resulting problem was that incoming rare book and manuscript acquisitions piled up in the upper floors of the Tower. Ransom himself kept stacks of purchased material in closets in his Main Building office. His secretaries merely typed notes about the arrivals, and these were of course incompatible with any conventional library methodology. In Todd's opinion, Harry Ransom's compulsion was collecting, certainly not cataloguing, and this predilection of his would become grounds for criticism in later years. Gradually, in Todd's view, Ransom, Hudspeth, and F. Warren Roberts (who had finished his UT English Ph.D. in 1956) virtually ran the Rare Books Collection as far as acquisitions, exhibits, and publications were concerned. Still, Todd found little to complain of in the results.[23] T. S. Eliot's visit drew such a crowd that Gregory Gymnasium had to be used for his reading. When the Alfred Knopfs came to town, Ransom personally designated the guest list.[24] Winfred P. Lehmann would marvel at the upshot: "One dinner and Knopf gives him his entire library!"[25] What Ransom said, went—largely because of his track record for producing miracles. It became sufficient for Frances Hudspeth to telephone someone on campus and tell that person what "He" (her exclusive term of reference for Ransom) wanted done.[26]

As Ransom stepped up his book-and-manuscript-buying campaign, he encountered and formed a working alliance with one of the most flamboyant American book dealers of the twentieth century, Lew David Feldman, and his eponymous House of El Dieff (pronounced "L-D-F") of Jamaica, New York. Educated by his father to be a rabbi, Feldman had rebelled and joined the Marine Corps. He was rumored to harbor an ambition to become recognized as a latter-day A. S. W. Rosenbach (1876–1952), the legendary American bibliophile and book dealer. F. Warren Roberts judged this latter-day aspirant to be pretentious, a poseur. But there was one peculiarity about the showy, extravagantly attired Feldman (he affected a cloak and a cane)—his shrugging indulgence about late payments—that Ransom found enormously helpful while he was trying to put together the funds for large purchases. According to Roberts, Ransom came to owe Feldman hundreds of thousands of dollars for months, or even years at a time, and Feldman was willing to wait patiently. "We essentially used him as a bank," Roberts said.[27] In fact, records indicate that in 1970 Ransom was in debt to the House of El Dieff for a total of $3,125,126.86, with payments scheduled through 1973.[28] By 1972 Feldman was still due $1,005,510.83.[29]

In an early letter to Feldman in 1957, following a visit to Feldman's bookshop and residence, Ransom sketched out the literary figures in whom he was especially interested: "Twain, Whitman, Poe, and others. . . . In the general plan, as I see it, we should move along a very wide front. The exceptions which I would make are only those unlikely to arouse much interest among graduate and undergraduate students or those who simply could not be built up effectively and economically in Texas. For instance, I would be completely disinclined to buy a small cache of Emily Dickinson papers. Important as she is, her manuscripts belong at Harvard, not at Texas. A distinguished collection of Dickinson books and criticism, however, would interest me immediately."[30] Ransom assured Feldman in 1958 that "you are not adding materials to a parvenu collection; the Research Center will be a foursquare library." But a postscript added a precautionary afterthought: "I am going to arrange during the summer and early autumn to space out the 'public relations' announcements of our program. . . . We do not want to give the impression that Texas is raking in indiscriminately a lot of books simply for the pleasure of raking them in. This plan is carefully calculated to advance scholarship and to give our younger people a laboratory for ideas."[31]

Feldman soon began bidding on behalf of UT at book auctions, following the instructions Ransom gave after perusing the catalogs issued in advance of auctions—buying, for example, a Walt Whitman collection at the Guffey Sale in 1958.[32] Sometimes, when the catalogs miscarried or there were other delays, Feldman took it upon himself to bid without authorization for an item he felt almost positive that Ransom would want. For example, he revealed to Ransom that he had bought a copy of Hawthorne's first novel, *Fanshawe* (1828), extremely rare because the author attempted to acquire and destroy its entire edition. Feldman termed it "certainly the finest recorded copy," but added, "Have no hesitancy, regardless of our former conversations and correspondence, if this purchase were to embarrass you for any reason whatsoever, pass it by."[33] When Feldman boldly asked for permission to consider himself "your sole American Auction agent," Ransom replied that "the Regents are going to balk at any kind of exclusive appointments, I gather; but we'll be able to work out a sensible arrangement for auctions, especially if we can get a sizeable fund in the Friends of Library office." By 1959 Ransom was showing a degree of connoisseurship, writing Feldman that "the Sotheby catalogue for April has come. Like the cowboy who visited the fashionable salons of Neiman-Marcus in Dallas, I am much comforted by the sight of so many things I do not need."[34]

In 1962 Ransom was again reminding Feldman (and possibly himself as well) that "we should consider the prospects of complete collections and libraries as against acquisition of small collections of manuscripts and extremely rare books." He also gave a green light to acquiring "collections on the history of Texas, the Southwest, and the western United States; the notable collections already at Texas on Latin American countries; the history of science collection, in which we have barely a start; and the theatre collections, already supported with tremendous generosity of the Hoblitzelle Foundation."[35] Although Ransom continuously employed as well the services of the Brick Row Bookshop, the Gotham Book Mart, the Jenkins Company, and other book dealers, especially Marguerite A. Cohn's House of Books in New York City, his business transactions with the House of El Dieff were extensive and his correspondence with Feldman especially cordial and specific. Feldman profited from the relationship primarily because he consistently kept Ransom informed of East Coast developments in the book world and he made the UT library one of his very top priorities. Moreover, he visited Austin and knew how to stay in touch with a restless client who had this tremendous desire to build up a superb collection of rare materials within a few years. His easygoing attitude about Ransom's line of credit was crucial, since rare book auction firms have rigid stipulations about sales and payments. But this close association with Feldman would penalize Ransom in the jealous circle of rare book dealers.

After the deaths of Feldman (in 1976) and Ransom, Charles Hamilton, a prominent New York City bookseller, would give vent to vile innuendo in a book titled *Auction Madness: An Uncensored Look Behind the Velvet Drapes of the Great Auction Houses.* According to Hamilton, "the ability to bilk one's clients at auction is a fine art" requiring animal-like cunning, ethics, and acquisitive drive. "All these feral qualities were uniquely fused in the late Lew David Feldman. . . . This exquisitely tasteless man . . . limped about with Mark Twain's silver-headed cane and a supercilious sneer on his fat upper lip." Allegedly, "the best deal Lew ever worked out was with the University of Texas where his 'arrangement' with . . . Harry Ransom blew in a gusher for both men. They made millions by bilking the University Library. They bought virtually worthless collections privately, then sold them to the university at an immense profit."[36]

But the evidence does not support these allegations. The invoices from Feldman suggest that if some prices were slightly high for their time, others were assuredly low. Feldman did bill UT for his professional "services" in locating, negotiating for, evaluating, and cataloging potential purchases, yet while these costs sometimes ran into the tens of thousands of dollars they were not frequent enough to make anyone "rich." F. Warren Roberts, who personally checked many of the itemized invoices during this period, utterly refuted the rumors of padding or kickbacks. As for Ransom's supposed wealth, said Roberts, he was only modestly well off (leaving aside Hazel's inheritance from her parents), and his comfortableness resulted from investments, frugal living, and the advantages of having a car and a house provided for him as a UT administrator.[37] Other interviews with book dealers, colleagues, and friends tend to vindicate Ransom completely from such charges. A chapter in Nicholas A. Basbanes's *A Gentle Madness: Bibliophiles, Bibliomanes, and the Eternal Passion for Books* (1995) very credibly exonerates Ransom by disclosing the flimsiness of Hamilton's evidence and the unreliability of his source for information.[38] Ransom himself commented to a former student, Robert Barnes, that "the only way to keep library acquisitions from being criticized is not to get any. I am looking forward to the day when I can retire and raise petunias; meanwhile, I am reconciled to commotion."[39]

Among those chagrined by the calumny of Hamilton's attack was Anthony Rota, son of the eminent London antiquarian book dealer Bertram Rota; both father and son had known Ransom through years of transatlantic correspondence and visits to Texas. "It's absolute rubbish that Harry was on the take," declared the younger Rota emphatically during an interview in 1989. "Charles Hamilton died soon thereafter, and I hope it was of remorse." Rota could only imagine that envy and the desire to write a good-selling book led Hamilton to include these unfounded claims. "We dealt with Harry for years and years, and he never took anything more than a lunch off us." Even Rota had to admit that "UT *was* a slow-paying customer—eighteen months was nothing for them at all. I used to say that UT was a very good customer, and if we had two customers that good it would bankrupt us. That's why Harry used Feldman so much—he would carry him indefinitely. He never charged interest, but the price most probably reflected the anticipated delay in payment." Rota conjectured that "Harry wouldn't have agreed to interest." The thing was, "Harry knew the Regents adored him, knew the same quality of materials would never be available again, knew nobody else could get the money for the Humanities Research Center, so he acted."[40]

One regent marveled how Ransom "is able to get money for books anywhere." Likewise, A. W. Yeats recalled that "he would tap every butcher and baker and undertaker in Texas."[41] Ransom's instinctive strategy of appealing to a broad base of support for research materials that could have multiple purposes and benefits is well illustrated in the plea for funds he released on November 18, 1957, when he had set his sights on purchasing a huge collection of Ellery Queen detective items. Rather than portray the 10,000 volumes as of interest solely or even primarily to enthusiasts of crime fiction, he insisted that "it would be the purpose of the proposed Collection to serve not only State agencies and other educational institutions, but also law enforcement officers, research workers, and writers concerned with the field." He closed with this appeal: "For the establishment of a law enforcement library, built around this Collection, $75,000 is needed."[42] Ransom secured an itemized inventory and savored the contents with anticipation: "First editions of approximately 95 percent of the detective-crime-mystery short story field, . . . and all of the 'high spots' in the development of the detective story novel." In addition, "a handwritten manuscript of the first Sherlock Holmes manuscript . . . , as well as the finest group of Sherlock Holmes first editions in the world."[43] Frederic Dannay (who collaborated with Manfred Lee in producing detective novels under the pseudonym "Ellery Queen") wrote on December 23, 1957, expressing pleasure that Lew David Feldman had arranged the procurement of Dannay's personal book collection. UT ended up paying $30,000 for the Ellery Queen Library—$15,000 from the Friends of the Library Fund and $15,000 from the W. C. Hogg Fund.[44] As one spin-off of the sale, Ransom and Dannay corresponded periodically about Dannay's coming to UT for a teaching and literary-magazine-editing appointment.[45]

In July of 1958 Harry Ransom made another acquisition about which he had delicately negotiated for four long years. As early as September 1954 Ransom had shared with this collector his "resolution to make here a live center for research and writing, not merely a museum of books."[46] The T. E. Hanley Library that he sought, rich in D. H. Lawrence materials, was also studded with gems in the form of manuscripts, typescripts, corrected proof copies, and first editions of Oscar Wilde, Dylan Thomas, George Bernard Shaw, Ezra Pound, T. E. Lawrence, James Joyce, Samuel Beckett, and other significant literary figures. Although Hanley (1893–1969) was a Harvard graduate and had already donated thousands of books to the University of Arizona and St. Bonaventure University, Ransom was able to catch and hold his attention while endeavoring to raise enough money to take possession of the balance of the entire collection. In Bradford, Pennsylvania, where Hanley had brick manufacturing and oil and gas interests, he and his uninhibited Hungarian-born wife Tullah (1924–1992) meditated upon the disposition of his monumental art, rare book, and manuscript holdings, thirty years in the assembling. (Oddly, Hanley casually stored these extraordinary items in his garage.) Ransom struck the right note with him by pledging that his library would become part of a "live center for research and writing." James H. Drake, a New York book dealer, assisted in arrangements for a partial sale, which the UT Regents approved in spite of its million-dollar price tag. (Through follow-up negotiations Ransom would land Hanley's remaining books and manuscripts for another $650,000 in 1964.) Richard W. Oram, whose library career at UT would be entwined with these materials, characterized the purchases as "a stupendous bargain" and "*the* defining moment in the early history of the Humanities Research Center."[47] F. Warren Roberts recalled the arrival of Hanley's collection "in a guarded truck caravan. . . . 'Nobody, . . . not even Harry, really knew what we had. . . . But when we started taking it out of those boxes—it was in no particular order, really—we were astonished. None of us dreamed of all the things that were in it."[48] Roberts added, "I shall never forget the excitement . . . as we opened package after package on the fourth floor in the old rare books library."[49] To Regent Merton M. Minter, Ransom wrote delightedly to explain that "Hanley has the omnivorousness of a collector and the altruism of a philanthropist."[50] David A. Randall, Rare Books Librarian at Indiana University, gamely sent congratulations on September 25, 1958: "I wish, of course, that Indiana could have had it—unfortunately the time was wrong for us—what with the building just going up and all. Ralph Collins is green with envy. . . . My best wishes for what you are doing—I'm all for getting books west of the Hudson."[51] Ransom replied with satisfaction and surely a little wishful thinking on October 2: "The Hanley Library is now settled—and mirabile dictu—catalogued, opened for research, and operating as part of the new Humanities Center." Candidly, Ransom added, "You scared us to death" during the months "when we are [sic] trying to bring the Library to Texas."[52]

A press release issued by the University of Texas News and Information Service on January 24, 1959, quoted Harry H. Ransom's defense of the new Texas location for the Hanley Library: "There was a time . . . when midwestern, southwestern, and southern libraries were 'way out there.' Now—with new systems of transportation and communication—Austin, for example, is literally in the middle of things, between two coasts, and between the lively social and economic developments in Canada and Latin America. It was partly because of this strategic location that Mr. Hanley consented to have his library established in Texas." Although Ransom had previously obtained (and the Rare Books Collection had also long possessed) holograph manuscripts by various British and American authors, it was really the magnitude and quality of the T. E. Hanley Library—with its manuscripts of D. H. Lawrence's *Women in Love, The Rainbow,* "The Prussian Officer," and an early version of *Sons and Lovers,* proof sheets of Ezra Pound's *Canzoni,* Shakespeare and Company's first edition of James Joyce's *Ulysses,* and George Bernard Shaw's annotated final proof of *Pygmalion,* along with many other treasures—that indelibly associated Harry H. Ransom's name with the two distinguishing hallmarks of acquisitions for the Humanities Research Center: an emphasis on the twentieth century, and auxiliary primary materials supplementing the first edition of a literary work.[53]

In spite of these many complicated distractions, Ransom never let go of a crucial vision that he had adopted with all the passion of which he was capable—the dream of erecting a commodious, up-to-date, multiuse undergraduate library that would serve as a center for campus cultural activities and attract the most gifted students in Texas. Two hundred thousand book titles were to be ordered for the sole use of students in this facility, he directed on July 24, 1958, combining three purposes: *"assigned reading, browsing and parallel reading,* and *teaching exhibit."*[54] In the *Daily Texan,* Ransom elaborated: "The Main Library was designed for the more mature student, one who has picked up a technique for 'getting at books.' This new Academic Center is designed strictly to give undergraduates access to the shelves. In this center, students just can't avoid coming in contact with books."[55]

The idea of students themselves being able to locate their desired library books on shelves within an "open" (non-restricted) area was still a relatively novel concept in the 1950s; most universities still relied on a laborious system of paging whereby students filled out library cards and waited many minutes while library workers entered restricted stacks and either returned with the volumes or with information that the books were already checked out. But Ransom noted that "excellent open-shelf libraries have been established recently at places as different as Harvard, Arlington, Rice, California, Oklahoma A&M, and Michigan."[56] When an English professor wrote to question the wisdom of Ransom's appointing eight student brainstormers to advise him on plans for the Academic Center, Ransom retorted, "I think that the ebullience of the undergraduates is understandable. Actually, don't you think that at least some of their notions should be incorporated in the building where we are to conduct a good deal of 'self-education'?"[57]

Graves Landrum as the UT business manager handled the increasingly complex paperwork for this new building and its furnishings; a letter of December 19, 1960, from Landrum to Chancellor Logan Wilson, by way of example, requested permission to seek "an appropriation of $190,000 from [the] Permanent University Fund" for equipment and interior decorations.[58] Ransom became persuaded that the top (fourth) floor of the new Academic Center should house "major special collections devoted to Americana, Texas subjects, the South, the history of the book, Latin America, the fine arts, and special exhibits." The other three floors "will be the undergraduate library."[59] It was Ransom's hope that the area between the Student Union and the new building would become a gathering point for students. A large flagstone patio with tables, chairs, umbrellas, and pools for fish and aquatic plants would link the two buildings. "Do you remember Beck's Pond by the Old Library?" Mrs. Hudspeth, writing on behalf of Ransom, asked potential donor Stark Young (1881–1963), a former teacher of English who had become a New York City novelist, journalist, essayist, and playwright. "And how much socializing went on there in days long past? Perhaps this patio will be the modern student's 'Beck's Pond.' It was by the old pond that I first encountered Mrs. Browning (Heaven forgive me!) when I should have been studying Greek irregular verbs or the atomic chart in chemistry. It is my extremely pleasant task to help Dr. Ransom in the development of the Center. This is the most stimulating and exciting project I've ever encountered. . . . Dr. Ransom has meant so much to this institution in so many ways that I can't begin to list them, but I believe the new Academic Center is the one for which he will be remembered most vividly."[60]

Who were the financial backers for this project? Essentially an amalgam of Austin, statewide, and national donors who believed in Harry Ransom's "magnet" vision.[61] The Garwood and Clayton families, joined by the

FIGURE 9.2

The Peter Flawn Academic Center (formerly the Undergraduate Library and Academic Center). Ransom kept abreast of library developments around the country and recognized that open-shelf libraries should become part of the university campus. He soon went about obtaining financial resources to provide this facility for the students. The fourth floor would house selected special collections. Margaret Berry, *UT Pictorial History,* 86, Center for American History, The University of Texas at Austin.

M. D. Anderson Foundation of Houston; the Tobin Foundation of San Antonio in cooperation with the Hobby Foundation of Houston; the Hoblitzelle Foundation, the DeGolyer Foundation, Mr. H. L. Williford of Dallas, and a group of South Texans. Many non-Texans also assisted the plans, including Alfred and Blanche Knopf, the publishers; E. L. Tinker, a New York financier; and Frederic Williams, the artist. Others made gifts of antiquities and portraits, including Jack Danciger of Fort Worth and T. E. Hanley of Pennsylvania.[62]

As early as December 31, 1957, Ransom had set out to coax his friend the Western writer J. Frank Dobie to grace the Academic Center with his personal correspondence and mementos. Ransom's initial letter to Dobie illustrates Ransom's ability to talk or write in the most intimate, confiding manner and to present a picture of possibilities encompassing the recipient's

FIGURE 9.3

Book dealers at the opening of the Academic Center, 1963: Jake Zeitlin, James H. Drake,
Frances Hamill, Bertram Rota, Margie Cohen, Lew David Feldman, Franklin
Gilliam. These were among Ransom's preferred book dealers when purchasing
rare books and manuscripts for UT. Harry Ransom Humanities Research
Center, The University of Texas at Austin.

most private and cherished aspirations. In this case, Ransom did deliver
handsomely on a promised fourth-floor installation:

> I see a great many libraries, and . . . most of them, one way or the other,
> lose the vitality of the minds who wrote the better books that line their
> shelves. There isn't a good Shakespeare Room in this country, although
> there are plenty of Shakespeare mausoleums and Shakespeare monu-
> ments and Shakespeare dissecting tables and Shakespeare repositories.
> The thing I am after is a Dobie Room. A capacious room in which
> things (including books and pictures) would get at people in the way in
> which you got at the younger, stiff-legged staff back in the thirties down
> at the bottom of B Hall. . . .
> I like you, and I have a good many sentiments about what you have
> been to all of us, and especially to me in becoming a Texan again. . . .

I would want in it a lot of humanity, some gusto, a proper sense of place— . . . and above all the vitality of faith in what is alive.[63]

Without any hesitation, Dobie replied on January 5, 1958, commenting that his legal will "didn't say anything at all about my manuscripts or letters, pictures, bronzes, artifacts, etc. In other words, it's no sort of will at all for me to have. I don't think my lawyer knows much about estate taxes. I know that the fellow who makes out my income tax is stupid and doesn't know straight up about anything. I had just as soon trust what you denominate 'the University's lawyers' on this matter as anybody else. I have a considerable amount of material ready for delivery now."[64] By May 12, 1960, Ransom was letting Dobie know that he was trying to achieve the rustic effect Dobie preferred: "I have given the go-ahead to the architects on the mesquite."[65] But a disappointed Dobie wrote resignedly to Ransom on December 8, 1960: "I guess it's no use to mention mesquite again. . . . The architects are used to fitting out penthouses on top of office buildings owned by oil millionaires. Very few of them love any wood or any stone because it expresses something of the life of a land."[66]

As finally agreed upon, the entire Academic Center building was to encompass 211,473 square feet.[67] The shellstone-, limestone-, and granite-façade structure opened in 1963 after a total expenditure of $4,700,000 for construction, furnishings, equipment, and books. During much of Ransom's lifetime it bore a fonder name than "Academic Center" among the UT students; it was often alluded to as "Harry's Place" because of Ransom's unrelenting devotion to it.[68]

Every arduous effort has its price, of course, and Ransom sacrificed many distracting pleasures in order to succeed as an influential administrator. In a letter written in the middle of the negotiations in 1958 over J. Frank Dobie's sale and contribution of materials to the Academic Center, Dobie paused to beg Ransom to undertake an essay Ransom had long intended to write. "I should be interested in seeing it in print. . . . But so long as you go on making speeches every time a can of tomatoes or peaches is opened somewhere in this country, you won't have time to withdraw and write. It takes withdrawing to 'see into the life of things,'" Dobie insisted.[69]

TEN

VICE PRESIDENT AND PROVOST

The summer of 1958 had its ups and downs for Ransom. On June 12, 1958, he wrote with near-incredulity to President Logan Wilson to register how "deeply distressed" he was "at the report in the administrative staff meeting, apparently originating in W. Gordon Whaley's Graduate School, that there is opposition among the faculty to the present program of acquiring library collections." This did not agree at all with his own impressions; "I know only one dissident in the faculty. . . . I wish to reiterate . . . that the needs of our library are appalling." Moreover, "by gift, stimulated largely in this program (no other comparable gifts having been received since 1918), we have acquired at least five times as much as we have bought." In a rare gesture of ultimatum (perhaps the sole such warning he ever issued at UT), Ransom concluded the letter by stating: "While I have enjoyed and have tried to work honestly at the routines of an ill-defined office, I cannot see in my present position anything more important than the building up of a research center and an undergraduate library. For that reason, I feel that I must now reconsider my whole situation here. The opposition of even a responsible minority of the administration and teaching staff to the library program would make my position, as I see my position, untenable. May we have a conference with [Graduate] Dean Whaley at any early date?"[1] The results of Ransom's line-in-the-sand pronouncement were satisfactory enough that his correspondence did not pursue this matter any further. It might be coincidental that the UT Regents' minutes of September 20, 1958, would include a resolution by Chairman John Leroy Jeffers, "on behalf of the Board," which paid tribute to Vice President and Provost Harry H. Ransom for "the imagination and enthusiasm he has exhibited in the acquisition of libraries and for his splendid work in interesting private sources to make contributions for the acquisition of these library collections."[2]

Then, also in June, he and Hazel traveled to Sewanee, where Ransom received an honorary degree of Doctor of Letters at the University of the South, a moving experience for Hazel as well as her husband. Ransom's university duties later required his traveling to Dallas, New Orleans, and Ohio, in the latter case to attend a meeting of the National Education Association. (The northern trip would be a relief of sorts, since, as he observed, "in August in Texas tumultuous joys usually have to do with swimming pools, shower baths, and the blessed snatch of breeze between 2:15 and 2:17 A.M.")[3]

Before those trips, the Ransoms took a vacation to Cuernevaca, Mexico, joining the Minters to visit Regent Joe C. Thompson and his wife, Peggy. Dr. Merton Minter was a physician and regent, and the Ransoms were becoming quite fond of businessman "Jodie" Thompson. What Ransom referred to as a "gracious interlude" in Mexico was followed by "Hazel's malady" and a mishap.[4] In a letter to Giles E. Dawson of the Folger Shakespeare Library, Ransom wryly reported, "After my return from Mexico, my wife fell critically ill and in the midst of these domestic turmoils, I managed to convert both a telephone pole and my Plymouth into trash (I escaped with only the penalty of several weeks inactivity)."[5] Hazel's illness, "which sounds more serious than it is," had been diagnosed as Meniere's Syndrome, "a rupture of a blood vessel near the inner ear," treatable with a prescription of anti-coagulants.[6] Both Ransoms, reluctantly taking time out to rest, recovered completely. By September 26 he could joke about the incident to Lawrence Clark Powell of UCLA: "I have been recuperating from a conclusive experiment: no driver can tear up a telephone pole and a Plymouth at the same time without some inroads into his correspondence. Fortunately, I do not write letters with either my nose or my knee; otherwise you would not be getting one even so late."[7] Such lightheartedness on Ransom's part was unusual, in Powell's opinion. "I never knew a man who laughed less than Harry Huntt Ransom," he recalled. "He was so earnest."[8] The formerly playful dean was being replaced by a more sober upper administrator.

On August 22, 1958, Ransom officially sought President Logan Wilson's approval to change the name of the Rare Books Collection to a more dynamic-sounding appellation, the Humanities Research Center, effective September 1, 1958. "The recommended title reflects more accurately the present character of this activity and its future development."[9] In a separate letter to the president, he stipulated the proposed salaries for the six people to be employed in the newly titled center for 1958–1959, requesting $5,088 for Frances H. Hudspeth, executive assistant.[10] On August 29 he admitted to the Curator of the American Literature Collection at the Yale University Library, Donald Gallup, that "we are in a state of inevitable confusion just now. Although the staff has done a heroic job of handling the incoming books and manuscripts, there is some chaos around the edges."[11] "It's important to get the collections while we can," Ransom said. "Scatteration can come later."[12]

When James Meriwether visited the East Coast in 1959, he picked up and relayed to Ransom some rumors of sour grapes about the seemingly unstoppable Texas campaign to buy collections at record prices; Ransom replied on August 19, 1959: "I am sorry that in this our life and among these our colleagues there is so much damn foolishness, including jumpiness and jealousy. Virginia has a great deal besides Thomas Jefferson to be content about. Their discomfort about Texas will give them ulcers if they are not careful. On the other hand, Texas is not going to sit still, and our contemporaries had better get used to the fact."[13]

While being vice president and provost meant that Ransom had the authority to undertake large-scale library projects and changes, he also gained a forum for addressing the entire faculty as well as the press. In his annual report delivered to the General Faculty on November 24, 1959, Ransom emphasized a momentous development: "The latest session of the Legislature freed the Available Fund. . . . This income is divided: one-third to A. and M., two-thirds to the University. . . . The expenditure of the Fund is no longer restricted to construction of buildings. On the other hand, *no buildings can be erected at the Main University from any other state moneys.*" One problem had become obvious: "Texas is the only great state university to which major buildings have not been given by private donors in recent years." The same address to the faculty sounded an optimistic note about the improving prestige of the university. "Time alters maps. . . . New axes of educational, political, economic, and social influence are forming. . . . The very geography of universities now gives Texas an advantage of travel. Austin is nearer to Los Angeles than New York is; Austin is nearer to New York than Berkeley is. But no advantage can be gained by sitting still in the middle. Advantage—professional, intellectual, institutional—lies in mobility."

Proceeding to praise the departmental "honors" courses, Ransom simultaneously made a plea for attention as well to "the student who is not academically superior but who is educable—and who . . . is likely to become an effective citizen, distinguished for the kind of civic usefulness without which the intellectual's own service to society would be theoretical and vacuous. . . . The student capable of a college education without academic honors is still a major responsibility of every state university."[14] The *Dal-*

las Morning News promptly editorialized: "The University of Texas is to be commended for the recent statement of Dr. Harry Ransom, vice president and provost, that 'educating the average student remains a major responsibility of the school.' In the welter and confusion following *Sputnik* I, some schools and educators lost a sense of perspective in their frantic efforts to increase the academic load, particularly in science courses. . . . It is encouraging to know that this great university is now, as always, being led by educators and scholars who have not lost compassion for the masses seeking higher learning."[15] Yet at almost the same time that Ransom was garnering this praise for an egalitarian approach to higher education, he was also touting the now-thirty-year-old Plan II program at UT, designed for "students coming from the top half of the high school classes," as well as the recently formed Junior Fellows. "We should plan to meet the superior student with good instruction, wide opportunity, and the time to take advantage of both."[16] Ransom personally ushered in the first class of Junior Fellows from the College of Arts and Sciences at the annual Honors Day convocation in April 1959. Selected on the basis of interviews, scholastic work, admission test scores, and high school records, these initial twenty-five designees gained scholarship assistance, special advising, an individual faculty adviser, and a privileged stack permit to the library. Ultimately there were to be one hundred Fellows.[17]

As a student, Shirley Bird Perry witnessed this period in Ransom's career. He arranged for teas to be held on the fourth floor of the Main Building and spoke at meetings in the Texas Union, recognizing student leadership in groups such as Mortar Board, Orange Jackets, and the Friar Society. When he spoke at these and other student gatherings he was, according to Perry, "very eloquent and articulate. We always left feeling good, convinced that the University had a visionary scholar, a true member of the intelligentsia, in that office." Only later on would she reflect (like many others who fell under his thrall) that it had been difficult to capture exactly *what* this revered leader had actually said—and of course in the 1950s students rarely thought to ask probing or hostile questions in his presence. "We viewed him with great affection and adoration." She noticed that he avoided letting students see him smoking. The story of how Harry and Hazel met had by then entered into the campus folklore, and was perceived by students as highly "romantic."[18]

Public addresses on the local and state levels became an almost daily routine during 1959. In effect Ransom did not merely deliver speeches; he reached out and enlisted each audience member in his near-sacred cause of promoting higher education in Texas. The Austin chapter of Sigma Delta

Chi, a national professional journalism fraternity, invited him to talk about "How Newsmen May Better Fulfill Their Obligations and Responsibilities from the Viewpoint of an Educator."[19] In March he spoke at the annual Texas Independence Day dinner for university alumni in the Baker Hotel in Dallas. Regent Joe C. Thompson introduced him there.[20] The next day he entertained the University of Texas Exes of Howard County at a dinner meeting.[21] Then he talked about "Democratic Education as a Continuous Process" at the Seventeenth Annual Southwest Conference on Adult Education at the Commodore Perry Hotel in Austin.[22] He also was the speaker at a dinner on November 20 for the first Texas Symposium on Nuclear Fusion at UT.[23] He addressed the Committee of 75 on the first anniversary of its existence, warning that "able students" are inclined to go where fellowships and scholarships are available and insisting that "this is not the time for Texans to kid other Texans into educational complacency. It would defeat the purpose of this committee."[24]

Part of his duties as vice president and provost included appearing before the Texas House Appropriations Committee hearings. "In the 25 years I've taught at the University, we have had the worst library anywhere," he told the committee members frankly. He sought funds to enhance research work and maintain the "all-state" character of the library as an "information center." He also argued that faculty salaries had fallen far below those at the University of California at Berkeley, the University of Virginia, and the University of North Carolina.[25]

He prepared for President Logan Wilson's consideration (on behalf of the Academic Affairs Committee) an analytical report on an issue that was troubling national universities: teaching evaluations. Among his points:

1. TEACHING evaluation is more important than TEACHER evaluation . . . because the latter gets mixed up with personalities; the former is clearly a matter of getting a good job done.
2. In a university as multiple in purpose as Texas, there can be no one standard (and no one method of estimate) in teaching. . . . The variety of methods among colleges and departments . . . is natural and necessary. . . .
3. . . . The full professorship should be given in 99 percent of the cases only to a man who has shown real ability to conduct research. Otherwise, the graduate faculty will deteriorate.
4. . . . Inarticulate, unpopular, uncooperative, and insurgent graduate directors are often the ones who turn out the really brilliant doctoral students.[26]

Ransom had a growing number of platforms from which to broadcast his ideas. On February 10, 1960, he addressed the nineteenth annual Junior College Conference at the Stephen F. Austin Hotel on the topic "The Junior College in the Future of Higher Education": "Unburdened by problems which beset complex colleges or large universities, the junior college may still be the institution where major problems in instruction are solved and major goals in experimental instruction are reached," he acknowledged, adding that the "thirteenth and fourteenth years in a continuous educational experience" can be "psychologically and socially significant as the 'buffer' between high school and senior college or university work."[27]

Many of his talks, of course, took place more informally on campus in the ebb and flow of academic debates. On December 9, 1958, for example, he had met with students in the president's Student Advisory Cabinet and heard their complaints about "oppressive" campus policies that verged on "Victorianism" (Richard Stanley), deans who were "too touchy" about student petitions (Frank Cooksey), and a reluctance to give "policy responsibility" to the University Women's Council (Cyrena Jo Norman). The grievances ranged from rules against kissing in front of dormitories or staying out late for academic functions to more abstract issues. Ransom, commending recent student participation and responsibility ("never before has it been so good") in events such as the OU (University of Oklahoma) Weekend and the Seventy-Fifth-Year Conference on Expectations ("I wish we could get the younger members of the faculty involved in the same way"), generally sympathized with the concerns about early closing hours on campus. "We're thinking seriously about keeping the new Undergraduate Library open until 12 or perhaps 1 A.M.," he promised.[28]

Logan Wilson could justifiably regard as one of his successes a shift away from an extremely conservative investment policy. In terms of the market value of its endowment, by 1963 the University of Texas possessed a $275,769,000 endowment, trailing only Yale and Harvard; four years later, it would have half a billion dollars, with only Harvard ahead of Texas. (All the same, in terms of actual dollar income per student, more than sixty institutions still surpassed Texas.) By 1972, with two-thirds of a billion dollars, yearly stock dividends alone would earn $11 million for UT. And then, additionally, the university owned West Texas lands on which 5,600 oil wells produced more than forty million barrels of oil annually in 1969. Two-thirds of that income, and the return from 130 gas wells, went to the University of Texas System.[29]

There were plenty of urgent uses for this income. A budget prepared by the Office of the Comptroller showed that during the fiscal year ending

July 1, 1960, the Main University campus would need a total of $5,075,300 for its ongoing construction projects, which included the Academic Center, the Business Administration-Economics Building, and the Art Building and Museum. Texas Western College (later to be renamed the University of Texas at El Paso) would require $1,413,750, and the Medical Branch at Galveston would spend $2,256,380.[30] On February 16, 1960, in an all-too-familiar situation, Ransom tried to placate a professor of the Department of Sociology by justifying why the Business Administration-Economics Building took precedence in the construction sequence. "The Empire State Building would have to replace the library and Wall Street structures put in place of our classroom buildings to satisfy the requirements of everybody deeply concerned with doing a good job at the University. Nobody is inclined to be careless, thoughtless, unconcerned, facetious, or penny-pinching about this project."[31]

Harry Ransom's efforts at diplomacy and total involvement in the future planning for the Main Campus were not going unremarked. Chemical engineering professor W. A. Cunningham expressed the opinion of many when he wrote to Ransom on August 24, 1959, to conjecture that "rather tempting lures [for outside administrative positions] have been cast in your direction. . . . We can ill afford to lose you for the quality we seek must necessarily start from the top. Harry, it has been a personal pleasure and a privilege to work with you. Your actions as Vice President and Provost have inspired confidence and a spirit of accomplishment among faculty members as nothing else has done during my 25 years or so on the campus. That which you are doing is appreciated by all of us, and I am sure that this personal 'thank you' of mine simply echos the feelings of a vast majority of this faculty. I pray that you will be among us for many years to come."[32] Ransom replied a week later: "At the end of a hectic summer, I cannot imagine a better piece of encouragement and cheer than your friendly letter. . . . Deciding to stay in Texas has been no difficulty for me, except in one instance. The decision, then, I want you to know, was clinched by a conviction that the University's future can count on loyalty exactly like yours. . . . I will try to live up to your encouragement."[33]

Such testimonials bolstered his resolve in the face of the occasional discouragements. At this level of office Ransom began learning firsthand the difficulty of extracting supplemental appropriations from the state legislature, and the uncertainty of all such political maneuvering. A UT Law School librarian, Helen Hargrave, wrote in February 1959 to report that she had conversed with a member of the state Appropriations Committee who initially "wondered why a man from the English Department was selected to appear before the Committee. Now he understands because you are the best and most impressive witness the Committee has had."[34] Ransom thanked her for the praise: "Encouragement like that certainly helps on these dim days."[35] But the same month he had to inform Professor Duane Howard that, owing to actions by the Texas Commission on Higher Education and the governor, "we now face a cut-back of nearly fifty thousand dollars in the general library operation provided by state funds."[36] Funding from private foundations was often no easier to obtain. Ransom's letter of October 18, 1960, to Professor Winfred P. Lehmann of the Germanic Languages Department betrays an uncustomary note of bitterness: "I do not mean to be cynical about [the Ford Foundation's] Mr. Melvin Fox's recent discovery of the University of Texas, but I can't resist pointing out that repeated visits have been made to Ford on the subject of area and language studies. I am willing, of course, to continue these visits *ad millennium*. That will be the year when Ford gives us a grant in the humanities. . . . In fairness to Ford, their policies do change—witness the recent decision to back our Engineering-Sciences Program very liberally."[37] Weak funding had consequences. On a typed list of National Academy of Sciences memberships at nineteen universities, Ransom noted in handwriting the disparity between the University of California at Berkeley (46) and even the University of Wisconsin (20) in comparison with the University of Texas (4): "Why *Cal.* & *Ws.* so far up?" he queried.[38] In a personal appeal to Governor Price Daniel, written on March 2, 1959, Ransom and Lanier Cox, Vice President for Administrative Services, "earnestly" urged that Governor Daniel reconsider state appropriations for UT and support "the minimum necessary to operate the Main University at a level consistent with reasonable growth and improvement." They identified teaching salaries as "our most critical need," followed by funding for libraries.[39]

By March 19, 1959, Ransom could write to his friend Richmond Bond of the University of North Carolina: "We are having our own discombobulations with the Legislature, but I am a confirmed optimist; I think that Texas will come through the underbrush, over the swamp, and across the desert sand."[40] By June 1 of that year, he could write more jocularly to Bond: "We have had a whirlwind year. Not all of it has been balmy breezes. I think . . . that the plan for development at the University will go along, despite the eternal political arguments and the infernal tax situation (Texas so far has no taxes of any sort to speak of)."[41] A contributing factor to the shortfall was the low tuition and fees for students, which in 1960–61 were less than half of what students paid in Ohio, and less than a third of what prevailed in Pennsylvania. Ransom faced a formidable political difficulty here: liberal

Democratic U.S. Senator Ralph Yarborough maintained a principled and adamant opposition to any hike in student tuition.

Resignations from boards and apologies for turning down invitations increasingly bespoke the press of Ransom's administrative duties. Writing to R. J. Lewallen, President of the Austin Chamber of Commerce, on February 1, 1960, Ransom asked him to excuse his absence from a major Chamber of Commerce event the preceding month ("influenza had made me a sorry example of Austin's citizenship"), and added: "Unless my schedule is clarified very shortly, however, I think that I should withdraw from the remainder of my term as a member of the Board of Directors and allow that place to be taken by somebody who is not under the iron rule of a calendar which external circumstances make for him."[42] He wrote to Jim T. Booth on August 23, 1960, to say that "I am deeply sorry that my summer has gone completely. I had hoped that I could put vacations into the weekends and in the remaining days make all the starts, stops, and circles which a long-delayed calendar required. The result has been chaos; I have done a few of the things I simply had to do and none of the things I most wanted to do."[43] On September 23, 1960, Ransom asked for the understanding of the faculty sponsor of Alpha Chi at Stephen F. Austin State College, explaining that reorganization plans at UT and "the oncoming problems of development in the legislative year" made it impossible for him to attend or speak at the Alpha Chi banquet the following spring.[44] Local club meetings requiring only one appearance and a brief speech were more feasible. On March 21, 1960, for instance, he managed to visit and speak to the Rotary Club of North Austin, which met at the Villa Capri Motel near campus.[45] At the same location on April 1, 1960, Ransom addressed the topic of "Life, Liberty and the Pursuit of Libraries" at a Conference of Southwest Foundations.[46] But his days were largely occupied with the legion of decisions and arbitrations that bedevil university administrators.

And then, with an almost startling suddenness, Harry Ransom was launched into a trajectory that intensified every pressure he had experienced and accentuated every opportunity he had envisioned. Meeting in Galveston, on Friday, May 13, 1960, the University of Texas Board of Regents announced that Dr. Logan Wilson had ended the speculation that he might resign from his $18,000-a-year position ("supplemented by private sources") as university president to accept a $30,000-a-year job with the American Council on Education; instead of leaving, Dr. Wilson would head the entire UT System with "no increase in his responsibilities" and a "salary adjustment." His new title would be chancellor, a position not appointed since Judge James P. Hart (under whom Logan Wilson had served as president)

FIGURE IO.I

President-elect Harry H. Ransom and Chancellor-elect Logan Wilson, June 1960. Ransom's and Wilson's personal styles were often contrasted. Together they ushered in a prosperous "golden era" of building at UT. Prints and Photographs Collection, Center for American History, The University of Texas at Austin.

resigned in 1952. The chancellor position had been abolished in 1954 after Wilson filled it temporarily in an acting capacity.

Dr. Wilson's replacement as UT president, effective September 1, 1960, was announced by Dr. Merton M. Minter of San Antonio, chairman of the Board of Regents. Some observers expected the appointee to be Dr. W. Gordon Whaley, graduate school dean since 1958, editor of the *Graduate Journal,* and an eminent cellular biologist. But the regents had looked in another direction. Logan Wilson had good words for his successor: "I am particularly pleased that Dr. Harry Ransom has accepted the presidency of the main university, where his fine leadership abilities and recognized educational statesmanship will lend added emphasis to excellence."

ELEVEN

UNIVERSITY PRESIDENT

One of Ransom's standard themes had become the irrelevance and fallaciousness of the image of the university as an "ivory tower." "That figure of speech . . . has no real educational significance today," he insisted. "In Texas the intellectual climber can see more from the top of an oil derrick or a power pole than from the ivory eminence," while in a former epoch, "the ivory tower was isolation, a kind of localized and self-attending splendor, precious and uncommunicated." An enormous change had occurred, according to Ransom. "Time was when a university's pursuit of truth was self-contained. Universities talked—when they abandoned the vital pleasure of silence—to themselves or to one another. Today it is difficult for a university administrator to be sure at any given time whether a scientist is in the classroom, a university laboratory, an industrial laboratory, or a conference combining elder and younger experimenters among academic and industrial personnel. . . . Whereas the 'pursuit of truth' once sounded like a tocsin for the mind which could not make a living pursuing anything else, that pursuit is now a common obligation of professors and graduate students, boards of directors and stockholders."

The stakes for research were immense, he asserted. In a previous age, "the common concerns of industry and education could be put in sonorous, if empty, terms: the cultivation of an intellectual commonweal, the general advancement of current social interests, the future good of society. These are now the stricter terms of our obligation: survival of mankind, defense of the country, guarantees of freedom through knowledge, advancement of science not merely toward new discovery but toward a new kind of life. If we were not alive to these concerns," he warned, "then one message from Moscow would alert us: Khrushchev's solemn announcement that Russia now has enough atomic warheads with enough mobility and enough accuracy of direction to destroy the world. Here is a new Samson indeed." In one of Ransom's most eloquent appeals on behalf of liberties, he implored that "science must stay inalienable from freedom." Furthermore, no one must lose sight of the fact that "the greatest beauty of science is its final impartiality: its sameness to all men at any one time. . . . Nothing is fairer than scientific principle."[1]

Making his first address to the General Faculty of the university since he assumed the presidency, Ransom struck a similar note. "University's 'Ivory Tower' Is No More, Ransom Says/Outside Influences Are Cited," announced an *Austin American-Statesman* headline on October 26, 1960.[2] Dr. DeWitt C. Reddick, Director of the School of Journalism, wrote Ransom "a personal note to express sentiments which I know are shared by University faculty members generally. After your talk on Tuesday, several faculty members on a walk across campus remarked on the rare qualities of vision and persuasiveness which characterize your leadership and arouse enthusiasm among those you contact. A few weeks ago I sat by a fellow faculty member on an airplane trip; and during the course of our conversation, he remarked, 'Harry Ransom is the best thing that has ever happened to the University.'"[3]

Dr. William C. Gardiner, a professor of chemistry and biochemistry who came to UT as a newly minted Harvard Ph.D. in September 1960, marveled at the eagerness with which between 200 and 400 members of the faculty left their offices and assembled for these periodic meetings called by President Ransom. Even though the topics on the agenda were usually noncontroversial, "they *looked forward* to hearing his remarks and wondered exactly what he would say. Ransom had a commanding academic presence—he was impressive in his use of diction, rhetoric, and humorous quips. As a longtime member of the UT community he had already earned and enjoyed the respect of his fellow professors. There was a genuine identification with and empathy for him. He was one of us who had done well and had earned the position of being our leader." On top of that, he "spoke with smooth self-confidence. Charisma emanated from him. He knew that he had achieved things worthwhile on the national scene and didn't mind sharing his eminence with us for an hour. His polished manner of address was nearly at the level of the political, so entirely was he the master of the craft of public address." Moreover, things were going well at UT—student enrollments were growing steadily, large new buildings were springing up around the campus, and faculty salaries were improving. The professors left those meetings with "a general aura of good feeling." Concluded Gardiner, "I have not heard of his like again on any campus across the nation."[4]

There were latent problems, however, such as lingering practices of racial segregation at UT and throughout Austin. Professor Gardiner sensed that the city he left, Cambridge, Massachusetts, "had been more reasonably integrated for the time." Here, "the movie theaters were still segregated, for instance; people of color attended movies on the east side of Austin. There were still a few of the infamous 'We Reserve the Right to Refuse Service to Anyone' signs visible in certain shops." The professoriate included no African Americans. Dr. Gardiner recalled that a leading member of his UT mathematics department once made an impassioned speech favoring the continuance of segregation at a faculty meeting in Batts Auditorium. The man asked rhetorically why Easterners came to Austin if they disagreed with Texas ways. All the same, Gardiner and most of those whose hiring Ransom had authorized elected to stay and collaborate in changing a social climate that had long prevailed.[5] When Ransom's friend William Friday of the University of North Carolina resisted political pressure and made a commencement speech advocating racial integration (garnering near-unanimous support from the North Carolina press), Ransom wrote approvingly: "As you know, I grew up on secondhand reports of what the University of North Carolina had meant to my forebears. What seems a great deal more important to me just now is what the University means to Southern education and American education in general. If you and Bill [Aycock] can make your Commencement lines stick (and I know you will), you will have done something more than notable for the state and all of us. I believe that you are accompanied—in purpose, in heart, and in spirit—by a much larger company of Southerners than some Southern cranks imagine. From this far distance, my affectionate admiration."[6]

Another decision that landed on President Ransom's desk was an inquiry on December 1, 1960, from an acquaintance in the Washington office of the USIA as to whether U.S. Senator George Smathers (Dem.-Florida) might be the University of Texas commencement speaker in May 1961. Mindful of prevailing tensions symbolized by black students' mounting protests about segregated and unequal dormitory and housing facilities, and of Chancellor Wilson's recommendation that the students eschew "forced integration" and resist "provocative demonstrations,"[7] Ransom's note to Frances Hudspeth rejected the proposed speaker as "too hot politically and not distinguished enough. Let's leave it at that."[8]

In October 1960, *Austin American-Statesman* reporter Ernestine Wheelock managed to obtain a thirty-minute interview with the newly installed president. Looking around her, Wheelock observed that "Dr. Ransom's office in the west wing of the Main Building looks down on the University's mall, where any time of the day he can see the students for whom he is hard at work. The presidential office seems a tranquil place, but even a visi-

FIGURE II.I

Students protest for integration of dormitories and athletics, 1960 (?). Student demonstrations represented the national mood toward full racial integration. By and large, these protests at UT ended peacefully. Ransom allowed most marches and rallies to take place, but formulated guidelines for the protesters to follow. Prints and Photographs Collection, Center for American History, The University of Texas at Austin.

tor is aware that he is in the midst of great activity. The effect of calm is achieved through its spaciousness and its pleasing color combinations and art objects. Soft green carpeting goes well with the walls, done in the palest of greens. . . . Decorative accents of the office are a very old Turkish brazier of highly polished brass and two portrait busts, one by [nineteenth-century American sculptor] Hiram Powers, and the other, a study by [British sculptor] Jacob Epstein." Wheelock's eyes also fell on "three telephones, a dictaphone, a much used typewriter, a large desk stacked with work, and a conference table."

Asked by Wheelock to compare the 19,000 modern-day UT students of 1960 with those of an earlier day, Ransom answered that "there are more married students; there is much more attention to what is going on in the world at large, partly because of the increased travel and better communication; and there is, besides, a tremendous increase in intellectual independence." What are the desirable goals of the faculty and administration of a major university? "To help uncover new knowledge and to help a constant succession of new students toward that knowledge." While believing that "every student who is well prepared for college should give himself a chance," Ransom conceded that "students who remain uninterested in study" should not be encouraged by their families "to stay in college merely for the sake of sentiment or social custom."

Concluding the interview, Wheelock asked a standard question of the university's sixteenth president: How would he define that elusive Texas goal of providing a "university of the first class" as mandated in the state Constitution of 1876? Ransom balked at the terms of the inquiry. "I wish we could quit worrying about adjectival descriptions of the University and get on with the substantive work. I think we could save a lot of time and avoid a lot of useless argument by changing our rhetoric. If Texans want the best university in the country, they can be sure that everybody in Texas and outside Texas will know when they have it."[9]

This willingness to comment for the record on a wide range of academic

FIGURE 11.2

Student demonstration to end "tokenism," November 11, 1967. Ransom and administrators throughout the nation faced a restless student population more demanding of rapid social change than previous generations had been. Prints and Photographs Collection, Center for American History, The University of Texas at Austin.

subjects delighted the entire news corps. According to one reporter, "newsmen saw in his remarks the promise of a more outspoken era at UT. . . . As a news source for the main campus, [President Logan] Wilson has been best known for his caution and decorum." The reporter was referring to an early pronouncement of President-elect Ransom, characterized in one published account as "chesty," and to his "tart-tongued reaction to newspaper stories about an expected 'tidal wave of students' at the University of Texas in September and plans for meeting the 'engulfment.'" Ransom shot back, "We are not operating a rabbit warren out here. It is a total fallacy to presume that we are frightened by or solely concerned with numbers. Our development program is only partly stimulated by the problem of classroom space. It is primarily concerned with improving the quality of instruction and research."[10] In a speech to the Sisterhood of Temple Emanu-El that Ransom had delivered in Dallas the preceding spring, he opened with the startling assertion that "in Texas, there is a large student exodus to other states each year. National Merit scholarship and Woodrow Wilson scholarship winners indicate plans . . . to leave Texas for good." Equally disturbing, "we cannot recruit faculties. The teachers do not exist. We can teach by movies, or by machines, but this does nothing for real intellect, character, citizenship, tolerance, compassion." Still, "we are doing a better job than ever before in educating individuals. . . . Individualism and individuality [are] the greatest hope we have."[11] Speaking to the Capital City Kiwanis Club, Ransom invoked ascent as a figure of speech in defending the UT admissions policy, which ensured that "the state university . . . is not a distant intellectual acropolis from which slow-marching students must be diverted." Instead, "the University of Texas has believed and still believes that there are different routes and different paces in this climb. It is determined to keep the paths clear for every student capable of reaching the top."[12]

Addressing 6,000 new University of Texas students undergoing orientation sessions in September 1960, the president, perhaps thinking of his own days at Sewanee and that serendipitous course from Professor Knickerbocker during one hot Tennessee summer, listed reading, talking, listening, figuring, and cultivating a "greater respect for the clock and calendar" as essential aspects of college performance, but advised his listeners to heed an equally important sixth element: "Exceptions you make to rules and regulations. . . . Silence. Silent cogitation. Random speculation. Woolgathering. Dreaming. . . . Some of the most memorable experience will be accidental, or incidental. You won't even know about some of it until much later, because there is a time fuse in intellectual development. Delayed explosions come long after the lessons are over. . . . Value idleness. . . . I mean intelligent loafing. . . . You'd better undertake lessons in living within your-self and living for whatever it is you are determined to become."[13]

Speaking at a luncheon meeting of alumni attending a seminar for their local officers, Ransom exhorted UT supporters not to cast the university's functions "in an 'either-or' frame." Quite frequently "the public sees us as if we were drawn up in separate camps: either teaching or research, either athletics or academics, either new intellects or new buildings, either the practical affairs of the citizen or impractical concerns of the scholar." The preferable approach instead is "a 'both-and' policy," he said. As an example, he cited the fact that "members of the football squad proved to be much better students than any 'average selection' you could make at the University."[14] To protect and advance the interests of the university, he even agreed to barnstorm the state in the company of the president and other officers of archrival Texas A&M University, speaking at breakfasts, luncheons, and dinners about the advisability of increasing the funding for state col-leges and universities. W. C. Magee of Houston, president of Tennessee Gas Transmission, loaned his airplane to the group to make the campaign feasible in a state the size of Texas. Eighteen cities and towns were on their schedule, including Beaumont, Tyler, Amarillo, and El Paso.

This presidential regimen of conferences and speeches curtailed the availability on which he had long prided himself. Access to the president of a swelling university was not so easy to guarantee as entrée to a dean or vice president had been. Linguistic expert Winfred P. Lehmann requested an audience with Ransom on September 9, 1960, by suggesting that "when you have some time, maybe I could penetrate the velvet curtain and have a chat."[15] Ten days later Ransom responded cordially, "All you have to do is rap smartly on the velvet curtain. It makes a large, booming sound."[16] But the whirlwind pace of his announcements and speeches netted Ransom more and more favorable notice. On November 8, 1960, Jack R. Maguire, Director of the Ex-Students' Association, prepared a resolution over an em-bossed seal thanking Dr. Logan Wilson and Dr. Harry Huntt Ransom for "the highest qualities of leadership" in taking the alumni group "toward the common goals of higher standards of excellence and eminence for The University of Texas."[17] Law librarian Helen Hargrave wrote to President Ransom on October 1, 1960, to praise a newsletter that Ransom had in-augurated: "The paper is a splendid idea—and a thoughtful one. Too of-ten faculty and staff hear about important university developments from outside friends or read about them in the newspapers. . . . Your plans and ideas have added a sense of excitement and anticipation of great things to come."[18] One unlikely person moved to praise Ransom for his initiatives was the Texas A&M Information Director in College Station, a former newspaperman who nevertheless admitted in a personal note that "you have been something new and rather startling in my 15 years of dealings with college and university administrators. . . . A breath of fresh air in the academic mausoleum is exhilarating. . . . You apparently believe that education is important in its own right, rather than as a means of providing an excuse for the continuation and expansion of The Institution. You even seem to think it is an exciting venture to which intelligent men can with pride devote their lives. As a Texan, I am pleased to have you at the head of my State's University."[19]

Shortly after Ransom accepted the UT presidency he had written to Regent W. W. Heath that he felt "a good deal more than pleased expectation. Friday the thirteenth was to the day the twenty-fifth anniversary of my interview for my first job at Texas, on May 13, 1935. During that time I've seen a good deal of muddlement, some conflict, and a few genuine defeats in the University's world. By and large, though, I think we have all been inclined to look on darker rather than brighter sides of the University's prospects."[20] In the opinions of many who knew him, this was possibly the most fulfilling period in Ransom's life. Although his earlier days as a dean had been gratifying, now he had the unprecedented adoration of the press, the taxpayers, the faculty, and the regents.

Ransom wholeheartedly supported the regents' approval on September 24 of a Ten-Year Development Plan intended "to place the University of Texas in company with the best institutions in the nation" and to give "first priority to greatly improved teaching and research, second priority to buildings." As Ransom phrased it, "We are determined that this University will furnish its students something more than sitting room." According to a news release, "key to the entire plan is the use of non-tax funds (endowment income, private and governmental gifts and grants) to supplement basic operating appropriations from the Texas Legislature." The aim was to raise faculty salaries, compensate outstanding teaching performance, improve teaching equipment, increase the number of classroom instructors for first- and second-year courses, and subsidize research projects. "This decision . . . attacks the main problem of greatness for The University of Texas," Ransom said in the news release. "It means that we can hold and add first-rate teachers and scholars."

Under the adopted plan, the Main University would benefit from $52,500,000 in new and improved buildings. Ransom's hand could especially be seen in the projected growth of major library collections and research equipment. Having rejected the idea of moving part of the campus

to the university-owned Brackenridge Tract in West Austin, the administrators and regents had decided instead to double the classroom space and
teaching laboratories and triple the faculty office space within a ten-minute
walking range of the existing campus. Ransom applauded this decision not
to split the campus into separate locations. "The result is an educational
plant which will be convenient for student use, and highly economical to
operate," he said. Ancillary research laboratories and storage facilities would
be located north of Austin at Balcones Research Center.[21]

Only the concept of a still-unbuilt multipurpose coliseum remained
unsettled, and Ransom wrote to Chancellor Logan Wilson on December 7,
1960, to recommend that the facility be designed to accommodate mixed
facilities including intercollegiate basketball, public events, academic conferences, commencement, musical performances, and university convoca-
tions. "Such a project would be supported mainly from gifts. . . . I assume
that neither the Central Administration nor the Regents would approve the
project until financing was assured."[22] The coliseum slowly took shape and
gained the necessary financing, though Ransom would not live to see the
resulting Special Events Center, eventually named the Erwin Center, open
for a wide range of activities in 1977.

Various people were beginning to give Ransom the lion's share of credit
for keeping the regents as well as the taxpayers satisfied about these ambitious building programs. Joe C. Thompson, whose term as regent would
end in June 1961, wrote to congratulate Ransom when the Ten-Year Plan
was approved: "You must feel good. . . . It is a great compliment to you. Not
one item was changed on your program. You were given a carte blanche approval to proceed. Yours is a big job; one filled with large responsibility, but
with full authority to work it out." The victory, Thompson wrote, was owing to "the manner in which it was presented to our committee."[23] Ransom
replied, "I am not underestimating the pitfalls and handicaps which we
face. Given this green light, though, we have no intention of sitting still."[24]

Part of Ransom's competency as president stemmed from the ease with
which he moved among businessmen and -women, something he was able
to do because of his sincere belief in their joint partnership in pursuing
social and academic ideals. Regent Thompson, speaking on the basis of his
broad experience as owner of the 7–Eleven foodstores chain, Oak Farm
Dairies, and other businesses, called Harry Ransom "the finest salesman
I've ever known."[25] Ransom, writing to the editorial office of *Harvard Business Review* after it requested his views about the relationship between universities and the business world, expressed skepticism about the efficacy of
questionnaires ("they usually get cursory treatment and statistical interpre-

tation") but identified "the most heartening development" as "the tremendously generous attitude of thousands and thousands of businessmen who have been willing to spend time on university campuses actually advising, criticizing, and helping in the enormous task of preparing men and women for American business." Ransom's final sentence had a familiar emphasis: "Business could help education most by giving education the necessary funds to employ better teachers, encourage better students, build better libraries, and in general provide better opportunities for getting [students] ready to live an intelligent (as well as a profitable) life in business."[26]

To reinforce the public's confidence in the regents and the administrators, Ransom was even willing to accept the challenge of a relatively new crucible for university presidents—the television interview. On November 28, 1960, he appeared as a guest on the weekly "Press Conference" produced by KTBC (Channel 7 in Austin). Ransom received a letter from George W. Hoffman, associate professor of geography, commending his nerve: "You certainly mastered some very tricky and difficult questions," Hoffman observed.[27] Ransom answered: "It is not my idea of a night's relaxation; but answering questions about the University—even when the questions are prejudiced—is going to be a necessary part of our future history."[28] Jim G. Ashburne, associate professor of accounting, wrote similarly: "I trust you will not think me presumptuous by wishing to express my sincere admiration of your TV performance last night. Your answers were direct and exactly right in my humble opinion. I just wanted to say so."[29] To which Ransom replied: "There are so many things we need to tell the state about both our needs and our opportunities that I am always glad to speak up when I get a chance."[30] In the interview Ransom had handled questions from reporters on subjects ranging from a proposed tuition hike to the need for better housing facilities for married students. He expressed doubt that the university could grow much larger by depending on its present number of faculty members. He called closed circuit television an exciting new development in the teaching profession, but said he did not believe it was an adequate substitute for individual student-professor relationships. Speaking without the advantage of a script, Ransom found himself pinned down as to the rank of the university against other national schools in terms of quality. "Dr. Ransom said he believed it to be ranked 'higher up' but not in the upper 10."[31]

Ransom himself had reason to pause at the end of 1960 and take stock of his professional achievements. The American Association of Land-Grant Colleges and State Universities in its December newsletter reprinted a paragraph about Ransom from a *New York Times* book review celebrating university libraries:

Actually, some of the most dynamic of Institutional collectors today are not even librarians. President Harry H. Ransom of the University of Texas is spending money on a Rosenbach scale to give his state a great research library, and is being damned by his competitors, as was Rosenbach by his, for raising prices. Combine a bookish and acquisitive academic administrator and a head librarian, and then watch the books fly through the air to that institution's stacks and vaults. Before joining the Guggenheim Foundation . . . , Gordon Ray, the scholar-provost of the University of Illinois, and Librarian Robert B. Downs formed such a team. At Indiana, President Herman Wells and Lilly Librarian David A. Randall have made Bloomington a synonym for books; while recently in Kansas the combination of Chancellor Franklin D. Murphy and Librarian Robert B. Vosper brought a renaissance in Lawrence. Now the transfer of Murphy and Vosper to UCLA has the West Coast quaking, and if Texas and UCLA meet head on, the bibliographical fallout will be fabulous.[32]

But Ransom's ability to focus solely on the Main Campus and its library was to be all too brief. His status abruptly changed again, as a headline in the *Austin American-Statesman* proclaimed on Sunday, December 11: "UT's Wilson Quits; Ransom Gets Post." Logan Wilson, who came to UT as president in 1953, had resigned as Chancellor of the University of Texas System to take the presidency of the American Council on Education in Washington, D.C., the position he had been considering the previous summer. Leaving a meeting at the Texas Western campus in El Paso, the regents released their announcement of Ransom's appointment as Wilson's successor. "Dr. Ransom becomes the third chancellor of the University system, after serving for one year as president of the Main University."[33]

Ransom would now inherit a system composed of the Main University campus at Austin and branch and affiliate schools at Galveston, Houston, Dallas, and El Paso. Another branch had been authorized at San Antonio. Dr. Wilson asked to be relieved as chancellor on March 1, 1961. Ransom would also hold the post of acting president of the Main University until the Board of Regents named a new president.[34] As president his salary had been $16,000, with a housing allowance of $1,500; his new position as chancellor of the UT System would earn him $18,100 plus a provided house and utilities.[35] In addition, during the 1960s Austin car dealer Roy Butler would insist upon presenting the new chancellor with an inexpensive lease on a Lincoln automobile, commemorating this arrangement with a memento for Ransom's office—a silver Lincoln hood ornament on a marble base inscribed "Dr. Harry H. Ransom."[36] All the same, Ransom would later confide to William S. Livingston: "I didn't want to become Chancellor—I took it because I didn't know whom they might put in otherwise."[37]

Longtime friend Richmond Bond wrote from North Carolina on December 12, 1960: "Bill Friday called this afternoon to tell me about Chancellor Ransom. Again the state and University of Texas deserve congratulations. You'll do a most excellent job, Harry, scholarly and imaginative and practical in both form and substance. I'm sure you've been put to some heart-mind-soul searching of late for the best solution."[38] Ransom replied four days before Christmas: "This administrative opportunity (like those that preceded it) appealed to me because I believe that I can help get things done that should be done. I have no intention of losing sight of library development or of the research and publication programs. As a matter of fact, the other branches of the University—like several of the independent institutions in the state—are ready for both programs."[39] A larger, multicampus perspective was already apparent in Ransom's thinking.

Accolades continued. The New Year's Day issue of the *Austin American-Statesman* evinced admiration by listing Ransom (and President Lyndon B. Johnson) among its year-end list of half a dozen prominent Texans of 1960 and selected Ransom as "Austin's Newsmaker of the Year": "Harry Huntt Ransom in just a few months as president of The University of Texas has won considerable community and state understanding of the aims of higher education in Texas. . . . He has lent dynamism to the acquisition by the University of important additions to the library. He has kept an open ear and an open mind to the role of the University in the community, its responsibilities not only to students but to wider society."[40]

Time magazine, whose editors Ransom had privately criticized two years earlier for their tendency to "treat Texas news as if it came from Mars or the moon,"[41] now commended Chancellor Logan Wilson and President Harry Ransom in a feature article in the January 13, 1961, issue. Wilson, *Time* wrote, brought stability to the campus after the tumult of the Homer P. Rainey firing in the 1940s. "A professional administrator, he did a remarkable job of remodeling his big main campus (19,500 students) and its five smaller branches." Giving Wilson the credit for attracting better teachers, requiring entrance tests for all students, launching a $35 million building program, constructing a new computer center and an atom smasher, and persuading the regents to "stop spending the income from the University's $360 million endowment (second only to Harvard's) on building alone," *Time* also judged that Wilson "coldly discouraged controversy" and deserved his "Great Stone Face" sobriquet. Ransom, on the other hand,

was "daringly different"; he made UT one of the country's richest reposi-
tories of rare manuscripts, nurtured the University Press, started the *Texas
Quarterly,* thought up the Academic Center, organized a Junior Fellows
program, and attracted a generation of bright young teachers.[42]

A preliminary fact-finding process for the *Time* article brought Ransom
into contact with Ronnie Dugger, then editor and general manager of the
Texas Observer, a political journal of investigative stories and opinion. Dugger had submitted background material to the *Time* editors, notifying Ransom on September 23, 1960: "Thanks very much for both interviews. Last
night I telegraphed a full report to *Time,* although of course I don't know if
they will be diverted from their paean to California by your most thoughtful dissents."[43] Subsequently Ransom sent Dugger a description of the UT
rare book and manuscript acquisitions between 1957 and 1960.

On November 4, 1960, Ransom wrote Dugger again about racial prej-
udice in Texas. "This is a problem in human relations that we shall not
live to see completely settled, but we work at it in good faith and in the
hope that while progress is slow, it *is* progress, and some day not too far
in the future the dignity and worth of the individual will be the criterion
for judgment, regardless of color, or religion, or economic or social status.
I have an infinite faith in the ultimate triumph of man's intellect over his
prejudices. Only time can prove me right or wrong."[44] Dugger responded:
"I have heard you described, in words attributed to you, as a high humanist. Your letter certainly expresses this. For myself, I do not have an infinite
faith in the ultimate triumph of man's intellect over his prejudices; but I am
thoroughly committed to the cause of that ultimate triumph. I believe this
makes me a low humanist." Concluding the exchange, Dugger averred: "As
the weeks pass I become even stronger in my conviction that you are the
best thing that has happened to the University of Texas in many years."[45]

TWELVE

THE CHANCELLOR

Ransom's ascension to the chancellorship was barely noticeable in certain respects. He had been a fixture of the University of Texas administration long enough that his transition to the highest post in the system might have seemed natural, almost inevitable. Still, there was one pronounced change for Harry and Hazel Ransom personally: they inherited Logan Wilson's handsome two-story home at 1610 Watchhill Road on the scenic west side of Austin. The regents allocated $10,000 to repaint and remodel the residence for the Ransoms. They would live there from 1960 until 1976.[1]

Despite the campus community's familiarity with its new chancellor, the student newspaper devoted a three-part series to the man who would succeed Logan Wilson as chancellor. Mrs. Frances Hudspeth informed the reporter, Hoyt Purvis, that Ransom "comes in as early as 6 o'clock, . . . and almost always by 8." He fingers a filter-tip cigarette as he "sits behind his desk and runs through his mail. . . . He answers some of the mail himself, and it isn't unusual for him to wheel around behind his desk and personally type some of his correspondence." "He is definitely the energetic type," says Mrs. Hudspeth. "He never has an idle moment [and] doesn't want one. Anyone who works for him is devoted. There's no urgency, but there's work to be done and we like to do it." After replying to the mail and writing some speeches, Ransom often "holds a staff meeting, likely to include Dr. J. R. Smiley, his successor as vice president and provost; Dr. O. A. Singletary, assistant to the president; and G. W. Landrum, business manager. Ransom ordinarily works in a luncheon appointment and goes strong all day before heading homeward at 5:30 or 6 P.M." As for relaxation, he "normally gets a portion of one day a week, plus occasional weekends for home life. He and his wife are fond of visits to the country, and Ransom gets away from everyday rigors with country strolls. The couple also attends a small Episcopal Church away from Austin."[2]

The alumni magazine *Alcalde* profiled Ransom for its March 1961 issue in a cover story produced by Jack Maguire, describing the fifty-two-year-old Ransom as "a stocky, friendly, bespectacled man wearing a crew cut" who would take possession of a suite in the east corridor on the same first floor as his former president's office. He would inherit the nation's fifth-largest educational enterprise. "A genuine intellectual who is uniquely articulate and disarmingly gregarious (almost everyone calls him 'Harry'), he neither likes nor has much patience for administrative detail. His long suit lies in selling higher education—and particularly The University of Texas—to its constituencies, and he does this with almost evangelical fervor." Characterized as "a hard worker," Ransom "doesn't golf or swim, dances only when a social occasion demands it, and rarely gets any kind of exercise except walking. He does a lot of that, and often reels off a couple of brisk miles before going to bed." His ideas about the libraries are particularly innovative. "In brick and stone, the Academic Center will express this philosophy of Harry Ransom. It will be a place where books will stand on open shelves, where students may come to relax and to think, to look at paintings and *objets d'art,* to listen to good music and to hold intelligent discussions."[3] Maguire quoted one colleague who said, "He seems to have an infinite capacity to assume that the most impossible sort of thing is going to happen—and then proceeds to make it happen—not worrying about the minutiae that trouble the 27 1/2 cent minds."[4]

Another observer praised Ransom's almost transcendent presence. "He walked into a room and everything stopped. . . . And if there was anything that people liked to do it was to give him things. A famous story about Dr. Ransom is that one day a man came out of his office and somebody who had been waiting outside said, 'What did he say?' And the man said, 'I don't know, but I just gave him twenty thousand dollars for his program.'"[5]

Margaret Berry first met Ransom in 1961, when she was doing her doctoral research on student cultural life at UT. Richard T. Fleming, founder of the University Writings Collection, a depository of materials related to the history of the campus, urged her to see the chancellor. She sat at the conference table talking with Ransom in his dimly lit office on the east side of the Main Building. (Numerous visitors confirmed that Ransom rarely if ever turned on the overhead lights in his offices.)[6] He possessed what Berry thought of as an "open-ended" personality; "if you went in with an idea, he would encourage it rather than squelch it." Some of his visitors probably would have preferred a straight "yes" or "no," but Berry liked this willingness to give the person an opportunity to try out a concept.[7] Professor Edwin T. Bowden also made this point. Ransom virtually never delivered bad

FIGURE 12.1

Ransom as chancellor, 1961. Ransom's term as president lasted a little more than a year, until Logan Wilson resigned as chancellor to take the presidency of the American Council on Education in Washington, D.C. Ransom then was appointed the third chancellor of the University System by the Board of Regents. Harry Ransom Humanities Research Center, The University of Texas at Austin.

news, never gave an outright "no," never discouraged anyone's initiative. "He was constitutionally unable to say 'no.' Everything was 'a fine idea.' He never offended anyone by an outright veto. . . . But his not saying 'no' didn't mean 'yes.' The tip-off was whether or not he added, 'I'll write a letter tomorrow.'"[8]

Philosophy professor (and future dean) John Silber echoed this general appraisal: "Harry was a constitutional optimist. He had a *vision* for this university. He recognized that it had the potential to be the finest state university in the country." At one point, a faculty curmudgeon in Romance languages, wanting more attention paid to faculty salaries, criticized this penchant of Ransom's by paraphrasing Isaiah: "Where there is *only* vision, the people perish." But Ransom remained undeterred in his crusade and unchanging in his personal attitudes. "He was *never* one to crush anyone's dreams," Silber would recall. "He could see the promise in ideas presented by someone else. Moreover, he was congenitally kind. Many of his efforts were directed toward advancing other people. Attractive and engaging in conversation, he could seem at the moment to share your dreams." His favorite phrase was "Now let's get down to brass tacks," followed by "All right, now let's get down to brassier tacks."[9]

Within a year Ransom would tap Norman Hackerman, the chairman of the Chemistry Department who had earned a doctorate degree at Johns Hopkins, to serve as his vice president of academic affairs and provost. Joseph R. Smiley (1910–1990), a Texan with a Ph.D. in French from Columbia University, had briefly held the same post before he was named UT president in 1961. Ransom and Hackerman would have a close ten-year association that intensified after Smiley left UT in 1963 to become president of the University of Colorado.

Even as merely the vice president, Hackerman essentially functioned as the CEO of the Main Campus, with the exception, of course, of any matters relating to the library and its research collections. The latter were invariably where Ransom's great interest lay. "Harry really preferred to be the president rather than the chancellor," Hackerman would later state. "But he didn't want to be president with someone else as chancellor." In the fall of 1962, when it appeared that Smiley would soon depart, Ransom brought Hackerman up to Ransom's little hideaway in the Tower and proposed the idea that UT *not* install another president. This expedient arrangement— whereby Hackerman took care of most Main Campus business and Ransom had no opposing chief officer—would last from 1963 until the fall of 1967, when Regent Frank C. Erwin, Jr., questioned the practice of not having a president at the Main Campus.[10] Henrietta Jacobsen (as well as others) would observe that Erwin seemed to change the organizational chart of UT every time he wanted to get rid of someone,[11] but in this case when the regents reinstituted the position of president and formed a search committee in 1967, Norman Hackerman became the president in name as well as fact and would not leave UT until 1970, when he accepted the presidency of Rice University. Hackerman chose psychology professor Gardner Lindzey as his vice president of academic affairs at UT.

Few people ever had Norman Hackerman's vantage point to see Ransom at work day in and day out. He noted that Ransom would usually light a cigarette if he became perturbed. However, the chancellor never actually seemed to enjoy the act of smoking—it was as though he had adopted a fad. He would puff on the cigarette, then blow the smoke right out as if barely inhaling. He would invariably light up at the Board of Regents meetings.

Hackerman noticed, too, that Ransom had a habit of telling people "no" without ever saying the word "no" itself. This disinclination, coupled with his poker face (often referred to as inscrutable), could lead to misunderstandings and problems. "Harry's method of telling you 'no' was to say 'yes.' He tried to let people down easily, and probably didn't realize what a thud it would be when they finally realized what had happened. He couldn't stand to injure *anyone*," Hackerman would recall. In especially trying situations Ransom would register an intent look sometimes, but never raise his voice in anger.[12] Pursed lips accompanied by the words "I'm surprised" were typically the extent of his expressions of disagreement or perplexity.[13]

Ransom would generally not get into any contentious issues that he could avoid, according to Hackerman. "He either worked them out, or else he got out of the way and let someone else handle them. Graves Landrum played the role of Ransom's protector, deflecting things that he did not think Harry would be interested in." Harold Billings, who had completed an M.L.S. degree at the University of Texas in 1957 and was assisting with Ransom's collections development programs, agreed that Ransom "succeeded largely because he found people like Graves Landrum and Frances Hudspeth to handle his details and protect him."[14]

Hackerman was an occasional guest in the Ransoms' home. Much like Harry, who disliked crowds and noise (and thus only attended football games obligatorily), Hazel Ransom did not enjoy putting on large affairs, but she did not mind entertaining small groups. She and Harry had the Hackermans up to their house in Pemberton Heights several times in the mid-1960s.[15] But other couples at UT retained a much different impression of their sociability. F. Warren and Pat Roberts sensed that Ransom was not close to anybody at all. "He never said, 'Come over and have a few drinks,'" Pat Roberts recalled, "even though we lived nearby." And the Ransoms would often leave parties early by giving the plausible excuse that Harry was "waiting for a telephone call."[16] Harold Billings noted that Ransom was so habitually formal that he kept his suit coat on even while working in the library stacks, and when Billings was a dinner guest at the Ransoms' house he found those occasions to be "cold and formal," despite Hazel's "gorgeous" appearance and "vibrant" manner.[17] When Hazel departed the room, the Ransoms' home felt "just as reserved as Ransom always appeared. At his warmest, there never seemed to be more than a thin tight smile. It was his words that were overwhelming."[18] On the strength of those words, however, Billings perceived that "an Athens-in-Austin atmosphere" had started to envelop the campus, even though he often suspected that Ransom "probably had no grand plan" and "made decisions in collection building as he went along," simply determined that his school not become "just another big State U." Ransom "had created this general intellectual ambience by stockpiling both human talent and library materials. He knew that if he brought enough of these together, some magnificent things were bound to happen."[19]

For a UT president becoming a UT chancellor in 1961, the problems and challenges mounted rapidly. His skills would soon be needed (and taxed) by a number of severe crises. One of the more notable was an imbroglio over the new $800,000 Forty Acres Club, a five-story private club at the corner of Guadalupe and 25th Streets across from the university, intended to offer dining facilities, a bar, a faculty lounge, meeting rooms, and hotel accommodations (forty-two rooms and suites on the upper floors). When contracts for construction of the building were awarded on January 19, 1961, a press release quoted Harry Ransom's comments: "Texas college and university budgets could not undertake such a project. It is therefore doubly fortunate that private enterprise has met this need with a site, a habitation, and a name."[20]

But the plan was taking shape in the 1960s instead of the 1950s, and scrutiny would be inevitable. A storm soon began brewing over the sensitive issue of racial memberships in the upcoming club. The director of the University of Texas chapter of B'nai B'rith Hillel Foundation wrote to D. M. "Buck" McCullough, one of the principals involved in creating the club, on February 8, 1961: "I was disappointed and shocked at the same moment to read in this morning's daily 'Texan' that the 40 Acres Club is to be segregated. I was about to make application for membership and send in my check but cannot do so under the circumstances. I simply will not join or be associated with an organization which discriminates against other humans because of race, color, creed or country of origin. May I suggest before you definitely finalize this segregation policy that you go through the files of the daily 'Texan' to read the names of the many faculty people who have protested the segregation policies of the University area business houses and theatres."[21]

Ransom was necessarily involved in the controversy from the beginning, since he was one of nineteen university members on the Advisory Committee for the Forty Acres Club. In a speech on January 30, Ransom had attempted to distance the university from the mounting dispute, assuring the community that "the University has not one cent, not one inch of land, and not one administrative assignment involved in the investment or the operation of the Forty Acres Club." He reminded the Ex-Students' Association that "the University during all my 26 years here has desperately needed a base on which it could feel itself socially, intellectually, at play, at ease, at work, in conference, part of this town, and of the very large body of citizens who studied here and then has gone elsewhere to live."[22]

What had appeared at first like a providential stroke of luck, the realization of a facility providing food and beverage services and meeting spaces that could bring Texas into the company of elite universities on the East Coast, within only a few weeks degenerated into a controversy certain to divide the faculty and exacerbate the traditional town-gown split—precisely the opposite of Ransom's goals. Between February 8 and 14, nineteen faculty members (including six members of the Sociology Department) sent letters to Ransom or McCullough protesting the segregation of the club and declining their memberships; seventy-two members of the faculty and staff signed petitions objecting to the membership policy. Professor of geology S. E. Clabaugh wrote to express his dismay to McCullough on February 13: "Could a visiting American Negro professor or guest lecturer be taken to the club as a guest?" Also, "if a Negro professor is employed by The University of Texas to teach on the 'forty acres,' is he barred from membership in the Forty Acres Club? Let me explain that these are very important considerations to all of my colleagues in the Geology Department, because we have many visitors of different races from foreign lands." Professor Clabaugh noted: "I am a native Texan as were several generations of my ancestors. . . . As a Texan and a southerner I am also deeply interested in the problems of our local racial minorities. I subscribe fully to the idea of complete integration."[23] Leonard Broom, Chairman of the Sociology Department, wrote to Ransom on February 10: "At least part of the difficulty that has arisen may be attributed to the ambiguous status of the Club and its sponsorship. . . . The curious juxtaposition of voluntary association, private enterprise and civic generosity are almost bound to generate tensions and to blur the development of responsible policy. . . . Clubs in general are most successful when management, policy and financial involvement are placed in the same hands." Broom added that Ransom had "my friendly and understanding sympathy" about the evolving conflict.[24] "Dear Len," Ransom replied, "I wish that everybody concerned with the University's more subtle problems would be equally judicious and equally constructive in criticism. I believe that the privately owned club (the initial advantage of which was—or appeared to me to be—its extremely low dues) might well consider a suggestion of stockholding by members of the faculty, alumni, and others."[25]

But then, just as suddenly as the furor had arisen, those behind the club efficiently defused the situation. D. M. "Buck" McCullough issued "To All Staff and Faculty Members" on Friday, February 17, 1961, a full description of the Forty Acres Club that contained no membership restrictions and promised that "the activities and programs of the club will be carried on in cooperation with the University Advisory Committee and will be designed to meet the needs of University faculty and staff."[26] The next day prominent Austin attorney and UT alumnus Trueman O'Quinn reported in a letter to Ransom that O'Quinn and Professors Leonard Broom, William J. Handy, Reece J. McGee, Roger W. Shattuck, and Charles A. Wright had met to seek a solution to the mounting disagreement. They had resolved that "the Forty Acres Club should be described neither as 'integrated' nor as 'segregated.' In view of recent developments, the club probably could not succeed if given either label." Moreover, "further publicity on the subject will be avoided, and spokesmen for the group will be Handy and Shattuck." As a gesture of goodwill, "the petitions in the President's office will be 'withdrawn.'" O'Quinn noted that "it was felt that the differences . . . should be worked out 'within the family' at the University without attracting the attention or inadvertently inviting the intervention of outside influences (including the press, members of the legislature, or mere busybodies)." Hereafter, "the faculty can demonstrate its good faith by responding with applications for membership, and the club principals can demonstrate their good faith by continued close cooperation with the University Advisory Committee in all phases of planning and building the club."[27]

In view of Ransom's close, continuing friendships with Handy and Shattuck in particular, it seems almost certain that he had engineered this meeting to seek a compromise and avoid the necessity of aborting the construction of the club. Broom wrote Ransom to say that he now believed "that the new statement prepared by Mr. McCullough's office solves the so-called integration issue, and . . . it is now possible to join the club without embarrassment." Broom added, "I want you to know that in all this brouhaha, I heard nothing but supportive comments about you."[28] Ransom himself wrote to the club owners on March 7, 1961: "I wish to congratulate the owners of this private club on making the prospect a reality. If there is one thing as important as the necessity of bringing the University community closer together it is the need of bringing the University closer to the alumni. I think that the Forty Acres Club, which allows for individual tastes, interests, and activities, will do a memorable job of unifying the community of interest in the University throughout the state."[29] By March 18, 1961, 600 people had already become charter members of the Forty Acres Club and Ransom could put this one crisis, his first of the sixties decade, behind him.[30]

A minor flap bordering on comic relief erupted with such fury early in 1961 that Ransom found himself pulled into an exchange of letters with a minor poet in Taos, New Mexico, and an embarrassed lecturer in Romance languages. A student-faculty poetry journal, *Quagga,* privately printed within UT facilities, had initially accepted and then rejected a poem. The irate poet wrote a series of letters to Ransom and the UT faculty member alleging that the editors' fear of "the wrath of the Baptist regents" had led to censorship of his poem. In a rare display of irritation, Ransom complained to the Printing Division of UT Press that "I am being deluged with peculiarly idiotic correspondence from people," and urged the staff not to take editorial responsibility for, let alone publish, periodicals and books that are not "official" UT publications.[31]

Far more welcome to Ransom—and now even more widely reported upon his assumption of the chancellorship—were the mounting public speaking opportunities upon which he continued to capitalize. In a bid to obtain a 14 percent budget increase, adding up to a total of nearly $25,000,000, Ransom addressed the state budget officers. "Last Chance to Be Great Seen for UT," read a resulting newspaper headline. For "historical and psychological reasons," he told the Legislative Budget Board and representatives of the governor's budget office, "This is the last biennium during the century [in] which Texas can really get on its way toward education leadership in the United States. . . . If we miss it now we will have missed it entirely." Compared to other great learning centers, Ransom remarked, the University of Texas receives "pipsqueak amounts for research."[32]

He also was capable of linking social principles with economics to encourage fellow executive officers of other academic institutions in his geographical region to risk reforms. In one of his most daring forays, speaking about the hazards of dogmatism, he told a general session of the Southern Association of Colleges and Schools, meeting at the Baker Hotel in Dallas: "We are in the South, but we are also in a world so contracted by communication, transportation and new universals that the whole globe, in effect, is smaller than the early confederacy of Southern States." He argued that educators should "insist that opportunity be provided according to ability, without regard to any other qualification or condition." Freedom is imperiled in Southern institutions of higher learning, he said, as long as "deadly" but "subtle" vestiges of "unfair discrimination" continue to prevail. These included "carefully rigged quotas for Jews in some professional schools," "silent provisos that are supposed to protect us against the foreigner," "unaccounted reservations" regarding Catholics, and "constitutional rights of the American Negro . . . so often proclaimed," but "still often lost in practice." In place of past habits of discrimination, Ransom urged administrators to usher "into being a new confederacy of intellectual and social confidence." Those Southerners who persist in supporting an outmoded "educational inferiority" will hinder "their industrial progress and economic independence," he predicted. Ransom's address ended with the admonition that "regionally we must face the double necessity of throwing off the sloth of unhopefulness and the satisfaction of the self-deluded. We must revive the grace, the spirit of adventure, and the ingenuity which informed the earliest educational plans of the South."[33]

Where the business community was concerned, Ransom's messages were conciliatory. Early in 1962 the chancellor acknowledged that "the impact on Texas culture by petroleum, cotton, cattle, lumber, transportation, and water resources is as important to complete cultural development as the collection and creation of great books, pictures, music, drama, and sculpture." Praising Dallas banker and theater-chain owner Karl Hoblitzelle before a New York City meeting of the business members of the Newcomen Society in North America, Ransom cited Hoblitzelle's "multiple vision" in making notable gifts that contributed to education, theater, medicine, and agriculture as well as succeeding profitably in finance and commerce.[34] At a hotel banquet for the Beaumont, Texas, chapter of the National Office Management Association, he urged that business and education cooperate in confronting a future that will see "technology . . . sweeping the country."[35] Asking the University of Texas National Corporations Committee in Dallas to encourage gifts to the university from business corporations, he said that such funds could provide superior research facilities and improve the faculty from "top to bottom."[36]

However, the educational experience itself was never far from Ransom's mind. In a talk to a district meeting of the Texas State Teachers Association in Amarillo on March 10, 1961, he defended grading systems against those people calling for their abolition. Grades "are the score which students make in their private game against ignorance," reflecting their "ability to pay intelligent attention to mental business." At the same time, he advocated three "freedoms" for students: "self-discipline" rather than "intellectual anarchy," the "freedom from mere fad," and the "freedom to make mistakes."[37] In August 1962, speaking at a Nuclear-Space Seminar in Amarillo, Texas, he warned the nation that "in an age when only intellectual advancement can save our skins and our reasons for citizenship[,] . . . the pleasures of the mind must not be made stale and unprofitable by sheer rigorousness or calculated regimentation. Learning can still be fun, whether it is learning to speak a strange language or launch a new rocket." Even so, "there is no way to make calculus chatty or cheerful for the well-adjusted, socially adept, self-satisfied student who has been encouraged to believe that all skills and all wisdom are equally easy to come by, if only one is lucky." Forecasting that the third great human age symbolized by orbiting rockets and satellites might "some day . . . be called the Scientific Revolution," he assured his audience that "the new educational geography will find every university next door to every other university with the same purposes. The sooner we join purposes and plans, the better for everybody concerned." Nonetheless, science and machines, no matter how sophisticated they eventually become, will never entirely replace the need for human beings. "Man's mind will not be out of a job after the next intellectual revolution."[38]

The pace of Ransom's speaking engagements and public appearances became so frenetic that he occasionally found himself caught off guard, despite Mrs. Hudspeth's near-infallibility in booking his talks. Graves Landrum, who primarily kept the financial picture in focus for Ransom, told a story of accompanying Ransom to the El Paso Country Club on November 30, 1962, for a reception and dinner for the Board of Regents hosted by the local Chamber of Commerce. The dinner was arranged as a special recognition for El Paso attorney Thornton Hardie, presiding chairman of the regents. During the dinner Landrum urgently caught Ransom's eye and pointed to the program; glancing down the printed list, Ransom saw to his astonishment that he—completely without any awareness of the fact—had been listed as the principal speaker. He blanched white for a moment, then turned the program over and began to write on it rapidly. Five minutes later he was introduced at the microphone and calmly—to Landrum's utter astonishment and lasting admiration—proceeded to deliver one of the best speeches of his life. Afterward, to an incredulous and extremely impressed Landrum, he laughed and made light of a mix-up that might have unnerved the most seasoned public speaker.[39]

Earlier in the year Regents Chairman Hardie had written to congratulate Harry Ransom on his appointment as a delegate to the Association of American Universities to the Quinquennial Congress of British Commonwealth Universities, scheduled to be held in London in July 1963.[40] Another honor soon came his way: the chairmanship of the Texas Rhodes Scholarship Selection Committee.[41] And as 1962 drew to a close, Ransom was named chairman of the executive council of the Commission on Colleges at the annual meeting of the powerful accrediting agency, the Southern Association of Colleges and Schools (SACS) in Dallas. He was also appointed to its Commission on Policies and Functions. The four-day meeting was marked by closed-door hearings on charges of political interference in university affairs regarding the attempt by African American James Meredith to gain admission to the University of Mississippi. Ransom found himself obligated to head a nine-member committee responsible for monitoring the situation at Ole Miss, which had been placed under "extraordinary status." He had the authority to dispatch committees of investigation and to call the fifty-three-member Commission on Colleges into special session to act on perceived violations of the Association's guidelines. "We will do anything to help Chancellor [John D.] Williams if the need ever arises again," he told the press.[42]

Ransom's ongoing columns in *Texas Quarterly* provided another outlet for his views. Predicting again that "the world is now on the verge" of a third great change called "the scientific revolution," he inveighed against "the idea that every college or university could be an intellectual realm in itself and sufficient to itself." Such an outmoded notion "is largely the product of social, administrative, and athletic rivalry among institutions, inculcated in freshmen and perpetuated by the oldest alumni." Consequently, "we have hardly discovered the benefits of interinstitutional cooperation."[43] In the Winter 1961 issue of *Texas Quarterly* he outlined the necessity for a state to possess "educated persons and a population that is constantly educable." Deploring the stereotypical image of "unbridled, uncurried, and uncompromising Texans sufficient unto themselves and vigorously contemptuous of everything not like themselves," which "grew from a misunderstanding of the defense mechanism of the frontier," Ransom urged that education needs in Texas begin to receive the same resources as oil, water, shipping, agriculture, and aviation. "Texas is ideally situated globally, internationally, and nationally to take advantage of the main characteristic of a new educational age: intellect in motion. Texas is no longer an out-post but a crossroads for this intellect. Its educational concerns in fields as various as scientific experiment, economic planning, philosophic discourse, the collection of knowledge, and the creative processes of the arts must be widened."[44]

Even with so many distractions, Ransom managed to keep acquisitions coming into the Humanities Research Center, now directed by F. Warren Roberts, the Ransom appointee who would oversee the collections from 1962 until 1978. At Ransom's behest, for example, Lew David Feldman made the winning bid ($16,000) for a rare, inscribed first edition of Lewis Carroll's *Alice's Adventures in Wonderland* auctioned by a New York City gallery.[45] But detractors in the book world continued to criticize the methods behind Ransom's collection. In 1961 the Earl of Crawford in Fife, Scotland (a trustee of the British Museum and other eminent galleries and libraries), queried Ransom about an article that had appeared in the Spring 1959 issue of *The Book Collector* alleging that a UT campus representative had bragged that "with the resources now at our disposal . . . we expect to disrupt all markets the world around in our search for significant material, particularly from 1700 onwards." Owing to the voracious Texas appetite, claimed the article, "the challenge is a formidable one, and not least to such experienced librarians as Provost Gordon Ray of Illinois, Robert Vosper of Kansas, and David Randall of Indiana."[46] Ransom replied to the Earl of Crawford's inquiry on February 9, 1962: "Let me begin by saying that the statement quoted from a 'correspondent' . . . has never been the policy of the University of Texas, is not the present policy, and so long as I am in office will never be the policy of the University." Instead, the object is "to provide adequate materials for the instruction of students and . . . to build collections suitable to the work of scholars." He reminded Crawford that "the rapid growth of any institution . . . is likely to encourage the exaggeration of both collectors and auction-room reporters. The University of Texas has repeatedly deferred to other libraries and to private collectors who indicated a special interest or a prior claim to materials of all sorts."[47]

An ongoing goal was an outstanding collection of Marcel Proust manuscripts, offered by Madame Mante-Proust but delayed by French objections. "We are no longer counting on this acquisition," Ransom acknowledged with resignation.[48] Bertram Rota of London, Ransom's designated agent, informed him on April 11, 1962: "I feel there is now no more than a faint hope that this great project (which we always recognized as dependent on the granting of an export licence) can succeed."[49] In May 1962, Rota's son Anthony sadly notified F. Warren Roberts that the French government had exercised its privilege and claimed Proust's papers for the Bibliothèque Nationale. "This action . . . is absolutely final and irrevocable. . . . We can all take a grain of consolation from the fact that we succeeded . . . in bringing things to a stage where only an export licence—one flimsy sheet of paper—stood between us and the successful conclusion of the deal."[50]

Still, the Rota firm kept up its endeavors to locate outstanding collections for Ransom's consideration. Bertram Rota informed Ransom on November 26 that the voluminous papers of the French-educated Romanian aristocrat, novelist, and playwright Princess Marthe Bibesco (1886–1973) represented "a very exceptional proposition from a very exceptional lady. . . . Her papers, ranging from Napoleonic times to the present and embracing a great many of the important literary and historical figures of her long lifetime, would provide an unrivalled picture of the cultural, governmental and high social life of Europe in the twentieth century, with roots stretching far back. Kings, Presidents, Prime Ministers, Generals and diplomats were her confidants. Writers from Marcel Proust to Jean Cocteau . . . became her friends." Among her holdings were "the private journal of Catherine the Great and the astonishing series of letters from [British] Prime Minister Ramsay MacDonald." Time, however, was crucial: "Princess Bibesco, now well into her seventies, constantly reminds me that she is not immortal and urges me to speed up the transfer of her papers to Texas. . . . So far you have bought four groups [of her papers] for a total of £15,000. . . . May I repeat my conviction that the whole archive will be of major importance and provide almost boundless opportunity for fascinating research in the future."[51]

Similarly, rare book dealer James H. Drake of New York City wrote on May 10, 1962: "It was wonderful seeing you and then the 'Colonel' [Hudspeth] last night, two of the nicest people I know." Drake presented "a sort of summary of the collection of books which we discussed in detail. There are about 500 cartons and I would estimate an average of 30 volumes to a carton which will be about 15,000 volumes. These books were collected over a period of almost 50 years." He ticked off a list of first editions that included Conrad, Whitman, Stevenson, London, Shaw, Wharton, James, Dreiser, Frost, "and many others," along with books relating to the presidencies of Lincoln, Wilson, Hoover, and Roosevelt. He particularly mentioned examples of early Texana, such as Kendall's *Narrative of the Texan Santa Fe Expedition* (1844) and Goddard's *Where to Emigrate* (1869). "We have only opened about 30 cartons out of the 500 and these are random selections," he noted. Knowing of Ransom's penchant for sifting through uninventoried books, Drake noted, enticingly, "I imagine there will be plenty of 'sleepers.'" He added, "In the last analysis it will be about one of the sweetest collections you can get for the money."[52]

The hectic pace of these acquisitions was not, predictably, without occasional mishaps. On June 23, 1961, Lew David Feldman sold the Humanities Research Center a portrait purportedly of the author Mark Twain painted by the gifted American artist Francis Davis Millet. The subject now is not believed to be Mark Twain, and the artist's signature itself is questionable. Feldman supplied no information establishing the provenance.[53] English professor Larry Carver recounts another story with an awkward outcome. On September 8, 1960, Feldman was the middleman when Ransom and F. Warren Roberts purchased a playful portrait of George Bernard Shaw and some whimsical book illustrations by a Polish painter who had moved to London, Feliks Topolski. Feldman vowed that the Shaw painting "will dominate any room you place it in" and would be worth $10,000, though he would charge much less. This sale led to an ill-fated plan for Topolski to paint caricatures of other modern authors for the HRC, the series to be known as the "Twenty Greats." Feldman declared that notion "a stroke of genius," and promised to get Topolski to consider a fee less than his usual $1,200–1,500 per portrait. Ransom gradually cooled on the project, however, even though Feldman anxiously reminded him, "Our recollection was that you were heartily in favor of the idea, and we proceeded on this basis." Two years later Feldman shipped the twenty paintings and requested $20,381.45. But when most of the sitters, including T. S. Eliot, Graham Greene, and Aldous Huxley, expressed emphatic dissatisfaction with their likenesses, Ransom pulled back from his intention to invite Topolski to Austin to give talks and to publish a catalog of the series (excerpts of which would have appeared in *Texas Quarterly*). Over the next decade a disgruntled Topolski continued to remind Roberts of these abandoned plans, and as late as 1971 Roberts tried to placate the disappointed painter by suggesting that the sitters' responses may have been "a compliment to your talent . . . because you seem to have a unique ability to extract submerged character traits."[54]

Ransom continued to combine a busy schedule of public appearances with frequent appeals for sustained support of the university. He thanked Elvin M. Smith of Houston for a "memorable experience at the Bluebonnet Bowl. Arrangements were perfect. Mrs. Ransom and I will always remember the event as a highlight in the way Texans do things."[55] At a luncheon, 160 members of the UT Development Board that had raised $5,100,000 in private gifts listened as he advocated salary increases, supplemental student scholarships, and funds to expand education through radio and television.[56] His phrasing remained both clever and insightful. Addressing an annual meeting of the Dallas Texas-Exes Club, Ransom characterized UT as being in a state of "perpetual transition," conceding that "television and teaching by television [have] convinced all of us mid-Victorian die-hards that while it won't save money, it can save something more valuable than money—time—while it effects the spread of knowledge, which is more valuable than either time or money." He added, "The tougher problem is to assure every superior student a superior education and to guarantee in Texas a higher education for every educable youngster. . . . The straight-A undergraduate will later make his own contributions to knowledge. . . . The C-average students may well provide means for making that knowledge effective in society."[57]

In this connection, Ransom often told an anecdote about how his "belief in a different standard for every student" had been brought home to him during his early days at UT. Teaching English composition to engineering majors, he had encountered one student in particular who experienced tremendous difficulty in composing an interesting, readable essay. In fact, Ransom all but gave up on him—"a hopeless individual," he decided after expending much effort in the student's behalf. One day, however, Ransom's car wouldn't start in the parking lot. This same student, passing by, noticed his teacher's plight, stopped and raised the hood, then made a few swift adjustments. When Ransom switched on the ignition, the engine turned over at once. The student commented matter-of-factly to the impressed Ransom, "You can write, I can fix." Ransom said he took away the lesson that many intelligent individuals possess specialized talents not readily valued by academics, but nonetheless worthy of respect.[58]

Ransom's daily duties included answering a procession of queries from regents. Vice chairman W. W. Heath (1903–1971), a wealthy Austin attorney who owned a ranch in Blanco County near Lyndon B. Johnson's, sent word through Landrum "that if the Legislature did not provide general revenue money for salary increases, then he wanted to know specifically from what source the monies were coming. . . . He said 'if you are robbing Peter to pay Paul, I want to know what you are robbing.'"[59] Even touchier issues presented themselves. Regents Chairman Thornton Hardie inquired into the lenient treatment of a student who had disrupted a campus meeting: "Here was an opportunity to demonstrate to the students of The University that the administration would take firm measures in a case of this character where students definitely broke up a meeting of the student assembly with shouting and with their personal presence. . . . I personally do not wish to forego this opportunity of letting the students understand that actions of this kind will not be tolerated!"[60] Hardie had also required Ransom to defend the university's ability in classroom teaching to "contrast the principles of Democracy and the principles of International Communism." Ransom sought to allay these misgivings by replying: "My own feeling is that our present strict requirement of Government 610 for all undergraduate degrees gives us ample opportunity . . . to convey positively and to all students a reasonable means of assessing the qualities of these conflicting systems." Furthermore, Ransom ticked off the professors who teach "more advanced level" courses in government—"an arch-conservative, High-Church Episcopalian," a person "who suffered bitterly and quite personally the defeat of Czech democracy," a top authority on the Russian revolution, and an expert on English and commonwealth subjects. "In other words, I think we are in a healthy, active, critical, aggressive state in these studies."[61]

For his beloved "book business" Ransom had now established separate offices higher up in the Tower on the fourteenth through eighteenth floors. Mrs. Hudspeth's office had become permanent on the sixteenth floor. She and her assistants stored the library materials as they arrived. Normally she left work at the end of the day with a multitude of letters, catalogs, bills, receipts, and inventories to sort for Ransom. From the official Chancellor's Office downstairs, Ransom, too, usually took work home for evenings and weekends. Henrietta Jacobsen became quite familiar with the large black leather briefcase he faithfully left with at the end of each day—a receptacle in which certain inquisitive letters from Heath and other regents might get conveniently lost for weeks at a time. A master of speed-reading, Ransom would check over and sign in a mere minute any typed document that Jacobsen had been asked to draft and placed before him.[62] Frances Hudspeth's secretarial reminder book for the period listed eight names and telephone numbers at the front: Governor Price Daniel's office and mansion, J. Frank Dobie, George Clark (Rotary Club), D. M. "Buck" McCullough, Walter Jenkins, Dr. Reginald Burbank, and Frank C. Erwin, Jr.[63] Two new names were of special note. Walter Jenkins (1918–1985) was a trusted political aide to Lyndon B. Johnson. New York physician Reginald Burbank was chairman of the Section of Historical and Cultural Medicine at the New York Academy of Medicine; the M. D. Anderson Foundation had purchased Dr. Burbank's rheumatology collection for the Houston Academy of Medicine Library.

A great many projects had been set in motion, including a proposal floated by Jack Maguire, executive director of the Ex-Students' Association, to house Lyndon B. Johnson's papers permanently at the University of Texas, possibly in a special Johnson Library. Maguire had written to LBJ, then U.S. Senate majority leader, about the idea as early as October 26,

1959, and two years later had reminded Ransom to bring up the proposal with Johnson.[64] In 1961 Ransom also wrote to John B. Connally of Richardson Oil, Inc., to "join the very large company of Texans who are delighted at the prospect of your assuming a central post in the Government of the United States," upon Connally's appointment by President John F. Kennedy to the post of Secretary of the Navy.[65] Texans were coming to play larger and larger roles in national and international spheres, as Ransom had anticipated. Having charted the course of his chancellorship, he now acted rapidly to squelch a story that he intended to accept a position with the Carnegie Foundation. "No, that is not true. . . . There is not one single smidgen of truth in the rumor," he stated categorically. "I am at the University to stay."[66]

THIRTEEN

CAMBRIDGE ON THE RANGE

In March 1963 Texas Governor John B. Connally, elected to office in November 1962, decided to invigorate the UT Board of Regents by appointing as a new member the perennial UT booster Frank C. Erwin, Jr. Erwin, who had finished a four-year stint in the U.S. Navy in 1946 and returned to UT to attend law school, was now an increasingly prominent trial lawyer in Austin with close ties to Lyndon B. Johnson and Democratic state legislative powerhouse Ben Barnes. In 1954 Erwin had married June Carr Houston, who belonged to the Good Shepherd Episcopal Church on Exposition Boulevard in West Austin, the congregation to which Harry Ransom had transferred his membership. Above all, Erwin had become widely known for his dedication to his alma mater. Harry and Hazel Ransom sent a congratulatory telegram to the new regent: "Hooray! Hooray! Hooray! We are all gleeful about the best possible news for your University. You and June are exactly what Texas needs and deserves."[1]

Two months later, Ransom took the step of meeting with an influential faculty group on the Main Campus, the appointive Committee on Budget and Personnel Policy chaired by Professor George Watt, to clarify his concept of the chancellorship in the evolving University System. A reorganization of the System by the Board of Regents, consequent upon President Joseph R. Smiley's acceptance of the presidency of the University of Colorado, was consolidating in the chancellorship the general administrative officers for both the Main University and the outlying institutions. Ransom had advocated this merger in a May 2 letter to the regents, promising to "curtail my speaking schedule in areas that are matters of public politeness rather than University significance. . . . The unification . . . will reduce by at least one-half the paper work of both, will eliminate the present confusions inevitable in dual authority and responsibility," and will result in "closer contact" among the various campuses.[2] One obvious benefit of the plan, of course, was that Ransom could thus retain the chancellorship and still directly oversee the growth of the Main University campus. There is a story that a certain regent complained to Ransom: "When you were President, you thought all authority should be vested in the President's office; now that you are Chancellor, you think it should lie in the Chancellory."[3]

To the entire General Faculty of the university, Ransom delivered an annual report on October 29, 1963, addressing this reorganization and the faculty's other concerns. As Ransom explained to the assembled professors, general administrative officers would henceforth serve both the Main Campus and the institutions beyond Austin. Dr. Norman Hackerman, a member of the UT chemistry faculty since 1945, had become the Vice Chancellor for Academic Affairs.[4] The highly likeable William D. Blunk, formerly an assistant dean of students, had been appointed Assistant to the Chancellor; he would coordinate development projects overseen by the Chancellor's Office. Dr. John Meaney, another Assistant to the Chancellor, would take charge of issues involving new academic programs. "On every score," Ransom said, "the Faculty Council should be the University's central academic forum. Its long history of faculty representation and its present vitality are among the University's greatest assets."

Repeating a statement he had issued three years previously, delineating practices of discrimination and intolerance, he took the opportunity to deplore the persecution of "the most important minority of all: the individual who according to conscience finds it necessary to assert himself against the regular order of the university community, the details of University regulations, and other customs and laws governing the society of which he is a part." With regard specifically to African American integration, Ransom pointed out that since 1961 the Board of Regents "have abolished rules governing public areas in the dormitories, dining and visiting privileges, and other living-unit activities . . . found unfair and unworkable." While restrictions about housing remained in force, he reminded critics that the regents had thus far approved the integration of the Texas Relays, the Longhorn Band, and the athletic stadium facilities.[5]

Nevertheless, Ransom had witnessed agonizing discussions by the Board about whether to take up what W. W. Heath termed the "highly controversial matter" of integrating the social areas in the women's dormitories (one alternative was to wait for the court system to adjudicate such issues and then abide by the decisions). Four additional steps toward total integration still remained: intercollegiate athletics recruiting, faculty membership, classified personnel hiring, and administrative appointments.

Another political issue directly involved the chancellor. Called upon to clarify the political rights of individual professors after several UT faculty members endorsed a Congressional candidate in an advertisement in the *Austin American-Statesman,* Ransom told the *Daily Texan* that as long as professors did not employ university facilities or offices, they might participate in promoting candidates. Such activity is a "normal exercise of the voter's function" but must never imply that UT as an institution endorses these candidates.[6]

Fortunately for someone increasingly swept into political arenas, Ransom's state and national stature was soon enhanced by encomiums lavished on him by author Willie Morris in an article about UT that appeared in the June 1963 issue of *Harper's* magazine. The chief officer of a system enrolling over 25,000 students on two campuses and in four medical schools and one dental school "is already something of a Texas legend. His enigmatic personality provides one key to the spirit of innovation which now characterizes the University of Texas," Morris declared. Although Ransom lacked the financial resources of a state like California, his "indestructible persuasiveness" had brought so many treasures to the UT library that UT had become "the terror of the book and manuscript market." Ransom was "a brilliant and intuitive educator" and "indisputably the most articulate academic spokesman ever to appear on the Texas scene." Admittedly "not the polished and self-contained administrator his predecessor, Logan Wilson, was," Ransom "has little patience with detail, and his critics say he sometimes promises too much without being able to follow through. But the net effect of his leadership has been to create a mood of hope in the top echelons of a vast academic hierarchy."[7]

The *Houston Chronicle* followed *Harper's* lead with a feature article headlined "He Believed in a Dream, And Made It a Reality" that recounted Ransom's humble origins and explained the secret formula for his rise: dreams and hard work. "His ability to absorb unlimited amounts of hard work amazes his associates. It is not at all unusual for him to spend 10 to 14 hours a day, seven days a week, at one of the several desks he has scattered over the campus. No 'organization man,' Ransom is an individualist who tries to gather equally rugged individualists around him. Impatient with rules himself, he imposes few on his organization." As a result, said the article, he has garnered "the respect of his peers in educational administration and a national reputation as a daring experimenter."[8]

Gradually becoming a celebrity of sorts in many parts of the state, Ransom stepped up his speaking schedule, which was augmented by interviews and his own writings. Far-ranging, the topics grew more personal and opinionated. He told the readers of the Summer 1963 issue of *Texas Quarterly* that young journalists should remember that "the dailiness of our knowledge . . . cannot relieve us of the responsibility of joining it to the timelessness of mankind's experience." In a rare bit of autobiographical indulgence, Ransom reached back into his past for examples of outstanding journalists, citing a publisher "in a little town in North Dakota" who, "like Socrates, . . . somehow succeeded in bringing philosophy from heaven down to earth." He also recalled and praised his Associated Press mentor Brian Bell, who "constantly interpreted the process of getting and writing news to newly hired newspapermen. He broke in reporters on facts. Truth and the historical interpretation of truth followed. But first, the facts." Although local journalism must preoccupy itself with news, "its wider profession should always be truth."[9]

When Abner McCall, president of Baylor University in Waco, and other educators recommended that a curb be established on private fund-raising by state colleges and universities, Ransom was quick to object in an interview published in the *Dallas Morning News*. (The proposal submitted to the Texas Commission on Higher Education would have prohibited spending state-appropriated money for organized fund-raising.) According to Ransom, the restriction on state funds would make public colleges dependent on federal funds, which (he noted) almost invariably came with strings attached. Moreover, he pointed out, a mere $79,000 expenditure on the UT Development Board during the previous year had netted more than five million dollars toward programs dedicated to "excellence."[10]

On the sensitive issue of race relations, a reporter for the *Dallas Morning News* quoted Ransom's editorial in *Texas Quarterly* as predicting that the "current crisis" in racial relations, far from heading toward violence, would ultimately produce a New South restored to its original place of cultural and economic leadership in the nation, a stature the region lost in the Civil War. Nearly fifteen years ago, Ransom reminded his readers, the U.S. Supreme Court in *Sweatt v. Painter* admitted African-Americans to the UT Law School as well as to the entire university because the "benefit of association" was seen as a vital component of racial equality.[11]

An op-ed piece written by Ransom for the *Houston Chronicle* conceded that difficult decisions confronted all school administrators. "We cannot assume that our church-related colleges can improve simply because they are long on doctrinal influence if they are short on libraries and laboratories. We cannot assume that miscellaneousness and popular obligations should damn state institutions to intellectual mediocrity." In any event, "we should quit discriminating against any able young Texan by having to tell him that for the very best education he had better leave the state for the East Coast or the West Coast. We should quit discriminating against the future of the state by concluding that what is necessary for Carolina or Massachusetts or Indiana or Minnesota or California is not also necessary for Texas. In short, we should quit trying to hitch our high ambition to low levels of opportunity." These exhortations concluded by insisting that "excellence is infectious."[12] The positive reception to this editorial emboldened Ransom to reach a publishing agreement with the *Houston Chronicle,* which headed one of his next contributions with the promise that henceforth Ransom's opinions and comments would appear "exclusively" and "regularly" in that newspaper.[13]

In a subsequent *Houston Chronicle* commentary, Ransom inveighed against too-rigid financial approaches to university budgets. His phrasing was quintessential Ransom. "The academic dollar cannot be accounted for like other dollars. It is not subject primarily to formulas of supply and demand. . . . Universities should make sense, discover facts, attain wisdom. Their business and their balance sheets concern ideas and new citizens, not dollar profits. They should not waste dollars; they must not waste minds."[14] In another contribution to the *Houston Chronicle,* Ransom argued that "early Texans thought more about us" and the welfare of our institutions "than we think about the society of 2063."[15]

John McKetta, Dean of the College of Engineering between 1963 and 1969, welcomed Ransom's receptiveness to new ideas. When McKetta would bring forward a fresh project that he was wary about putting to an initial faculty vote—the prospect of hiring M.D.s for an innovative bioengineering program, for example—Ransom would breezily advise him, "Johnny, just call it a 'test.' I have eighteen of those tests going on." After McKetta instituted the first classroom teaching effectiveness series featuring guest speakers, Ransom not only supported the concept but attended many of the lunchtime seminars and even spoke at several of them. "It was *great* to work with a guy like him," McKetta would say.[16]

In September 1963 Ransom traveled to England to attend the Congress of British Commonwealth Universities as one of the delegates representing the American Association of Universities. He was accompanied by representatives from Princeton, Columbia, Stanford, Northwestern, California, Pennsylvania, Illinois, and other premier schools, all of them sponsored by the Carnegie Foundation. After the meetings Ransom moved on to conferences in Paris and Rome.[17] Back home, he was named to a local Chamber of Commerce Presidential Committee to assist President Lyndon B. Johnson and his staff in their visits to Austin.[18] Presiding at groundbreaking ceremonies for the Newman Club, a new Catholic Student Center at Twenty-First Street and University Avenue intended to serve the more than 2,300 Catholic students, Ransom joined the director of the center, the chancellor of the Diocese of Austin, and the pastor of St. Austin's Church in addressing a small gathering. Ransom's remarks praised "organizations of this type" and hailed "the man for whom this movement is named, Cardinal Newman," who promulgated the idea "that religion and education were indivisible. I submit that a state university must realize that these two things are indeed inseparable."[19]

Speaking on a vastly different subject to members of the American Institute of Chemical Engineers meeting in Houston, Ransom characterized engineering as a "social force" and warned that "unless this generation produces a mobile, adaptable, intelligent, socially responsible and completely altruistic group of engineers, the rest of us are sunk." Anyone entering the field, said Ransom, must expect from the outset that within ten years his profession and job will already have been transformed by scientific advances. An engineering student "must equip himself to move among varying social groups and among conflicting scientific theories."[20]

Campus matters continually required the chancellor's attention. In Darrell Royal, a former Oklahoman hired away from the University of Washington, UT Austin had found a football coach who would win 167 games, three national titles, eleven Southwest Conference championships, and sixteen bowl games in twenty seasons as head coach before stepping down in 1976. Royal said later that he had the feeling Ransom "wasn't a real big football fan, but he certainly wasn't anti-athletics. In fact he was extremely supportive." Royal remembered that in 1962 or 1963 Ransom called him over to his office. "He told me he was pleased with the work I was doing, and he wanted to make a long-term commitment." The resulting full professorship for Royal—involving lecturing and "blackboard work"—was "*highly* unusual" in that day, possibly the first such innovation in the nation. Under the arrangement, Royal no longer needed a coaching contract; he had academic tenure instead. Some professors registered dissatisfaction with this method of keeping Royal at UT, but Royal himself found it "flattering and comforting that the Chancellor would think that much of me."[21]

Ransom also gave votes of confidence to students. In the Fall semester of 1964, Dave Oliphant, the student-editor of *Riata*, a literary magazine published twice annually, received a telephoned summons to Harry Ransom's office. Although Oliphant was a graduate student earning a master's degree in English, "it was like going to meet God," he said later. Ransom had noticed English professor Ambrose Gordon's praise for the latest issue of *Riata* in a *Daily Texan* review, and simply wanted to commend Oliphant for producing an issue of *Riata* that sold out its 1,500 copies.[22]

Owing to the tide of favorable publicity and his preceding years of teaching and service at the university, Ransom's initial stage in the chancellorship went swimmingly, better than he ever could have anticipated. Honors and appointments descended from every side. He was made the new chairman of the Air Force ROTC Advisory Panel to the Department of the Air Force, replacing the president of the University of North Carolina. This group of nine representatives from educational organizations guided the Secretary of the Air Force in devising policies for ROTC programs.[23] Trinity University in San Antonio conferred an honorary degree of Doctor of Laws on Ransom on May 27, 1963.[24] Two days later, Texas Christian University in Fort Worth likewise awarded him a degree of Doctor of Laws, and he was the commencement speaker to 640 graduates and their families.[25] As the good notices multiplied, raconteur and wit Cleveland Amory included a brief tribute to Harry Ransom in the second edition of the *Celebrity Register,* a compilation of brief identifications of "citizens more or less internationally known for conspicuousness in the public press": Ransom, said Amory, had "bought up every young scholar and old book in sight." Other Texans cited by Amory were then–Vice President Lyndon B. Johnson, Senator Ralph Yarborough, merchant Stanley Marcus, artist Tom Lea, J. Frank Dobie, Karl Hoblitzelle, businessman H. L. Hunt, and author Katherine Anne Porter.[26]

The library with which Ransom was now identified was likewise sharing his good fortunes. Tennessee Williams, aware that the Humanities Research Center already possessed numerous examples of his dramatic writings, donated manuscripts, personal papers, and other literary materials valued at some $50,000. Stanley Marcus of Neiman-Marcus in Dallas presented the Center with the original typescript of a William Faulkner book, *Miss Zilphia Gant.* Popular author Irving Wallace, a resident of Los Angeles, made a gift of manuscripts and papers, as did Thomas B. Costain of New York City. In 1964 the library obtained the manuscript of Somerset Maugham's *Cakes and Ale.* A collection of Hemingway letters and papers was acquired for $10,000.[27] When Parke-Bernet Galleries on Madison Avenue auctioned off the original manuscript of Joseph Conrad's novel *Victory* in May 1963, Lew Feldman of the House of El Dieff purchased it for the University of Texas. Numerous authorial corrections, additions, and cancellations gave Conrad's manuscript, completed in 1914 and published in 1915, a special appeal. The price of $21,000 for *Victory* was a record for a modern manuscript at a public sale, according to the *New York Times*. Notably, the previous record price—dating from 1960—belonged to the sale of E. M. Forster's manuscript for *Passage to India*, sold by Christie's in London for $18,200, which the House of El Dieff had also acquired and turned over to the Humanities Research Center.[28] In a complicated transaction negotiated by F. Warren Roberts and Bertram Rota of London in 1964, an enormous trove of Ezra Pound materials—including inscribed copies of Eliot's *The Waste Land*, thousands of letters, notebooks, photographs, hundreds of books from Pound's personal library, and a rich variety of manuscripts and proof sheets—was delivered for the sum of $250,000. Ransom himself wrote to Pound about the importance "that your archive be maintained as a unit and not dissipated in small lots here and there."[29]

The *Houston Chronicle* paid tribute to Ransom's achievements in this arena in a commendatory feature article in the Sunday section of the September 15, 1963, issue. "Last year," announced fine arts reporter Ann Holmes, "the University library nosed out proud Harvard in expenditures for rare books and manuscripts. . . . Credit for the magnificent collection is due largely to Chancellor Harry Ransom for his planning and fast footwork in the competitive world where coveted manuscripts leave an author's desk drawer and go to some institution. But which one? In the past most of them have gone to the major collections like those of Harvard and Yale in the East. Now that's changing." Frances Hudspeth, Ransom's executive assistant, had explained to Holmes that thirty years ago "the university was fortunate . . . if it had $500 to $750 a year to spend on rare books. And there was great excitement with the arrival of one fine book." By contrast, librarian Ann Bowden showed the Houston reporter the manuscript of Shaw's *Pygmalion* and explained that a scholar can additionally peruse 4,000 letters written by George Bernard Shaw and find seventeen of his plays represented by holograph or typescript versions. Also available was the manuscript of Faulkner's *Absalom, Absalom*. The new Academic Center Library, which would open on September 23, 1963, exemplified Chancellor Ransom's determination that modern libraries not serve as "mausoleums of dead ideas presided over by the undertakers of polite scholarship," wrote a rapt Holmes.[30]

Presenting the annual budget requests of the UT System to the Texas legislative committees on February 12, 1963, Ransom was characteristically succinct: "I am in favor of telling those constituents [the Texas taxpayers] exactly where we stand, exactly where we want to go, and exactly what they will get for what they pay."[31] Taking his own advice in a general statement he prepared in 1964 while seeking the state appropriation for the University of Texas System, Ransom informed the legislators that since the school was founded in 1881, the "essential test" had remained the same: that the institution "advance knowledge, and in advancing knowledge and communicating knowledge to students, that it serve the economical, social, and intellectual welfare of the people." Looking ahead to the 1965–1967 biennium, he insisted that "the time has now come to quit talking about future subjunctives. . . . By any objective standard it is now a 'university of the first class.' Among the 2,000 institutions in the United States with which The University of Texas is compared in various ways (for student performance, for educational opportunity, for faculty distinction, for research programs, for teaching, for educational facilities, for academic experiments . . .), the University is now ranked among the top 20." But the challenge had not ended. "Texans today cannot be complacent about any such status, simply because the chief characteristic of a 'first class' university is its dedication to constant improvement."[32] In other contexts, however, Ransom revealed impatience with some Texans' continual absorption with rankings. Addressing the General Faculty of the Main University on November 2, 1964, he urged "that the educational world should declare a moratorium on the use of mid-Victorian terms such as 'first class' and mid-century jargon about 'excellence' and get on with our work. When excellence arrives, when the first-class quality arises, this academic quality requires no trumpets. Labor gets it, and only hard labor maintains it."[33]

Soon after the Academic Center opened, Ransom happily announced to a reporter for the *Daily Texan* that "we were told that it would take three years for the students to get used to using the building. . . . The fact that students began using it very quickly is not only an interesting contradiction to what experts said, but it's encouraging." Julius Glickman, student body president at UT in 1963–1964 and later an attorney in Houston, would recall how cooperative Ransom was about the new campus facility. "Through Harry Ransom," Glickman said, "we received publications and student newspapers from various colleges around the country and put them in that Center and it became a kind of reading room for students." When UT students began "stump speaking," exercising their free-speech prerogatives on current affairs in front of the Academic Center, "Dr. Ransom had some reservations about where we were speaking," yet "he never tried to stop it." All in all, Glickman "found Dr. Ransom to be a human person but very strong willed when he wanted something."[34]

Even as president, Ransom's accelerating pace of activities had started to induce signs of stress. Hazel called Henrietta Jacobsen one day and asked her to check Harry's shoes—Hazel had found one brown shoe and one black one under the bed. Henrietta looked and confirmed that the UT president was indeed wearing mixed colors. A male student assistant was dispatched to his home to retrieve a matching mate. In another instance a campus policeman called the Main Building to report that Ransom had left the engine running with the doors locked in the Lincoln Continental that UT leased for him.

The fifty-five-year-old Ransom told a student interviewer in 1964 that with the chancellorship, "it's never the same day and no Monday is ever like any other Monday, and that is part of the pleasure." He spent his mornings responding to mail and conducting office work; most afternoons were taken up with meetings. "To avoid getting caught in a routine," he said, "he and his wife vanish on the weekends. Leaving Friday or Saturday, they pick a direction and drive as far as they can before Monday morning. This is his way of getting to know Texas and the Texans he wants to educate."[35]

Wherever he and Hazel ventured in the state, Harry Ransom was more and more likely to be recognized because of the frequency with which his photograph was accompanying articles about the progress taking place at the University of Texas. And now visitors to the new Academic Center would encounter his visage on canvas. The UT Dads' Association had commissioned Houston artist Robert Joy to execute an oil portrait of Chancellor Ransom. The official presentation of the portrait took place at the Dads' Association executive committee breakfast on the Saturday morning of the Texas Roundup festivities, April 4, 1964. Regent Jack S. Josey of Houston, Dads' Association President, presided at the 8 A.M. ceremony in the Driskill Hotel.[36] E. G. Morrison made the presentation remarks, saying that "*progress* and *growth* are words you readily associate with Harry Ransom. . . . This was to be expected when we turned the place over to Harry." Above all, Morrison said, "He is a man who *gives* and *commands* the priceless gift of *loyalty*. The story goes that a certain professor blew up one day and told the University big wheels: 'You can all go to hell—everybody except Harry.'" In the matter of tactics, "Harry Ransom prefers to *reconcile* men and work things out—not *separate* them and fight it out. . . . But he has the courage to defend the genuine lines, and to fight for them if necessary." The portrait depicts, added Morrison, "a fellow with brains, common sense, book-learning, and respect for things of the spirit. . . . They are rarely found in combination. . . . He is a dreamer who can wake up and *do* what he dreamed about."[37] In accepting the portrait on behalf of the university, Regents Chairman W. W. Heath said that "a great University System must have a really great leader. The chief responsibility of any Governing Board is to provide that leader and to unitedly back him." Ransom is truly "one of America's greatest educators and administrators. . . . He is recognized as such in educational circles throughout the world." Heath referred to Ransom's dream of "a great library—for no University is great without such a heart."[38] The painting itself, publicly viewed for the first time that morning, depicted a seated Ransom wearing an academic robe and regalia, posed against a background of library bookshelves and holding a large volume on his lap. He looks up at the viewer, his left hand caught midway in the act of turning a page. An antique bust looms over his right shoulder. In his opulence, the studious Ransom bears resemblance to a prominent Medici, a discerning, prosperous patron of literature and the fine arts.

In point of fact, of course, Ransom's days were hardly as relaxed as the portrait implied. Ransom told the Association of Governing Boards of State Universities and Colleges at its October 1964 meeting in North Carolina that, owing to new technology in mass communication, "there is

FIGURE 13.1

Anna Mae Morrison, artist Robert Joy, Elva Josey, Hazel Ransom, and William D. Blunk with portrait of Ransom, 1964. The UT Dads' Association commissioned Houston artist Robert Joy to produce an oil portrait of Chancellor Ransom, which was hung in the Peter Flawn Academic Center. Harry Ransom Humanities Research Center, The University of Texas at Austin.

no longer a comfortable lag between an educational event and its editorial interpretation." Consequently, "it is much more difficult for truth to overtake misunderstanding once educational policy has been printed or aired." Chief among the concerns was the concept of academic freedom, for which Ransom had a winning definition: "That within the bounds of law and with respect to the rights of others (including the rights of an institution to be represented by more than one tongue or pen), the scholar is obliged to pursue the truth as he sees it."[39]

Day to day the chancellor's time was sometimes occupied by less weighty but equally crucial matters. The Longhorn football team had been unbeaten in 1963, gaining its first national championship, yet there were unfounded rumors of the coach's imminent departure. (Darrell Royal had been contacted by his alma mater, the University of Oklahoma, but he "didn't want to leave," he decided, because Harry Ransom "had shown his confidence in me.")[40] Ransom himself was said to be considering a post at George Washington University.[41] Among the library personnel Ransom tried to recruit in 1964 was Decherd Turner, who had been assembling an impressive collection of rare books for the Bridwell Library at Southern Methodist University since 1950. Despite an offer of three times his SMU salary, Turner resisted Ransom's entreaties, largely because Ransom was evasive about his title and responsibilities. "Your particular talents would be very helpful to us," Ransom assured Turner. "We'll work everything out when you come."[42] (Much later, Turner would move to UT Austin and serve as director of the Humanities Research Center from 1980 until 1988.) Another uncommon—and stinging—defeat for Ransom was the purchase on May 15, 1964, of the Louis H. Silver Collection by the Newberry Library of Chicago. Mrs. Hudspeth received a wire indicating a switch in the family's plans to sell the holdings to Texas. For $2,687,500 these important English and Continental first and early editions, mostly from the Renaissance, would become the most significant addition of rare books to that date for the Newberry Library headed by Lawrence W. Towner. Ransom thought of contesting the matter in court, but decided it would not reflect well on UT to be involved in a lawsuit with a family; he did, however, give a deposition in a legal action brought by the book dealer, John F. Fleming, who had brokered the abandoned arrangement.[43] Chagrined that a lower bid had been accepted, Ransom wasted no time in diverting the $2,750,000 he had raised for the Silver Collection to other acquisitions instead.[44]

More far-reaching and positive in its implications was the regents' decision (by a 6–1 vote, two members being absent), announced by Chairman Heath on May 16, 1964, to take the final step in racially integrating "all teaching and non-teaching personnel, housing and other facilities, and units of the entire University of Texas System." Heath certified the ten locations affected: the Main University in Austin, the Medical Branch at Galveston, the Southwestern Medical School at Dallas, Texas Western College at El Paso, the Dental Branch at Houston, M. D. Anderson Hospital and Tumor Institute at Houston, the Graduate School of Biomedical Sciences at Houston, the McDonald Observatory at Fort Davis, and the Institute of Marine Science at Port Aransas. A new paragraph was added to the Regents' Rules and Regulations forbidding discrimination "on account of his or her race, creed, or color" in areas of admission, education, employment, promotion, "student and faculty activities conducted on premises owned or occupied by the University, and with respect to student and faculty housing." Heath defended the regents' pace of actions since 1961. Whereas "some feel we have been too slow, others that we have been too fast," Heath said, the Board nonetheless had completed the challenging task of integration "without troops, marshals, violence or bloodshed."[45] Dramatic results were straightaway discernible. In the spring of 1964 the campus interfraternity council voted to permit black men to participate in rush activities. In May 1964 a twenty-eight-year-old African American faculty member, Dr. Ervin S. Perry, was hired as an assistant professor in engineering.[46] Summer seminar participants found that their housing was already integrated.

Watching this progress, Ransom was moved to advise other Southern schools to emulate UT's lead. Testifying in Houston in April 1964 at a trial on a suit brought by Rice University trustees seeking a new interpretation of its founder's racially exclusive stipulation dating from 1891 (a change opposed by a group of former Rice students), Ransom said that Northern universities are recruiting "the best Negro brains in the South" as the result of foot-dragging efforts at integration. Moreover, race restrictions made it impossible for the modern university to "attract both federal and foundation research grants." Ransom told the jury that the University of Texas had found it difficult to attract top-notch faculty members before segregation at the school was ended.[47]

Meanwhile, back home in Austin, the regents' chairman W. W. Heath continued to make his wishes on various matters firmly known to the chancellor. On June 9, 1964, he wrote Ransom to express his opposition to a push for increasing the faculty's participation in selecting future chancellors. Concerning "the circumstances of your selection as Chancellor," he reminded Ransom, "it would have been a mistake to have delayed our action until other ambitious persons could have attempted organization of faculty cliques." Heath further pointed out that since the various components of the UT System had little consultative role in the choosing of a chancellor, why, then, should the Main University Faculty Council be so presumptuous as to "unilaterally spell out the 'ABC's' of how the Board of Regents should go about selecting a Chancellor for the whole University of Texas System? . . . It has no more right to originate and spell out the details of how the Board of Regents shall discharge its responsibilities than the Board of Regents has to tell the faculty how they shall conduct their classes."[48] Two months later, requesting a status report on miscellaneous matters, Heath registered his concern about a request that university facilities be established in Corpus Christi. "I am categorically opposed to proliferation of the Main University by setting up Main University programs away from Austin in widely separated portions of the State. They will be difficult to administer and supervise. Since the University was located in Austin by a vote of the people, serious legal questions exist. Worst of all, if we start this sort of thing, I am afraid we will have opened Pandora's box."[49] Ransom's reply on August 10 acknowledged that "the University is being approached by almost every large community in the State which does not already have a four-year institution. . . . The administration is unanimous in resisting all such proposals." At the same time, Ransom urged that limited, specific, and related programs be considered for locations in Corpus Christi, Smithville, and San Antonio (including a Center for American Studies at the latter, connected to the South Texas Medical School).[50]

Again the honors and offers seemed to mount for Ransom. In 1964 he was elected to serve as the twenty-third member on the Board of Directors of the American National Bank, an announcement made by A. C. Bull, chairman of the board.[51] But the largest appointments and most promising connections now came from a source farther East—from the native son who in 1963 had ascended to the United States presidency upon the assassination of John F. Kennedy. In April 1964 Ransom became a new member of the committee that handled the estate of U.S. Supreme Court Justice Oliver Wendell Holmes, who had bequeathed it to the government to finance a history of the court.[52] Other appointments followed. In October 1964 President Johnson convened college student-body presidents from across the nation in Washington, D.C., to announce the creation of a new program known as White House Fellows. Fifteen student-body presidents were to be chosen in the future to assist the Executive Office in paid positions. Harry Ransom of the University of Texas would be among the committee of nine college and university administrators (which also included Ransom's great friend William Friday, President of the University of North Carolina) that would make the selections. Following a White House dinner for the students, Johnson spoke "on subjects ranging from Viet Nam to his daily agenda." Ransom accompanied Greg Lipscomb, UT Students' Association president, to the conference, traveling by airplane. President Johnson surprised Lipscomb by saying that he sometimes read the *Daily Texan*. "Be sure to beat OU next weekend," he enjoined the pleased UT student.[53]

In August 1964 Ransom returned to Washington at the invitation of President Johnson to attend what was billed as "an intellectual convocation of the states," joining nearly eighty other educators to exchange information with the President about studies their schools were conducting for state governments and to discuss regional cooperation.[54] Ransom was appointed to chair the committee of seventeen Southern delegates. The conference included a luncheon with the President at the White House. Urging the chancellors and presidents to be on the lookout for talented young people who might enter public service, Johnson offered to telephone likely candidates himself to persuade them to try to become "Abraham Lincolns or Oliver Wendell Holmeses or Arthur Vandenbergs or Sam Rayburns."

This Washington connection with a sitting President deeply interested in higher education was registered powerfully at the May 1964 commencement on the UT campus, where President Lyndon Baines Johnson stood before Chancellor Harry H. Ransom to receive an honorary degree of Doctor of Laws, both of them wearing academic gowns, and then turned to deliver the commencement address.[55] Mrs. Johnson received an honorary Doctor of Letters degree that same night; she sat next to Harry Ransom on the stage of the Austin Municipal Auditorium, where the ceremony had to be moved because of heavy rains.

As another sign that President Johnson and his family had successfully been brought into the circle of the friends of UT, shortly thereafter Mrs. Lady Bird Johnson, who herself held two degrees from the university (and whose daughter Lynda Bird would receive her B.A. degree from the school) made an unannounced visit to the campus and spent two hours touring its environs in the company of W. W. Heath, chairman of the Board of Regents, Frank C. Erwin, Jr. (UT regent and national Democratic Party committeeman), Chancellor Ransom, Frances Hudspeth, and an unidentified "official from the National Archives." Although Ransom characterized the two-hour visit as a "social" one, several people saw Mrs. Johnson standing for long minutes on the terrace of the Main Building where Miss Ratchford had once maintained a little garden, gazing across the campus toward a hillside location where Harry Ransom was pointing. Frank C. Erwin, Jr., was seen carrying what appeared to be a roll of building plans.

Clearly something major was contemplated, although few of the students milling about on the Main Mall glanced up at the bareheaded First Lady in her green dress and simple black coat. Among her stops that day was the recently opened Academic Center.[56]

Enormous and lasting as were these repeated encounters with Potomac power and influence, the signal event for Ransom in the mid-sixties probably was his introduction to a national television audience. On Sunday, March 1, 1964, the CBS network broadcast "Two College Presidents: An Exchange of Views," a televised program in which Hughes Rudd interviewed John Sawyer, president of Williams College, and Harry H. Ransom, chancellor of the University of Texas. Filmed three days earlier in Williamstown, Massachusetts, where Williams College had been founded in 1793, the show contrasted a private school of 1,100 male students and 650 New England acres against a coeducational institution of 22,000 students, 1,400 faculty members, and 1,100 acres. Even the styles of the respective presidents differed visibly on the screen. Sawyer was far more active with his hands in making his points. He wore a tweed suit, Ransom a dark one. It was Sawyer who generally took the initiative and gave the more elaborate comments. Ransom was attentive and intense in listening and replying, typically narrowing his eyes in concentration when concluding the most potent part of his answer. The camera lights emphasized deep clefts in his chin and forelip. Ransom was quick to smile, but even the smile seemed categorizable as "intellectual." He responded succinctly and then briefly amplified his ideas. When Rudd asked Ransom what arguments could be made on the side of the hugeness of a university over a small college like Williams, Ransom replied that he himself "went only to relatively small men's schools east of the Mississippi," but that "the advantage, it seems to me," is "the complexity, the variant interests, the tremendous miscellaneousness, variety, sometimes conflict of activity." Warming to his subject, he added that "the institution where I now am has infinitely more means of helping the individual student than the smaller colleges I once knew." He also remarked that one should "remember that these youngsters are going to live typically in fairly good-size towns."

On other topics, Ransom asserted that "we have a deep obligation to the American Negro, to the youngster with a Mexican background . . . in a very broad band of the Southwest, to the student with an Oriental background." Rudd asked if Ransom meant "a kind of a racism in reverse. You'd almost be getting into a quota system," and Ransom explained that "we can't arrange a neat mosaic of minorities. This would be the most stultifying possible thing, both to the minorities and to the total educational picture." Rudd queried Ransom about whether there wasn't "a limit to this proliferating student population at campuses like yours." Ransom said there was no "mystic number," but that certainly an institution has become too large if "effective communication . . . breaks down," impairing "the effective exchange of . . . knowledge."[57]

Although the interview was not presented as a competition, the fact that it took place in Sloan House, the traditional home of Williams College presidents, and the requirement that Ransom several times explain the advantages, if any, of a large Southwestern state university gave his appearance a crucial symbolism. The feeling was, as he returned home, that he had represented Texas and its premier state university very much to their credit in a national exposure.

Ransom and the Main Campus received another prestigious plug in the form of a cover-story article by New York University professor David Boroff, titled "Cambridge on the Range: The University of Texas," in the June 20, 1964, issue of *Saturday Review*. Although alleging that the school "tends to be shrill, naively promotional, aggressively quantitative," the author conceded that "many observers consider it among the top twenty universities in the country. . . . It would now like to be among the top ten." He quoted one professor's remark that "there is nobody nearby we can look up at," and concluded that "U.T. is now part of the mainland of academia, irrevocably divorced from the dingy poverty of Southern higher education."

Presiding over this main campus with a $400,000,000 endowment—as well as a College of Arts and Sciences bulging with 9,000 majors—is "the University's able Chancellor," who fought for an undergraduate academic center. Boroff reviewed the faculty—old Southern gentlemen ("a dying breed"), leathery old Westerners (Dobie is "now retired" and historian Walter Prescott Webb "was killed in an automobile accident last year"), "academic carpetbaggers" imported from the East and Midwest "presumably to give the place some intellectual dash," and "scientists, brash and confident." Among the "outrageously confident" faculty, Boroff spotlighted "a kind of inner brain trust of younger men—'Harry's boys'—beginning to age, alas, who are close to Dr. Harry Ransom, the Chancellor, and who, in effect, have a *carte blanche* to try anything. They have given the University a certain exuberant flavor. Ransom himself is the new breed of Texan. Urbane, Yale-educated, he is the spearhead of the drive toward excellence." The bottom line for Boroff and the *Saturday Review:* "Texas is a place to watch."[58] Editor and columnist A. C. Greene of the Dallas *Times Herald,* applauding Boroff's article, commented that UT's prominence "is returning national interest on its investment." Greene saw this as proof that Texas was on the right track. "The grumbling among some Texas exes that the 40 Acres is 'becoming more of a Yankee school than a Texas school' stems from the very things Boroff finds for approval."

As another sign of Ransom's achievement and status, the Board of Regents resolved itself into an Executive Session on November 7, 1964 (allowing them to meet with only the regents and their secretary Betty Ann Thedford present), whereupon Regent Frank C. Erwin, Jr., moved that a plaque honoring Harry Huntt Ransom be prepared for installation in the Undergraduate Library and Academic Center (its language to be supplied by Regent Wales H. Madden, Jr., an Amarillo attorney). The plaque would read: "A wise leader who would dream must also reason and inspire lest even his most noble goals escape attainment. To Harry Huntt Ransom, we here affirm our profound appreciation. Through his vision, his suasion, and his able direction, this building came into being."[59]

FOURTEEN

A UNIVERSITY IN TRANSITION

On March 16, 1965, students and faculty members gathered in Batts Hall Auditorium to hear a keynote talk by Chancellor Harry H. Ransom titled "State of the University," which would launch the fourth annual convocation in the Texas Today and Tomorrow series. His audience would then fan out to attend and address alumni receptions. Ransom's speech identified UT's present "chief characteristic" as "transition," reporting that "most of the deficiencies" detected in 1958 by the Report of the Committee of 75 had been "remedied," but meanwhile "new priorities" had emerged. Even so, "historic milestones have been passed," including integration of minorities, inter-institutional cooperation, and the "freeing of the Available Fund from routine support of Main University operation . . . as a means of improving academic quality."

In an oblique response to the mounting demand by students across the country that they be allowed to evaluate their professors, Ransom reflected on "the painful process of judgment" in fully grasping an instructor's worth. For one thing, he observed, "much of the best teaching brings its influence into full force long after the student is out of class." Still, "the best teachers . . . are usually well known by their colleagues in a discipline and by students," as well as by alumni. Everyone should bear in mind the reality that "publication is in some respects the most difficult kind of teaching. . . . It is remembered for substance, not legitimate or doubtful tricks of presentation. It is subjected to long scrutiny rather than temporary impression." Basically, then, "the main point for a university . . . is to do everything possible to locate the effective teacher. Once located, he should be cherished."

Resuming his theme of "educational transition," he mentioned the need to expand "the boundaries of university geography. On this new map, such programs as international exchange and junior years abroad must be redrawn. What was once mere educational tourism has become citizenship in the world of the intellect." He closed by reminding his listeners that "by every ancient academic principle, the university is the critic of its own society as well as its servant. By every theoretical and practical tradition, we are required to join our dreams . . . with rigorous self-criticism." He predicted that the "next decade" will impose "changes" that will sometimes be "uncomfortable," and that "ambition, ardent conviction, hard work, honesty, and tolerance will have to be mustered."[1] Shirley Bird Perry, a UT student during the 1950s and then program director in the Texas Union (and eventually a vice chancellor of development and external relations and senior vice president), testified that these exhortations "made students feel that they were part of an important enterprise," and "sent them off on fire, eager to spread the word about UT's mission."[2]

When Ransom (along with DeWitt C. Reddick of the UT School of Journalism) spoke at the mid-winter conference of the Texas Press Association at its meeting in the Commodore Perry Hotel in Austin, he told the luncheon group that "the prissiness and pride of academic division must give way to the excitement and reward of sharing knowledge." He added, "Public and private education, with all the neat distinctions inherited from the past, must give way to cooperation in a common cause. The old competition may have been innocent fun in 1925; in 1965 it is dangerous and damaging foolhardiness."[3] A similar visionary message infused Ransom's dinner address at the annual meeting of the Texas Institute of Letters in Houston, which that day paid tribute to the late J. Frank Dobie, who had died in 1964, with talks by Dr. Mody C. Boatright (1896–1970), UT Press Director Frank H. Wardlaw, and others.[4]

Members and even former members of the Board of Regents continued to express concern about perceived inroads on the regents' prerogatives. Ransom assured Thornton Hardie of El Paso (whose term had ended in 1963) that "during the innumerable sessions of the 'Committee of 75' I was one member who kept insisting that every activity of the new coordinating board be qualified by some such phrase as 'with due regard to the authority and responsibility of the individual governing boards.'"[5] Ransom invariably took opportunities to praise Regents Chairman Heath's "remarkable sense of public trusteeship." Heath's attributes "add up to a kind of professional selflessness," wrote Ransom. "I have never known a man who could start out completely opposed to a proposition, be convinced by argument on the other side, and then support with vivid imagination and courageous sense that same proposition." He added that Heath "has been a history-making chairman because he has been devoted both to the tradition and the future of the University."[6] In a draft of an admiring testimonial, Ransom declared that Heath possesses the "ability to change . . . as the evidence under the glass of whatever wisdom God gives him, indicates." Where education is concerned, "he is as inquisitive as a prosecuting attorney and once convinced about an educational proposition, or converted to one he originally doubted or opposed, he is as relentless as a crusader."[7] And yet mutters of dissent arose occasionally among the Board of Regents. One regent was heard to ask, dismissively, "Why are we spending all this money on a bunch of old, *used* books?"[8]

Another round of rumors swept the campus and the state in March 1965 to the effect that Ransom would be leaving for a government post, perhaps at the federal level. "Friends of Dr. Ransom have said they didn't believe he would ever leave The University of Texas for another university but that he might be persuaded to enter government service. He has often said that he has always been happy at The University of Texas," reported *The Daily Texan,* "and would be content here going back to teaching English." Ransom himself denied that there was any "immediate prospect of his resignation."[9] W. W. Heath stated unequivocally, "He's not going anywhere." Heath said that the regents had conferred with Ransom and had received guarantees that he planned no moves. "He says his roots are deep here," added Heath.[10] Ransom's intensifying ties to the LBJ Administration were presumably the basis for these periodic speculations, and there undoubtedly had been some discussions regarding possible roles for Ransom in the President's commitment to higher education. In 1965 the President would name Ransom chairman of the Commission on the Patent System, and in 1966 would appoint him to the President's National Advisory Committee on Libraries.[11]

Providing another possible source of gossip about Ransom's ties with Washington, Heath and the regents had been negotiating with President Johnson about his papers coming to the University of Texas in return for the creation of a school perhaps to be called the LBJ Institute of Public Service, a proposal very close to Johnson's concept of federal and state responsibility for training the next generation of government leaders.[12] By May 11, 1965, Heath could send Ransom, Frank C. Erwin, Jr., and new Regent Frank N. Ikard the second draft of a "Letter of Intent from University of Texas for the Lyndon Baines Johnson Presidential Archival Depository." The proposal stressed that the "richness" and "fullness" of the nation's knowledge and understanding of the "historical heritage" of a President's papers depend upon their "completeness," the "care" of their preservation, the "adequacy" of the museum facilities, and "their general *accessibility* and availability for *scholarly* research and study." Echoing some of Ransom's previous language, the document went on to assert that the university's "responsibility to develop tomorrow's leaders, capable of making intelligent decisions for the future, can be greatly advanced when the inquisitive mind has available at the university the research collections from which a comprehensive view of the age in which we live can be obtained." The university pledged itself to provide "not less than fourteen (14) acres within the principal academic environs," to grant President Johnson the right of "approval" for architects, design, and "physical relationship with other University facilities," and to "make available at its expense adequate, convenient parking facilities." In turn, the administration, operation, protection, maintenance, and staffing of the Presidential Library, as with other presidential libraries, would be "at the expense of the United States of America."[13]

Lady Bird Johnson wrote to W. W. Heath from the White House on February 5, 1966, to express her pleasure about "the tremendously fast progress Dr. Ransom and the Committee are making on visiting schools and planning for the budget, curriculum, and so forth." She recommended a number of schools of public administration that should be investigated as models, and attached several lists of people at Harvard, Cornell, Berkeley, and other institutions and programs who might be considered for the new directorship.[14] William S. Livingston soon took charge of a committee to work out the details, arrange the budget, and select a dean. Regent Frank C. Erwin, Jr., would write to Livingston on September 12, 1966, to suggest Secretary of State Dean Rusk, Professor Eric F. Goldman of Princeton, and Dr. Otis Singletary (former assistant to the UT president, first Director of the Job Corps, former Chancellor of the University of North Carolina at Greensboro, and Vice President of the American Council on Education in Washington) as candidates for the deanship.[15]

Even with the protective buffer of so much favorable coverage of his activities, Harry Ransom seemed to sense a pending change. His public speeches began to stress the inevitable limitations of time. Addressing the Texas Press Association meeting on January 23, 1965, for example, he stated bluntly that a "sense of urgency is inescapable in Texas. . . . Already it is past noon on the East Coast, from which we got most of our direct educational impetus, and early evening in the university quadrangles which formed our heritage, partly in Europe. It is not yet high noon on West Coast campuses with which we are more closely timed in history." He went on to speak of Lyndon B. Johnson as the "Texas president [who] has put the nation's schools into a kind of limelight." Moreover, "the Governor of Texas has focused . . . the action of his career upon educational advancement," he said, referring to John B. Connally, who held office from the election of 1962 until the election of 1968, when he would decline to run.[16] Connally, benefiting from a state sales tax adopted by the legislature in 1961, had advocated larger appropriations for colleges and universities.[17]

Invited to speak on Law Day in Fort Worth on April 30, 1965, Ransom invoked the Magna Carta, the Napoleonic Code, the Bill of Rights, and "marble figures blindfolded by impartiality and holding scales sensitive to individual rights," together with the symbolic frontier "star." He urged citizens to make a greater effort to "support those laws which are viable, just, and effective; and to participate in changing those laws which are not." Alas, "many citizens vacillate between awe and annoyance, between lyric pride and manic depression in the realm of law, from the policeman on his beat to the most recent decision of the Supreme Court." Closing with a historical survey of the connections between law and education, he recalled that "law, as it educates the citizen in each era of his experience, is continuous. We should keep its books wide open at those pages which have announced unforgettably the inseparable connection between the privilege and the responsibilities, the rights and the obligations of citizenship."[18]

A series of decisions by the Board of Regents reached between 1963 and 1965 reunited the UT System and the Main University.[19] In 1965 Ransom produced a fascinating document, "Memorandum for the Organization Committee," with the intention of influencing the concept of his office. Observing that "the present chancellorship is quite different from the UT System presidencies of Dr. Painter and Dr. Wilson" as well as from "the Chancellorship of Mr. Hart," Ransom noted that the chancellorship is also "not comparable" to the chief academic posts in the California, North Carolina, or other complex university systems. Some chief academic officers have "grown up in administration by slow degrees like Chancellor [Herman] Wells of Indiana, President Friday of North Carolina, and President [Fred Harvey] Harrington of Wisconsin." Others have "been suddenly elevated like President [Robert] Goheen of Princeton (who was an assistant professor of Classics when he became president)." Still others have been "'imported' from business or another university, as were Presidents [Robert] Odegaard of Washington, [Harlem] Hatcher of Michigan, [Nathan Marsh] Pusey of Harvard, [Herbert Eugene] Longenecker of Tulane, [Kenneth] Pitzer of Rice, [O. Meredith] Wilson of Minnesota, and [Franklin] Murphy of UCLA." A few have been "brought over from law or medicine like [W. Clarke] Wescoe of Kansas, [J. Roscoe] Miller of Northwestern, or [Kingman] Brewster of Yale." By contrast, Ransom pointed out, "the present chancellor has been at Texas since 1935 in a miscellany of assignments. I am primarily a native Texan and a teacher. . . . The Board knows that

I have never made any pretense to being an 'administrator.' . . . I came into administration more or less by accident and stayed in it only because I believed that the University could project a future for future students." With unusual candor Ransom admitted that "at various times I have felt completely frustrated and defeated by operations of current students, resident faculty, alumni, citizens, and members of the Board. This occasional gloom has always been dispelled by the belief that the Regents (and everybody else in the University community) constituted an educational organism—not an organizational structure."

To continue as chancellor, Ransom indicated, he would need certain "essentials." These included "the confidence and the friendship of the Board, . . . which has been the main reward of my 'administration,'" and supplemental funds for endowment, professorships, fellowships, and buildings "in all institutions." Additionally, "on a more personal count," he stipulated that he wished to continue six specific projects in whose establishment he had "been deeply engaged." The first of these activities, naturally, was "*Library development generally.* . . . Texas has made real progress in this field." He also wanted to develop "*History of Science Collections,*" a "*History of Law Collection,*" and a "*History of Medicine Collection.*" Then, too, he wanted backing for *Texas Quarterly;* "established in 1958, the Quarterly has had unexpected success—especially abroad." Finally, he asked for "*Special Programs for Honors and Unprepared Students.*" After all, "I participated in the founding of Plan II, established the Junior Fellows Program, and suggested the Provisional Admission plan for 'ineligible' students. I should like to continue in at least distant relation to these programs and when I leave the Chancellorship, work in them directly."[20] In other words, having arrived at the pinnacle of university power, he presented a culminating wish list reflective of projects he had brought with him up through the ranks—wishes resembling more the dreams of a scholar-teacher-rare book librarian than the *realpolitik* demands of a survivor who had scaled the slopes of Texas academe and now could virtually dictate the terms of his tenure as chancellor. But these were also the kind of negotiable objectives— institutional, constructive, tangible—that had endeared him to the Board he served and the faculty he represented.

Ransom's era predated any of the Open Meetings or Open Records restrictions; as chancellor he had direct access to the Board without going through a president or explaining his agenda to the press. To each meeting of the Board he habitually carried an orange folder (known in the aggregate as his "orange books") containing items he had often not bothered to discuss with his associates. Their contents included the outlines of proposals and topics that Ransom personally thought were important enough to bring before the Board.[21]

He also had the privilege of writing directly to the Board Chairman at any point, and by June 21, 1965, Ransom was pressing Heath about several matters (though "no crashing crises") during Bill and Mavis Heath's vacation in Honolulu, which Ransom apologized for interrupting. His letter to Heath gives a glimpse of how Ransom approached the improvement of faculty salaries and other budget items. "I received a *'preliminary'* budget of the Main University on *June 18,* as I left for a Washington meeting. I have got copies for Graves [Landrum] and Frank Graydon to analyze. We will have a general review tomorrow, June 22, or Wednesday, June 23. When Hackerman returns, he and I will go over the document on June 30, and there will be a final *administrative* review of recommendations on July 1, anticipating your Executive Committee review soon after your return." Having received a generous appropriation from the Legislature that year, Ransom urged that UT make a "point of *showing* real progress" in support for faculty and academic programs.

Ransom also shared with Heath some of his organizational concerns. Vice Chancellor Hackerman understandably wished for "a much more nearly complete and final delegation of authority for operation of the Main University." Ransom also reported on federal grant approvals for buildings in the UT System and lamented that ("in Washington, I was told unofficially") three other Texas schools had been ranked ahead of UT on proposals to the National Science Foundation. A decision was needed on whether to proceed with financing membership in a council to administer research programs in high-energy physics using reactors (only UT and Rice had been invited from Texas by the National Academy of Sciences to join this council); Ransom felt that the doctoral work, prestige, and future potential warranted the annual cost of $100,000. Ransom fretted about a "major problem ahead of us" if the U.S. Office of Education made good on its public announcement that Health, Education, and Welfare grants would no longer be awarded to any universities having official connections with fraternities and sororities that discriminate in electing members. Similarly, the new Civil Rights Act conceivably made the university responsible for knowing and distinguishing among the various rental practices of the owners of private housing.[22]

Less than a year earlier Ransom had informed another correspondent that he took special pride in moving beyond "the appointment of the first Negro professor. We now have the second—a woman."[23] But it was the surge in library acquisitions that usually caught the attention of the press.

FIGURE 14.1

Norman Hackerman, Joseph R. Smiley, Regents W. W. Heath, Walter P. Brenan,
Wales H. Madden, and John S. Redditt, with Harry H. Ransom at the Electrical
Engineering Research Laboratory, University of Texas, date unknown. These seven men
were instrumental in making numerous decisions affecting UT's future. Harry Ransom
Humanities Research Center, The University of Texas at Austin.

"UT Raids Treasure Trove," read one headline in the *Houston Post* on February 6, 1966. According to its reporter, Gayle McNutt, "many serious English scholars who wish to do original research on some of their best-loved
writers and poets" such as Kipling, Shaw, and Lawrence have been obliged
to forsake their homeland and "come all the way to Austin, Texas, to get
at the material." F. Warren Roberts, director of the Humanities Research
Center, explained that the differing tax laws of the United States and Great
Britain partly accounted for the HRC's success in building a priceless collection. In the United States, "a man in a higher income bracket can make a
$1,000 donation to a library and it may actually cost him only $150." Meantime, "in England, tax laws are favorable to money from foreign sales."
Consequently, book dealers handling British items found it more profitable to sell to American buyers. "As one UT librarian put it, 'We don't call
them, they call us.' She said the UT library may get 10 or 15 letters a day
from English book dealers offering material for sale." A literary writer and

editor for the *London Sunday Times,* William Rees-Mogg, lamented that "this is the last decade in which it is at all possible to form any sort of proper university collection of English literature and the opportunity is already slipping fast away. The University of Texas has been taking it—we have not."[24]

Newspaper reports of the HRC's conquests mounted on an almost weekly basis. Lew D. Feldman, declining to identify the purchaser for whom he was acting as an agent, bought for $4,500 the holograph manuscript of the Reverend Charles Monroe Sheldon's *In His Steps,* which, prior to the Topeka, Kansas, author's death in 1946, had sold twenty-three million copies—supposedly more copies than any book in its time except the Bible.[25] Feldman also successfully, amid British chagrin, bid $95,200 for Robert Herrick's seventeenth-century "Poetical Commonplace Book," a manuscript in verse and prose described by Sotheby's as "the most remarkable literary discovery to have been sold in our rooms in the memory of any of the present partners."[26]

Virtually everything Ransom did now attracted notice. When he finally shook the hand of a similarly named Harry H. Ransom with whom he had frequently been confused—Harry Howe Ransom, a professor of political science at Vanderbilt University who was visiting the UT campus—their brief meeting was reported in the campus newspaper. The Ransom from Vanderbilt told a reporter, "We are like two Lloyd Russels [*sic*]. We need to write a letter to the *Times* and say, 'We wish to state that neither of us is the other.'" He added that the two "are not kin, at least not close enough to do either any good."[27] The combination of J. Frank Dobie's and Harry Huntt Ransom's names as co-editors (along with Mody Boatright) of a reprinted Southern Methodist University Press edition of *Mustangs and Cow Horses* (first issued in 1940) was sufficient to draw a page-long, admiring review in the July 2, 1965, issue of *Time* magazine.[28]

Periodically the faculty loyalty oath emerged as an issue. Author and educator Howard Mumford Jones wrote from Harvard University on September 21, 1965, to explain that "Professor C. L. Cline of the English Department has been gracious enough to ask whether I might not like to return to Austin to teach for some limited period of time." Arrangements had been completed for Jones to arrive "for the term beginning February 1, 1966," but Jones registered disgust over one detail of his contract. "At no time during our conversations or in correspondence has anyone mentioned the disclaimer or loyalty oath required of your faculty. . . . Attached to the form is a list of scores of organizations alleged to be subversive or disloyal on the ground that they appear on some other list compiled I know not how." Jones was prepared for a confrontation. "I have combated this kind of oath all my life as a member of various state universities and of Harvard University. I once declined to teach during the summer at the University of California because that institution then demanded an oath like yours." He concluded by castigating the oath as "an affront to me as a responsible American citizen who has worked for his government and several times taken an oath to defend it" and announcing, "I hereby resign my post as visiting professor at the University of Texas." Observing that Jones had sent a copy of his letter to the *American Association of University Professors Bulletin,* Ransom elected to sidestep this invitation to engage in a national public debate with an eminent humanist, merely making a note at the bottom of the Jones declaration: "I do not answer letters which are released simultaneously to the press. H. R."[29] The oath requirement would soon be abolished at UT as at other schools.

A far happier development was the announcement by the White House on August 9, 1965, that President Johnson had accepted the proposal by the University of Texas to provide facilities and a site for a graduate school that would be known (in the initial stages) as the Lyndon Baines Johnson Institute of Public Service. During Lady Bird and Lynda Bird's visit in 1964, the site had been approved. The school would house Johnson's presidential papers and offer scholars and students a broad historical picture of his administration. No fund drive would be needed; the financing would come from university resources. It would be the first presidential library to be provided entirely by an institution of higher learning; the previous libraries—those for Hoover, Roosevelt, Truman, Eisenhower, and Kennedy—had been paid for by private subscription.[30] Ransom, Chairman of the Board Heath, and several regents stood at President Johnson's side as he told of this decision.

After such a high-profile day in Washington, Ransom's campus duties seemed tame by comparison. Public speaking opportunities arrived regularly, however, in spite of the chancellor's earlier stated intention to curtail these engagements. On September 8, for instance, Ransom spoke in Houston at a meeting of the Women's Institute, where his remarks on the renaissance of interest in the arts applauded a changing climate. Even "the foot-weary male blinking his way past an exhibit in the wake of a wife set upon culture," he said, might result in an "accidental collision" with the arts so that "a few hearts and heads are never quite the same again." The creation of museums, the generosity of art patrons, the growth of performing arts centers, and the flourishing book trade were making Texas "an enjoyable place to live." Now the greatest need was "for better taste." After all, "in 1965, it would be easier for a Texas painter, musician, or writer to seek exile on the Gulf Coast than in Paris."[31]

Pulled into a swirl of formal social activities involved with the chancellorship, Harry and Hazel Ransom—he in tuxedo, she in an ornate empire gown, pearl necklace, and long white gloves—greeted long lines of faculty and staff at an annual reception at the Westwood Country Club on Tuesday night, September 28, 1965.[32] His deliberate, reserved manner scarcely belied the fact that his mind was far more absorbed with campus developments. Within Ransom's office, for instance, Mrs. Hudspeth, whose husband was becoming more helpless physically though staying mentally alert, herself suffered a coronary occlusion and spent most of the summer of 1965 in the hospital. Once back in the office, however, she told a correspondent that she enjoyed her work "even more after the enforced rest." Her return was marred by a fire on the twentieth floor of the Main Building, the damage from which she dismissed as being "very slight. Papers and radio had us burned out, and all sorts of wild rumors were floating about that the research collections or theatre collections or manuscripts, etc., etc., were destroyed." She had to reassure one donor, Leo Perper of New York City, that "nothing of yours was harmed or even threatened."[33] The Ransoms had been vacationing at the Karl Hoblitzelles' summer home in Cape Cod at the time of the fire.[34]

When Ransom came to deliver his annual report to the General Faculty of the Main University on November 15, 1965, he took note of the formation of the Coordinating Board that had replaced the Texas Commission on Higher Education to oversee the network of junior colleges and "a fast-growing state system." Arlington State College had now joined the UT System, and the South Texas Medical School at San Antonio and the Graduate School of Biomedical Sciences were making progress. Ransom took pride in reporting that average faculty salaries by rank had "at last" reached levels comparable with those of other leading state universities. He gave credit to Lieutenant Governor Preston Smith and Speaker of the House Ben Barnes for supporting faculty "fringe benefits," which Ransom preferred to call "'faculty effectiveness programs,' ranging from retirement and leaves of absence to insurance and support of travel." Asked about the university's plans regarding future enrollments, Ransom criticized any university that "simply keeps sprouting at random, spilling over into the society which surrounds it." The model is one that "can grow with deliberate checks, balances, and selective expansion. . . . In such a plan, the chief expanding points are usually fields of graduate study and postdoctoral work."

FIGURE 14.2

Chancellor and Mrs. Harry H. Ransom and Chairman of the Board of Regents and Mrs. W. W. Heath, Westwood Country Club, Austin, September 28, 1965. The Ransoms sometimes attended formal university functions like this one. Heath was a close adviser to Ransom during these years. Harry Ransom Humanities Research Center, The University of Texas at Austin.

Alluding to a "critical shortage of library, seminar, and carrel facilities," particularly on the graduate level, Ransom announced that the regents had in August 1965 "approved in principle my suggestion of a Graduate Library Center," a concept that would evolve into a spacious separate structure housing the Humanities Research Center. This move would devote "the entire quadrangle on the southwest corner of the Forty Acres to . . . the verbal disciplines, chiefly the humanities." Ransom also told his faculty audience that the regents had "approved . . . the development of a fine arts complex on the east side of the campus."[35]

FIGURE 14.3

Ransom and Regent Wales Madden, date unknown. Harry Ransom Humanities
Research Center, The University of Texas at Austin.

The year 1966 brought on vastly different events, some of them extremely
unwelcome, though things started out on a typically confident note. Ransom told the Graduate Club at its weekly Thursday luncheon meeting in
February 1966 that graduate students must abandon the "quill pen age"
and embrace technology and teamwork for their research. Very few graduate students, he said, are adequately informed about what is available in the
application of modern technology to research. Ransom predicted that the
time was coming when students could instantly and easily obtain information from Washington "or even Tokyo" through technology. Urging graduate students to adopt the concept of collaborative research, he also called for
greater clarity, succinctness, and focus in graduate theses and dissertations;
a clear, concise essay is preferable to a murky 500-page book, he said.[36]

Yet despite ongoing efforts to bridge misunderstandings and instill positive feelings about the entire university experience, such as the Texas Today and Tomorrow series, Ransom and his fellow administrators found
themselves encountering a national phenomenon of deteriorating faith in
ordinary relations between universities and their students.[37] The Gulf of

Tonkin incident in 1964 had led the United States into a deepening involvement in South Vietnam, and college campuses had now become sites of
resistance to the military draft. A caustic underground publication in Austin, *The Rag*, had begun disseminating passionate commentaries on LBJ's
war, the Free Speech Movement at the University of California at Berkeley,
UT civil rights worker Dick Reavis's jailing in Alabama, and other political
stories, packaging these articles and editorials around psychedelic artwork
and local retail advertisements. In November 1966, for instance, *The Rag*
would announce forthcoming speeches on the UT campus by Chicago-
based community organizer Saul Alinsky and Dr. James Allen Williams of
the Sociology Department, the latter of whose topic was "College—A Con-
veyor Belt to Conformity."[38] The often-satiric style of *The Rag* was lively
enough to garner attention in many sectors of the community; even Graves
Landrum conceded that it was truly an entertaining publication, "if you
weren't involved."[39]

But Ransom, unfortunately, as the living and breathing symbol of everything UT aspired to be, was yanked publicly into the fray. An episode
involving the so-called Texas Student League for Responsible Sexual Freedom, which advocated the abolition of laws regulating prostitution and
other sexual crimes, serves as an example of the various causes and issues
with which Ransom more and more had to contend on a weekly and sometimes daily basis. There had certainly been nothing like this at Sewanee,
at Yale, or even in earlier epochs at UT. An administrator had few prec-
edents (and almost too much advice) in trying to negotiate areas of agreement where common sense and established behavior had formerly provided
guidelines. As *Time* magazine reported in March 1966 (in a vastly different
kind of article from the one that had earlier extolled Ransom's effectiveness, this one spicily titled "The Free-Sex Movement"), "The Texas Student
League for Responsible Sexual Freedom has 18 members so far, led by Senior Tom Maddux. He contends that limiting birth control pills to married
women is 'ridiculous,' society's attitude toward homosexuality is 'hypocriti-
cal,' and laws against sodomy should be 'stricken or radically changed.'" A
photograph of nude students cavorting in a Berkeley apartment accompanied *Time*'s article.

At UT the issue revolved around the group's demand that it be given
official recognition by the university. On March 15, 1966, sixteen days after
the formation of the Texas Student League for Responsible Sexual Freedom, Chancellor Ransom issued a strong letter rebuking the student group
and denying it the status it had sought. Graves Landrum testified that this
was not a hard decision for Ransom to make. "He looked upon these things

as disturbing impediments to the educational purpose of the University."[40] Ransom acted a day after State Senator Grady Hazlewood of Amarillo attacked the University of Texas for allowing the group to operate on the campus at all. Noting that it had chapters at UCLA, Stanford, and Berkeley, he vowed: "I will never vote for another appropriation for the university as long as that group of queer-minded social misfits remains officially approved to operate on the university campus, using public facilities to wage a campaign to abolish our criminal laws."[41] The League then appealed to W. W. Heath, Chairman of the Board of Regents, "for reinstatement as a University of Texas approved organization."[42]

Dozens of responses poured into Ransom's office, nearly all of them concurring with one professor who wrote to "strongly support your position and action" and to assure Ransom "that practically all faculty members in the Grad. School of Business feel as I do."[43] A letter backing Ransom arrived from a faculty member in the Department of Geology, and an associate professor of chemistry expressed regret that "the campus and the community as a whole have been subjected to an increasingly anarchistic and petulant attack by various groups. The firm exercise of proper authority will, I hope, rectify this. . . . I extend to you my wholehearted support."[44] Two of the three professors who had initially sponsored the League retreated from its demands at a press conference on March 16, indicating that they "personally disapproved of actions of the League and/or others in distributing the material."[45]

H. J. "Doc" Blanchard, the State Senator from Lubbock, reminded Ransom that the "Cross case" had already focused "unfavorable" attention upon UT and that the "conduct of students" at UC Berkeley—site of the incendiary Free Speech Movement in 1964—and at UCLA "is a disgrace and a matter of national concern."[46] In the James Cross murder case in 1965, two young female UT students, stopping by a male acquaintance's apartment after arriving in Austin, had been lured into accepting his invitation to use his bathroom shower. Their gruesome murders had drawn attention to the increasingly casual social style of co-ed apartments and dormitories, and made manifest the end of the *in loco parentis* era of supervision of students at universities. Many state residents were puzzled or even outraged by this recent and monumental shift in mores at the state university they loved and about which they felt so proprietary in part because of Ransom's outreach efforts.

Regents chairman W. W. Heath issued a press release on Friday, April 1, 1966, following an afternoon session of the Board, stating in part that "no administrative Head has ever possessed the complete confidence of his

Board to a higher degree than does Chancellor Harry Ransom."[47] But the controversy dragged on even after the League seemed to be soft-pedaling their effort for formal university recognition.

In the middle of that flap, a newly formed Texas Students for Free Speech demanded an end to the censorship of any material published in student publications or distributed on campus. "No person or committee . . . should decide what students are to be allowed to publish, distribute, or read," declared the resolution. Another part of the document asked the university to cease its practice of approving organizations and to allow any organization composed from the "academic community" to use university facilities.[48] Clearly the mood of the campus was reconfiguring, and a chancellor merely dedicated to improving university budgets, faculty morale, library facilities, student programs, and public relations was no longer going to be seen as adequately engaged in the truly vital issues by activist factions of the students, faculty, and community.

Ransom's earlier speeches and letters within the past two years had expressed optimism about and urged patience with the so-called campus radicals leading protests across the nation, and had indicated that people should not view their goals—but only their methods—as being much different from the concerns of earlier generations of students. But now in 1966 he faced pronouncements and decisions of a more committed and less trusting (and far less respectful) element than he had ever encountered as a student, teacher, or administrator. The ordeal of these repeated confrontations would tax his energies, slow his agenda for the university, and ultimately wound his chancellorship. To the state as a whole and to the regents, particularly Frank C. Erwin, Jr., he could no longer give the impression of rather effortlessly grasping and answering the deepest needs of his campus, and of pointing the faculty and students toward the highest possible ideals of the academic enterprise. The dawning age of student revolt permitted no one his former status of unruffled decorum and unquestioned wisdom— not even Chancellor Harry Huntt Ransom.

Still, Ransom continued his upbeat messages. As the guest on a Wednesday night television program, *Men and Ideas,* he converted part of the televised interview into a tribute to librarians who are "understanding," helpful, courageous, interested in books, and become "everything from technicians to tele-communication experts." He attributed the strength of his own education to a librarian who had given him the run of a library when he was only seven years old.[49]

However, careful not to seem overly partial to any one facet of the university operation, even its library system, Ransom took pains to convey his admiration for the College of Engineering, among other technical fields he supported generously. Addressing a banquet celebrating the completion of a three-week Conference on Engineering for Executives, Ransom proposed a future conference devoted to engineering as an essential force in American culture. He observed that engineers had recently advanced many aspects of culture, mentioning language laboratories, microfilm, and instantaneous communication. The future would depend on engineers staying aware of their responsibility to society, he said. "The agencies of discovery are going to have to join us in updating the practicalities of living."[50] Dr. John J. McKetta, the dean of the College of Engineering who introduced Chancellor Ransom at that banquet, had developed an ever-increasing respect for this administrator whose own background, interests, and training were so remote from disciplines like engineering. "He was on our side all the time," he later said of Ransom. "He appreciated the sciences and engineering, and only lamented that he couldn't understand more about their discoveries." And Ransom had a knack with words that McKetta admired: "'Here is the gist of the subject,' he would say. 'Now let me dilate this.'"[51]

Enthusiastic approbation for Ransom held firm around the state. On May 30, 1966, Austin College in Sherman, Texas, presented Harry Ransom with a doctorate of humane letters because "your vision, forthrightness, and discernment have contributed greatly to the growing prestige of Texas letters." Ransom delivered the commencement address that night.[52]

As rocky as 1966 had been during the spring, that summer a completely unthinkable event ripped apart the peace of the University of Texas main campus. Shortly before noon on August 1, 1966, a swelteringly hot day, twenty-five-year-old Charles J. Whitman, a UT senior architectural engineering student and ex-Marine from Florida, took the elevator of the Main Building to the twenty-eighth floor observation deck, armed with a scope-sighted .30 caliber semi-automatic carbine and backed by a formidable supply of additional weapons, ammunition, food, and water. He then began a methodical killing spree, targeting the minuscule human beings walking about below him on the campus and in front of the businesses lining the west side of Guadalupe Street. A total of fourteen people died from their wounds, and thirty-two others were injured, many of them very seriously. Whitman would not stop his deadly fire on pedestrians for nearly an hour and a half, until two police officers reached the observation deck, confronted the gunman, and killed him with shotgun blasts. Police would later discover that Whitman had also killed his wife and his mother, making a total of sixteen murdered. It would be one of the worst mass shootings in U.S. history, and the first large-scale slaying to take place on a university campus. A book and then a movie depicted how an ordinary summer day had been turned into a nightmarish scenario of sudden death. In some respects the campus community would bear the scars of this event through the remainder of the twentieth century.

For Ransom, the connection with this crime was immediate and proximate. He was upstairs on the sixteenth floor with Mrs. Hudspeth when the shooting commenced, and they both stayed there as the drama unfolded above and below them. He had access to a police radio and could follow the efforts to halt the rampage. Graves Landrum was on the first floor, sitting at a desk looking out an east window. For a time Landrum supposed the invisible missiles raising puffs of concrete that looked like chalk dust and the reeling, hiding students were parts of yet another staged student demonstration on the mall. Then he saw a man lying nearby, holding his arm and looking down at his own blood. "My God," Landrum realized. "That man's been shot!" Next he noticed that bullets were hitting Gregory Gym. He reached for the telephone and called upstairs, learning that Ransom had access to a PAX (internal campus) line, but that his Centrex (outside line) line did not work. Since Landrum's Southwestern Bell telephone line functioned, he could relay Ransom's calls to various parties who needed to know what was happening.[53] The chancellor and his staff were in shock. Unable to leave the building, they could only listen to news of the mounting toll. The first regents to reach the scene were a shaken W. W. Heath, who came to Austin by airplane, and Frank C. Erwin, Jr., who arrived after the killer was dead. Huddling with Erwin, Landrum, and Amy Jo Long at the close of a ghastly day, Ransom said over and over again that Whitman "was *not* a Texan," as though the fact somehow consoled or explained.[54] Local announcer Neal Spelce delivered a national CBS-TV report so effectively that Ransom was not required to give an immediate national interview, a great relief to him. In a joint statement issued with Heath, Ransom praised the police and UT staff for their bravery in assisting the wounded during the ordeal. "It's incredible and it was heart-lifting, the way people helped," said Ransom at a subsequent news conference. He dismissed classes for the following day, Tuesday, and arranged for the official flags to fly at half-mast.[55]

There were many long-term consequences, as might be expected. One of them was almost inevitable: the observation deck atop the Tower was closed temporarily while the campus recovered some of its equilibrium. But Ransom's inclination was to resume the illusion of normalcy as soon as possible, and he agreed to reopen the facility several weeks after the calamity.[56] Equally characteristic of Ransom's thinking was the fact that UT soon thereafter expanded its psychological counseling for students, establishing a twenty-four-hour telephone hotline staffed by university personnel that would receive more than half a million calls during the next quarter century.[57]

The toll went even beyond the lives and families so deeply affected by Whitman's monstrous deed. The entire state of Texas winced under the glare of the news cameras covering another hideous act of violence that followed within only a few years the assassination in Dallas of President John Fitzgerald Kennedy. For Austinites specifically, it would mean putting up with decades of visitors asking at once to see the infamous "sniper's tower" before showing any interest in the monumental achievements of the university itself—its magnificent library, innovative faculty, selectively chosen students, awesome athletic teams, sprawling campus, and countless awards.

As things settled down, at a Board of Regents meeting at the Shamrock Hilton in Houston before the Bluebonnet Bowl football game on Saturday, December 17, 1966, Preston Shirley, chairman of the University Development Board, would present Chancellor Ransom with a $1,000 gold watch because of his "outstanding dedication, devotion, and effectiveness." However, Frank C. Erwin, Jr., ominously, would choose that same meeting as the place to recommend that the university administrators study the feasibility of splitting the ballooning 16,000-student College of Arts and Sciences into smaller divisions, either as two schools (Arts, Sciences) or a number of colleges.[58] A showdown over this drastic proposal would loom on the horizon.

The year 1966 still had one more important and saddening development in store for Chancellor Ransom. On Thanksgiving eve he sat reflectively at his desk looking out the window across a dreary, deserted mall. Before him lay a dark walnut, glass-lined cigarette box for his Parliaments, presented "In Grateful Recognition of Your Significant Contributions to the University of Texas Medical School at San Antonio." On the nearby table rested another cigarette box, also with a glass interior, made of Philippine mahogany. Visible as well was a commendation from the U.S. Air Force "for rendering meritorious service . . . from December 1962 to December 1965 as a member of the Air Force ROTC Advisory Panel to the Department of the Air Force."[59] None of these mementos was capable of cheering the chancellor on this long evening. He smoked and mused at his typewriter as he prepared a personal note to W. W. Heath. From time to time he paused to read the statement Heath had distributed to the Board of Regents on November 5. "I have resigned as Chairman of the Board of Regents," he announced there. Heath explained that "business and professional commitments in the months ahead make it impossible for me to give this vast University System the time required of the Chairman." He devoted a separate paragraph "to express my special thanks to Chancellor Harry Ransom and to his gracious wife. Without their unwavering support and their personal friendship with my wife and me, I could not and would not have continued in this office a second term. I am proud that I am the only Regent now on this Board who originally participated in the selection of Dr. Ransom as head of this great System. I have been asked by many the question, 'Of what official action are you most proud?' My reply is, 'My motion in El Paso in 1960 to elect Dr. Harry Ransom as head of this great University System.' There is no doubt in my mind that he is the greatest educational leader anywhere."[60]

Now Ransom, writing to Heath personally, poured out his gratitude: "I have innumerable things to thank you for: most of all, for your friendship. For candid advice. For generous encouragement. For your willingness to listen. For understanding Hazel and me, and our joint concern about the University. . . . For understanding my limitations as an 'administrator'—something I did not plan to be or expect to become. For giving me the most rewarding months of all my thirty-one years at the University. . . . If I can still type when I retire or resign, that is the chapter of educational history I will write."[61] This was his most explicit reference to any contemplation of retirement since 1949, when he had noted "1965/1969" as possible retirement years.

A new Chairman of the Board of Regents took office on December 1 and announced a reshuffling of committee assignments. He wrote his fellow regents of his "deep gratitude for the honor and responsibility which you have imposed on me. I am not unaware that nearly every person who has ever attended the University has an earnest desire to serve on the Board of Regents."[62] This new, opinionated chairman was Frank C. Erwin, Jr.

FIFTEEN

PREROGATIVES AND PROTESTS

Gradually, almost imperceptibly, Harry Ransom was accruing his first set of persistent negatives. A miscellaneous group of detractors had effected an alteration in his status, not among his immense core of admirers, but with those dissatisfied with the directions in which UT was moving. Obviously to a certain extent it was not precisely *him* they were after; he simply embodied (in their eyes) rank, protocol, tradition, privilege, power—in other words, the "establishment"—that the younger professors of the 1960s and their students instinctively targeted. He was not the first or by any means the only university administrator of that generation to endure public abuse—Roger Heyns of UC Berkeley and numerous other authority figures suffered vastly more slings and arrows from Vietnam-era student demonstrators and their sympathizers. But still it seemed an unwelcome reward for his years of single-minded service to the ideal of the university, a mean-spiritedness he could hardly fathom. He tried to leave behind him each incident and snide attack, but they had begun to accumulate. The chancellor, once almost untouchable, had become a mere fallible mortal to sizable dissident sectors within his constituency.

It might be said, of course, that he was simply discovering the price of becoming a legend. Chancellor Ransom's title and reputation even got turned into literary material. One example originated from William Burford, an assistant professor of English at UT Austin who had resigned and then unavailingly sought Ransom's assistance in rescinding his resignation. Subsequently Burford wrote a bruising poem, "The Chancellor," and collected it in a volume published by W. W. Norton & Company in 1966. "He purses his lips . . . Something does not quite please him today," opened the poem, which went on to refer to "that close-clipped bullet head," "rising authority," and reliance on subordinates "who do what he thinks." Though Ransom is not named, the poem's title, its allusion to "past days . . . when they laughed that he might be chosen," and Ransom's well-known habit of puckering his mouth when concentrating guaranteed that the verse would be passed around campus among those who had reason, real or fancied, to resent Ransom's rise to eminence.[1]

Another, more daring foray against Ransom's formerly sacrosanct dignity had appeared in print in 1961. The wife of a member of the UT English Department wrote a *roman à clef* murder mystery, *Close His Eyes,* under a pseudonym ("Olivia Dwight")—a secret identity quickly deciphered because she used her maiden name.[2] In *Close His Eyes,* assistant professor John Dryden is hired by "a large university in the Middle West with about twenty thousand students and a damp climate." Upon introduction to its president, Horace Wooten, Dryden sizes up a man "a bit shorter than I am and much solider. He had . . . a square, heavy face, very closely shaved, with a small, firm mouth and a consciously shrewd expression." Dryden quickly learns that the president has instituted a lecture series. "He gets as many famous men as he can to come here and talk. . . . It's supposed to be good for you, rubbing elbows with greatness." President Wooten's administrative assistant, Miss Crabbe, a woman only four feet tall, sits in a revolving chair, her metal crutches leaning against the wall. "Her legs were useless." In earlier years Wooten "had been an authority on Victorian poetry. . . . and had suddenly been chosen to be the new president of the University at the beginning of its uranium expansion (or explosion)." Dryden deduces that "the friendliness forced on him by his job wasn't natural to him. . . . If he wasn't naturally the solitary contemplative type, he was definitely unsocial. Misanthropic, even." At the novel's climax, Miss Crabbe, "spiteful, petty, and tyrannical," kills herself out of love for Wooten.

According to a professor of communication, "*Close His Eyes* spread like wildfire through the campus." Miss Crabbe, with her severe disability, seemed to conflate Mrs. Hudspeth's dedication to Ransom and her husband's crippled, bed-ridden condition—and Mrs. Hudspeth was "truly crushed" that the book had emerged from an apparently ungrateful English Department. The ridiculing novel had the effect of diminishing the apparent invincibility of the Ransom-Hudspeth combination.[3]

Ransom also drew the enmity of an even more bitingly witty and skillful writer. Nearly a decade earlier, Hazard Adams, an assistant professor of English whom Ransom had recruited from Cornell as one of his bright young men (and who had earned a B.A. degree from Princeton University and taken a Ph.D. at the University of Washington in 1953), grew utterly disenchanted with Ransom and the entire university.[4] When he came to write a satirical work of fiction, *The Horses of Instruction*—taking the title from a line in William Blake's *Proverbs of Hell* ("The tigers of wrath are wiser than the horses of instruction," presumably seeing himself as one of the tigers)—Adams scattered Harry Ransom's mannerisms and endeavors through the novel, particularly in the character of "Henry Hastings, the Fastest Dean in the West," jocularly known as Hasty Hank Hastings.[5] "He wore black horn-rimmed glasses. His face was not deeply lined, his complexion fair." He wore "a mandarin smile," and "spoke rapidly in a clipped way," but was plagued by "natural shyness." Hastings's university "had built up a certain notoriety for seeking out the papers and libraries of almost anyone involved in modern letters." Dean Hastings, too, has inaugurated a lecture series, this one called the Critique of Culture Series. "The older professors . . . had been told—and not too obliquely—by Dean Hastings that the series was for the younger people and to stay in the background." Those on the Series Committee call themselves "Henry's Hasty Boys."

One of Hastings's grandiose plans is "a journal of culture and the arts." His loyal secretary Mrs. Bolyard (called by some "Old Mama Bolyard") protects him "with a vengeance"; she is his accomplice in frustrating the hopes of those whom he inveigled into expecting immediate publication or eventual hiring. He has a "favorite expression," according to a character named Jason Talbot: "Let me parenthesize for a moment." His "vague enthusiasm coupled with a sentimental desire to please" necessarily "made 'no' an obscene word." In the end, the dean becomes a university vice president. "But with the younger men, where he most desired to succeed, he had failed."

In his better moods Ransom could construe these gibes, typical of the satiric 1960s, as being tributes of a sort; the University of Texas had grown so large, rich, and complex that New York City publishers had become receptive to books and poems mocking its administrators and faculty. This was essentially the first generation in which Texas public officials, including even figures in higher education, attracted enough national attention to be perceived as subjects worthy of ridicule and exaggeration.[6]

More troublesome, because more directly involved with Harry Ransom's agendas as chancellor, was the small but growing minority of faculty and staff members disillusioned with his modes of administration. Such cavils had been festering for several years. In 1964, Horace Busby, a UT graduate and longtime speechwriter for Lyndon B. Johnson, had sent a confidential note to a person awaiting word from Ransom about former UT President Joseph R. Smiley's qualifications to be considered for another post: "This is gratuitous and presumptuous of me to intervene, but I think you should know that among Harry's best friends his habit of delayed replies—or non-replies—to bothersome detail is legendary. . . . Those who wish Harry Ransom well, as I do, also wish that he would learn to reply to requests for information as he always promises so earnestly to do but so seldom does."[7] Betty Gibbons, who had worked for Joseph Smiley until he went to Colorado, resolutely declined Ransom's offer to take her into the chancellor's office. She sent him a blisteringly critical letter explaining how much she disliked the way Ransom conducted his office, and Ransom replied in strong terms, for him.[8] She was, however, expressing the opinion of a number of staff workers who had observed his laissez-faire style of management. Various observers told Joan Simpson Burns "what a haphazard administrator he was."[9] Those he had thus disappointed usually wanted more day-to-day managerial direction; they disliked his tendency to allow staff members to discover their own assignments, methods, and schedules.

And yet Ransom could indisputably motivate people, and his adherents were as yet legion, unfazed by these cavils, and far more vocal than his detractors. He still had firm footing throughout the state and on the campus. The Chancellor's Council, for instance, a group of dedicated University of Texas supporters he organized as a source of special funds for crucial projects, numbered 165 founding members by January 1967, including Dan C. Williams of Dallas, Mr. and Mrs. Lloyd W. Birdwell, Alfred A. Knopf, Mrs. A. J. Oppenheimer, C. B. Smith, Sr., and Dr. Edward L. Tinker. Each had pledged to contribute $10,000.[10] Whatever else might be said, Ransom was also able to point to impressive university growth. In 1956 UT Austin had awarded 130 doctoral degrees; by 1966 it was conferring 350 Ph.D.s. In 1956 private donors had contributed $3,000,000; ten years later, spurred by the Chancellor's Council, they gave $9,000,000. Only two UT departments had been nationally ranked in 1956, whereas twenty-one held this status in 1966. Thirty-five endowed professorships and chairs were now appointable; there had been none only a decade earlier. (President Peter T. Flawn would later build on Ransom's achievement in this area and increase these endowed posts exponentially.) The Permanent Endowment, known as the Permanent University Fund, was nearly $200,000,000 greater than in 1956, amounting to $478,000,000.[11] *Life* magazine pronounced the University of Texas to have been "pushed along by another man with a dream. Harry Huntt Ransom, a heavy, bespectacled man of graceful intellect. . . . is making it an important university nationally. Ransom is rare, an administrator with a classical sense, and he believes that research facilities for the humanities—books and libraries—should match the laboratories for the sciences. For 10 years he has pushed this dream and in that time he has assembled one of the world's great collections on the 20th Century."[12]

Hazel Ransom, too, continued to score points with the press. Her formal portrait—she stood, slim and demure in a scalloped two-piece dress and pearl jewelry, with one hand resting on an upholstered chair— appeared beside a flattering feature article in the January 22, 1967, issue of the *Austin American-Statesman*. Hazel there reminisced laughingly that she had married Ransom "so they could be 'quiet and intellectual' together. But the long evenings in their library with the fire going rarely materialize. Instead, Chancellor and Mrs. Ransom are more likely to be entertaining 600 guests. . . . She may be hostess to faculty members one day, alumni the next, state officials the next, visiting dignitaries the next and . . . the next, anyone from Stravinsky to Erle Stanley Gardner."[13]

On the Austin campus, however, divisive issues were heating up in unforeseen ways. The presumed advantage of having a Texan in the White House was being offset by the mounting opposition to him among university students and professors. President Johnson's escalation of the Vietnam War elicited a large protest advertisement in the *Austin American-Statesman* on March 5, 1967, signed by 150 faculty members. Addressed to "Dear Mr. President," the letter reminded Johnson that "some of us lived in Austin when you were a resident here, and many of us expect to be here when you return. We address you as neighbors, past and future. . . . We strongly urge you to order an immediate halt to our bombing of North Vietnam." The co-chair of the faculty objectors was one of Ransom's recruits, Roger Shattuck.[14]

But this was a comparatively sedate form of dissent. On Friday, April 14, 1967, the UT chapter of Students for a Democratic Society (SDS) sponsored an appearance and speech by radical activist Stokely Carmichael, leader of the Student Nonviolent Coordinating Committee, prime minister of the Black Panther Party, and a national figure in both the "black power" and anti-war movements.[15] Suddenly the chancellor found himself embroiled in tumult even greater than what he had experienced during the preceding year.

Carmichael's appearance set the stage for heated struggles between the administration and the student activists. When SDS members defiantly scheduled an unauthorized campus rally for Sunday, April 23, Ransom interpreted it as a direct challenge to the normal regulations necessary for orderly meetings. He issued a public announcement prohibiting the SDS rally. "Any student organization deliberately ignoring this decision will be eliminated from the list of General Student Organizations," warned Ransom. "Students participating in such activities will be referred to a discipline committee. The University is a public institution, but the present administration will not allow this fact to be used as an excuse for flouting

FIGURE 15.1

Hazel Ransom as chancellor's wife, 1967 (?). Hazel Ransom, ever the charming hostess,
also devoted her life to the university. She would remain a very private person, but later
edited Harry Ransom's speeches and essays. Harry Ransom Humanities Research
Center, The University of Texas at Austin.

recognized authority by students or non-students on University property."[16] The move was unpopular among many students, even those not directly involved in the rally. One male student wrote plaintively from Brackenridge Hall to lament that "for nearly four years I admired your policies with regard to students on this campus. . . . I find that I have respected a ghost."[17]

The SDS group went ahead with an unauthorized on-campus Sunday rally to announce protest demonstrations during Vice President Hubert Humphrey's scheduled visit to Austin and his planned address at the State Capitol, whereupon Regents Chairman Frank C. Erwin, Jr., drove his burnt-orange Cadillac onto the campus and openly stood nearby during the speeches. Some of the students' placards read "Our Conscience Will Not Be Ransomed." Subsequently Ransom announced that charges would be filed against "certain students" for violating a chancellor's order, and a number of names were referred to a disciplinary committee. Robert S. Strauss, an attorney with Akin, Gump, Strauss, Hauer, and Feld of Dallas (and the future national Democratic Party chairman), sent a sympathetic letter to the *Daily Texan* editor: "I think Dr. Ransom's stand was proper and courageous. . . . I think this is the first letter I have ever written to an editor."[18] And Wales Madden, Jr., who had retired from the Board of Regents in 1965 and now practiced law in Amarillo, wrote: "Harry—I know these are tedious times for you. Frank & you have done an excellent job with the demonstration."[19]

Ransom's explanations, clarifications, and justifications of his action stretched into the next month.[20] His original order of April 22 banning unauthorized meetings had stressed that the "University of Texas has regularly encouraged the expression of student opinion." On May 2, seeking to stem criticism of his decree, he announced that he had appointed Professor Millard Ruud of the Law School to chair a faculty advisory committee that would examine the "legal aspects of issues now confronting the campus." Ransom attended a meeting of the Committee on Academic Freedom and Responsibility on May 1, at which he defended his policies.[21] On Wednesday, May 3, the chancellor's office issued a five-page "Statement of Chancellor Harry Ransom" responding to various accusations. In that document Ransom traced his legal authority for banning unauthorized campus rallies to the Rules and Regulations of the Board. "I am willing to stand on the record of my office from April 1, 1961, through May 2, 1967, as that record reflects my concern for freedom of opinion, freedom of expression, and freedom of action under law." The call for non-students to attend the rally showed "callous disregard . . . for the safety of those individual members of the University who have a right to use the campus on Sunday for their individual purposes. It was a clear proclamation that one group proposed to take over the campus."

Appealing for the return of decorum and good faith in campus dialogue, Ransom revealed that he had "received both at my home and my office specific threats of retaliation against me or my family if I prevented such meetings." He mentioned that he had "canceled participation in the President's Commission on White House Fellows, a national meeting . . . , and other appointments of first consequence to the University or me personally." Returning to the campus from sessions of the Association of American Universities, he said, he had found himself called upon by "more than fifty separate student, faculty, and civic groups" to discuss the situation. He insisted that the rules of the university had "taken into full account such national statements as that of the American Association of University Professors concerning academic freedom of students." He iterated his continuing support for "such spontaneous activities as Stump Speaking," provided that "it is approved through proper channels." Finally, Ransom called for the preservation of "common freedoms and joint responsibility," and the repudiation of "fear, recrimination, suspicion, falsehood, personal vilification, and callous self-interest which are now evident in some quarters." In his strongest language to date, Ransom avowed that he was "not willing to buy an illusion of local academic calm and tranquillity at the cost of flouting national, state, or local laws. I am not willing to demonstrate university freedom by flagrant violation of the University regulations and deliberately destructive incursions against the real purpose of academic freedom and responsibility."[22]

Confidential notes kept by a secretary during Ransom's report to the regents in May 1967 testify to the chaotic set of challenges he had faced. "I will make some swift and dangerous generalizations," he said in that meeting. "I think it is referable to something called Berkeley. It is not comparable with Austin, because Austin isn't Berkeley. We are faced with a real blessing in Austin with the State press and local press having been supportive in the best way by advertising sensationally only occasionally the happenings on this campus." For example, he noted, when he had visited Washington, D.C., "the *Washington Post* ran a special issue sneering at American University . . . in effect asking why don't these students raise a little hell?" After Stokely Carmichael's visit was announced, telephone calls to Ransom's office had claimed that Carmichael would not leave the campus alive. "I went to the FBI. . . . I was literally afraid something would happen to Stokely Carmichael and his staff. We let him stay here because the peace officers said we can control one spot but if you deny him, we will have an equal number of brush fires around the campus which we cannot control. Stokely Carmichael came late, made an extraordinarily dull talk, bored everyone to death, and left. I don't know what the response in SDS was to that flop." One regent asked, "How many professors do we have leading this show?" adding, "I don't see why we reward people who are going to be problems." Ransom admitted that some faculty members "will fight for an idea and forget the practicalities," but said, "if we start firing them, I would rather face the SDS." Erwin expressed exasperation: "The Board has no idea how much this administration has been demoralized for three months. Why should we pay people of this quality and ability to spend their time in meetings to decide how to handle SDS?" Regent and corporate executive William H. Bauer said, "I think Harry and this group have handled it beautifully. It could not have been handled better."[23]

The end of spring semester classes (an event welcomed by college administrators across the land in 1967) abated the SDS acrimony, but Ransom had other matters to occupy his mind. At the same regents' meeting in May, Frank C. Erwin, Jr., had again raised his idea of creating "three identical" Arts and Sciences colleges. The matter had come up in a discussion about the difficulty of providing adequate academic counseling for students in a single college of such size. Vice Chancellor for Academic Affairs Hackerman had commented that within Arts and Sciences "there are 5,000–6,000 kids who do not know what they want to do and don't fit in and they are the ones who give us the trouble." Ransom expressed skepticism about the hope that mere counseling might stem student unrest. Mainly, he said, with the growth of apartment complexes, there is "the fact that these kids no longer live in the university. They are living out in the world."[24]

The realm of book lovers still offered Ransom a coveted refuge. "I am glad to be in Pittsburgh, talking about books," he began in a speech to the Pittsburgh Bibliophiles on May 18, 1967. He centered his remarks on the book collection accomplishments of the University of Texas, praising his predecessors. "Neither the depression nor discouragement . . . dampened the spirit of Professor R. H. Griffith and his associate, Miss Fannie Ratchford," Ransom testified. He dismissively referred to himself as "the Chancellor of Secondhand Books" bedeviled by "many of the bookish sins." He lauded as a blessing the nine-member Board of Regents, whose "attitudes . . . have varied from strenuous enthusiasm to patient acceptance of what seemed to them more often than not inscrutable eccentricity." He recalled one regent who finally declared, "Well, incunabula [books printed before 1501] seem to be what I can do without, but if the University can't, I second the motion to approve the purchase."

Among attendant problems, Ransom mentioned in Pittsburgh the zeal of scholars who demand "the day after any acquisition is announced . . . instant and exclusive access to all the collection's materials." He also disputed the "mindless argument . . . that prices have risen because of the Texas program." As Bertram Rota once commented, and Ransom here repeated, 'There is always an underbidder.'" (In other words, it takes more than one bidder to drive up a price.) Ransom said he foresaw a future consisting of "a world well populated by learned people who believe that the real book is a mere curiosity and the electric or electronic device the only true recorder and dispenser of knowledge."[25]

Such prophecies about technological innovations by no means betokened a lessening of the acquisitive spirit Ransom had instilled in the HRC. The *New York Times* reported on November 22, 1967, how, merely by "raising his eyebrows," the irrepressible Lew David Feldman, owner of the House of El Dieff and agent for Ransom's HRC, had purchased $19,200 worth of W. Somerset Maugham's effects from his villa on the French Riviera that were auctioned in London at Sotheby's. Feldman had bid on every manuscript by Maugham and every book from his library.[26]

Other diversions in 1967 took Ransom's mind away from the acrimony of campus protests. In the summer, at a special stockholders meeting in St. Louis, Ransom was elected to the Board of Directors of Southwestern Bell Telephone Company. That same year Ransom was initiated into the Alpha Rho chapter of Alpha Phi Omega, a national service fraternity.[27] Another success was the landing of Sigmund Koch, formerly of the Ford Foundation, for one of the "university professorships" that Ransom had created to stimulate interdisciplinary studies and liberate gifted individuals from departmental controls; John Silber, Donald Weismann, Donald S. Carne-Ross, and William Arrowsmith already held such unfettered appointments. According to one envious description, Koch "got an endowed chair there, a university-wide professorship, no departmental duties, collaborative support from three departments—fine arts, psychology, and philosophy—[could] pick his own students and his own courses, make what public lectures he wants to, go away on his own research, nine-month contract each year, tenure, big salary— . . . better than Harvard in the humanities and social sciences."[28] Silber, acting as a go-between, wrote to Ransom on June 14, 1967: "Your letter to Koch is perfect—Harry at his very best. . . . I think you'll get Koch. Unless he has far greater immunity than the rest of us, he's been ransomized."[29]

Ransom wrote a personal letter to Frank C. Erwin, Jr., on July 21, 1967, urging that professional librarians be removed from their present personnel classification and be listed in a separate category similar to that devised for administrators. "It will do a good deal for morale and recruitment," he wrote. He also cautioned Erwin "that the almost completely public context of future meetings may require private and gentle suggestions by the Chairman that . . . every comment had better be considered publishable. We've narrowly escaped hammering by the press and broadcasters on personal, offhand remarks in committee meetings."[30] (Erwin's own off-the-cuff sallies had probably been the most inflammatory.) At the next regents meeting, on July 28–29, the Board officially confirmed the final name of a new program: The Lyndon Baines Johnson School of Public Affairs.

Consequential events of various sorts were occurring with a whirlwind intensity. June Carr Erwin, whom Frank Erwin had married in 1954, lost her battle with cancer in September 1967. When Erwin suffered this bereavement (he never remarried), the last link holding him to his law practice and keeping him out of an almost completely political life dropped away. He became a regular sight at the Forty Acres Club or the Quorum Club, often staying late into the night to drink Scotch and talk with friends and acquaintances.[31] Norman Hackerman, for one, thought that Erwin became "more despotic" after June Carr Erwin's death. Whereas before Erwin had been "bright" and "rational," with "lots of ideas" but "willing to debate and even *concede* if he got the impression you knew what you were talking about," subsequently he was "tougher to deal with," a man who "wouldn't brook any interference," someone inclined toward "arguments rather than debates." Hackerman doubted that Ransom enjoyed this emerging side of Erwin, since "'arguments' call for truculence, unlike 'debates.'"[32] Meanwhile, the death of the dean of the College of Arts and Sciences, J. Alton Burdine, suddenly opened up that position during the month of September, when Erwin was preoccupied with June's illness, death, and grief over her death. John Silber, whom Ransom had talked into declining a handsome offer to chair the Purdue University Philosophy Department in 1965, accepted this deanship.[33]

But the shift that truly startled the campus was a recommendation by Harry Ransom himself, acted upon by the Board of Regents' Committee on Administrative Organization on Saturday, October 7, 1967, that the office of president for the Austin campus should be reestablished. Ransom had been doing double-duty as Chancellor and Acting President (at a salary of $42,000), but under his own proposal he would yield the duties he had held as chief administrative officer of the Main Campus. He pointed out that in the past six years the System had grown from eight to twelve institutions, the faculty and staff had swelled from 10,300 to 18,800, and student enrollment System-wide had mounted from 25,000 to approximately 53,000. Frank C. Erwin, Jr., greeted the motion by declaring that "Harry Ransom has undoubtedly had greater and more significant influence on the academic development of the University at Austin than any other individual in history." Erwin added that "relief from day-by-day administrative detail is essential if the University system is to capitalize on Dr. Ransom's magnificent leadership on the wider issues confronting higher education in the state."[34] English professor Robert Wilson would recall an impression around campus that Ransom might welcome the chance to move out of the line of fire inasmuch as police had to be posted in the stairwells of the Main Building to evict student demonstrators trying to break into Ransom's office.[35] Numerous people logically assumed that Ransom anticipated with relief the arrival of a president who could function as a buffer between campus protesters and the chancellor.[36]

In effect this development would return the administration to the separate chancellor-president arrangement prevailing prior to Joseph R. Smiley's resignation as president in 1963. (Even during Smiley's term in office, Ransom had in truth yielded few of the prerogatives he had previously enjoyed as president in 1960 and 1961.) A ten-member committee would select the eighteenth president, Dr. Norman Hackerman (1912–2007), before 1967 ended. Ransom explained that he would remain "in charge of general budgetary, developmental, and planning activities. I will also continue in direct charge of programs of the Academic Center, the Humanities Research Center, special library collections, and the *Texas Quarterly*."[37]

No written communications seem to exist regarding the actual background of Ransom's request for reassignment, but it is hard to avoid the assumption that Frank C. Erwin, Jr.'s, wishes were involved. Even if Ransom had come up with the idea of relinquishing the presidency on his own, Erwin presumably could without much effort have dissuaded him from pursuing the request. Whatever the case, the net result of Ransom's withdrawal from the Austin campus meant that he no longer held day-to-day authority over the campus he had served with such dedication, and that Frank Erwin, a frequent visitor to that campus, and the other regents now had an opportunity to choose a new president who would run its daily operations and deal with student disruptions.[38]

With this speculation in the air, Ransom's annual report to the General Faculty on October 19, 1967, his tenth and last as president, afforded unprecedented drama. He began his remarks by recreating for them the "completely free," "furious," and "sometimes irrelevant" General Faculty meetings he had witnessed when he first arrived at UT in 1935. He waxed

FIGURE 15.2

President Lyndon Baines Johnson and Regent Frank C. Erwin, Jr., date unknown. Frank C. Erwin, Jr., served on the Board of Regents from 1963 until 1975, and was its chairman from 1966 to 1971. He frequently visited the Main Campus and, according to numerous observers, closely oversaw university affairs. He gained many admirers for this degree of daily involvement, but just as many detractors. Margaret Berry, *UT Pictorial History*, 102, Center for American History, The University of Texas at Austin.

nostalgic in recalling the "verbal pyrotechnics" of physics professor William Tyler Mather, English professor J. Frank Dobie, chemical engineering professor Eugene P. Schoch, English professor Robert Adger Law, engineering professor Thomas U. Taylor, law professor Ira Polk Hildebrand, English professor R. C. Stephenson, history professor Milton R. Gutsch, Greek professor William J. Battle, English professor Hanson Tufts Parlin, "and many others." These articulate debaters, Ransom said, intrinsically knew "what the University community was." Praising the university's spirit of "tolerance and toleration," he called for it to retain "the ability to live with tension."[39]

The *Dallas Times Herald* reported that "Harry Huntt Ransom departed the University of Texas presidency this week with no pomp and little ceremony." Reporter Ann Watson mentioned that "some observers see a possible personality conflict between Ransom and the present chairman of the board of regents, Frank C. Erwin, Jr. Erwin, an Austin resident, has taken an unusually active role in university affairs. He spoke to student demonstrators at mass protests last spring." The *Times Herald* article also alluded to charges by some students that Erwin, a National Democratic Committeeman from Texas, had been anxious to thwart demonstrations against the visiting Vice President Hubert Humphrey so as "to prevent embarrassment to President Johnson in his home state."[40] Linguistics professor Robert D. King, later Dean of the College of Liberal Arts, witnessed an instance when Erwin stepped forward to speak at one of the anti–Vietnam War rallies. Erwin told the students about his military credentials from World War II and "then he said, basically, that no, the University would not be doing whatever it was the protesters wanted it to do. Then he just walked off. Walked off the South Mall. That was Frank Erwin: say it straight and get out."[41]

Ransom now found his duties considerably streamlined. He was no longer responsible, among other things, for chairing the General Faculty and making the annual report; representing the campus to the regents on budgetary matters; overseeing the Advisory Committee on Policy; communicating with the Student Cabinet; conferring with deans, departmental chairmen, committees, and other groups from the faculty and staff; consulting with students and student groups on matters relating to regulations; or meeting with alumni groups. He made a list of these "major exclusions" on November 1 for Acting President Norman Hackerman, and the tone seemed regretful. ("The most difficult problem will be equating Austin with Arlington and El Paso. . . . I will not be in Austin so regularly as before.")[42]

On November 30, 1967, Ransom had the satisfaction of announcing, with Frank C. Erwin, Jr., and Joe M. Dealey, a new award recognizing "persons who have excelled in voluntarily assisting advancement of The University of Texas System and have demonstrated concern for the principles of higher education generally." It was to be named the Santa Rita Award in honor of the first oil well brought in on Permanent University Fund lands on May 28, 1923, a development that had changed the possibilities for higher education in Texas. Thus far oil and gas production had yielded approximately $500 million for the Permanent University Fund, an endowment invested and whose income was divided between the University of Texas System (two-thirds) and the Texas A&M University System (one-third). Now an award—one to be presented occasionally when individuals deserved to be honored—carried the name of this fortuitous gusher that had heralded the golden era over which Ransom had presided.[43]

SIXTEEN

A CHANCELLOR'S PROPHECIES

Always an admittedly "private" couple, Harry and Hazel Ransom enjoyed other personal diversions besides their drives through the Texas countryside and weekends at the small ranch house in the Hill Country southwest of Austin. For one thing, Ransom continued to write his surprisingly bold, often whimsical poems. Hazel called these "his sincere, unpompous view of his total world," theorizing that "he wrote for himself . . . to relieve tedium, to explode an impatience, to exercise his risibles, and sometimes to express a deep sentiment." Ransom modestly said that he hoped his "verse" might attain the relationship to poetry that "a personal letter sometimes bears to the essay."[1] The titles of these poems suggest the patterns of his travels, studies, and concerns: "War Correspondent," "Ward 37," "Soldier's Lent," "City Morgue," "Reflecting Pool, Lincoln Memorial," "Main Street," "Autumn Remembered," "Separation." He had submitted a few poems to newspapers, magazines, and arts journals during his younger years, but most of his efforts went unpublished during his lifetime.[2]

One of Hazel's favorites,[3] "Possessions," alludes to Austin and lists sights that stir the poet's deepest reverence:

> I have owned beauty momentarily— . . .
> Lines of type, new cast from matrix—hot
> And shining words in clean reverse of sense— . . .
> Green-gray aging of a fieldstone fence,
> Orange blossoms after rain at dawn,
> An air by Thomas Moore on Liffey's bridge, . . .
> Impudent clover sprouting on the lawn,
> New-minted aspen leaves on Poudre's ridge,
> My stubby bucket bumping down the well,
> Two London hawkers crying pennyware,

Skygoing violet on Mount Bonnell,
And wooded roads that climb hills, anywhere.

A poem titled "Frontier Museum" meditates: "We brought prim order out of old wild living; / . . . The spinning wheel is polished, ready, threaded . . . / Even the longhorn spoons are sterilized. / No trace of years appears upon the labels, / We note their pristine wording as we pass; / The lighting's indirect upon the tables . . . / The bright estate of muskets under glass." Another poem, "To Every Man a Heath," echoes Ransom's conversations with J. Frank Dobie about an individual's need for "that eternal part / of every man, a heath / owned by the heart." In another mood, Ransom's "Homecoming" advises the reader not to "believe we pass this way no more. / We come again, but it is night-time then; / and then, for us, no light behind the glass, / no latch out at the door."[4]

Another outlet was Ransom's steady stream of small pen-and-ink doodles and sketches, sometimes of such quality that his secretaries quietly preserved them. Typically they consisted of four or five lines loosely suggesting an animal, mythical or real, a flower, a face, a figure, sometimes a landscape. He adorned his notes, drafts, and schedules with these Thurberesque decorations.[5]

Even in his disengaged role as chancellor, having given up the combined office of president, Ransom could not escape the pressures of periodic political convulsions on the Main Campus, and both the university and the Chancellor's Office had to operate in the ensuing years on two levels simultaneously—a lofty reaching for large goals, and a week-by-week scramble for effective stratagems and legally defensible positioning vis-à-vis demonstrations and accusations by student activists. A column by commentator Jimmy Banks that appeared in the March 1, 1968, issue of the *Dallas Morning News, Houston Post,* and *Fort Worth Star-Telegram* inveighed against the disrespect shown President Johnson by the campus for which he had done so much. Banks told of the tremendous number of policemen required to ensure Johnson's security at an event in Gregory Gymnasium. "The men were state and local police and Secret Service agents and their mission was simply to get President Johnson inside the building and away again safely. . . . The objective was to protect the life of the President of the United States." Banks had seen someone throw a soft-drink bottle at the President's car. "This is academic freedom?" Banks mentioned that regents chairman Frank C. Erwin, Jr., "drew one of the greatest ovations of the evening" at a celebration honoring Gov. John B. Connally by saying: "When we have reached the point where it takes 300 armed policemen to keep the President of the United States from being embarrassed on the University of Texas campus, then we should re-examine the goals of higher education." Amy Jo Long of the UT News and Information Service sent this column to Ransom, who answered, "Thank you. I got it hot & heavy in Dallas."[6]

During the Fall 1968 semester a locally volatile issue provided SDS with another opportunity to assemble students in a large rally—the controversy surrounding SDS's faculty adviser, Lawrence Caroline, an assistant professor of philosophy. During a speech on the state capitol grounds in October 1967, Caroline had called for a new American revolution. Ransom became a repository for Erwin's disgust over the notion that such an individual had to be kept on UT's payroll. On March 29, 1968, Erwin forwarded to Ransom a copy of a telegram Erwin had received from Texas legislator Charles R. Scoggins of Corpus Christi: "ACADEMIC FREEDOM IS COMPROMISED BY THOSE WHO ABUSE IT BY THEIR EXTREMISM. I PERSONALLY TELEPHONED ASSISTANT PROFESSOR CAROLINE TO VERIFY THE ACCURACY OF SPECIFIC ITEMS CONTAINED IN THE NEWS REPORTS. . . . HE VERIFIED THEM ALL TO ME AND REPEATED HIS ADVOCACY OF REVOLUTION AND THE ABOLITION OF PRIVATE PROPERTY IN AMERICA. CAROLINE'S CONTINUED ASSOCIATION WITH THE UNIVERSITY OF TEXAS GIVES HIS VIEWS A CLOAK OF PUBLIC LEGITIMACY. THIS ASSOCIATION MUST BE TERMINATED NOW." "Mr. Scoggins has released the telegram to the press, and I am besieged by them for comment," wrote Erwin. "It . . . appears that Mr. Caroline is determined to continue his recurrent acts of irresponsibility and bad judgment. I doubt that we can indefinitely tolerate Mr. Caroline if we are to command the confidence of the people of Texas."[7] Ultimately the Philosophy Department faculty did not renew Caroline's contract because of his failure to complete his doctoral dissertation and other alleged shortcomings as an assistant professor, but Erwin's public pronouncements on the case, though they temporarily placated critics of the university, complicated the judging of Caroline's academic credentials. Student protests were unavailing in getting Hackerman, Ransom, or the regents to reconsider Caroline's termination.

Harry Ransom, thoroughly cognizant of possible damage to the reputation of, and legislative appropriation for, the university, commented publicly as little as possible about the campus unrest. In the course of addressing a Salesmanship Club meeting at the Dallas Athletic Club on January 18, 1968, for instance, he was far more interested in stirring his audience with projections of higher education in the future than discussing the protest movement. "Newer generations of students will be more mature in every sense of that word. . . . There will be many more graduate and post-doctoral students. More will be married. Many will be given to greater perception. . . . Gladstone's studying Greek at eighty used to be only an anecdote; tomorrow, elder citizens will be bent on getting into unknown realms before and after retirement." Additionally, "carefully packaged" types of knowledge will become antiquated; "overlap of information, interchangeable phases of technology, and possible unities of wisdom all demand new interpretation of what we once called 'comparative' or 'general' studies. . . . Communication," Ransom predicted, will "be increasingly a two-way process."[8]

In spite of periodic discouragements and alarms, Ransom's first year outside the presidency offered him distinct pleasures. One of the chief of these was the duty of writing to Miss Ima Hogg of Houston on March 12, 1968, to notify her that she would be the first recipient of the UT System's Santa Rita Award. "It is fitting," he assured her. "You personify the Texan the award honors."[9] Among other philanthropic gifts, Ima Hogg had presented to UT, in 1964, the Winedale Stagecoach Inn near Round Top, following her restoration of this historic property. Arrangements were made for the official presentation of the Santa Rita honor to take place while she visited Austin for the dedication of the Will C. Hogg Building, formerly the old Geology Building before its renovation.[10]

In 1968 the University of Texas at Austin received the Institute of International Education/Reader's Digest Foundation award for distinguished service in international education. Ransom traveled to the Institute's headquarters at the United Nations Plaza in New York City to attend an award dinner and accept the citation. Fred W. Friendly, the Ford Foundation's television adviser, made the presentation, praising UT for "its pioneering role in international education and for the breadth and quality of its international programs." Under the auspices of the International Office, Friendly said, "more than 10,000 foreign citizens have studied at The University of Texas. . . . Thousands of Texas students have studied abroad under reciprocal exchange programs with foreign universities."[11] On November 10, 1968, Ransom also had the satisfaction of announcing that the Board of the Americas Foundation was conferring a special citation to the UT System for contributing to "inter-American understanding and friendship" through the Institute of Latin American Studies (directed by Professor Stanley R. Ross), the accomplishments of librarian Nettie Lee Benson of the Latin American Collection, the Mexican fieldwork of medical students from the UT Southwestern Medical School at Dallas, and other projects and programs.[12]

FIGURE 16.1

*Harry H. Ransom, Ima Hogg, Regent Jack S. Josey, and Hazel Ransom, Winedale
Stagecoach Inn, Round Top, Texas, 1964 (?). Ima Hogg donated this restored
historic property to UT prior to becoming the first recipient of the UT System's Santa
Rita Award in 1968.* Harry Ransom Humanities Research Center, The University
of Texas at Austin.

Honors and awards continued to descend upon Harry Ransom as well,
in part reflecting his reluctance to shed very many of the functions and
responsibilities of his former presidency. (The new president, Norman
Hackerman, like Joseph R. Smiley before him, had come to terms with
this disinclination on Ransom's part to share or delegate those duties and
prerogatives he enjoyed.) In December 1968, for instance, he was named to
the executive committee of the Carnegie Foundation for the Advancement
of Teaching, whose board of directors he had joined in 1962. The two other
members of the executive committee were Robert F. Goheen, president of

Princeton University, and Frederick L. Hovde, president of Purdue University.[13] He likewise joined the board of directors of the National Space Hall of Fame. He was selected for the Commission on Education for Health Professions within the National Association of State Universities and Land-Grant Colleges. He assumed the presidency of the International Library Commission. He became a delegate of the Association of American Universities to the National Commission on Accreditation. The Texas Council on Economic Education appointed him to its executive committee.[14]

A United States Senate Sub-Committee on Education met on March 29, 1968, in the Academic Center Auditorium at the University of Texas at Austin for a hearing on S. 3098, the Higher Education Amendments of 1968. Chancellor Harry Ransom welcomed the group and presented an "overview." Nowadays, he said in his opening remarks, "education at every level grows obsolescent by the year and not by the decade." Accordingly, "we must bring in a new population of learners." Decades in advance of governmental insistence regarding special services for the disabled, Ransom here called for "new academic understanding" of people with handicaps—whether "environmental, physical, social, or psychological." Such individuals merit "opportunities for them to realize their full potential." His report praised President Johnson's "imagination, courage, and a sense of hard reality" in his messages to Congress on issues of education. "It is . . . my strong recommendation to this Committee that the Congress enact the proposed amendments to the Higher Education Act," he concluded.[15]

On May 12, 1968, Ransom had the privilege of announcing a tribute to the man who had in effect launched Ransom's career in administration. Upon the recommendation of faculty committees and the administration, the Board of Regents named the English Building in memory of Dr. H. T. Parlin (1879–1951), who had come to UT sixty years earlier (in 1908) to teach in the English Department, assisted Dean Harry Benedict in Arts and Sciences, and assumed the deanship of that College in 1928. Ransom's news release credited Parlin with "skillful management of depression-era budgets" and "the earliest conception of Plan II." He also mentioned Parlin's "quiet sense of humor" and "enduring respect for individual students."[16]

The regents' acquisition in 1968 of a building at 601 Colorado Street and another edifice nearby, both in downtown Austin, would soon enable the chancellor to move off the Austin campus and preside amid historical commodiousness. Without any payment required, the UT System obtained two buildings offered by the federal government as surplus property: a former federal courthouse built around 1880 and subsequently named O. Henry Hall after the American short-story writer who once had resided in Austin, and Claudia Taylor Johnson Hall (named in honor of Lady Bird Johnson), erected early in the twentieth century and until 1965 the post office location on West Sixth Street. Under the agreement, UT could use the structures rent-free for thirty years, provided it maintained them properly and preserved their historic value. In 1998 they would then transfer free and clear to university ownership.[17] Ransom initially hoped that these buildings could function as a mini-campus for the Extension Division of the Main Campus, and he resisted the idea of moving the System office. He fundamentally believed that the chancellor should be based on an academic campus, telling Graves Landrum, "Downtown you just become a business office."[18]

At a hearing of the Texas College and University Coordinating Board held in Austin on June 21, 1968, Ransom discussed enrollment projections for the state through 1980. In his opinion, part of the anticipated increase in students could be taken care of by accelerating and enriching the high school curriculum, and then giving collegiate academic credits through advanced standing examinations. The California system of admitting students only to a specific designated campus did not win Ransom's endorsement; "Texas students cannot be arbitrarily assigned to attendance at one institution or another," he said. Praising the Texas legislature, which had increased funds for higher education by "231 percent" in the past eight years, Ransom fretted nonetheless that "a rapidly growing State already ranking fourth in population is still thirtieth among the states in per capita expenditures to operate colleges and universities." Perhaps surprising some of those on the Coordinating Board, Ransom insisted that "the private college or university is absolutely essential," not only because it will absorb 25 percent of the enrollment, but because "the nature of the private institution is part of the viable tradition of American educational opportunity, basic to the highly individual choices of the student, invaluable in cultivating the kind of enlightened citizenship which no formulary and no statistic can express."[19]

Within the UT System itself, decisions had to be made. Ransom brokered an agreement joining together the University of Texas at Arlington, the University of Texas Southwestern Medical School in Dallas, and the Southwest Center of Advanced Studies into an education consortium for North Texas, headquartered in Dallas. The resulting Excellence in Education Foundation included among its assets 250 acres of land and buildings worth $11,000,000.

In advance of the regents' meeting in Midland in July 1968, Ransom proposed ("because time is short") that President Hackerman review the "availability" of the five prospective deans nominated by Professor William

FIGURE 16.2

Harry Ransom in the Wrenn Library, 1968. Vogue *magazine (April 1968) used this photograph in declaring the University of Texas libraries "a scholars' Eden" due to Harry Ransom's guidance.* Harry Ransom Humanities Research Center, The University of Texas at Austin.

S. Livingston's committee for the recently established LBJ School of Public Affairs. Owing to the newness of the institution and the distance of Texas from Washington, D.C., and the two coasts, Ransom wrote Hackerman: "I assume, as I am sure you do, that none of these prospects will be easily persuaded and that all may refuse. Surely Lincoln Gordon is beyond our reach."[20] When the Lyndon B. Johnson School of Public Affairs ultimately opened in 1970, its first dean was John A. Gronouski, the former postmaster general in the first years of President Johnson's administration and later his ambassador to Poland.

A nice bit of magazine publicity landed Ransom's way in April 1968, when the elite magazine *Vogue* ran a cluster of modishly photographed profiles of Texas personalities such as Mrs. Henry E. Catto, Jr., Mrs. Clint Murchison, Jr., and Mr. James J. Ling. A photograph and a paragraph also introduced Dr. Harry Ransom, Chancellor of the University of Texas (described as "an enormous sprawl of education throughout the state"). He was characterized as "a scholarly administrator with a mild, bookish air who introduces himself to students with, 'I'm Harry Ransom.'" Ransom was the only Texan to receive a full-page portrait, showing him seated behind five elaborately bound editions, the ornate bookcases and carved doorway of the Wrenn Library framing his black glasses, white shirt, striped tie, and serious mien. "Under the Ransom guidance, the University of Texas libraries—and they are immense—have the definitive collection of D. H. Lawrence manuscripts [and] manuscripts of George Bernard Shaw. . . . The enormous vault holds . . . a scholars' Eden," *Vogue* assured its readers.[21]

Ransom no longer made an annual address to the UT General Faculty, but on December 6, 1968, he delivered a report at the second yearly meeting of the Chancellor's Council in Austin. Wryly he recalled that "in the fifties, the American campus was criticized most often and most severely for apathy, idleness, and addiction to personal security." By contrast, "in the sixties, criticism has been directed universally at rebellion, disruption, disorganization, and irresponsibility." He conceded, however, that "in the sixties, academic dialogue has often degenerated into shouting matches. In both periods, more attention and more interpretation should have been focused upon the majority of students who insisted upon going about the hard business of getting their own education in their own way." Above all, he insisted, "the fact that discontent has surfaced [in the 1960s] is not an academic phenomenon; it is a condition common to political, industrial, and religious movements all over the world."

At the close of his report, Ransom noted with pride that the System, formerly destitute with regard to honorific appointments, now boasted more than sixty endowed academic positions. He also pointed to the potential for continuing education endeavors made possible by "the [Joe C.] Thompson Conference Center, rising on the East Campus." Acknowledging the problems of the moment, Ransom urged the Chancellor's Council to understand that, during a decade that "many pundits have chosen to label an age of educational chaos, every university requires a truly open forum. It should be open to evaluation of apparent success, confession of obvious error, problems and perplexities, needs and opportunity." Within such frank exchanges, Ransom said, "the System can attain those high goals constantly redefined by every generation."[22]

SEVENTEEN

STAYING THE COURSE

Early in 1969, Ransom was confronted by a truly pivotal decision. Frank C. Erwin, Jr., had completed his six-year appointment to the Board of Regents, and his reappointment was by no means assured. Some felt that his future on the Board hung by a thread while the newly elected governor, conservative Democrat Preston Smith, sorted over his options. Erwin had unquestionably done the university many favors with his political connections, astuteness, and energy, but a number of observers—even those not affiliated with the faculty, which had begun to distrust and dislike his intrusions—viewed certain of his tactics as heavy-handed and needlessly combative, even provocative. Ransom, however, steadfastly faithful to the chairman of the Board, elected to write to Lieutenant-Governor Ben Barnes on February 8 to spell out some reasons for reappointing Erwin. The UT administrators, he assured Barnes, were "joined, without exception, in admiration and gratitude for Mr. Frank Erwin's service." Countering likely rumors, Ransom, choosing his words carefully, added that "Mr. Erwin is capable of vigorous disagreement and allows disagreement from administrators. Intellectually he is one of the most gifted Regents since the time of Ashbel Smith. . . . Mr. Erwin's service to the University of Texas is truly historic—in its loyalty, its candid independence, and his constant support of every object which he believes serves the interests of education and the citizens of Texas."[1] Though aware of this crucial gesture by the chancellor, Erwin did not make any response until April 1, after his nomination had received approval and his chairmanship of the Board had been reconfirmed. At that date he wrote to "Dear Harry" rather formulaically: "The press of other matters has prevented me from expressing to you sooner my sincere appreciation for the assistance which you so generously gave me in connection with my reappointment and confirmation to the Board of Regents. I shall try hard to discharge the duties of that office in a way that will deserve your continued support." But in a longhand postscript Erwin added, quite personally: "I am more grateful than I can say for the support & assistance that you gave me and for your letter to Ben."[2]

Coincidentally, a few weeks earlier—on March 17, 1969—Ransom had written a letter (marked *"Private and Confidential"*) indicating that he was seriously considering taking over the reins at another school. A recent luncheon in San Antonio with Gilbert Denman, a Trinity University trustee, had been "heartlifting," he wrote to Trinity president James Lawrie. "I have discussed the conversation with nobody—*nobody*—but Hazel," he stated. The San Antonio institution tempting Ransom was, rather surprisingly, a Presbyterian-related school founded in 1869 that enrolled fewer than 3,000 students and had fewer than 300 faculty members. The only graduate programs it offered led to master's degrees. The library holdings did not yet even approach half a million volumes, whereas the UT libraries would soon reach the six-million mark. On the other hand (to speculate about a few thoughts that might have crossed Ransom's mind), there were virtually no student protests, the humanities programs were respected, and he would arrive on the Trinity campus as such an illustrious figure that he could direct the university's development without much interference from skeptical trustees or recalcitrant professors. Moreover, the 100-acre campus afforded a pleasant view of portions of the sprawling multicultural city of San Antonio. The possible relocation would bring him a simpler, lower-key academic existence, enabling him to return to a private school having resemblances to Sewanee, and yet offering the familiar scenes of Austin only an hour and a half away and views of the Texas hill country just over a rolling ridge to the west.

Specifications about the post, Ransom brushed aside. "Lengthening experience has convinced me that both 'tables of organization' and 'job descriptions' mean only what the people involved in them are capable of becoming. To me, the best description of this prospect is the opportunity of working under such men as I have met at Gilbert's luncheon." Regarding money, he explained: "As you know, I would have left the state long since if either salary or other emoluments had much to do with my idea of an administrative appointment." He enclosed a separate sheet revealing what his recommended salary at the University of Texas for 1969–1970 would be: $49,000. He assured Trinity that he would "wind up our talk well before the end of April. No matter what the event, Jim, you can count on my steady support."[3] But the Ransoms found reasons by that date not to change their place of residence.

With the departure of Lyndon B. Johnson from the White House and of

John B. Connally (following four terms) from the Texas Governor's Mansion, after 1968 the past tense began to creep into summaries of Harry Ransom's career: he "*was* co-chairman of a Presidential Commission which last year recommended major changes in the U.S. patent system. He is a *former* member of the President's Committee on White House Fellows, *former* president of the Council of Southern Universities, and *former* chairman of the executive council of the Commission on Colleges of the Southern Association of Colleges and Schools. He *was* a member of the Texas Governor's Committee on Education Beyond the High School." So read a paragraph in the *Texas Times* issued in March 1969 (italics added).[4]

To his good friend Allen T. Hazen, the prominent bibliographer of Samuel Johnson and other eighteenth-century figures who was now living on Riverside Drive in New York City, Ransom mentioned his recovery from temporary physical decrepitude. "Last year was a dismaying one for me," he wrote on July 29, 1969, "—a continuing lesson in humility. I had boasted too often about never being ill: in short order, I had three serious bouts with phlebitis. What had always sounded like a funny word turned out to be a wretchedness. Now I'm completely well, my only prescription after this recent interminable 'check-up' at the Medical Branch being daily strenuous walks." Praising Hazen's three-volume *Catalogue of Horace Walpole's Library,* recently published by Yale University Press, he reminisced to his former Yale classmate that "back to 1932 . . . lie the happy memories of friendship. I owe you more than I shall try to say, more than you know." Telling Hazen about leaving the presidency, Ransom merely referred to his having "got out of daily administrative duties." He characterized his chancellorship responsibilities as embracing twenty institutions and being "focused on planning, policy, and development—which my best friends here say is [a] high-sounding job description of a sinecure. Not quite. Foundations are clamming up, as you know; and the Federal programs douse even my optimism."[5]

In July 1969 the staff of the HRC prepared a brief typescript history and description of its collections, calculating that they embraced nearly 4,000,000 manuscripts, 1,200,000 volumes, and 2,000,000 photographs, and reflecting the Board of Regents' approval in 1967 of the design and construction of a new structure to house "this growing mass of source material to serve the needs of the faculty, the graduate student, the visiting scholar." The report quoted an unidentified "visiting scholar-librarian, who holds what is perhaps one of the four most important jobs in his profession in this country, as saying that 'the University of Texas has telescoped seventy-five years of arduous library building into a scant ten years of Herculean effort.'"[6] The

Humanities Research Center was also fostering spin-offs that enriched the general understanding of the printed word; for example, it now underwrote various activities related to the history, composition, manufacture, and collection of books, including an annual Lew David Feldman Lecture Series. Sir Frank Francis, former British Museum director and principal librarian, became its second featured speaker on December 5, 1969. Feldman himself had attended the first lecture in 1968, delivered by Dr. Frederick R. Goff, chief of the rare book division of the Library of Congress.[7]

An HRC-sponsored lecture at UT by John Lehmann on March 12, 1969, ultimately fetched a superbly valuable dividend. Several months after Lehmann, a British poet, essayist, editor, novelist, and travel writer, returned home, the July 10, 1969, issue of the *Times Literary Supplement* carried an immensely laudatory article, "John Lehmann on a Visit to the Humanities Research Centre, University of Texas." In one fell swoop all of Ransom's efforts seemed to have been validated on an international basis. Lehmann took the unexpected position that he was unable to "see what injury is done by the export of British literary archives to institutions in the United States of America; institutions which share a common heritage of language and civilization with us, and which have the resources to care for them in the most devoted way." After all, British institutions "were fast asleep until Texas woke them."[8]

Within two weeks the *Dallas Morning News* crowed about "the full-page encomium of the University of Texas' Humanities Research Center" in the "magisterial *Times Literary Supplement*. London, it seems, is more aware of our intellectual wealth than we are." The *Dallas Morning News* observed that Lehmann was essentially "praising the vision of Harry Ransom in correctly seeing that a great opportunity was at hand for Texas to do something largely left undone."[9]

As welcome and gratifying as Lehmann's opinion was, it would soon be overshadowed by a more monumental recognition. Almost as though in disbelief, Ransom wrote to the eminent British authority on books and libraries, Anthony Hobson, at his London address to certify the rumor. Hobson replied placidly on October 28, 1969, corroborating what Ransom had heard:

> Many thanks for your enquiry about my book "Great Libraries." The text is now complete and the book should appear next year, in American, English, and French editions.
>
> It will consist of historical descriptions of thirty-two libraries, arranged chronologically from the Capitular Library of Verona, the only

collection to have had a continuous existence since antiquity, to Texas University Library. . . .

I've included Texas in the book for various reasons: it illustrates a modern version of this association, with the Regents of the University taking the role of the patron; and its expansion and rise to prominence have been as rapid and remarkable as the British Museum's expansion under Panizzi in the 19th century, or the Vatican Library's in the 17th. I've also drawn a parallel between Texas and the Lovenjoul Library at Chantilly. Spoelberch de Lovenjoul set out to collect not only all the manuscripts of a few contemporary authors—Balzac, Gautier, George Sand, and Sainte-Beuve—but as much surrounding documentation as possible. Although his collection (which now belongs to the Institut de France) is far smaller than yours, it has long been an indispensable place of pilgrimage for all scholars studying these authors, just as Texas will certainly be the centre of future scholarship on English and American twentieth-century literature.[10]

The sense of relief and gratification that washed across Harry Ransom's soul was probably unrivaled in his life. His library projects had been ranked among the greatest archives in the history of world civilizations, and this hosanna was uttered less than two decades since Fannie Ratchford blustered and begged for relative pittances to maintain her rare books collection. Nothing in his remaining years would quite match the exultant thrill of Anthony Hobson's vindication of his vision.[11]

But trouble loomed in the form of the resumption of clashes between protesters and the university administration, with Regents Chairman Frank C. Erwin, Jr., continuing his prominence amid the escalating confrontations. In a year when U.S. B-52s intensified their bombing of Cambodian sanctuaries, the trial of the "Chicago 8" began, and large anti-war demonstrations took place around the country, the UT campus was not immune to unrest. Indeed, the atmosphere crackled with so much tension that almost any incident, however non-political, could turn into a cause. When picketers protested the removal of trees along Waller Creek for an enlargement of Memorial Stadium, Erwin showed up to approve the arrest of dozens of tree-climbing objectors. Students struck back by dragging the tree limbs uphill to the Main Building and depositing them in vast disarray in the doorway to President Hackerman's office. A dispute over the admission of non-students to the Texas Union Chuck Wagon on November 10, 1969, resulted in property damage and more than thirty arrests.

Such was the prevailing climate when 242 members of the UT faculty convened on October 28, 1969, to vote on a resolution asking Frank C. Erwin, Jr., to resign his position as chairman of the Board of Regents. In vain Chancellor Ransom and President Hackerman rose to remind the professors at the meeting of the good works that Erwin had done on behalf of the System. Professor Clarence L. Cline, recent chairman of the English Department, sent Erwin a letter the next day (with copies addressed to Ransom and Hackerman) to explain Cline's personal decision to oppose the resolution. Many of the people assembled, he told Erwin, had likely decided in advance not to heed the pleas of Hackerman and Ransom. "Certain statements attributed to you—sometimes calculated to irritate—influenced yesterday's vote. . . . I am not sure to what extent you realize that in this permissive age faculties are suspicious of and rather generally resent any discipline and all authority. . . . What this really means is that the General Faculty tends to regard itself as the real University, with officials and Regents as servants, possibly necessary and certainly to be disregarded and unvalued. . . . I have every confidence that you are tough enough not to be deeply wounded by what happened yesterday and that your love for the University is too great to let it sour you toward the University."[12] Despite such individual expressions of accommodation, however, the fact had become public that neither Harry Ransom nor Norman Hackerman could influence an increasingly organized and vociferous element of their faculty, let alone the rowdy, nonconformist faction among the students, and the chief regent had been embarrassed by disparaging remarks and a rebuking vote orchestrated by his campus opponents.

As 1969 drew to an end and a new decade beckoned, the *Dallas Times Herald* ran a two-part feature article written by Ernest Stromberger summing up the state of the University of Texas and discussing its future. Currently the largest university west of the Mississippi except for the University of Minnesota, UT ranked in the top 10 percent nationally in virtually every category, but "the going seems rougher than ever." Stromberger pointed out that "the faculty is being paid better and enjoying a higher degree of academic freedom than even they expected, yet they are grumbling at the Board of Regents more than ever. . . . General Electric Corp. recruiters canceled planned job interviews on the campus rather than face a threatened demonstration by radicals." Nonetheless, the article agreed with President Hackerman that "the university edged into [the] nation's top 20 schools about four years ago."

The article also quoted Charles Alan Wright, law professor and president of the UT Faculty Senate, who said the university was "engaged in an experiment of making a provincial university of limited talent into a great national university. . . . When I go back East, . . . people speak of the university with a respect they didn't have 10 years ago. . . . We hardly ever lose someone [in the law school] we want to keep, and we're able to raid other universities for faculty." Despite classes sometimes containing 400 students and one student dormitory housing 3,000 people, said Hackerman, "we had a larger percentage [enrollment] increase than other schools. If people are better looked after on small campuses, why don't more people go to small colleges?" Dallas junior Steve Van added that UT's size is "the way we're going to have to live in the future. . . . The university is a microcosm of the world, and part of college life is learning to survive in the world."[13]

In a similar article written by Leslie Taylor, the *Austin American-Statesman* noted, accurately as it would prove, that "some manner of restructuring of the College of Arts and Sciences which handles more than 60 percent of the student body can be expected in the next year." The regents, meanwhile, had installed a new amendment to their Rules and Regulations, one that prohibited the chancellor or president or their representatives from negotiating with persons engaged in disruptive activities. The regents also altered the quorum for the General Faculty from 40 members to 225 members, seeking to ensure that a small faction of instructors could not dictate the proceedings of a meeting. Very soon the regents were expected to adopt a "student academic freedom" clause to prevent the repetition of an incident that had occurred in the Fall 1969 term when a history instructor refused to allow access to his classroom to a uniformed Army officer who had legitimately registered for the course.[14]

An ominous air of expectancy hung over the campus. Intuitively, Dr. Clifton M. Grubbs, Jr., a popular professor of economics and winner of multiple teaching awards, wrote to his chancellor on January 17, 1970, to attempt to "span some of the years . . . in the life and times of a very precious human being, Harry Ransom. A man who more than twenty years ago . . . took the time one day to treat a hunger-filled kid from Fort Worth as a potential gentleman. Later on, after some polish by Harvard and unpolish by the Marines, it was my honor to join the faculty of the University in 1965. When I came here there was magic in the air. You had done something to the University which made me feel that I too was important, that great events were in the making, and that if one of my own lectures failed, all the events would come to ruin. . . . Now, of course, hard times have come, but I want you to know that I shall remain to carry on the best I can the old dream . . . . I too was one of your sons."[15]

EIGHTEEN

"MR. UNIVERSITY"

The new year of 1970 opened ordinarily if busily for the Ransoms, with Harry telling one correspondent, artist and illustrator John Groth of New York City, "I have been up in the air (coast to coast), under the weather (sniffling around the clock with Cotton-Bowl sneezes in between), or completely inundated by the damnedest tax-foundation-budget muddlement in history."[1] (UT had recently defeated Notre Dame 21–17 in the Cotton Bowl in Dallas.) Ransom still typed approximately one-third of his own letters (though he lamented that "my typing—of which I was once quite proud—gets jumpier with the years"). But more of his letters were handwritten, in a script that had now assumed a horizontal, slanting-to-the-right aspect, with near-perfect stylized loops and an almost machine-like, stenciled appearance.

In a candid interview with the *Houston Post*, Ransom rehearsed his views of the current generation of students: though they were "better" than those who came before them, nonetheless many were still "not well prepared," particularly in knowing "how to read, how to concentrate and read and be critical about the result of reading." He recommended that a student preferably develop "an ability really to enter into a serious conversation—because he is going to get into serious conversation, domestic, community, legal, and professional when he gets out—than to deal simply in the clap-trap of college life. I dealt a great deal in clap-trap when I was an undergraduate student myself," he admitted. As for what makes the best teacher? "The quality that is most important is intellectual curiosity in the teacher himself. Unless that is there, he isn't likely to recognize it in the student." How does one motivate a teacher? "To some, it really means something to be rendering a social service. This is an abstraction. It's merely an idea, but it is very powerful with some teachers. To some it means a great deal to stay in contact with a guaranteed liveliness, creativeness in the realm of thought."[2]

Spring arrived on the campus, bringing warm weather and the relaxed mood of a concluding semester. A nostalgic mood was evident in Ransom's correspondence. When psychiatrist James A. Hall, M.D., of Dallas wrote on April 2, 1970, to say, "I think of you, with gratitude, from time to time—and tell colleagues that you were my first psychotherapist, way back in Plan II," Ransom replied the next day: "Lengthening memory at UT would put Plan II at the top of all my rewarding experiences here."[3] The month of May 1970 began propitiously with a flattering profile of the chancellor in the *Daily Texan*. That article mentioned Ransom's "public relations" role ("an average of two speeches a week") and emphasized his significant influence on the process of selecting a new president for UT Austin. (Dr. Norman Hackerman was leaving to become the fourth president of Rice University in Houston.)[4]

Ransom was still conducting his business from an office on the first floor of the Main Building, but the chancellor's office would move downtown into O. Henry Hall, the former federal building, in July 1971. Ransom told several people that he was not looking forward to leaving the campus, though he acknowledged that it made sense symbolically for the UT System offices to operate at a distance from the Main Campus so as not to give other sites and campuses any impression of favoritism. Graves Landrum was one of those who pointed out that the UT components outside Austin might feel like stepchildren if the chancellor remained where he was, whereupon Ransom remarked, "Then maybe they need a different chancellor."[5]

On the national scene, the Vietnam War continued to stir protests that culminated in the Kent State University shootings. President Nixon's dispatching of U.S. troops into Cambodia intensified the situation to the point where nearly 450 colleges and universities across the country either closed or were declared to be "on strike." The crucible for UT Austin arrived on Friday, May 8, 1970, when an estimated 20,000 demonstrators, largely UT students, marched through downtown Austin in the streets and on the sidewalks. "Peace Now" and "Free Bobby Seale" (a national Black Panther leader), they chanted as they passed the Travis County Courthouse and headed for the university campus, where they disbanded peacefully, many pausing to wade in Littlefield Fountain.[6] Ransom and Graves Landrum had been part of a university team anxiously negotiating with city, state, and federal authorities about parade permits and security arrangements. Ransom had favored giving the protest organizers the benefit of the doubt and avoiding confrontation, according to Landrum, but these days it was Norman Hackerman rather than Ransom who made most of the final determinations about handling these increasingly volatile student demonstrations. As with other matters, Hackerman would say later, "Harry stood above the fray. He didn't like to deal with these things." Both Hackerman and Ransom were grateful that no one was hurt. "When the kids were up in the trees down on San Jacinto," recalled Hackerman, "we were lucky to get away with that one."[7] Now the lack of incidents during the huge march was the cause of similar jubilation. As the protesters dispersed amicably, Ransom, watching nervously from a window in the Tower, was nearly tearful with relief, and he impulsively patted the shoulders of several worried UT officials and staff members whose own children had been among the marchers.[8] So much violence had occurred during similar events on other campuses that the UT administrators could scarcely believe their good fortune at avoiding injury and destruction in Austin.

Students gradually returned to their Spring semester classes and Ransom's daily regimen accordingly took on a normal look. On May 24, 1970, Dean John Silber of the College of Arts and Sciences (signing himself, archaically if half-seriously, "your obdt. servt.") sent Ransom a report on "Problems and Programs, 1967–1970" detailing the recent history of his college. "If in these pages you find anything truly imaginative or supportive of individual students and humane values in education, please take unto yourself all the credit. You have been my guide and inspiration for fifteen years. I hope you will not be too disappointed in your student. I have often felt deeply unworthy to follow in your footsteps as Dean of the College of Arts and Sciences. Let me take this occasion to thank you again for all that you have done for me—both personally and professionally. I owe you so very much."[9]

At a meeting of the Board of Regents in El Paso on Friday, May 29, 1970, Ransom witnessed the regents choose a 600-acre site for the UT San Antonio campus, approve a rule prohibiting the use of campus facilities by student organizations when more than three non-students or non-employees were in attendance, and reject as too high a bid to construct the new Communication Building for $9.19 million. He also heard President Norman Hackerman's recommendation that the twenty-five departments in John Silber's Arts and Sciences College be grouped into four separate, smaller divisions. This reorganization would result in the Colleges of Humanities, Natural Sciences, and Social and Behavioral Sciences, plus a Division of General and Comparative Studies. There is no indication that Ransom made any objection to the proposal.

In this same session the regents named Dr. Bryce Jordan, a music scholar who had been vice president for student affairs at UT Austin since 1968, as

FIGURE 18.1

Protesters march toward the university campus, May 8, 1970. Not since the firing of President Homer Rainey in 1944 had Texas seen a massive demonstration of this scope: 20,000 marchers. The bombing of Cambodia by U.S. troops prompted 450 colleges and universities across the nation to go "on strike." Students did not attend classes and instead sought ways to "end the war in Vietnam." Margaret Berry, *UT Pictorial History,* 329, Center for American History, The University of Texas at Austin.

president ad interim of UT Austin effective July 1, the date when Dr. Norman Hackerman would depart for Rice University.[10] Hackerman insisted then and thereafter that he did not at all feel pushed out. Rice truly needed him, presented an interesting challenge, offered him research facilities on a par with those at UT, and reminded him of Johns Hopkins University, where he had earned two of his chemistry degrees. He left Austin with a determination to pitch Rice University to the Houston community as an overlooked jewel.[11]

During a mysterious executive session that lasted for hours and piqued the curiosity of onlookers, the regents summoned William S. Livingston, Charles A. ("Mickey") LeMaistre, and others who came and went gravely.[12] Then, suddenly, an era was over. An announcement issued that afternoon following the regents' meeting shook the UT System and electrified the press across the state. "Dr. Ransom Quits as UT Chancellor" read the large headline of the *Austin American-Statesman*.[13] "Ransom Resigns as UT Chancellor" reported the *Dallas Morning News*. The Board stated that "at his request" Ransom had resigned effective January 1, 1971. Regent Frank N. Ikard, chairman of the Committee on Administrative Organization, said that Ransom would be named chancellor emeritus beginning on that date. Insisting that Ransom was merely changing positions rather than retiring, Ikard said: "In this new position, he will continue to be active in administrative work, which will include regular consultation with the board on all matters. . . . He will also continue system development, especially in the field of research collections, endowments, and foundations." The Board took no immediate action in naming, or even in specifying a procedure for selecting, a new chancellor.[14] Deputy Chancellor Charles Lemaistre, former executive vice chancellor for health affairs, was appointed interim chancellor.

Despite Ikard's assurances about the continuity of Ransom's affiliation with the regents and the System, the departures of Ransom and Hackerman seemed suspiciously abrupt to many observers. The relative silence of Frank C. Erwin, Jr.—who passed up opportunities to comment on Ransom's resignation—bred rumors that the regents chairman might have orchestrated, perhaps through veiled threats against some of Ransom's favorite projects, the chancellor's exit. For one thing, it was known in many quarters that neither Hackerman nor Ransom had shown the alacrity that Erwin desired about dividing up the huge College of Arts and Sciences. Hackerman had initially told the regents he was waiting for "spontaneous nucleation."[15] Such was the potency of these surmises about manipulation that they held sway with a majority of the UT community for the better part of the next

FIGURE 18.2

Former chancellor Harry H. Ransom and acting chancellor Charles A. LeMaistre, Board
of Regents meeting, summer 1970. On May 29, 1970, Ransom resigned as chancellor,
effective January 1, 1971. He was named chancellor emeritus upon this retirement
date. Prints and Photographs Collection, Center for American History,
The University of Texas at Austin.

two decades, casting a shadow over Erwin's reputation as a champion of
UT's best interests. Fairly or unfairly, whether by plot or coincidence, the
apparent demotion of the best-known and most popular administrator in
the university's history had occurred on Frank Erwin's watch, and he would
bear the consequences. As with every other development for which some
people blamed him, Erwin shrugged off the criticism and poured himself
back into matters at hand. It would vastly and misleadingly oversimplify
the matter to say that the alumni and Texas taxpayers in general were divided between those who backed Erwin and those who supported Ransom,
because there were thousands who admired the dedication of both men,
but it is probably true that there was an element, especially among the UT
alumni, willing at least to give Frank Erwin credit for trying to find administrators with more eagerness to crack down on demonstrators who in the
opinion of many graduates were despoiling a great institution and a scenic
campus.

Ransom himself stressed his pleasure in accepting the new emeritus responsibilities: "I am looking forward to the new role in which I may serve all the institutions in the System. I am deeply grateful for the Board's confidence and generosity." (Among other things, the new appointment would enable Ransom to remain in the Watchhill Road residence he had been provided by the Board of Regents.) But many commentators seemed to assume that Ransom was merely displaying his characteristic loyalty to the university to which he had devoted his life since 1935. The unmistakable diminishment of his duties sparked numerous conjectures regarding hidden motives. "There has been speculation that Ransom became increasingly unhappy with intrusion into administrative affairs by the strong-willed chairman of the board of regents, Frank C. Erwin," noted the *Dallas Morning News*. "Speculation was that Erwin [had in 1967] backed Hackerman for president of the Austin campus because he wanted someone who would be tougher on campus dissidents than Ransom." Yet the same article pointed out that "insiders who should know" consistently said that Ransom's resignation "was strictly his own idea." Moreover, Norman Hackerman scoffed at the rumors: "My own belief is that after 30 years of administrative work it gets a little tiring. There's a lot of sameness to it. In the time remaining to him I think he wants to make a maximum effort on the book side . . . and fund development."[16]

The testimony of Ransom's wife and friends would seem pertinent here. Hazel Ransom emphatically denied, in the years following, that Harry received any form of ultimatum or was under any pressure to tender his resignation. Graves Landrum, Ransom's longtime financial guide, likewise disputed the ubiquitous stories that his superior had been forced out of office. Nor was Ransom's stepping down solely the result of continuous campus demonstrations, argued Landrum (a band of demonstrators had finally succeeded in actually entering Ransom's office, and one protester had reportedly even pounded on Ransom's desk), though they were "one of the factors" that led Ransom to realize he was feeling "tired" as well as "frustrated." He "wasn't protecting anyone or anything" by announcing his retirement in such unruffled language, nor could he have identified one particular straw that had broken the camel's back, according to Landrum. As for the timing, well, it had been in El Paso exactly ten years earlier that he had accepted the chancellorship, and so he thought it would be fitting to let go of the office in the same city after exactly a decade.

By Landrum's convincing account, nobody knew that Ransom would be resigning except Hazel. Landrum was out of the room, preparing a presentation on the site selected for the new UT San Antonio campus, when Ransom broke the news to the Board of Regents. Regent John Peace, who would take over the chairmanship of the Board in 1971, came out after Graves Landrum's report and told him that Ransom had resigned unexpectedly. Landrum was "floored." Ransom then called him up to his hotel room to explain that he had not wanted to give Landrum any opportunity to try to talk him out of the move. During that conversation Ransom emphatically denied that he was forced out. "This was my decision," he told Landrum. He firmly assured Landrum that it was strictly a burnedout situation. Ransom reminded him that five to eight years is the normal length of service for someone in a demanding position like that of chancellor. He spoke to Landrum of his wish, if possible, to return to some classroom teaching.[17]

Arthur H. Dilly, LeMaistre's assistant, speculated also that Chancellor Ransom, cognizant of Erwin's ambition to establish a UT campus in every metropolitan area in Texas, did not relish the prospect of overseeing this burgeoning administrative growth.[18]

Another valuable source, Board of Regents member Jenkins Garrett, Fort Worth attorney and noted book collector, vehemently denied that Ransom was forced out of his position. "We Regents were stunned when he told us he was leaving," Garrett maintained. "It took us a while to figure out a way to keep him around so that he could still influence things. We even gave him the same salary as a sign of our gratitude." Garrett was aware that "there were rumors at the time, though we disputed them. It became just another way for Arrowsmith and other people angry about the aftermath of the breakup of the College of Arts and Sciences to retaliate against the Regents." Garrett's impression was that Harry Ransom "was tired out by the student activists, by someone banging his sandal on his desk, by their incessant demands and demonstrations. He wanted to step back from it all. He was just too *gentle* a person to put up with all that turmoil, week after week."[19] Clarence Cline likewise corroborated the toll these interruptions were taking on his friend. Cline saw Ransom after one of these disruptive "incidents" (their word for them), and noted that "his face was gray and his manner tense."[20] During these years Ransom conferred frequently, sometimes almost daily, with William D. (Bill) Blunk, who had been named executive director of development in 1965 and had served as executive secretary of the Chancellor's Council and the University of Texas Foundation since 1967. Blunk's job involved the cultivation of strong private support for the university, but Ransom came to depend on this genial, efficient man, who held a master's degree from Austin College and had been a teacher and administrator before joining the UT staff in 1948, for advice about decisions and timing as well. Blunk later told Cline that after several especially wounding episodes with protesters Ransom began to say it was time for him to quit. "Not now, not now," Blunk counseled. But finally the time came when Blunk agreed, "You're right. Now *is* the time." "And that's when Harry resigned."[21]

It also appears important to record the fact that, even decades after Ransom's death, not a single individual could be found who would come forward and offer evidence that Ransom had told him or her that he was forced from office, or that Erwin or anyone else ever confided any role (or, for that matter, any degree of elation) in Ransom's resignation. If this was indeed a conspiracy on Erwin's or another's part, then it remains perhaps the best cover-up ever orchestrated at a large university where very little else seemed to remain a secret over any period of time.

Still, disbelief and cynicism vied with regret as letters poured into Ransom's office and commemorative but indignant editorials erupted in the state's leading newspapers. Former Regents chairman Merton M. Minter, M.D., sent a typical note from San Antonio to "Hazel and Harry": "Once in a hundred years a great university may be blessed with the leadership you have given . . . . I hope you may be able to take a deep breath, go back to your beloved books, spend some happy hours together, and have some time for those who dearly love you."[22] Former Regent Lyde (Mrs. Charles) Devall of Kilgore sent word to "Dearest, dear Hazie and Hal": "Friday night Charley and I were listening to the news and there was just one brief statement from El Paso. . . . I felt like King Arthur when he said 'The old order changeth, yielding place to new.' . . . It was a bad time. But now what I want to say is thank you, both of you, for the time, the talent, the patience, the forbearance, and the multitude of other virtues that have gone into the building of a university that even our illustrious forebears could call 'first class.'"[23]

The *Houston Chronicle* worried that Ransom's retirement "will deprive his growing, progressive system of an able administrator." The editors went on to speculate that "Dr. Ransom might have stayed on as chancellor had he not wearied under the pressures of his job. A man in such a position finds himself trying to please regents, students, faculty, alumni, benefactors, and legislators. In this time of social upheaval and changing attitudes, particularly in our academic communities, that may be next to impossible."[24]

On June 7, 1970, Ransom took a few days off to return to North Dakota, where the University of North Dakota in Grand Forks conferred on him the honorary degree of Doctor of Literature.[25] When he returned to Austin, the stack of rueful letters was growing. Anna T. Painter, widow of UT President Theophilus S. Painter, commiserated from Austin: "I was very sorry for the sake of the University but glad for you two. . . . Administrative positions today are no fun but I do feel you both did much for the University and will be missed." Mrs. Painter added, "My dearest hopes are that the University can get a real *academic* leader who can quiet all these revolutionary tendencies."[26] Former Governor John B. Connally wrote from Houston under the letterhead of Vinson, Elkins, Searls & Connally: "For the University, I am sorry—for you, I am glad. You have earned the surcease from the grind. You are entitled to take it a bit easier and do the things that please you the most."[27] When Ransom wrote to Lady Bird Johnson on June 18, 1970, to apologize for the fact "that we could not join your guests at the Ranch last week," former President Lyndon B. Johnson replied personally: "Lady Bird was so touched by your letter . . . she wanted me to read it, too. I've finished it as she did . . . with a grateful heart. You've always given us friendship without reservation."[28]

Another political figure, Democratic Congressman J. J. Pickle, took note of Ransom's change of title: "How we will miss the clairvoyant brilliance with which you have led our great school, and how many of us as individuals will feel a personal loss that you are not our spokesman whose words and voice are always toned to the theme of academic excellence." Representative Pickle assured Ransom that "you will always be held in respect and genuine appreciation by those who know what a great sacrifice you have made."[29] Texas Governor Preston Smith and former Texas Governor Allan Shivers wrote similarly.[30]

Other people who contacted Ransom had little association with politics. Frank Dobie's widow, Bertha, for instance, wrote from 702 Park Place in Austin "to thank you for having raised the University of Texas from mediocrity to distinction, many others helping but you the causative. Especially close to me is all that you have done to commemorate Frank in public talks, published writings, and the Dobie Collection made permanent and finely housed."[31]

In June 1970 Ransom's attention was temporarily distracted by Frances Hudspeth's serious health problems. Ransom wrote to former First Lady Mrs. Johnson that "news from the hospital this morning is good: Mrs. Hudspeth seems to be in a chipper mood. She is a very great lady."[32] A few days later he explained to another correspondent: "My work is sobered by Mrs. Hudspeth's second heart attack. (She is now out of 'intensive care' and on the way to recovery, but will be away for about six weeks.)"[33] Until her illnesses Mrs. Hudspeth had often served as an in-house sounding board for Frank C. Erwin, Jr., who liked to eat a sandwich in her office while drawing out her opinions.[34] Her rapport with Erwin and the Johnsons as well as other important Texas and national figures had long benefited Ransom, but for some time her fabled energy and vibrancy had been in decline.

Various correspondents sought to perceive latent reasons behind Ransom's retirement. The most probing letter arrived from a former UT administrator, Dr. John W. Meaney, now a professor at the University of Notre Dame. Meaney exhorted Ransom not to leave with "a quiet quitting." In Meaney's interpretation, "the basic problem, of course, is not the personality of Frank Erwin, his love of his Alma Mater, and the kind of bear hug that results in such administrative dislocations, such meddling. The real problem is the built-in politics that results from having the Board members nominated by the governor."[35] But Ransom's reply was calming. "It would take a book—or two—for proper answer," Ransom wrote. He reminded Meaney that throughout the United States "we are steadily moving through faster and faster change to 'managerial administration'—streamlined, efficient, economical, impersonal." He explicitly denied that the planned division of the College of Arts and Sciences had anything to do with his resignation. Yet he conceded that "I did resign suddenly and without discussing the move with anybody but Hazel. My main reasons were that the whole board was present when I made the decision in El Paso the day before the session; there were few controversies on the agenda and none relating to my office; I had rounded out exactly ten years . . . ; and younger men suitable to the new age of 'operation' were available." Even so, Ransom mentioned suggestively that "obviously that is not the whole story."[36] (One indication that this was a somewhat simplified version of the events is William S. Livingston's revelation that he, Livingston, had already been asked to substitute for Ransom in speaking at the UT El Paso commencement, which would occur just a day or two after the regents' meeting.)[37]

John McKetta, executive vice chancellor for academic affairs, had not attended the regents' meeting in El Paso, so "it was a *real* surprise for me when he informed me that I should start reporting to the deputy chancellor." McKetta sensed that Ransom had essentially been deposed. "Dr. Ransom looked so *hurt*. I could tell it wasn't his own decision to step down." Ransom suggested that McKetta should stay on for at least six or eight months to make things look better. "Johnny," he said to McKetta, "the University is bigger than we are. If the news gets out that two, three, or four of us are leaving at one time, it will hurt the University. We must not harm the University."[38] William S. Livingston, however, then vice chancellor for academic programs, recalled that LeMaistre came up to him during the regents' meeting in El Paso "and said that 'the Board' had asked for resignations from McKetta and Livingston."[39] Both men complied. Raymond Vowell, vice chancellor for public affairs, also resigned after that meeting, almost surely by request.

Two other bombshells were about to hit Texas, enveloping Ransom's departure in a larger drama. Newspaper headlines across the state on June 29, 1970, trumpeted comments that Norman Hackerman, the outgoing UT President, had made during an interview for *Capitol Eye,* a weekly television-radio news program: "Texas U. Chief Hits Regents" (*Texarkana Daily News*), "Hackerman Says Erwin Interferes with Management" (*Jacksonville Journal*), "Regents Said Taking Too Much Power" (*Denton Record-Chronicle*). Hackerman urged that the "operations of an institution be in the hands of the academic community—and that governing boards set policy and philosophic tone." For example, Hackerman said he did not consider it "appropriate" for Frank C. Erwin, Jr., chairman of the Board of Regents, to have directed the bulldozers in the dispute over the stadium and the trees along Waller Creek. Hackerman also disagreed with Erwin's recent suggestion that universities and colleges should rely more on managerial personnel instead of academics to run universities. "I think it's wrong," said Hackerman. "Look back to the '50s when college presidents were retired generals or important people in industry and so on. It seems to me this is not the best way to get administrators."[40] Editorialized one newspaper, the *Abilene Reporter-News:* "It is not the board's place to pick out which trees can be cut and which editorials must be censored in the campus newspapers as has happened in the last year or so. . . . It must hire first rate administrators and let them do their job. . . . When men of the caliber of Hackerman and Dr. Harry Ransom, who unexpectedly resigned as chancellor of the entire system, resign, it is time for the regents to start asking questions of themselves."[41]

As though these events were not unsettling enough for the alumni to absorb in rapid succession, on September 12, 1970, Regent Jack S. Josey of Houston, president of the Josey Oil Company, announced in a press statement his resignation as vice chairman of the UT Board of Regents, commenting that "the chairman and indeed the Board should have a vice chairman whose ideas and views on *methods* and *procedures* are more closely akin to the chairman's views."[42] The *Houston Post* reminded its readers that it had previously raised questions about Erwin's conduct: "Just what is going on at the University of Texas? Is a policy of rule or ruin being pursued? Is a great institution being re-molded to fit the ideas and concepts of one man?"[43] Ransom wrote to Jack Josey within two days to declare that "the lessons you have taught me about integrity over the years are unforgettable. . . . You . . . have been so deeply and selflessly devoted to our University that each of us has been held steady by your spirit."[44]

Other storm clouds churned on the horizon. While the well-publicized resignations had been engulfing the Board of Regents, a related set of disputes on the Main Campus began to receive almost equal attention from the press. In a face-to-face confrontation in July 1970 between Erwin and John Silber, the dean who was resisting the dismemberment of his College of Arts and Sciences because he (correctly) perceived it as an effort to get rid of him, Erwin informed Silber that he would soon be removed from office. Aware that controversy would result, Erwin told Silber, point blank, "John, I'm going to make you famous. I'm going to fire you as the dean of Arts and Sciences." The meeting took place in Professor Donald L. Weismann's office, and Erwin began by asking Weismann not to leave. Silber was caught off guard by Weismann's presence and by Erwin's straightforward declaration.[45] That same day, after Silber balked at submitting his resignation, President ad interim Bryce Jordan recommended, and newly appointed acting chancellor Charles A. LeMaistre put into effect, the firing of Silber as dean.[46] Detailed accounts of this scenario subsequently appeared in numerous publications; it became a cause célèbre even among elements of the UT faculty not given to activism and was a sensational incident recited at gatherings of professors on the East and West Coasts for many years thereafter, coming to epitomize regental interference in academic affairs. Erwin, recalling the event seven years later, said that military draft–avoiding students and other students who "didn't know what to major in" had drifted into the College of Arts and Sciences until "more than half the students at the university" were registered in a single college that absorbed "more than half the budget." Silber, Erwin said, "through no particular planning on his own part, suddenly was in control of more than half of everything at the University. And this simply made Arts and Sciences an administrative monstrosity. It gave him disproportionate control of things."[47]

The episode, though immensely notorious, not only failed to hinder but on the contrary propelled the career of the mercurial John Silber, who soon went on to become president and then chancellor of Boston University and a national commentator on trends in higher education. Further resignations followed and magnified Silber's firing, including those of classicist William Arrowsmith, who departed with a public condemnation of the regents' actions,[48] and French teacher Roger Shattuck, who left in 1971.[49] Classicist D. S. Carne-Ross accompanied Silber to Boston University, as did psychologist Sigmund Koch. Thomas Gould, another classicist, took a position at

Yale University. History professor Vartan Gregorian, a Stanford Ph.D. who had come to UT in 1968, promptly resigned as director of the Plan II program to protest the elimination of the College of Arts and Sciences and the creation of four different colleges in its place, "which was contrary to the will of the majority of the faculty." His resignation was also in protest of the "shabby treatment" of John Silber. Gregorian left the university in 1972 for the University of Pennsylvania, where he served as a dean and provost before becoming, in succession, president of the New York Public Library, president of Brown University, and president of the Carnegie Corporation of New York.[50]

On September 14, 1970, Silber wrote emotionally to Ransom: "I know I let you down in important ways. The timing was wrong. I tried to do in two years what might have been possible in three. The apprentice cannot fail his master without regret and, if he loves his master, without personal sorrow. And it's hard for you, too, because the sorcerer has also let down the apprentice. At the critical moment your magic was gone."[51] By Silber's account, Ransom seemed "crushed and disappointed" and had tears in his eyes when he met with Silber after the firing. "You have just witnessed the final scene in *Titus Andronicus*," Silber remarked. (Shakespeare's character Titus Andronicus wreaks revenge at the end of the play by feeding a queen's sons to her in a pie and then stabbing her, but is himself fatally killed amid a gruesome bloodbath.)[52] Norman Hackerman's analysis was that Ransom would have had to give up some points—conceivably many points—in a bruising struggle to save Silber, and that was not Ransom's way of conducting himself.[53] William S. Livingston, too, related how Ransom "would sit in the corner at a Regents' meeting and let the Regents go after someone without raising a finger."[54] Much later, Silber would be more frank: "He should have been able to defend me," he said of Ransom. "But he was compromised. He should have been able to oppose the disunifying of Arts and Sciences."[55] Silber told another interviewer that "Ransom is not a scrapper, never was a scrapper. He's not a tough guy. He's not equal to a fight with Frank Erwin."[56]

Actually it was Norman Hackerman, not Ransom, who had appointed John Silber dean of the College of Arts and Sciences. As a philosopher Silber had formerly studied Immanuel Kant, but his scholarship gave way to academic politics after Hackerman discerned that Silber possessed the intellect and fire for an administrative post. Over the ensuing decades, even after Silber left UT, Hackerman would watch him become an astute administrator interested in the care and management of academic institutions. It pleased Hackerman to see his judgment vindicated; Silber did not shoot off in all directions as dean, but focused his energies. Yet whereas the College had always been the larger part of UT, under Silber it became (sadly, in Hackerman's eyes) controversial.[57] On the other hand, despite Silber's reputation at UT as a flaming liberal, he had sometimes joined with Frank C. Erwin, Jr., in going out onto the quadrangle and debating the leaders of student demonstrations. One such unlikely Silber-Erwin pairing took place during a rally featuring Larry Caroline, the assistant professor of philosophy whom Silber had hired. Erwin later admiringly told the assistant to the vice chancellor for academic programs Kenneth Ashworth, "Silber could beat down those arguments, and if he couldn't win he would question Caroline's ancestry back three generations."[58]

But those moments of camaraderie had not protected the dean. Silber would subsequently say that his speeches across Texas on behalf of liberal causes and in defense of UT had alarmed Erwin, who had one of Silber's speeches at Baylor School of Medicine in Houston (about the AMA's policies) recorded for review. When Silber received a standing ovation from affluent UT donors at the Mansion on Turtle Creek in Dallas in 1969 after addressing a fund-raising event, speaking without notes and tackling the public perception of the beards on campus and the partial nudity in a UT theatrical performance, Erwin perceived—rightly, Silber conceded thirty-five years later—that Silber was nursing political ambitions about controlling the liberal wing of, if not the entire, Democratic party in Texas. According to Silber, it was his rising statewide popularity, together with the growth of his College, that doomed his deanship.[59] Erwin shrugged off speculation that powerful Democratic party figures were behind Silber's ouster, telling Kenneth Ashworth shortly after the firing: "I didn't need any instructions from LBJ, Connally, Ben Barnes, or anybody."[60]

Even prior to Ransom's retirement and Silber's firing there had been problems with some of the projects that they both had supported. Now there began a full retreat from various experiments, such as the National Translation Center directed by Keith Botsford and its journal, *Delos,* which had depended more upon personalities than the durability of organizational structure. To many people in higher education across the nation, the chain of resignations and closures in Austin would amount to what was sometimes hyperbolically called "The Sack of Athens in Austin." Ransom commented little on these passing changes that washed across the surface of his university. As he had always done in the past, he seemed intent upon allowing people to find, without interference on his part, the destinies they were bound to reach. For him it had been Austin and its campus; for other administrators and faculty members it might be somewhere else in the world at large. He wrote heartfelt letters of regret about their leave-takings but stopped short of accepting or assigning blame and merely wished them well.

Personally there was the passing embarrassment for Ransom of pulling back from large-scale commitments as well as minor promises. To one collector he wrote on July 13, 1970: "Because I have resigned the Chancellorship and we all are now in a period of quick but officially uncertain transition, I am not able now to proceed with negotiations for the great Volterra Library. . . . It will always be the envy of scholars; it would have been a source of great pride to bring it to Texas."[61] The popular and outgoing Vartan Gregorian, who had joined the vanguard of faculty members seeking to block Erwin's strategies, was indignant upon seeing that the administration had marginalized Harry Ransom and stripped his office of its university seal and sumptuous desk. Gregorian visited Ransom repeatedly in an attempt to enlist his support for the unity of the College of Arts and Sciences and the rights of the faculty, but instead found "a man whose power and self-respect had slipped through his hands. He was now a chancellor who could not talk." Waving a cigarette in the air, Ransom would only say, "Bless you, my son, bless you, my boy."[62]

Ransom joined in hosting a dinner for President ad interim Bryce Jordan at the Commodore Perry Hotel in Austin on the evening of Friday, September 18, in advance of the opening football game against the University of California at Berkeley. Speakers included Erwin, Ransom, LeMaistre, and Jordan himself.[63] Jordan received a standing ovation following his remarks. The *Texan* editor noted grumpily that Erwin referred to the possibility that Jordan might become president "ad infinitum" rather than "ad interim."[64]

An article Ransom had already prepared for *Family Weekly,* debating the case in favor of large universities against arguments mounted by Dr. Leland Miles, president of the 2,000-student Alfred University, appeared nationally on September 13, 1970. It was essentially Ransom's swansong as far as this sort of public relations promotion was concerned. Representing a school enrolling 40,000 students in 100 buildings worth $200 million on 262 acres, Ransom highlighted "individual opportunity" involving "choice of courses, choice of companionship in groups, choice in the use of each day's hours." He touted the advantages accruing from the continual flow of public entertainments, lectures, and exhibits. Ransom's concluding paragraph about "the essence of a student's education" depending principally upon his ambition, breadth of his search for knowledge, and "depth of his understanding of what he had learned" was vintage Harry Ransom, the kind of rhetoric that had always made his university proud.[65]

Not so enjoyable were some of the other spin-offs from this season of unrest. On September 24, 1970, Ransom dutifully notified Bryce Jordan, in elegantly precise handwritten script, that he had "received two anonymous calls—Monday and yesterday—both of which I take to be only vicious jest. Each call threatened the bombing of the Computer Center, the Academic Center, and the 'Rare Books Library' (Stark?), as well as the 'burning of the general library catalogue.' (No mention of ROTC)." Advising Jordan that "we should be alert," Ransom noted that inasmuch as the messages "were *verbatim* identical, they should probably not go unnoticed."[66] After all, such malevolent acts as the destruction of library catalogue-card trays, the burning of libraries and other buildings, and even the bombing of campus facilities were happening with astonishing frequency at schools such as San Francisco State University, the University of California at Berkeley, and the University of Wisconsin at Madison. In some locales, marches and demonstrations seemed to be on the brink of giving way to engaged terrorism.

Letters of thanks from prominent Texans continued to accumulate on Ransom's desk. Leroy Jeffers, an attorney with Vinson, Elkins, Searls & Connally in Houston who had served on the Board of Regents from 1953 until 1959, wrote that "your retirement from the Chancellorship necessarily marks the end of a truly great epoc[h]. As the inspired and inspiring, articulate spokesman of The University of Texas System and its planner and leader, you have brought it not only great libraries, great scholars, and great grants but also a vision of greatness itself. No passing flurry of discord will ultimately dim this vision."[67] Tom Sealy, the attorney from Midland, Texas, who had been a regent from 1951 until 1957, applauded "the tremendous contribution you made to the University of Texas System," adding that "because of your personal eminence in the field of education, you . . . earned for the University of Texas at Austin a preeminent position as one of the half dozen outstanding institutions of higher learning in these United States. While we will miss you tremendously, the Ransom 'touch' will long endure."[68] John S. Redditt, the Lufkin attorney who had served on the Board from 1961 until 1964, wanted Ransom to know that "you have made a record as one of the great men of the United States."[69]

A climactic duty remained for Ransom to perform before his retirement. On November 6, 1970, he met with the Chancellor's Council in Austin to deliver a final report. "My last comments to the Council are an expression of gratitude," he began. "Both the Council as an organization and the vigor of its growth have been heartening. The roll has increased from 42 members in 1965 to more than 300 members in 1970." In a rare reference to the tumult that the nation's campuses were enduring, Ransom alluded

FIGURE 18.3

*Former chancellors Logan Wilson, Harry H. Ransom, and James P. Hart, dedication
of Burdine Hall, December 14, 1970.* Prints and Photographs Collection, Center
for American History, The University of Texas of Austin.

to "innumerable educational perplexities of the decade" that "might have
been disastrous had The University of Texas System not had support of
such friends as this membership." He listed twenty "notable accomplishments" in which the Chancellor's Council members had participated, citing the new Joe C. Thompson Conference Center in Austin, assistance to
disadvantaged and disabled students, travel grants for graduate students,
subsidies for conferences, help in acquiring four art collections and conducting teacher-evaluation surveys and two library surveys, editorial support for a volume highlighting 100 modern books, and loans for students
in emergency situations. Concluding his brief remarks, the chancellor said
that "the greatest boon of all has been the friendship of the members of the
Council. . . . My chief official duty after January 1 will be to live up to that
friendship."[70]

As the year wound down to the final month of Ransom's chancellorship,
a succession of evaluative feature articles marked the end of his tenure.
Texas Times commemorated Ransom's retirement by reprinting a speech
Ransom had made on March 7, 1964, to honor Dr. John Flowers upon his
retirement as president of Southwest Texas State University. In his 1964

talk Ransom had kiddingly congratulated Flowers on "not having to get up early to read the student newspaper so as to answer with reasonable moderation the other papers who want to make a college crisis out of one paragraph of undergraduate midnight musing," as well as "not having to attend a social function when he wants to read a book." A university president, explained Ransom, has "a full, free, uninstitutionalized life . . . only between Breakfast and Church on Sunday."

Professor Clarence L. Cline, a longtime friend and former chairman of the UT English Department, prepared personal reminiscences for a special issue of the *Texas Times* dedicated to Harry Ransom. "My wife and small daughters were devoted to Mrs. Ransom, . . . and many of our Saturday evenings were spent in the company of the two at a local Mexican restaurant," Cline wrote. "It was on one of those evenings at a corner table in El Matamoros that Mr. Ransom remarked, with a casualness as if he were telling us that he had bought a new suit, that he had been offered and had accepted the office of Dean of the College of Arts and Sciences." In Cline's opinion, while "others of us" might have come up with certain of his ideas, "none of us could have approached the sheer number or the brilliance of them, and not one of us could have persuaded the Regents to put them into execution."[71] Another article quoted the observation of Henrietta Jacobsen, director of special programs in the office of the chancellor for the University System, that in spite of the stress and magnitude of the task of creating a university of the first class, Ransom invariably retained an "inherent dignity" along with "unfailing good humor and courtesy." A mournful Graves Landrum, vice president for operations, pointed out the difficulty of assessing the achievements of someone "who had done everything at an institution" in such a wide variety of posts and capacities. "He has been Mr. University to a number of people," Landrum remarked.[72]

NINETEEN

FAREWELLS

When Harry Ransom became the first chancellor emeritus ever appointed for the University of Texas System, on January 1, 1971, the outlines of his existence reassuringly bore a marked continuity with the years that had gone before. His residential address was still on Watchhill Road, and his salary remained essentially unchanged. The regents invited him to attend their meetings as an adviser. He went on editing *Texas Quarterly*. He retained his presidency of the International Library Commission; memberships on the executive committee of the Carnegie Foundation for the Advancement of Teaching, American Council on Education Commission on Academic Affairs, and the permanent committee of the Oliver Wendell Holmes Devise for the history of the Supreme Court; delegate status from the Association of American Universities to the National Committee on Accreditation; and board memberships of the National Space Hall of Fame, Texas Council on Economic Education, Amon Carter Museum of Western Art, Southwestern Bell Telephone Company, and Austin National Bank. He was a fellow of the Texas State Historical Association and a member of the Texas Institute of Letters, the Philosophical Society of Texas, and the Grolier Club of New York City. However, his speeches, once so extremely frequent, now became unusual events.[1]

At his campus office a large portrait of Winston Churchill, whom he much admired, hung prominently in the same place as ever on one wall; he rotated numerous other paintings on loan from the art collections, but Churchill glowered down perennially.[2] A bust by expressionist sculptor Jacob Epstein (1880–1959), "Ole Pinager," remained as the only piece of sculpture in the office. "I keep him around to keep me humble," he told Kathleen Gee.[3] Ransom still could ride the Tower elevator to visit his staff and his priceless acquisitions in their temporary quarters—artworks on the seventeenth floor, theatre arts on the nineteenth, F. Warren Roberts's director's office on the twentieth, Mrs. Hudspeth on the twenty-first (her office often so filled with cardboard boxes that a visitor had to slide along the wall), his own "library" office on the twenty-second, and the treasure room on the top floor. According to Hazel Ransom, only one disappointment marred his arrangements for this new phase, a long-taken-for-granted assumption rebuffed when the routine request was made: he learned that he would not be invited to return to teach in the UT English Department.[4] His good friend Clarence L. Cline was no longer its chairman, and departures, retirements, and deaths within Ransom's home department, coupled with the recruiting of numerous new faculty members unable to recall Ransom's exceptional teaching or the glorious years of his innovative deanship (and in no mood to accommodate the wishes of an upper administrator linked with Frank C. Erwin, Jr.), combined with other factors to frustrate Ransom's desire to re-enter the classroom.

But many other compensations offered themselves. On January 8, 1971, the UT News and Information Service issued an announcement celebrating the official publication of *Great Libraries,* the book by Anthony Hobson of Sotheby's auction house in London.[5] Although Ransom had received advance word about *Great Libraries,* now he and the UT community finally had the delight of studying and circulating its declarations. Hobson included only five U.S. libraries among the thirty-two distinguished institutions he selected for inclusion—Harvard University, Yale University, the Pierpont Morgan Library in New York, the Henry E. Huntington Library in San Marino, California, and the University of Texas Library. He gave Ransom credit for launching a "huge programme of acquisition . . . such as had not been seen in the USA since Henry E. Huntington's death." Hobson likened UT Austin to "an active volcano; it is impossible to tell in which direction it will erupt next." He cited Ransom's transportation to Austin of the entirety of Evelyn Waugh's library, shelves, and furniture, the papers of astronomer Sir John Herschel, and the Gernsheim photographic archive as indicative of the manner by which Ransom elevated the standing of the Humanities Research Center.[6]

Another confirmation of the stature of the Humanities Research Center came in the form of a report on its "achievements and prospects" submitted by Gordon N. Ray of the Guggenheim Foundation on January 26, 1971. Based on his visit to Austin in November 1970, Ray's analysis asserted that "the development of the HRC over the last 14 years represents one of the great achievements in the entire history of book and manuscript collection." Ray singled out Harry Ransom, who in 1956 "first began to realize his breath-taking inspiration of creating in the southwest a collection of rare books and manuscripts that would rival those of such long-established

FIGURE 19.1

President Richard M. Nixon at podium, (left to right, first row) Harry H. Ransom, First Lady Pat Nixon, Regent Frank C. Erwin, Jr., President Lyndon B. Johnson, First Lady Lady Bird Johnson, dedication of the Lyndon Baines Johnson Presidential Library, University of Texas at Austin, May 22, 1971. Planning for the library had begun in the mid-1960s, when Lady Bird Johnson visited the UT campus escorted by Ransom, Erwin, Heath, and Hudspeth. Prints and Photographs Collection, Center for American History, The University of Texas at Austin.

eastern universities as Harvard and Yale." He found the necessary money from Texans and non-Texans whom he "infected with his own enthusiasm," and achieved "a burst of acquisition unmatched since the great days of J. Pierpont Morgan and Henry E. Huntington."[7]

Meanwhile, the opening and dedication of the Lyndon Baines Johnson Presidential Library, postponed from autumn 1970 because of construction delays, was finally scheduled for May 22, 1971. Designed by the architect who had created Yale's rare book library, the LBJ Library contained a lecture hall and a 1,000-seat auditorium. Perhaps because of the potential for political demonstrations, the timing of "the dedication itself will now occur after most of the local University population is scattered," Ransom mentioned.[8]

An article in the March 21, 1971, issue of the *Houston Chronicle* was accompanied by a photograph of "beauteous Hazel Ransom" wearing "a stunning long-sleeved print gown." A tuxedo-clad Harry Ransom stood beside her as usual in the picture, but his appearance was dramatically altered. Gone was the robust, slightly stocky, hale face of old, instead replaced by a smiling, wearier-looking, almost gaunt Ransom.[9] Moreover, Ransom seemed to be experiencing a fresh awareness of his mortality. Various people noticed earnest efforts on his part to curtail his smoking habit, first switching to long, filter-tipped cigarettes and then trying to stop altogether.

In the spring of 1971, Ransom continued to inspire students. He was the guest speaker at the Phi Beta Kappa initiation dinner at UT Austin. Having long been a member of the national honor society, Ransom told the students who were being tapped that they should carry out the rest of their lives so that it would not be the last honor they would receive. Elaine Shelton, one of the riveted initiates who heard him, would find these words acting as a catalyst for achievements in her eventual profession, adult and continuing education.[10]

Ransom himself received an honorary Doctor of Humane Letters degree conferred by the University of Dallas on May 23, 1971.[11] That event was followed on Thursday, May 27, by a signal ceremony in Austin bestowing on Ransom the gold medallion and leather-bound volume—symbols of the coveted Santa Rita Award he had helped create—at a campus luncheon following the regular meeting of the UT System Development Board. The *Austin American-Statesman* news photo of the event again captured a thinner, more diminutive Ransom.[12]

A few weeks later, on Thursday, June 17, Ransom addressed two hundred librarians and scholars at a pre-conference dinner meeting ("artichokes, steak, and red wine") for the Rare Books Division of the American Library Association at the UT Alumni Center. The guests "settled back with an anticipatory murmur," according to one account of the dinner, since they "knew that Dr. Ransom had done much to transform Texas . . . into the bookman's promised land."[13] Talking there that night to a roomful of kindred spirits, Ransom described his discarding of earlier notions about what constituted "literature": "The history of design and architecture, maps and charts, the western novel, detective fiction, and the little magazine . . . are mixed examples." He expressed his hope that libraries will continue to be "one of the few social contexts left capable of making both peace and unity feel completely at home."[14]

John Silber, having ascended to the presidency of Boston University, remained critical of Frank C. Erwin, Jr., but laudatory of Harry Ransom. On

July 30, Silber wrote to Ransom himself: "I was never a nomad; so it is hard to fold my tent and steal away. I feel like one of those live oaks ripped out on campus to make room for a new building. . . . You called forth from me and the rest of 'Harry's Boys' the best that was in us, stuff of which we had only the vaguest inkling. We accomplished a few things beyond our capacities for no better reason than that you believed we could."[15] Ransom's reply is unknown, but he had written to Silber earlier, on January 11, 1971: "You cannot change Boston—or the educational world—overnight in your new role. What you can do, with the sense and support of your board and other colleagues, is to start programs which have been left to palaver in most institutions. Expectations of you may go high enough to be handicaps. Haul them into reality."[16]

A humbling honor now descended: Mr. and Mrs. Jack S. Josey (he the Houston oilman who graduated from UT with a B.S. in Petroleum Production Engineering in 1939, and retired from the Board of Regents in January 1971) commissioned a large bronze bust to commemorate Ransom's achievements. Charles Umlauf, a UT professor of art, was selected to create the likeness.[17] Hazel and others close to Ransom were bothered by the rugged features that Umlauf was molding into the face, but liked the sculptor's efforts to capture Ransom's cerebration and intensity.

During this period Ransom continued to utilize the fourth floor of the Academic Center as an entertainment facility. A photograph taken at one luncheon showed Ransom seated at a table with Regents Rabbi Levi Olan, Jack S. Josey, former Governor and Mrs. John B. Connally, Mrs. Perry Bass, Frank C. Erwin, Jr., and former President Lyndon B. Johnson. He sometimes even held candlelight dinners there for groups of library supporters, who emerged under a Texas moon to stroll about the well-lighted quadrangle area and talk over the stimulating book-talk they had just enjoyed.[18]

After Ransom stepped down from the chancellorship, the budget for the HRC as a whole became far smaller and less dependable. Kathleen Gee was flabbergasted that in the first year he was out of office the direct amount available dropped precipitously from $2 million to $300,000 a year. During that period Mrs. Hudspeth herself occasionally met with Frank Erwin to implore him to authorize the funding of specific purchases, and windfalls did occur sporadically. That this decrease more or less assumed a permanency was partly due to modified priorities at the university, but also stemmed from the fact that Ransom in his emeritus position could no longer argue for the HRC's vital importance during the final stages of budget decisions. Even so, he had not been left without effectual means of making and keeping influential friends for the HRC. In addition to the lunches, dinners, and special events he arranged in the Academic Center for supporters and potential friends of the Humanities Research Center, he also discovered the popularity of his practice of lending works of art or rare books from the library's collections to campus and state figures involved in the budget process. From time to time he would contact Kathleen Gee to say, for instance, "Kathy, Speaker of the House Price Daniel, Jr., needs some paintings." She would promptly deliver several canvases to the Speaker's quarters in the State Capitol Building a few blocks south of campus. These loans of artworks and books to elected politicians, reminders of the value and beauty of the university collections, became a tradition that went on for many years.[19]

Frances Hudspeth made the arrangements for Ransom's social affairs, though her health was faltering. After her second heart attack she had said that she wanted above all to see Harry Ransom installed in the new Humanities Research Center he had worked so long to envision and prepare. But when he did move in, she found herself hospitalized and had to be content with his description of the desk awaiting her in a freshly decorated building.[20] Then, on Saturday night, January 29, 1972, Mrs. Frances Hellums Hudspeth, executive assistant and office manager of the UT Humanities Research Center, died, never having made the move to her new quarters. She left a husband, Jack C. Hudspeth, a sister in Chicago, and three nieces and a nephew in Austin. The family asked that memorial contributions be made to the Multiple Sclerosis Association, to fight the disease that had wasted Jack. One measure of her standing was the list of honorary pallbearers: Harry Huntt Ransom, of course, but also former President Lyndon B. Johnson, Frank C. Erwin, Jr., Charles A. LeMaistre, Graves W. Landrum, E. D. Walker, F. Warren Roberts, Carl Eckhardt, Thomas M. Cranfill, Clarence L. Cline, W. D. Blunk, and a dozen other identifiable names from the campus and city communities. The day after she died, Ransom issued a statement saying, "Mrs. Hudspeth's lifetime of devoted service to the University has few parallels. Her influence ranged from very young students to distinguished patrons of learning. Her most remarkable quality was complete loyalty. That quality was supported by heroic devotion to her ideals and a deep wisdom which touched many of the University's greatest accomplishments."[21] Harold Billings, who had been associated with the University of Texas Library since 1954 and would serve as the General Libraries director from 1977 until 2003, put the future state of things quite simply: "The day that Frances Hudspeth died, the Ransom University died with her."[22]

The seven-story Humanities Research Center, nestled within a grove of live oak trees at 21st Street and Guadalupe, opened on February 7, 1972, to those engaged in scholarly research. Only the Dobie Room, Tinker Room, Hoblitzelle Room, Josey Room, Erle Stanley Gardner Room, and the Knopf Collections retained their original locations on the fourth floor of the Academic Center.[23] Ransom designated himself as "Director of Special Collections," which allowed him to move intricately (and protectively) into the HRC operations while leaving F. Warren Roberts in figurehead control. Dr. David Robb Farmer, a UT Austin Ph.D., soon became the assistant director of the HRC, also teaching courses in the English Department. William R. Holman, former director of the San Francisco Public Library, was named Humanities Research Center librarian, and John R. Payne, hired in 1958, took up the duties of associate librarian.[24] It required half a dozen conferences in Ransom's new HRC office suite before Dr. Maria X. Z. Wells overlooked her misgivings and accepted the curatorship of the extensive new Italian collection in 1972. Although she pointed out that she had no bibliographic training, Ransom soothed her concerns: "With your background, you can, I am sure, master the necessary terms. And you have the knowledge, and can truly *understand* these Italian-language manuscripts." "When Ransom was in power," she said afterward, "everything was possible." But she soon began to worry about whether he would be leaving behind a strong enough infrastructure of leadership when he eventually departed.[25]

On May 12, 1972, the Colorado School of Mines conferred an honorary degree of Doctor of Engineering on Harry Ransom. It was his eighth and final honorary degree.[26]

Another tempting offer from a Texas school now materialized for the last time. On August 22, 1972, Dr. Herbert H. Reynolds wrote from the Office of the Executive Vice President for Baylor University in Waco: "It was a distinct privilege to visit with you last Spring and to have the honor of inviting you to become the first recipient of our Endowed Chair for Robert Browning Studies."[27] Robert Browning's poetry had long delighted Ransom, and the Armstrong Browning Library on the Baylor campus contained the world's largest collection of materials related to Browning and his wife, Elizabeth Barrett Browning. Nevertheless, Ransom replied candidly on August 29: "I have a contract with the Regents until September 1974. . . . I also have a moral obligation to complete, if I can, the history of our recent library development and a small volume of comment on higher education. . . . I wish that time (and timing) could justify longer delay in joining my gratitude and my regret."[28]

Harry Ransom and his Humanities Research Center caught the attention of the *New York Times* yet again in January 1973 upon the stunning

FIGURE 19.2

Harry H. Ransom and a model of the Humanities Research Center. Ransom's dream of a facility to house a world-class library became a reality when the Humanities Research Center opened on February 7, 1972. Harry Ransom Humanities Research Center, The University of Texas at Austin.

purchase, for $125,000, of the 400 long-lost letters exchanged between Emperor Ferdinand Maximilian and his Empress Carlota, whom Napoleon III had appointed to rule Mexico. Ransom declined to provide details about how he obtained the collection, except to confirm that the Belgian royal family had released the correspondence. The sensational purchase caused *Times* reporter Martin Waldron to praise "a library that already lures scholars from all over the world and outdraws the Texas football team for alumni support." Waldron identified Ransom as "a one-time newspaperman and now chancellor emeritus . . . whose 15-year search for rare books, manuscripts and papers has been so successful that rival collectors of several nations have wished that he would retire."[29]

Ransom had become known as the friend of university presses as well as libraries, and on June 19, 1973, he was the invited speaker who concluded a meeting in Austin of the seventy-member Association of American University Presses. Ransom argued that the "intellectual standards of a university can be judged" to an extent on the basis of the caliber of its press. He warned that current university journals are "two, three, or four times too long to be readable or economically printed. . . . Brevity is a goal much to be desired." New technologies would offer different methods of publications, and he predicted that "the opportunity offered by these new developments" would be "as great as the obligation to maintain old standards of service to knowledge."[30]

When President ad interim Bryce Jordan turned over the presidential office in July 1971 to ecologist Stephen H. Spurr, whose Yale University degree in forestry had taken him to a vice presidency and deanship of graduate studies at the University of Michigan before he was recruited by Charles A. LeMaistre, Harry Ransom thereby had the distinction of having known ten men who had held the UT presidency, excluding himself. Although Frank C. Erwin, Jr., nominally yielded the Board of Regents chairmanship to John Peace of San Antonio from March 1971 until January 1973, and then from January 1973 until December 1975 saw it go to Houston attorney and banker A. G. McNeese, Jr., who was serving his second term as a regent, many observers felt that Erwin retained his immense influence and continued to call the shots on many key issues. Erwin and Spurr reportedly clashed over Spurr's push for funding a Welch Hall addition for the sciences rather than following through on preliminary plans for the Performing Arts Center that Bryce Jordan had championed. Nonetheless Spurr presided over the approval of the Perry-Castañeda Library plans, the Texas Swimming Center, and eventually the Performing Arts Center. But Spurr admitted that he was not used to the Board of Regents being so actively involved in what was transpiring on campus. Spurr brought in Ronald M. Brown from the University of Michigan in 1971 to serve as vice president for student affairs, and in 1972 summoned W. Rea Keast (1914–1998), a former department chairman and dean at Cornell University and the beleaguered president of Wayne State University during incendiary times in Detroit, to chair the UT English Department within Dean Stanley Werbow's scaled-down College of Humanities.[31] A specialist in Restoration and eighteenth-century British literature—and most notably a scholar of the English dictionary prepared by Dr. Samuel Johnson—the engaging Rea Keast soon became a candidate to be "director" within a concept being floated among the regents and administrators. The new entity would consolidate all of the research materials at the various UT Austin libraries such as the Barker Texas History Center into a comprehensive unit, tentatively called the Division of Special Collections, to simplify budget procedures, clarify personnel decisions, and develop more logical collections development policies. Along with Keast, Gordon Ray of the Guggenheim Foundation, Stephen McCarthy, president of the Association of Research Libraries, and purportedly Ransom himself (a less and less likely prospect as the months went by) were considered for this post by a committee reporting to President Spurr, though nothing about these plans had been officially announced. One impediment was the strenuous opposition of Regent Jenkins Garrett, among others, to the idea of placing the HRC under the control of the General Libraries, as that larger organization was called after 1972.[32]

Ransom, now settled into an office on the third floor of the HRC (in later years it would become the Tom Lea Suite, a conference room adorned by Lea's paintings of Texas and the Southwest), was near Director F. Warren Roberts's office on the same floor. Physically as well as mentally, Ransom seemed protected at last from chanting students and campus politics in general; uniformed guards in the lobby of the high-security building, after all, controlled ingress to the elevators. But the rumors, maneuverings, and speculations about the library restructuring, while following patterns of behavior familiar enough to Ransom from his years among the cognoscenti in the Main Building, became tiresome. His future was clarified in September 1973, when the Board of Regents announced that Harry Ransom would undertake, with their authorization and support, a history of the University of Texas from 1883 until 1961. This would clearly be Ransom's final service to the university, and offered him an enviable opportunity to interpret for future generations the events that he had witnessed. Ransom moved his office across the campus from the Humanities Research Center to Sid Richardson Hall, where the Eugene C. Barker Texas History Center (later renamed the Center for American History) had been located since 1971.

Esther R. Moore went with Ransom to Richardson Hall. Tall, lanky Moore, highly competent, became Ransom's executive assistant but always maintained that she "did *not* replace Mrs. Hudspeth—she was irreplaceable." Moore had worked in the president's office at the University of Arizona for six years before beginning duties as an administrative assistant in Ransom's office in 1969. She brought focused professionalism to every task, though she also had a wryly humorous side. She found him "so educated, so intellectual. I had never finished college, yet he could sit down and talk with me—or a janitor or an elevator operator—without ever seeming condescending. He was able to 'connect' with people at all levels." Another thing she admired was "his way of putting words together, his turn of phrases. I liked working for him because I liked the way he used the English language. Even much later, I enjoyed reading over what he had said or written."[33] A young Ralph L. Elder would also assist him one summer, apprehensive about being in proximity to such an august personage. Would he be difficult, demanding, judgmental? To Elder's relief Ransom immediately revealed himself as "the prototypical Southern gentleman" and "a joy to work with."[34]

Jo Ann Bardin, preparing a news release (dated August 21, 1973) that reviewed the highlights of the Humanities Research Center, included Ransom's opinions about the futility of isolating the humanities from other human attainments: "It seems to me impossible to understand science without understanding the human beings who are the users and innovators of science. . . . The most important impulses of the humanities and the sciences interlock. The humanities have benefited vastly by science and technology. For example, look at the technology of communication; if it were not for science we would still be in the quill pen era."

Student protests had dwindled across the nation, and large-scale demonstrations became virtual rarities after the military draft was ended in 1973 and the Vietnam ceasefire accords were signed. But in 1974 there appeared an acerbic book, written by the publisher of the feisty *Texas Observer*, that would haunt the political atmosphere of the University of Texas for decades to come. Ronnie Dugger's *Our Invaded Universities: Form, Reform, and New Starts* purported to confirm many of the allegations by campus activists regarding the triumph of corporate greed and the defeat of valorous professors and truth-seeking students. The clearest sign that Dugger's book was a product of the late 1960s and early 1970s was its basic premise that collusions among financiers, business tycoons, corporate attorneys, public officials, and university administrators lay behind nearly every significant campus development. A powerful, interlocked elite seemed to monopolize decision-making at the institution. Harry Ransom received a mixed treatment in *Our Invaded Universities*. Dugger recalled meeting him in out-of-the-way bookstores and tobacco shops in Washington, D.C., and other cities, and liked the way "he listens, and by what he then says, you know that he is hearing what you say." Although charmed by Ransom's manner, Dugger ultimately dismissed Ransom as "soft," a "man with a pliant way in words" whose "special collections were his priority, not the faculty's or the students'—they hardly even knew about them."[35] *Our Invaded Universities* correctly discerned the magnetic attraction of the university for those with major political, financial, and legal influence, but it failed to recognize the generous and socially constructive benefits accruing from these collaborations. Above all, the book showed profound blind spots, especially in its refusal to acknowledge the indelible value of Ransom's Humanities Research Center, and likewise in its indifference to the resulting national and international renown that UT reaped.[36] Margaret Berry, the author of a series of historical monographs tracing the history of the University of Texas at Austin, found Ronnie Dugger himself "very likeable," but lamented his tendency to be "*so* negative—always looking for something wrong."[37]

President Spurr underwent open-heart surgery in June 1974 and did not resume a vigorous schedule, working only half days. On September 23, 1974, just after classes had convened for the Fall term at the Austin campus, Chancellor Charles A. LeMaistre met with Spurr and delivered an unexpected ultimatum: resign or be fired. Refusing to submit the requested letter of resignation, Spurr was removed from office the next afternoon.[38] The reasons behind the firing were not immediately made explicit, but newspaper reporters attributed it to LeMaistre's eroding confidence in Spurr's loyalty, Spurr's tendency to consult directly with certain regents rather than go through the chain of command, LeMaistre's discontent with the management of the special library collections, and Spurr's stubbornness about acceding to some of Erwin's stipulations concerning social and sports arrangements. One published rumor held that Erwin and Spurr had clashed over the list of people to be invited to pre-football-game parties. Moreover, Spurr perhaps unwisely had scheduled his visit to Big Bend National Park on the weekend of the annual Texas–Texas A&M football square-off. Arthur H. Dilly, an executive assistant to the chancellor, would characterize Spurr as an administrator unable to adapt to the Texas ways of doing things, "an absolute academic, resistant to athletics," and "not a warm personality."[39]

Issues regarding Ransom's successor in the HRC and whether the momentum of his acquisition program should be maintained apparently played a role in Spurr's removal. In October 1974 Spurr told a special Faculty Senate committee that LeMaistre and Ransom, along with Regents Jenkins Garrett and Edward Clark, had "enthusiastically concurred" with Spurr's choice of Keast to take Ransom's place in the Humanities Research Center, but that Garrett subsequently became unhappy with Spurr's handling of the Keast appointment and "accused me of having downgraded the directorship of the HRC. . . . It is quite likely that Dr. LeMaistre was influenced by the anger of Regent Garrett in reaching his decision that day to dismiss me."[40]

Chancellor LeMaistre's appointment in 1974 of Dr. Lorene Rogers as the president ad interim—after the faculty search committee had twice refused to include her in the list of candidates submitted to the regents—triggered a series of explosions registering mounting resentment against regental conduct. A Texas-born biochemist who had received her Ph.D. from UT Austin in 1948, she had conducted research on the congenital effects of nutrition and chemicals and had served as a vice president since 1974. Rogers was UT's first female president and, for that matter, the first woman to head any American university of UT's size and prestige.[41] Yet faculty and students rallied on the West Mall to call for her resignation, and some departments canceled their classes to protest the lack of faculty and student consultation. A year later, when the Board of Regents (narrowly, by one vote) confirmed her permanent appointment as president, the General Faculty, several hundred strong, met in the LBJ School Auditorium and adopted three measures: (1) Members of the Faculty Senate would hereafter not attend any University Council sessions, which would mean that the University Council would be unable to produce the necessary quorum to hold official meetings; (2) Faculty would not accept appointments by the president to any University committees; and (3) Faculty would not attend commencement ceremonies. These practices were widely accepted and observed, seriously hampering and challenging the legitimacy of university decision-making.[42] (Professor of law Charles Alan Wright, the previous chairman of the Faculty Senate, and a few others objected to those strategies, arguing that campus cynics were permitting their antagonism toward the chancellor and the regents to spill over onto Dr. Rogers.) Within this context of animosity and distrust, President Rogers made a succession of moves that sent waves of shock through portions of the library sphere that Ransom had fostered, and in their aggregate they amounted to a seismic shift in appropriations, emphases, and personnel. The era over which Ransom formerly presided had now definitively closed.

In the meantime, however, and as though in compensation for what was occurring and what was yet to come, the UT Board of Regents voted unanimously on Friday, September 20, 1974, to rename the building occupied by the Humanities Research Center. At the subsequent meeting of the regents on Friday, November 1, 1974, Frank C. Erwin, Jr., presented a resolution for adoption and inclusion in the minutes; he recited the offices that Ransom had held "as an educator of national eminence," and then went on: "Throughout his years of administration Dr. Ransom never lost sight of the importance of libraries to a great university. The Library was both his first and a continuing professional love. . . . In recognition of the key role of Dr. Ransom in the development of the collection, the Board of Regents does hereby resolve that the building housing these books and manuscripts be dedicated as a deserved honor . . . and . . . be named and known as the Harry Ransom Center. May it long stand as a monument to his genius."[43]

In January 1975, President Lorene Rogers made newspaper headlines around the state by signaling a drastic reevaluation of previous policies: "UT Stops Paying Library's Bills" (*Fort Worth Star-Telegram*), "Cutbacks

FIGURE 19.3

Chancellor Emeritus Harry H. Ransom, UT Lutcher Conference Center, San Antonio, Texas, 1974. This snapshot of Ransom is a favorite among those who remember him for his congenial manner and ability to put others at ease. Harry Ransom Humanities Research Center, The University of Texas at Austin.

Put HRC in Debt" (*Austin American-Statesman*), "Power Play Seen in Halt of UT Library Bill Payments" (*Dallas Times Herald*), "Library Hassle Feeds UT Fires" (*San Antonio Express*).[44] The Board of Regents had appropriated $400,000 to the Humanities Research Center, but Rogers issued a presidential order for the university accounting office to stop disbursing the funds until a team of experts could conduct an "objective" examination of how the money was being spent. (This group would eventually conclude that the record-keeping had unquestionably been inadequate.) "HRC has been experiencing personnel problems as well as criticism that money has been wasted," she said. "I am waiting until these problems can be resolved to be sure the money is spent as it was intended to be." Embarrassed library officials had no choice but to ignore repeated telephone calls from irate book dealers, insurance companies, and other creditors owed hundreds of thousands of dollars in unpaid bills. Several unnamed library employees tipped off newspaper reporters that a "power struggle" among HRC Director F. Warren Roberts, Special Collections Director W. Rea Keast, President Rogers, and Chancellor LeMaistre was responsible for Rogers's order.[45]

Whatever the causes, the aftermath of this disagreement was sweeping. The books, manuscripts, photographs, and artworks stayed where they were, but library administrators who had lost favor moved on. F. Warren Roberts was allowed to retain the HRC directorship until 1978, while others were removed more promptly. Among these was Rea Keast, who talked several times with Lorene Rogers and the regents about what he considered to be his laudable intentions in an effort to persuade her to give him a chance to implement ambitious plans for reorganization and review.[46] Nevertheless, she abolished his recently created position as Director (or Coordinator—references differ) of the Division of Special Collections and asked him in December 1974 to return to the UT English Department, which he had formerly chaired and where he would teach until his retirement in 1980. During the period when President Rogers was making up her mind, Keast conferred repeatedly with Harry Ransom in his suite in Sid Richardson Hall amid tables piled high with folders and photographs of UT figures and campus scenes. Ransom assured Keast that he had his best interests at heart and was trying to use his remaining influence to smooth things over.[47] Compounding the generally damaging situation was the cumulative effect of a 1969 tax reform law that essentially ended large deductions for gifts to non-profit organizations; libraries and museums consequently found that writers, composers, and artists were becoming far more inclined to sell their manuscripts, correspondence, compositions, and paintings rather than donate them to universities.[48]

For Harry Ransom in his Sid Richardson Hall bunker on the east side of the campus near the LBJ Library, the collisions and collapses were at a bearable remove. Occasionally, in spite of flare-ups of his phlebitis with pre- scribed spells of bed rest, there were even gratifying reminders of the glory years. In 1975 Dean Stanley Werbow, President Rogers, and the Board of Regents approved a new annual prize, the Harry H. Ransom Award for Teaching Excellence in the College of Humanities. The final possible cam- pus honor came to Ransom on Friday, October 24, 1975, in the Lyndon Baines Johnson School Auditorium, when he sat beside five other recipients of the University Distinguished Alumnus Awards to watch a tape of CBS television news anchorman Walter Cronkite (himself a previous honoree in 1964) narrating highlights of their lives. (Ransom technically qualified for the University's Ex-Students' Association Alumnus award because he took graduate courses at UT between 1935 and 1937.) He received a heavy bronze commemorative medallion inside a large walnut box with an in- scribed plaque announcing the fact that the Ex-Students' Association, "in recognition of professional attainment, participation in alumni affairs, and service to Alma Mater, hereby elects Harry Huntt Ransom Distinguished Alumnus 1975." A reception and buffet after the ceremony allowed Ransom to greet many of his former colleagues and longtime friends.[49]

Ransom's years in the top echelon at UT were additionally memorial- ized in 1975 by the publication of Joan Simpson Burns's unconventional but informative 511-page study, *The Awkward Embrace: The Creative Artist and the Institution in America: An Inquiry Based on Interviews with Nine Men Who Have—Through Their Organizations—Worked to Influence American Culture* (New York: Alfred A. Knopf, 1975). Quotations from interviews largely conducted in the summer of 1967 enabled Burns to evoke the hey- day of Ransom's chancellorship. A postscript recounted Ransom's retire- ment and concluded that "the dream of a community of scholars on the plains of Texas was shattered."[50]

As 1976 opened, Ransom became more fully absorbed in sifting through photographs to make selections for the history of UT he had been commis- sioned by the regents to prepare. May Ellen MacNamara ("Mrs. Mac"), an administrative assistant since 1972 in the HRC's photograph collection on the sixth floor, often saw this "very quiet, reserved man" as he toiled on the project. "He wanted it just right. He spent many months digging." She made arrangements to reproduce the scenes and portraits he was deciding to use.[51]

The Ransoms spent the third weekend of April at their Dripping Springs ranch house, where Hazel's parents had resided since moving from Dallas

FIGURE 19.4

Maurice F. Granville, Mario Efrain Ramirez, M.D., Jack Wrather, Liz Carpenter,
Harry Huntt Ransom, Ben Foshee Love, University Distinguished Alumnus Awards,
October 24, 1975. This award by the university's Ex-Students' Association also honored
Granville, chairman of the board and CEO of Texaco, Inc.; Ramirez, a Rio Grande
physician and judge; Wrather, a Los Angeles executive and investor; Carpenter,
former White House secretary and Lady Bird Johnson's staff director; and
Love, CEO of Texas Commerce Bank in Houston.
Ransom was eligible for the award since he had taken graduate courses at the university
in the mid-1930s. This award would be his final campus honor. Prints and Photographs
Collection, Center for American History, The University of Texas at Austin.

in the 1950s. Whenever Harry and Hazel visited that country home they
stayed in living quarters at the rear; the now-elderly Harrods, assisted by
several attendants, lived in the front. The couples shared meals. After dinner on Sunday evening, Harry held hands and laughed with Hazel. Later he
moved to the back of the house to work, and Hazel alternately read, watched
television, and napped. Early the next morning, on Monday, April 19,
she went back to join Harry. She stood at the doorway transfixed with horror and then knelt frantically to touch her husband where he lay beside
the bed. "He was gone," she realized almost at once. She rushed to get her
father, who called Dr. Ace Alsup in Austin, the physician to Hazel and her

father. The doctor arrived to confirm Harry Ransom's death and place it at approximately 4:00 A.M. on Monday, April 19, 1976. Dr. Alsup drove a shocked Hazel back to her home in Austin. Ransom's phlebitis had been under control again, thanks to a blood thinner he was taking. He had no history of heart problems, and no medicine for high blood pressure had been prescribed. Chronic sinusitis had been his only ongoing ailment. He had stopped smoking several years previous to his demise.[52] Nonetheless, the family and the doctor agreed that an autopsy would really serve no purpose. Nothing could change the fact of his loss. The official cause of death was listed as infarction of the heart; in other words, a heart attack. He had died at the age of sixty-seven.

Because Ransom had been, in Hazel's phrase, such a "private" person, she made arrangements for a small funeral to take place the next day, Tuesday, April 20, at the Weed-Corley Funeral Home on North Lamar Boulevard. Mrs. Lady Bird Johnson attended, as did Frank C. Erwin, Jr., Frank Wardlaw, Margaret Crow, the faithful Graves Landrum of course, and a few other close friends. The Reverend Charles A. Sumners officiated. Burial took place in Austin Memorial Park. Frank Erwin made it known to Hazel that he was tremendously disappointed in the decision only to hold private services; he had wanted a large public rite.

Literally sick with grief, Hazel Ransom was haunted by guilty reasoning: "If only I had been sitting right there beside him, maybe I could have helped him," she kept telling herself. The doctor assured her repeatedly that the heart attack was evidently so massive that probably even a physician standing ready in a fully equipped hospital cardiac room could not have saved her husband's life. Still, her mourning continued unabated for days, and her haggard condition rendered it inadvisable for her to leave the house on Watchhill Road.[53]

In the end, however, Hazel's wish for privacy yielded to the opposing view represented by Frank Erwin. Harry Ransom had dedicated his life to the University of Texas, had become completely identified with its growth and stature, and could not depart from the scene without the valedictories deemed proper for someone of his station and attainments. First came the newspaper headlines in the city. "Heart Attack Fatal to Ransom" and "Ex-UT Chancellor Harry Ransom Dies" reported the *Austin American-Statesman* in various editions.[54] Amy Jo Long of the UT News and Information Service now had the lugubrious task of issuing a final press release on behalf of the administrator she had esteemed and served for so long. She summarized his education, offices, achievements, and honors, emphasizing that "throughout his career in teaching and administration, Dr. Ransom's principal concern was the individual student."⁵⁵ President Lorene Rogers gave an immediate statement in reaction to the news: "During more than 40 years . . . Dr. Ransom made thousands of converts to the life of learning. His contagious enthusiasm brought excitement to the classroom and attracted many friends to the University. In his public speeches and private conversations, he expressed brilliantly and gracefully his dream of what the University could become. Much of that dream was realized under his inspired leadership."⁵⁶ Allan Shivers, Chairman of the UT System Board of Regents, said, "No one has done more for the university than he has done. He probably contributed more to the greatness of the University of Texas at Austin than any other individual."⁵⁷ Democratic Governor Dolph Briscoe called him "a great educator and a great Texan" and said that "his passing is a great loss to the state of Texas."⁵⁸

Newspapers across the state, from Freeport to Fort Worth to Kilgore, carried front-page articles headlined with variant wordings of "Former UT Chancellor Succumbs." Brenda Bell of the *Austin American-Statesman* termed him "The King Arthur of UT's intellectual Camelot during the heady 1960s."⁵⁹ His death rated two columns in the *Mexico City News*. An obituary appeared prominently in the *International Herald Tribune*, published in Paris. The *Washington Post, Baltimore Evening Sun*, and *Cleveland Press* devoted respectful stories to Ransom's demise. Morris Kaplan, writing the obituary for the *New York Times*, quoted New York City book dealer John F. Fleming, who recalled how, upon meeting Ransom, the Texan vowed: "I'm going to form a great collection of books, equal to the collections of Harvard or Yale."⁶⁰

Meanwhile, administrators on the UT Austin campus elected to honor the memory of Harry Ransom with a public commemorative assembly at 2 P.M. on Tuesday, May 4, 1976, in the Lyndon Baines Johnson Library Auditorium. Four speakers—two from the faculty, one from the administration, and one from the regents—were soon announced. On the day of the memorial service Hazel Ransom still felt too ill (and, one suspects, too loyal to Harry's passion for privacy) to attend. What the *Austin American-Statesman* pointedly called "a sparse crowd" and the *Daily Texan* termed a "sparse audience" spread itself out thinly amid the plushness of the large auditorium. Harry Huntt Ransom had obviously become, to the majority of students and faculty, a venerated name rather than a beloved person. Reporter Brenda Bell observed that "his departure from the hurly-burly of big university power politics" had been so complete that "he appeared to vanish from the scene. . . . He could be seen gliding in and out of Regents' meetings, a solitary, enigmatic figure with a half-smile on his face. Students and others . . . hesitated to approach him, as one would shy from approaching a legend or a ghost."[61]

President Rogers opened the services by averring that "this institution will never forget what Dr. Ransom has done for it. . . . His name will be honored and will be praised as long as this university shall stand and scholars find their way here." Logan Wilson, former UT Austin president and System Chancellor, spoke next, saying that Ransom's successes were evidence that "outstanding academicians" can handle "the uncertain perils of full-time administrative posts." Wilson reminded the audience that "Harry Ransom's heaviest responsibilities of leadership" occurred during "the 1960s, a decade of turbulent change," when some universities "were torn by strife from which they have not yet recovered." Ransom's institution, however, "kept an even keel and moved steadily ahead."

President Rogers then introduced Joe B. Frantz, who praised Ransom's administrative skills: "Funding, though fundamental, was relegated to its proper position as a detail. He worked with no fixed idea except one: if it is good, go after it." Moreover, "Ransom had an almost unerring sense of timing." We honor him most if we somehow can recapture that elusive zest and build on the resources he left behind."

Dr. Donald L. Weismann's voice "grew blurry with emotion," noted the *American-Statesman,* as he recalled drinking Jack Daniels whiskey and broiling steaks over an open fire with Ransom, Frank Wardlaw, Roy Bedichek, and Walter Webb at J. Frank Dobie's ranch, Paisano. "Harry Ransom's *modus operandi* was that of an artist—a contemporary maker, a creative formulator. . . . His medium, so to speak, was his teaching and his role as administrator. . . . Coping with the rich complexity of people, situations, and operations fired up Harry. . . . As with the painter or the novelist, he often worked in a trial-and-error pattern—trying and abandoning, trying and saving, incorporating. . . . Harry's dream . . . was that old dream of the artist—to discover and implement the means by which the disparate elements in human experience and institutions could be brought to a good coherency, an integrity, a purposeful unity."

The last speaker was former Regent Frank C. Erwin, Jr., whose service on the Board had ended in January 1975 but whose clout with the legislature as well as the current regents was still taken for granted. Quoting from the poetry of Keats, Tennyson, Hardy, Bridges, and Yeats, Erwin extolled the class in English literature he had taken from Ransom thirty-five years earlier. Erwin's lengthy accolade went on to recall that "the waves of controversy that periodically wash across this campus never wet his feet, and he wisely refrained from engaging in the sometimes acrimonious disputations in which others became involved. As a result, he stood straight and tall above the skirmishes, and he served as a constant reminder to all that the main business of this institution is to provide the best possible education for its students . . . [and] to develop and support the best possible collegiate community of scholars and scholarship."[62]

But it was Charles A. LeMaistre, Chancellor of the UT System, who perhaps most eloquently paid tribute to Ransom in the period shortly after his death, releasing a succinct statement that was quoted in various memorial articles. LeMaistre wrote: "When in the light of history the life of Harry Huntt Ransom is revealed in true measure, we will ever more come to know that we have been in the presence of extraordinary greatness."[63]

TWENTY

LEGACIES

Harry Ransom's place in Texas letters continued to come under discussion in the ensuing months. Lon Tinkle, professor of French at Southern Methodist University, author, and book critic of the *Dallas Morning News,* referred to Ransom's passing as having "deprived the state of its number one tastemaker and intellectual leader. . . . The Humanities Research Center is a symbol of that bedrock base for civilization: a great library in which mankind may quietly yet creatively study mankind in its most enduring monuments."[1]

Within a few weeks of Ransom's death, the UT Board of Regents took two actions to commemorate his life's work. First they adopted a resolution that reviewed the offices he held and asserted that no other person had "left so great an impression upon the University." The regents predicted that "many of those who survive him will remember 'The Ransom Years' as the halcyon years of the University." Moreover, "for fifteen years Harry Ransom was universally recognized as the greatest single builder of libraries in the world."[2] Chairman Allan Shivers also announced the establishment of the Harry Ransom Memorial Rare Book Fund to collect private contributions to purchase books and manuscripts for UT Austin. By November 30, 1976, the fund totaled $30,326.77, along with donated books valued at $17,100.[3]

In September 1976, President Lorene Rogers announced that the pictorial history of the University of Texas begun by the late Chancellor Emeritus Harry Ransom under a special assignment by the Board of Regents would be completed by history professor Dr. Joe B. Frantz and Dr. Margaret C. Berry. For many years Frantz's office had been above Ransom's, and he had enjoyed regular access to the president and chancellor; they had met for coffee and walked together "on five minutes' notice."[4] Berry, a fourth-generation Texan from Navarro County, had earned her doctorate in Student Personnel Administration in Higher Education at Columbia

University in 1965 and served as dean of women at East Texas State University before joining the UT administration as associate dean of women and then director of developmental programs for the Office of the Vice President for Student Affairs. Dr. Berry's dissertation, "Student Life and Customs at The University of Texas, 1883–1933," qualified her to contribute substantially to the project. She found it eerie to be moving into Ransom's deserted Richardson Hall suite to work on the book among the silent piles of manila envelopes, papers, and photographs, "like walking into Dr. Ransom's personal domain."[5]

Frantz and Berry were able to establish the fact that Ransom had decided a book of photographs should come out first, before a detailed history, but they found no prepared introductions, texts, or detailed captions—only five or six outlines, from which Frantz and Berry selected one to implement. Each of Ransom's outlines was divided into topics ("Administration," "Campus," "Faculty," "Sports," "Ex-Students") and then treated chronologically within that category. Ransom seemed to have been especially interested in collecting and comparing histories of other universities. He had made many notes about the history of Yale University in particular. Clearly he was interested in looking at a time-line chronology to see where UT fit into the national picture of institutional histories. Ransom's book, Berry could tell, would have been a multivolume, scholarly compendium.

The project started to run into snags in 1977. Lorene Rogers became unhappy with Frantz's lengthy and opinionated introduction and his tendency to insert anecdotes into picture captions. Delays proliferated. On September 1, 1979, Peter T. Flawn, the Yale-educated eminent geologist and former UT San Antonio president, ascended to the UT Austin presidency. Flawn, after seeking the advice of a regents' committee, UT Press director Jack Kyle, and others, elected to sever Frantz's ties with the book project and rely entirely on Berry to provide a straightforward introduction as well as purely informational chapter headnotes and factual picture captions for a one-volume illustrated history.[6] Margaret C. Berry's 425-page compendium, *The University of Texas: A Pictorial Account of Its First Century*, was published by the University of Texas Press in November 1980. A color portrait of Harry Ransom adorned its dedicatory page, embellished by quotations from the tributes to Ransom uttered at the commemorative assembly in 1976.[7] Frantz provided his own disgusted version of these developments (for which he did not blame Berry) in his rollicking *The Forty-Acre Follies* (1983), a partisan look at selected episodes in UT's history, which he conceded "is not a balanced account. . . . This is the story of a living, evolving institution through my eyes."[8]

For Hazel Ransom, life on Watchhill Road revolved at first around the condolence letters that arrived by the bundle. Regent James E. Bauerle, D.D.S., of San Antonio wrote: "I will miss Harry more than ever on the day in May when the Board meets next. He always [sat] in the same area of the room with a pleasant, understanding look on his face and was always ready to advise."[9] Betty Boatright, widow of the former UT English Department chairman Mody C. Boatright, commiserated: "What can I say other than [that] both Harry and Mody did what they wanted to do, which must mean they had a good life. . . . You made Harry a beautiful wife, as well as a most helpful one."[10]

Matthew M. Gouger of Waynesboro, Pennsylvania, phrased the thoughts of many:

> My admiration for him knew no limits. Much will be written about him using the descriptive terms—scholar of the first ranks—able administrator—forceful leader—articulate—perceptive—delightfully charming—loveable and wholly trustworthy. I know because I used those words in giving [author] Jim Michener my impressions of Harry one time. But, I added this—"Dr. Ransom is one of the very few men I have ever met I could label as a true patrician," and he was.
>
> But, Hazel, to these virtues MUST be added, his complete devotion to you. He adored you, and a warm light came to his eyes when he spoke of you (and he did most frequently). . . . You gave him so much genuine happiness, and made his life so complete. . . . I have never seen love, loyalty, and gallantry so magnificently displayed as by you when gross and stupid people had hurt him. I shall always cherish the memory of having witnessed two thorobreds [sic] standing tall in adversity and so in love.[11]

Whatever consolation Hazel was able to find in such testimonials and encouragement, her own situation was drastically altered. In November 1976 she made a final relocation, leaving the two-story, university-owned and furnished Watchhill Road residence with its library and sun room, and moved into a much smaller (one-story, two bedrooms and a study) house on Stamford Lane. One task was spared her. Her husband's private library contained no rare books or valuable manuscripts to dispose of; he had resisted the urge to acquire any because of his concern about giving any appearance of conflicts of interest. As a consequence she had difficulty finding a new location for what was, after all, merely an English professor's miscellaneous collection of reading materials. Concordia Lutheran College in Austin accepted a few books as donations, and the volumes she felt sentimental about went to the Humanities Research Center. The latter included inscribed copies of Dr. Warner Barnes's bibliographies of the Brownings' poetry, Morris Leopold Ernst's *Privacy—The Right to Be Let Alone* (1962), Erle Stanley Gardner's *The Desert Is Yours* (1963), Bertrand Russell's *Autobiography of Bertrand Russell, 1872–1914* (1967, inscribed by Lew David Feldman), and Clarence L. Cline's edition of *The Letters of George Meredith* (1970).[12] Household items including furniture and other pieces were auctioned off to benefit scholarships sponsored by the Ex-Students' organization.[13] There was not a single work of art in their Watchhill Road home, or one piece of exquisite china, that had not been loaned to the chancellor's residence by the HRC. Hazel was essentially left with clothing, personal mementos, and photographs of Harry Ransom and her. The rest of the trappings of her married life vanished.

She did, however, keep the little ranch-retreat, though its mortgage would not be paid off until 1989. Hazel's mother, Lee (Curtin) Harrod, suffered a stroke a few months after Harry's death and had to be taken care of in a nursing home until she died in 1981. Hazel's father, (Andrew) Cray Harrod, was able to live independently until a few days before his death in 1984.

Hazel Ransom eventually devoted herself to transcribing, editing, and supplying contextual notes for her husband's writings, speeches, poems, and drawings. Under her hand appeared, among other titles, *Snow in Austin* (1986),[14] a photographic record of that rare climatic phenomenon, and *Chronicles of Opinion on Higher Education, 1955–1975,*[15] a wide-ranging compilation of Harry Ransom's statements, elaborate or pithy, drawn from many sources. During the presidency of Lorene Rogers, Chairman of the Board of Regents Allan Shivers suggested that Hazel Ransom's editing projects be adequately underwritten. Upon returning to the UT campus, Hazel was surprised to find more than the office space (on the third floor of Walter Webb Hall, above the Faculty Center) and secretary (Lynda Hester) she had hoped for; there was also a half-time salary attached to Hazel Ransom's appointment as a Special Publications Project editor. In that two-room suite she received visitors from time to time who wanted to talk about the old days. Even for these she preferred scheduled appointments, avoiding if possible the impromptu and the casual. She disliked having people, even friends, merely knock on her door to converse. "It's just not in my makeup," she explained.[16]

As the months passed in 1977, Hazel Ransom was caught up in preparations for another commissioned portrait of her husband, this one presented by Mr. and Mrs. Halsted B. Vander Poel. On August 27, 1977, she sent numerous photographs of her husband to Mme. Elizabeth Shoumatoff of Locust Valley, New York, writing, "I have thought often and happily of the portrait of Harry that you are doing." In a note attached to a facsimile of Houston artist Robert Joy's portrait of Ransom, Hazel observed that "his hair was a darker brown than this reproduction shows." To one photograph of Ransom she attached another note: "His hair was never grey. He was never old." In additional notes Hazel tried to give the artist a feeling for her subject: "He wore the 'crew cut' in the late fifties and early sixties, in spite of my protestations." He had "lovely hands." He frequently displayed a "slight smile." "He often composed his work 'on typewriter.'" "In a social context of some hilarity, he managed subdued mirth."[17]

It is the custom at the University of Texas at Austin to commemorate the death of a faculty member by the report of a Memorial Resolution from a specially appointed faculty committee to the General Faculty through its secretary. On September 2, 1977, a committee consisting of Professors Clarence L. Cline (chairman), Joe B. Frantz, and Wayne H. Holtzman (President of the Hogg Foundation) submitted its Memorial Resolution, surveying Ransom's career in detail. The committee prophesied that "when the history of The University through the year 1971 comes to be written, no one within its pages will be found to have held so many positions of importance or to have left so great an imprint upon The University. . . . When all else may be forgotten, the Academic Center and the Harry Ransom Center will stand as monuments to his genius and his foresight."[18]

Institutionalized recognitions of Harry Ransom and his staff also began to take visible, permanent shapes. Charles Umlauf's bronze bust of Ransom, a gift of Mr. and Mrs. Jack S. Josey, graced the lobby of the Humanities Research Center.[19] Within the outer foyer of the same HRC lobby, university administrators in 1972 mounted a large bronze wall plaque, sculpted by Waldine Tauch, honoring "Frances Hellums Hudspeth/1907/1972/whose long service to the University community was filled with steadfast devotion and complete unselfishness." Hudspeth's head and shoulders appeared in bas-relief at the center of the plaque.

Tributes to Ransom took other forms as well. A majestic one that he assuredly would have relished was the purchase by the University of Texas, on June 9, 1978, of one of the forty-eight surviving copies of the Gutenberg Bible, the first book printed (in Latin) with movable type. German inventor and printer Johann Gutenberg produced this epochal two-volume work around 1450, and Carl Pforzheimer acquired it in 1923 from the Earl of Carysfort. UT was given an opportunity to purchase it for $2.4 million from the Carl H. and Lily Pforzheimer Foundation. Only four other complete copies had previously been brought to the United States: those at Harvard, Yale, the Pierpont Morgan Library, and the Library of Congress. Professor William B. Todd and his wife, Ann Bowden, reported on the condition and quality of the book at a meeting of the forty-five-member executive committee of the Chancellor's Council held in the Dallas residence of Mr. and Mrs. Trammell Crow. Tyler oilman Ralph Spence and the executive committee then led a fund drive to meet the stiff price, asking donors to give at least $50,000 apiece before the June 9, 1977 deadline expired on the option to purchase the magnificent copy. Baker Duncan of San Antonio, Rex Baker, Jr., of Sugarland, Dr. and Mrs. Clarence L. Cline of Austin, Mr. and Mrs. Trammell Crow, the Johnny Thompson family, and Mrs. Eugene McDermott (all of Dallas); Walter Sterling, Paul Barnhart, John H. Duncan, Joe Walter, and Mr. and Mrs. Jack S. Josey (all of Houston); Burton E. Grossman of Mexico City, and other Chancellor's Council members promptly pledged a total of $1.4 million. The UT Board of Regents (in an executive session on the final day of the option) then added the remaining $1 million to the amount and voted to place the copy on display in the HRC in memory of Harry Huntt Ransom, who had vainly endeavored to bring this elusive iconic treasure to the university. Ralph Spence called UT a worthy guardian for the "source and origin of the explosion of knowledge and education." Dr. William B. Todd spoke of it as "the whole embodiment of what we believe in, what we hope for, and what has been done." He remembered Ransom's alluding to it as "a landmark of western civilization." Arthur H. Dilly and Ralph Spence were bluntly concise about the new acquisition: "Instant ivy."[20] During UT's Centennial Observance of 1983, the treasured object would make eighteen stops in Texas cities, commencing with Spence's hometown, Tyler.[21]

Meantime, the library that Ransom had founded was undergoing rapid changes in personnel. F. Warren Roberts announced his retirement effective May 31, 1978, and President Lorene Rogers named John R. Payne as acting director for a few months until she appointed art critic and historian Carlton M. Lake to succeed Payne. President Rogers announced her own retirement in December 1978 and was succeeded in office on September 1, 1979, by Peter T. Flawn. On June 1, 1980, President Flawn named a new director of the HRC: Decherd Turner, founding director of the Bridwell Library at the Perkins School of Theology at Southern Methodist University, whom Ransom had unsuccessfully tried to bring to UT in 1964. During Turner's HRC directorship he would purchase Robert Lee Wolff's huge collection of Victorian novels, an additional collection of British literature from the Carl and Lily Pforzheimer Library, Edith Wharton's long-hidden letters to her lover Morton Fullerton, and other dazzling prizes. However, Turner came to regard preservation rather than acquisitions as the primary goal for the next era. Acidic paper was the main enemy, and special laboratories undertook the costly process of halting the accelerating deterioration of books and manuscripts. The Graduate School of Library and Information Science had to be relocated from the fourth floor of the HRC to the Education Building in order to free up space for this operation.

Gradually the major players during the Ransom years passed from the scene. The regents abolished the position of vice chancellor for operations upon Graves Landrum's retirement on December 1, 1978, from full-time employment, though he would continue to assist the UT Chancellor's Office in a reduced-service capacity until December 1988, completing forty-four years of service to the university. Landrum, whom Ransom had always considered indispensable, would die on April 22, 1995. W. D. (Bill) Blunk, UT System executive director of development, executive secretary of the Chancellor's Council, and Ransom's affable confidant, had died after surgery for a ruptured esophagus at the age of fifty-nine on February 23, 1976, only a few months before Ransom's death. Fannie Ratchford, who had hovered protectively over the UT Rare Books Collection until she relinquished that responsibility to a young dean named Harry Ransom, had died two years earlier, on February 9, 1974.

An unexpected heart attack carried away Frank C. Erwin, Jr., on October 2, 1980. Several thousand people turned out for a memorial service for Erwin staged in the new Special Events Center, which would subsequently be named in his honor. UT officials were prompt to praise his "strong will, extensive research, and sincerity." Though a writer for the *New York Times* magazine took a swipe at the "political meddling" of "the hard-drinking Mr. Erwin, in his orange Cadillac and orange raw-silk blazer,"[22] Nettie Lee Benson, former director of the Latin American Library, commented, "In all my experience, he was the only regent who ever visited the library. He walked around and asked us if we had enough space. . . . He promoted the library."[23] A decade and a half after Erwin's death, a poll of selected UT administrators, faculty members, and ex-students would rank Frank Erwin among the "top ten" people who had influenced the university in critical ways during its history. Dr. Lewis Gould, historian, called him "a master power broker." Dr. Don Carleton, historian and executive director of the Center for American History at UT Austin, said, simply, that "his power and influence largely created the University as we know it today."[24] Many alumni would continue to believe that Erwin had preserved the integrity of the university by courageously standing up to those misusing its prestige and influence during a decade of extraordinary campus turbulence when administrators appeared to temporize and equivocate. Others familiar with Erwin's tactics, like former vice president Kenneth Ashworth, felt that he remained too powerful for too long.[25] Harold Billings, the longtime director of the UT General Libraries, believed that after a certain point Erwin became "a negative force" in the university's drive to join Berkeley and Michigan among the very top state universities.[26]

In 1981 Donald L. Weismann added a coda to the Harry Ransom story by publishing a whimsical novel, *Follow the Bus with the Greek License Plates,* in which private detective Harry O. Hydal undertakes an odyssey from Texas across the North American continent. During the journey Harry summons up memories of a group of four assistant professors "recruited by the enterprising Dean Alfred A. Carson. These Young Turks had in common "lots of energy, knew their stuff, sharp, courageous, irreverent, hard workers and full of visions of what education could be." They also shared a reverence for their dean: "There seemed no limit to what Al Carson could dream up right there in front of you. And he had the language, the voice to do it, a mellifluous poetic chant that exorcised logic and made a believer of you right on the spot." In their salad days, "there was great good fun, the feel of life, high-bar intelligence swinging, a swaggering irreverence, booze, food, a feeling of strength and real work to do."[27]

The publication by the University of Texas Press in 1982 of eighteen of Ransom's most significant essays and speeches in *The Conscience of the University and Other Essays,* edited by Hazel Ransom, stirred renewed interest in Ransom. In a press release, Hazel recalled that "the post-Sputnik period, with its rush to technology and science, traumatized educators everywhere. . . . Harry was one for standing a little stiller. . . . He certainly believed in a broad, liberal arts education." Editing the book had been difficult, she said, "because I had been so close to the man as well as the scene. . . . We worked together and thought together and relaxed together. When you are that close to someone else, his death leaves you feeling amputated."[28]

Madame Shoumatoff's painting of Ransom, completed in 1978, was officially hung in the inner foyer of the Humanities Research Center at an invitation-only ceremony in 1983 that drew several hundred of the Ransoms' longtime admirers. The painting depicts a seated Harry Ransom wearing academic regalia (but capless) and holding a large book. A brilliant scarlet hood loops under Ransom's tie and sweeps across a black gown tinged with purple. Ransom looks up from his reading—three other volumes lie on the library table to his right, two of them open—and smiles slightly and enigmatically at the artist who has apparently interrupted his reverie. Books tightly packed together on shelves form a partial backdrop. His face is highlighted so that shadows define the familiar cleft on his chin and other contours of his forehead, cheeks, and neck.[29]

On December 9, 1983, the UT Board of Regents renamed the library collections and related research functions previously known as the Humanities Research Center; thereafter, they would be referred to as the Harry Ransom Humanities Research Center.[30] Other collections on campus were being named for people connected with their establishment, and Hazel Ransom had decided to approach the chairman of the Board of Regents, who then conferred with the president and chancellor before making the alteration. Some on campus wondered if this appellation was a long-planned shift that explained the original parallel initials, but the "HR"/"HRC" similarity was entirely a coincidence, according to Miguel Gonzalez-Gerth, Hazel's confidant and adviser during this period.[31]

The next year, Dean Robert D. King of the College of Liberal Arts announced that Harry H. Ransom had posthumously been awarded the 1984 Pro Bene Meritis Award, intended to honor individuals who had made distinctive contributions to the College.

Ransom's repute on the campus seemed to rise as the 1980s progressed. Decherd Turner marveled at this "amazing apotheosis" for the administrator-librarian who had "essentially been booted out," in Turner's words, yet whose memory again became "green and good."[32] For instance, the *Daily Texan*'s review of Harry Ransom's *The Other Texas Frontier* (1984), gathering six important essays edited by Hazel Ransom, reminded students that "Harry Ransom played an integral part in the educational and literary growth of the University for over 40 years."[33]

Harry Ransom had already been gone from the scene for twelve years when alumni, faculty, administrators, and friends of the University of the South and the University of Texas convened in Austin in May 1988 "to pay tribute to one of Sewanee's most distinguished graduates, Harry Huntt Ransom, A'24, C'28, H'58." Invited by Sewanee administrators Robert M. Ayres, Jr. (vice chancellor), W. Brown Patterson (dean), and George Core (editor of the *Sewanee Review*), 200 guests assembled at the Harry Ransom Humanities Research Center. The crowd heard the HRHRC compared to the British Museum and the Bibliothèque Nationale and hailed as "the Fort Knox of modern literature."[34]

A year later, on Monday, May 1, 1989, eighty people gathered in the Knopf Room on the fourth floor of the Peter T. Flawn Academic Center, formerly known as the Academic Center, to listen to readings of Harry

Ransom's poems as showcased by Hazel Ransom in *The Song of Things Begun*.[35] In prefatory remarks at the event, Chancellor Hans Mark spoke of Harry Ransom as a "genuine intellectual," someone who "lived the life of the mind" and successfully combined the talents of an academic leader with those of a politician. A man who "understood how to use words" (indeed, poetry represents "the highest use of words"), Ransom also grasped "what it is we are here to do at a university." Dr. Kurth Sprague of the American Studies program and Dr. Miguel Gonzalez-Gerth, the last editor of *Texas Quarterly* (who had become Hazel's trusted friend and frequent escort), read verses that drew mainly upon Ransom's wartime service and the academic milieu.[36]

A nationally distributed Associated Press article written by Jules Loh in December 1991 blanketed Texas and the nation with headlines such as "Harry Ransom's Vision Put UT Library Out Front" (*Houston Chronicle*), "UT's Rare-Book Library Is Worth a Ransom" (*San Antonio Light*), and "A Cultural Heart of Texas" (*Riverside, California Press-Enterprise*). Loh credited Ransom with setting out in 1957 to assemble "a 'Bibliothèque Nationale,' a great national library for the state of Texas. . . . Now, about 10,000 scholars a year from America and abroad trek to the library named for him." Loh was less than charmed by the "stern lines" of the HRHRC building, "a great box of an edifice," whose formidable design seemed reflective of an earlier decade when campus administrators felt themselves to be under siege. But once inside, Loh found himself "awed" by the sight of the Gutenberg Bible and, six floors above, "a mannequin wearing Scarlett O'Hara's dazzling green dress." He surveyed samples of the "million books and 9 million manuscripts." To Loh, "there was something decidedly Texan about the forthright way Harry Ransom went about collecting manuscripts and papers, sometimes dealing directly with the author."[37] In the early years of the twenty-first century, Loh's unfavorable impression of the HRHRC's "fortress"-like architecture would be rectified by an extensive renovation of the ground floors that introduced windows and exhibition areas and showered the interiors with Texas sunshine. This spacious redesign was made possible by the transfer of the Huntington Art Gallery from the first and second floors of the HRHRC to a separate new facility, the Blanton Museum.[38]

In the face of heightened competition from other institutional buyers, Ransom's lingering charisma gave UT an advantageous leverage with certain writers. James A. Michener, author of the Pulitzer Prize–winning *Tales of the South Pacific*, as well as *Hawaii, Centennial, Texas, Alaska*, and numerous other best-selling books, had purchased a residence in West Austin when he was writing his epic *Texas*. Michener and his wife, Mari, formed an attachment to the University of Texas largely through the auspices of President Peter T. Flawn and the regents, but also partly through the reputation of Ransom, whom Michener thought of as "avuncular" and "having that quality of embracing you." The Micheners and Ransoms saw each other socially from time to time. "He was a good man to do business with," said Michener. "Judicious." It surprised few people when, having already made a gift of his collection of twentieth-century American paintings (and specifically citing Harry Ransom's collecting abilities and his editing of *Texas Quarterly*—especially one "Image of Spain" issue—as primary reasons for making this decision), the eighty-five-year-old Michener announced in 1992 that he was donating his papers, including notes, drafts, correspondence, and clippings, to the Harry Ransom Humanities Research Center.[39]

Another echo of Ransom's life reverberated on June 11, 1992, when the UT System Board of Regents appointed HRHRC director Dr. Thomas F. Staley, a prominent James Joyce scholar with a Ph.D. from the University of Pittsburgh, to the Harry Huntt Ransom Chair in Liberal Arts established by C. B. Smith, Sr., Nash Phillips, and Clyde Copus. Staley, a former Provost and Vice President for Academic Affairs at the University of Tulsa, had replaced Decherd Turner as the HRHRC director in 1988.

On Saturday, August 28, 1993, Hazel Louise Harrod Ransom died at the age of seventy-three, after several years of treatment for heart disease and breast cancer that eventually metastasized into her lungs. At her death she was an honorary member of the executive committee of the UT Chancellor's Council, a member of the President's Associates, and a member of the Liberal Arts Foundation Board. She had received the Pro Bene Meritis Award from the College of Liberal Arts in 1991. Dr. Margaret Berry described her as "a scholar, and . . . a hostess deluxe as first lady of the university."[40] Funeral services were held at the Good Shepherd Episcopal Church. Hazel Ransom was survived only by a cousin in Houston. Pallbearers at the service included a chancellor, Dr. Hans Mark, and a future chancellor, Dr. William H. Cunningham, along with Graves Landrum, Dr. Gerhard J. Fonken, Lowell H. Lebermann, Frank E. Scofield, and Lonnie L. McKinney. Dr. Gonzalez-Gerth's remarks reminded those attending that after the "untimely death" of Hazel's husband, she extended his impact by "editing his unpublished essays, lectures, and poems, and by continuing to support the programs he had envisioned and established."[41] Burial took place in Austin Memorial Park. As executor, Dr. Gonzalez-Gerth disposed of her house, the ranch retreat, artworks, and investments with Merrill Lynch. Bequeathing her parents' estate as well as her own, she left an endowment of more than two million dollars for new HRHRC acquisitions. A graciously furnished space on the second floor was named the Hazel Ransom Reading Room.[42]

An unexpected avocation of Hazel's came to light in 1996, when the University of Texas published a limited edition of 400 copies of *A Vacation in the Sun and Other Stories,* a fifty-one-page paperbound collection of her short fiction edited by her literary executor, Dr. Gonzalez-Gerth, and dedicated to "The family of Joe C. Thompson, Sr." In an introduction Dr. Gonzalez-Gerth explained that "when it came to her own creative endeavors, she felt compelled to prevent them from shifting her attention from her primary purpose during her married life, which was to remain her exemplary husband's helpmate" (5). Gonzalez-Gerth gathered nine briskly narrated pieces here that ranged from the tersely probable to the wildly fanciful.

A year later, in 1997, Hazel Ransom's master's thesis, *Elizabeth Barrett Browning: Poet-Reformer,* appeared in a limited-edition monograph of 200 paperbound copies edited by Miguel Gonzalez-Gerth and published by the University of Texas. This volume additionally included Hazel's notes and drafts for a proposed doctoral dissertation on Shakespeare's soliloquies, along with a study of two folk motifs traceable through tales in early Europe as well as modern-day America. Dr. Gonzalez-Gerth's introduction reminded readers that Hazel Ransom had selflessly laid aside these scholarly pursuits because "her time and effort were inevitably claimed by the precedence of her husband's highly significant academic and institutional projects."

Under Thomas F. Staley's direction the Harry Ransom Humanities Research Center continued to be a high-stakes player in the bidding for major collections related to literature and the arts, winning, among others, the papers of such diverse figures as James Jones, Don DeLillo, Leon Uris, and Isaac Bashevis Singer. Staley's HRHRC obtained the archives of British playwright Tom Stoppard, spent $5 million in 2003 to acquire the much-sought-after Bob Woodward–Carl Bernstein Watergate papers, and in 2005 announced the addition of Norman Mailer's papers for an outlay of $2.5 million. Mailer's archives, stored in nearly 500 boxes, included 25,000 letters as well as manuscripts, screenplays, photographs, and notebooks.[43] In part Staley was able to consider new purchases because of an enthusiastic advisory council he created in 1990, spearheaded initially by Henrietta Jacobsen, Ransom's former assistant.[44]

When *Texas Alcalde* in 1993 polled Dr. Robert Berdahl, president until 1997 of UT Austin; Dr. Margaret C. Berry; Dr. William H. Cunningham, Chancellor; Dr. Lewis Gould, UT professor of history; Dr. William S.

Livingston, Vice President and Dean of Graduate Studies; and five other knowledgeable people regarding the ten most influential individuals in the history of the University of Texas, the votes for Dr. Harry Huntt Ransom surpassed those for George Washington Littlefield, Frank C. Erwin, Jr., Ashbel Smith, Darrell Royal, J. Frank Dobie, Dr. Homer P. Rainey, Beauford Jester, Dr. Lorene Rogers, and all other nominees. Historian participant Jim Nicar gave the most powerful reason for honoring Ransom: "To many, he epitomized what the University should always be." He quoted former University of California president Clark Kerr's jocular lament: "Each time we hear about a new library find in some odd corner of the world, . . . it turns out Harry Ransom already has his Texas bookplates pasted over it." Lewis Gould hailed the way "he fostered the philosophy that high standards for educational performance could offset some of the leveling tendencies of state-supported higher education." Livingston said that Ransom "exemplified the excellence that he proclaimed as the institution's goal."[45]

Harry Ransom also made a lasting impression on Robert D. King, the linguist who in 1979 became the first dean of a reconstituted College of Liberal Arts. King came to think of Harry Ransom as a "bridge personality" between the "mesquite intellectuals" (Dobie, Webb, and Bedichek), who distrusted academic degrees, refused to disguise their rougher qualities, and enjoyed outdoor life, and the enormously different kind of campus life that followed—more sophisticated, culturally rich, citified. According to King, Ransom understood the worth of something homespun, but at the same time he knew what people on both coasts were thinking. "We were good, but we were regional. That is how Harry Ransom found us. What he left us was a university nationally ranked and unashamed." As the years passed, Ransom's own reputation grew so towering, remembered King, that in the end he came to seem rather forbidding to many faculty and students, though this was through no fault of his own. In person he remained immensely approachable.[46]

A book-length poem published by Dave Oliphant in 1983, *Austin*, compared Harry Ransom to the early Texas historical figure Stephen F. Austin. Oliphant, who as a student was in awe of Ransom, had joined the staff of the Humanities Research Center and become the editor of its *Library Chronicle*. Oliphant's greatest regret, shared by various members of the university community, was that *Texas Quarterly* survived its founder and editor by only a few years. The loss of Mrs. Hudspeth had been a blow to its fortunes, depriving the journal of its longtime managing editor. Dr. Miguel Gonzalez-Gerth and Dr. Thomas Cranfill jointly brought out *Texas Quarterly* after Ransom's death in 1976, and David Price continued to oversee its design and production. But funds for continued publication evaporated amid President Lorene Rogers's doubts about the caliber of HRC management. The Winter 1978 issue (vol. 21, no. 4) announced the immediate termination of *Texas Quarterly.* "A king's tributes die with him," dryly observed one member of the UT staff many years later. "The journal was so driven by Harry Ransom that it was bound to succumb upon his demise."

Those not within the realm of the humanities had likewise experienced Ransom's reach and harbored grateful memories. Dr. Earnest Gloyna, member of the National Academy of Engineering and dean of the UT College of Engineering from 1970 until 1987, recalled Ransom as, above all, "an individual who did not set his own body of knowledge above other people's disciplines. True, he put millions into rare books, but he didn't forget about engineering education and labs. I never felt he wanted to relegate engineering to a second-class citizenship." Indeed, Gloyna contended that "Ransom was the administrator who brought the total culture of our campus together. . . . Lots of business and engineering people across the state didn't have the same vision as his, but even they made financial contributions, accepting his argument that possessing and displaying examples of our literary past was important for our national and international image. And Ransom knew that we also had to go out and get the money for superior students, professors, and teaching and research laboratories." Gloyna summarized it like this: "In engineering we call it 'risk-assessment'— Ransom took a calculated risk that he could sell the idea (and his purchases) to the faculty, regents, and public. And he succeeded."[47]

Dr. Gerhard J. Fonken, former executive vice president and provost, concurred that Ransom's great ability was his willingness to "understand, appreciate, and support all elements of the University. He had no bias in favor of one area or another—except the library, but that too goes beyond the parochial bounds of any discipline or school." As an example, Fonken cited Ransom's interest in professor of chemistry Dr. Roger J. Williams's work on the role in health and nutrition of the B vitamins.[48]

National commentators recognized Ransom as a distinctive academic type. Dr. Clark Kerr, the much-quoted university administrator and authority on institutional management who was formerly president and chancellor of the University of California System, observed that Ransom managed to avoid "a common mistake" often made by university administrators who take on the vast responsibilities of overseeing a major institution: "Falling into the habit of merely *reacting* to the multitudinous pieces of paper that cross their desk." A few recognize the danger of this numbing syndrome and "select half a dozen projects that, amid the daily urgency and chaos of their enterprises, they hope to accomplish before leaving office in five or six years, nudging these along whenever time and energy allow." A very few others, in Kerr's view, perceptively recognize the odds against completing even so modest an agenda in the press of speeches, lobbying, and negotiating, and "settle instead for a single envisioned achievement"— and this latter strategy essentially became Harry Ransom's choice, though he brought other, less colossal projects to the point of completion as well. But primarily after his retirement and death he would be identified with the conceptualizing and founding of the Humanities Research Center. "To have assembled a premier collection of rare books and manuscripts generally ranked in the top dozen of its kind in the world is a very unusual and significant achievement," acknowledged Dr. Kerr.[49]

Harry Huntt Ransom's attitudes were so adaptive that he still serves as a relevant model for educators even as the demands of the Information Age become more and more insistent. His mental habit of expecting continual transfigurations, of endeavoring to retain the finest elements and traditions while building toward a still-crystallizing future, is a valuable perspective that he wanted to pass on to the generations that followed. The changing nature of teaching and research intrigued rather than repelled him, an advantageous outlook in an impending era of redesigned and "virtual" universities. Since he himself predicted that digital and network information systems would supplant old-fashioned bookshelf libraries, his tremendous degree of flexibility about the very concept of "education" should be remembered. Ransom encountered much new terrain. But he accurately gauged and mastered the public policy arena, taught himself how to speak to legislators' concerns, thrived on the shift to federal controls and funding, and welcomed the challenge of outside fund-raising. He led the way in accepting and promoting racial equality, barrier-free learning for the disabled, hybrid disciplines, electronic instruction, perpetual learning, and the computerized campus.

Eventually, however, he concluded that his time had come and gone. He foresaw that a trend toward meticulous record-keeping, strategic planning systems, emphasis on "accountability" at all levels of organization, specialized consultants, transient CEOs, proliferating legal tests, and operational streamlining—in other words, what he termed "managerial administration"—was likely to follow in the ensuing decades. He was not at all intimidated by this emerging pattern; he simply intuited that its relative anonymity and formulaic rigidity did not fit his strengths, and he bowed to its efficiency as much as its inevitability. Frank C. Erwin, Jr., may have sent the warning signal that Ransom's individualistic style of administration was nearing its expiration date, but in any event Ransom's energies appeared to be ebbing. He had always felt that he was an anomaly anyway—an English instructor who had risen from the ranks without any preconceived ambition to head a university—and by 1970 he was prepared to yield to pressures for different modes of governance.

In the wake of his administrative successes a resolute crusade by the UT System Board of Regents, the Chancellor's Council, the College of Liberal Arts, Hazel Ransom, and Ransom's legion of admirers preserved a collective memory of Ransom's idealistic principles of higher education. The enduring legacy of Ransom's unflagging conviction about the destiny of the University of Texas as a national influence and international presence and his determination to construct a magnificent library amply fulfilled his vision of the university as intellect in motion. Pursuing those aims, Ransom earned title to the native heath he said everyone deserves.

NOTES

PREFACE

1. Michael Barnes, "The Treasures of the Ransom Center," *Austin American-Statesman,* Sunday, 17 February 2002, http://www.statesman.com/specialreports/content/specialreports/ransom/17profileransom.html, 11/18/2005.

2. Herbert Marder, "The Biographer and the Angel," *American Scholar* 62 (Spring 1993): 231.

3. The phrase "intellect in motion" appeared in Ransom's "Educational Resources in Texas," *Texas Quarterly* 4 (Winter 1961); reprinted in Harry Huntt Ransom, *The Conscience of the University and Other Essays,* ed. Hazel H. Ransom (Austin: University of Texas Press, 1982), 25; and in Harry Huntt Ransom, *Chronicles of Opinion on Higher Education: 1955–1975,* ed. Hazel Ransom; foreword by Hans Mark (Austin: University of Texas at Austin, 1990), 42.

CHAPTER ONE

1. Ransom family record, 1942, Harry Ransom Humanities Research Center, University of Texas at Austin (hereafter cited as HRHRC).

2. C. H. Bridges, letter to Mrs. Herbert Norris, Jr. [Minnie Ransom Norris], 30 January 1929. Bridges was returning to Norris her copies of historical references to Matthew Whitaker Ransom and Robert Ransom, Jr. (Center for American History, University of Texas at Austin; hereafter cited as CAH). Her documentation included pages from *The Civil War Dictionary,* 679, and *Clark's History,* Vol. 1, 402, and Vol. 5, 277. A fuller account of the brothers' Civil War service is found in William J. Kimball, "Ransom's North Carolina Brigade Served the Confederacy Bravely," *Civil War Times Illustrated,* May 1962, 45–47 (PH in CAH).

3. George S. Wills, Westminster, Maryland, letter to editor, *Alumni Review,* Chapel Hill, North Carolina, 1935 (CAH).

4. Joan Simpson Burns, *The Awkward Embrace: The Creative Artist and the In-*

stitution in America (New York: Alfred A. Knopf, 1975), 58 (based on interviews she conducted in 1967).

5. Harry Huntt Ransom, Sr., letter to *Austin Statesman,* 26 January 1895 (HRHRC).

6. Mrs. H. E. Barnett, Jr., letter to HHR, 26 August 1957 (CAH).

7. Harry Hunt Ransom, Sr., letter to James Stephen Hogg, 12 August 1904 (HRHRC).

8. HHR, "Sherman Goodwin," in *The Other Texas Frontier,* ed. Hazel Ransom (Austin: University of Texas Press, 1984), 55.

9. Minnie Ransom Norris, letter to HHR, 9 March 1954 (CAH).

10. HHR, "The Educations of a Doctor," *Texas Quarterly,* Summer 1966; reprinted in *The Conscience of the University,* ed. Hazel Ransom (Austin: University of Texas Press, 1982), 67; reprinted in *Chronicles of Opinion in Higher Education: 1955–1975,* ed. Hazel Ransom, foreword by Hans Mark (Austin: University of Texas at Austin, 1990), 184; hereafter cited as *Chronicles.*

11. HHR, letter to John W. Gardner, Carnegie Corporation, New York City, 22 May 1957 (CAH).

12. Mrs. Donald L. [Olive Ransom] Nelson, letter to HHR, 20 January 1965 (CAH). Nelson knew Ransom's father as "Uncle Henry." The proposition that the senior Ransom himself was likewise christened *Henry* Huntt Ransom gains support from the *Alumni History* (1935 edition), University of North Carolina, which listed him as *Henry* Huntt Ransom (p. 512), based on the University records of 1883–1884, 1884–1885, and 1885–1886 (Wills, letter to the editor, *Alumni Review,* 1935). Wills himself mentioned that he knew the elder Ransom in college as "Henry."

13. HHR, letter to Mrs. Cartes (Katherine) Pauls, 30 April 1956 (CAH).

14. Quotations and allusions employed without citation in this and the following chapter were drawn from autobiographical notes set down by Harry Huntt Ransom, evidently sometime in the 1950s. He merely identified them as "Chronology" and appeared to have multiple purposes in mind in collecting these remembrances, including the possibility of producing a memoir or a series of sketches (PH of MS in the Hazel Ransom Collection, now in the HRHRC; hereafter cited as "Chronology").

15. Burns, *The Awkward Embrace,* 58.

16. "525 Woodland Avenue," *Homes* 2, no. 11 (May 1912): 6.

17. Hazel Ransom, letter to author, 14 January 1993.

18. Burns, *The Awkward Embrace,* 58.

19. HHR, note to "Daddy," undated (HRHRC).

CHAPTER TWO

1. "K-K-K-Katy," words and music by Geoffrey O'Hara (1918). Subtitled the "stammering song," it became one of the most requested humorous songs of World War I.

2. Hazel Ransom, interview by author, Austin, 17 January 1990. She recalled hearing that the senior Ransom moved to Maryland to be near family members who could attend to his medical needs.

3. "Chronology."

4. Arthur Ben Chitty, interview by author, Sewanee, May 1990.

5. HHR, "The Educations."

6. *Sewanee Purple,* 28 October 1925, Archives and Special Collections, Jessie duPont Library, The University of the South, Sewanee, Tennessee. Hereafter cited as USouth.

7. "Chronology."

8. HHR, letter to "Commandant of Cadets," 5 October 1923 (HRHRC). Hazel Ransom, interview.

9. Hazel Ransom, interview.

10. Robert Sherrill, *Texas Observer,* 23 December 1960. Also cited in Burns, *The Awkward Embrace,* 59.

11. Marion G. Ransom, letter to Colonel Cravens, 14 November 1921 (USouth).

12. HHR, "Service," *St. Andrew's Cross,* May 1924 (cited by editor, *St. Andrew's Cross,* 26 March 1924). PH of essay and letter in HRHRC.

13. *The Little Tiger* [Sewanee Military Academy Junior Yearbook], 1922–1923, 57 (USouth).

14. Stuart Maclean, letter to HHR, 21 May 1924 (HRHRC).

15. DuVal Cravens, letter to HHR, 2 June 1924 (HRHRC).

16. H. M. Gass, letter to HHR, 26 June 1924 (HRHRC).

17. *Sewanee Purple,* 28 October 1925 (USouth).

18. Official Transcript of Harry Huntt Ransom, The University of the South, 23 May 1942 (HRHRC).

19. Knickerbocker taught as a full professor of English at Sewanee from 1926 until 1942. In 1948 he would become an English professor at Emerson College in Boston, Massachusetts.

20. HHR, letter to William S. Knickerbocker, 29 November 1934 (USouth).

21. HHR, letter to William S. Knickerbocker, undated (USouth).

22. DuVal G. Cravens, Jr., interview by author, Sewanee, May 1990.

23. HHR, "While Presses Wait," *Cap and Gown* [sophomore yearbook], 1926 (USouth).

24. *Sewanee Purple,* 13 October 1926 (USouth).

25. HHR, "A Plea for a Cultural Education," *Sewanee Purple,* 13 June 1928 (USouth).

26. Margaret T. Corwin, Executive Secretary to Wilbur L. Cross, Dean of the Graduate School at Yale University, letter to HHR, 20 February 1928 (HRHRC).

27. Frank Smith, letter to HHR, "Wednesday" [1928] (HRHRC).

CHAPTER THREE

1. "Jewel," postcard to "Aunt Het" [Mrs. Jesse B. Templeton], undated (HRHRC). The Templetons were related to John Marks Templeton, who was born in Winchester, Tennessee, in 1912, graduated from Yale in 1934, was selected as a Rhodes Scholar, and became a billionaire by developing globally diversified mutual funds. His extensive philanthropy, which included the Templeton Library in Sewanee, would gain him a knighthood from Queen Elizabeth in 1987.

2. Hoyt Purvis, "Dr. Ransom's Father Gives Academic Mark," *Daily Texan,* 13 December 1960, 1.

3. Burns, *Awkward Embrace,* 59.

4. W. L. Bevan, letter to Harvard Law School, February 18, 1929 (CAH).

5. HHR, letter to Marion Ransom, 7 August 1929 (HRHRC).

6. Graduate School Scholarship Record, Yale University, 23 May 1942 (CAH).

7. HHR academic record in Sewanee Alumni File (USouth).

8. Jean Barron Hurlbut, notice of rental, 28 July 1930 (HRHRC).

9. HHR, "Personal History Statement," March 1953 (CAH).

10. Edgar S. Furniss, Dean of the Graduate School, letter to HHR, 12 November 1932 (HRHRC).

11. Purvis, *Daily Texan;* see also HHR, TS recollections to assist Hoyt Purvis, undated (CAH).

12. L. M. Taylor, letter to HHR, 24 August 1934 (HRHRC).

13. Joseph Jones, letter to author, 12 May 1989.

14. "Harry Ransom: Speaker at Birthday Luncheon of Shakespeare Club," undated newspaper report, undated (HRHRC).

15. HHR, letter to Knickerbocker, 29 November 1934 (USouth).

16. HHR, letter to "Tony," 26 February 1935 (USouth).

17. Membership card, Modern Language Association, 1935 (CAH).

18. Clarence Cline, letter to author, 29 August 1991.

19. Margaret Cousins, "The Beatific Memories of an English Major," in *Texas, Our Texas: Remembrances of the University,* ed. Bryan A. Garner (Austin, Texas: Eakin Press), 1984, 24.

20. Daniel Morley McKeithan, "Yet Autumn Remembers" (unpublished memoir), 1983, 70 (CAH). The author discovered this typescript in 1987 in Calhoun 306, the late Professor McKeithan's office at the University of Texas at Austin. McKeithan's detailed chronology and characterizations of the UT English faculty were invaluable.

21. McKeithan, "Yet Autumn Remembers," 70.

22. C.[larence] L. Cline, Powell Stewart, and Wilson Hudson, "Report of the Memorial Resolution Committee for Alice Lovelace Cooke," Documents and Minutes of the General Faculty, University of Texas at Austin, 20 June 1991, 19044–19055.

23. Cline, letter.

24. *University of Texas Bulletin,* 1 November 1937.

25. Leo Hughes, interview by author, Austin, 22 December 1989.

26. Wilson Hudson, interview by author, Austin, 5 January 1990.

27. Cousins, "Beatific Memories," 23–24.

28. Willis Pratt, interview by author, Austin, 18 October 1989.

29. HHR, "Observations on the Establishment and Early Administration of 'Plan II,'" undated TS, University News and Information Service files.

30. H. T. Parlin, "The New Way to the B.A. Degree," *Alcalde,* February 1935, 103–104.

CHAPTER FOUR

1. Robert Wilson, interview by author, Austin, 19 December 1989.

2. Virginia (McNutt) Stansbury, telephone interview by author, Beaumont, 2 December 1989.

3. HHR's class notes (CAH). Dr. Miguel Gonzalez-Gerth of UT Austin found Ransom's copy of Bennett's *New Latin Grammar,* used at Sewanee Military Academy in 1923. Even then, Ransom doodled. The book bore the Greek letters of his fraternity, a cartoon profile of a football player, and a pipe-smoking instructor—very likely Major Gass, his classics professor (HRHRC).

4. Mrs. V. H. McMillan, letter to HHR, 29 December 1938 (CAH).

5. Clarice (Hollman) Neal, interview by author, Austin, 5 April 1991.

6. Margaret (Doggett) Crow, telephone interview by author, Dallas, 13 August 1991.

7. Ray Past, letter to author, 26 September 1989.

8. Helen (Shudde) Hill, interview by author, Austin, November 1990.

9. Leslie Donovan, "First Lady of UT System: Graciousness Marks Hostess," *Austin American-Statesman,* September 1969.

10. Hazel Ransom, interview by author, Austin, 17 January 1990.

11. Hazel Ransom, interview. "I majored in Ransom," an older Hazel admitted.

12. Joseph W. McKnight, letter to author, 2 December 1990.

13. Margaret (Swett) Henson, interview by author, Austin, 13 June 1990. Swett married in 1943, reared five children, earned M.A. and Ph.D. degrees, published books on Texas history (one of them winning the Summerfield G. Roberts Award), and taught history courses for more than a decade in Houston-area colleges.

14. Ransom lecture notes (CAH).

15. Wilson, interview, 1990.

16. Roger S. Plummer, letter to author, July 1989.

17. William Christian Smith, Jr., interview by author, Austin, 6 October 2004.

18. Frank Erwin, "In Commemoration of Harry Huntt Ransom," *On Campus,* 10–13 May 1976.

19. Deborah Lynn Bay, "The Influence of Frank Erwin on Texas Higher Education," doctoral dissertation, University of Texas at Austin, 1988.

20. Chadwick Oliver, interview by author, Austin, 21 November 1989.

21. Redding Sugg, Jr., interview by author, Fredericksburg, Texas, 23 March 1990.
22. Past, letter.
23. Redding Sugg, Jr., letter to author, 11 July 2007.
24. Past, letter.
25. Charles Hagelman, interview by author, Austin, 27 April 1991. Hagelman would become a Byron specialist and chair the English Department at Northern Illinois University.
26. Shelby Hearon, "Owning Jolene," *Alcalde*, September/October 1989, 36.
27. Wayne Rogers, letter to author, 31 August 1992.
28. George O. Marshall, Jr., letter to author, 23 October 1989.
29. Robert J. Barnes, telephone interview by author, Beaumont, 7 May 1991.
30. Past, letter.
31. HHR, "The Teacher," reprinted in HHR, *Chronicles*, 103–104.

CHAPTER FIVE

1. Evelyn (Buzzo) Moorman, letter to author, 20 October 1989.
2. HHR, "Chronology."
3. Moorman, letter.
4. HHR, "From a Gentleman in Edinburgh, 1769: An Early Sidelight in Literary Property," *Sewanee Review*, July-September 1936, 366–71.
5. HHR, "Riddle of the World: A Note on Pope and Pascal," *Sewanee Review*, July-September 1938, 306–11.
6. HHR, "The Rewards of Authorship in the Eighteenth Century," *Studies in English* 18 (1938): 47–66.
7. "Some Legal Elements in Elizabethan Plays," *Studies in English* 16 (1936): 53–76.
8. HHR, "Date of the First Copyright Law," *Studies in English* 20 (1940): 117–22.
9. HHR, "The Brownings in Paris," *Studies in English* 21 (1941): 147–63.
10. Application for Fisk Teachers Agency, Chicago, 25 January 1940 (CAH).
11. HHR, TS recollections of his visit to England and Ireland in 1939 (Collection of Hazel Ransom, HRHRC).
12. Picture postcard, undated (CAH). Though a historian at heart, unfortunately Ransom never dated any photograph he kept.
13. HHR, typescript and manuscript notes collectively titled "And So to War" (Collection of Hazel Ransom, HRHRC).
14. HHR, TS of recollections.
15. Press release, UT News and Information Service, 1940 (CAH).
16. HHR, TS of recollections.
17. (Doggett) Crow, interview.
18. Florence Heller, "City of Flint's Voyage Was No More Exciting Than Dr. Ransom's," *Daily Texan*, 30 January 1940 (CAH).

19. HHR, "Galway: The Night the *Athenia* Went Down," in *The Song of Things Begun*, ed. Hazel H. Ransom (Austin: The University of Texas at Austin, 1988), 50.

20. Heller, "City of Flint's Voyage."

21. HHR, notes (Collection of Hazel Ransom, HRHRC). By the year 2005, largely on account of Ransom's impetus, UT's library holdings—8,482,207 volumes—would rank below only eight American universities: Harvard, Yale, UC Berkeley, UCLA, Illinois at Urbana–Champaign, Columbia, Michigan, and Cornell (*Chronicle of Higher Education,* 20 May, 2005, A19).

22. Robert Wilson, interview by author, Austin, 18 December 1989. Heller, *Daily Texan,* notes that Ransom "had been denied shipment of 6,000 microfilms he'd made in connection with his research work." A UT News and Information press release (21 April 1942) reported HHR's statement that UT might become the wartime depository for more than 1,750,000 frames of microfilm records from the International Copyright League's historical commission. HHR chaired the commission. At the time a decision was pending as to whether to deposit them at UT or at the League offices in New York.

23. Frank Dobie, letter to HHR, 29 March 1941 (CAH).

24. Preface supplied by F. E. Abernethy, Secretary-Editor of the Texas Folklore Society, in letter to author, 25 April 1991.

25. Sunny (Neeley) Thurmond, telephone interview by Irene Wong, Tyler, Texas, 11 September 1992. Like Evelyn Buzzo, Sunny found Ransom's mother good company. She would visit Marion often during Ransom's early months on military assignment in Florida.

26. Frances "Sug" (Mueller) Danforth, telephone interview by Irene Wong, Austin, 11 September 1992. "We never dreamed he would be President of the University in those days," recalled the former Sug Mueller.

27. *The Self-Pronouncing New Testament* (Philadelphia: National Bible Press, n.d.) (HRHRC). On the verso of the endpaper he recorded the names of his mother's cousin and his two half-sisters: "Miss Grace McIntosh . . . Victoria," "Mrs. Harold J. Darcy . . . N. O.," and "Mrs. Jean Barron Hurlbut Asheville, N. Carolina."

28. HHR, telegram to Mrs. Marion G. Ransom, 27 July 1942 (HRHRC).

29. HHR, letter to Major Gass, 9 August 1942 (USouth).

30. Wilson Hudson, interview.

31. Willis Pratt, interview.

32. HHR, telegram to Mrs. Marion G. Ransom, 5 November 1942 (HRHRC).

33. Newspaper clipping, undated (HRHRC).

34. "Separation Qualification Record," Army of the United States, 1946 (HRHRC).

35. *Daily Texan,* 13 December 1970 (CAH).

36. "Report of the Memorial Resolution Committee for Harry Ransom," Documents and Minutes of the General Faculty, 2 September 1977.

37. Playbill (HRHRC). Hazel lived in Alexandria, Virginia, at this time, so possibly they attended this performance together.

38. Gerald Langford, interview by author, Austin, 10 September 1990.

39. "Legion of Merit Awarded UT Prof," newspaper clipping, undated (HRHRC). Ransom was one of six officers to receive this award for public relations, including Major Benjamin J. Grant, Jr., who knew Ransom in Orlando and was responsible for bringing Ransom to Washington.

40. Purvis, "Dr. Ransom's Father Gives Academic Mark."

41. HHR, memorandum to Colonel Bowman, 15 May 1946 (CAH).

42. Kenneth R. Williams, letter to HHR (CAH). Williams, Director of the Educational Services Division, wrote to Ransom: "I indeed regret that circumstances did not permit you to work with us."

43. Newspaper clipping, undated (HRHRC).

44. HHR, letter to "Darling" (Hazel), 10 August 1946 (photocopy in author's possession). In 1990, while researching Ransom's birthplace for this book, the author dropped into a bookstore in Galveston—that of Frank I. Mapes, 1919 Strand—and mentioned the biography project. Mr. Mapes produced some letters written by Hazel to Ransom; they had been tucked into some books that he purchased. Mapes gave the letters to the author, who returned them to Hazel. In gratitude, Hazel showed the author Ransom's corresponding letters written to her. When Hazel died in 1993, the executor of her estate, Miguel Gonzalez-Gerth, did not find these among her possessions; presumably she had destroyed this correspondence. Thus, the letters quoted here constitute the only glimpse of intimate devotion that the author can document in their very private lives.

45. HHR, letter to "Darling," 12 August 1946 (photocopy in author's possession).

46. HHR, letter to "Hazel darling," 4 July 1946 (photocopy in author's possession).

47. Arthur H. Scouten, letter to author, St. Germain-en-Laye, France, 16 February 1991. After holding the instructorship at UT Austin from 1943 until 1946, Scouten, a specialist in seventeenth- and eighteenth-century British drama, went on to a distinguished teaching career at the University of Pennsylvania.

48. Burns, *Awkward Embrace*. 71.

49. HHR, letter to "Hazel darling," 4 July 1946.

50. HHR, letter to "Darling," 16 August 1946 (photocopy in author's possession).

51. HHR, letter, 10 August 1946.

52. Hudson, interview.

53. Pratt, interview.

54. HHR, letter, 12 August 1946.

55. L. L. Click, letter to HHR, 21 April 1947 (HRHRC).

56. Mrs. Charles E. Goodell, letter to HHR, 4 June 1948 (CAH).

57. Hazel Ransom, interview.

58. Marriage Service Book, Memorabilia Box 1 (HRHRC). The bridal register at Trinity Episcopal Church in Galveston, Texas, lists only the Reverend John Caskey and a relation of Edward H. Gibson, the officiating minister, as the Ransoms' witnesses.

59. The house, located at 2428 Jarratt, was purchased from a professor of Romance languages, Carl Alvin Swanson, who had taught at UT for nearly thirty years. Ransom paid $500 down and contracted to pay $100 a month.

60. Hazel Ransom, interview. At the end of a dinner party in 1989 at the home of Chancellor Hans Mark, Hazel Ransom was chatting in the front foyer with the present biographer's wife, Irene. They were talking about Irene's children when Mrs. Ransom, waiting for her escort, Dr. Miguel Gonzalez-Gerth, leaned toward Irene and confided, "You know, Harry really wanted to have a son."

61. "Ransom Rites to be Held at Trinity," newspaper clipping, undated (HRHRC).

62. Marion Ransom's funeral service program, Trinity Episcopal Church, Victoria, Texas, 1 September 1953 (HRHRC).

63. HHR, letter to Allen Hazen (CAH).

64. HHR, letter to Mrs. George W. Goodson, 15 August 1960 (CAH).

CHAPTER SIX

1. Jeri Clausing, "Creators of 'The Fantasticks' Celebrate UT Roots," *On Campus*, 4 March 1991, 3.

2. "Load Sheet in English," Spring 1949 (CAH).

3. "UT Faculty Council Report on Modified Service," 13 December 1949 (CAH). Ransom also continued his scholarship, publishing "Ownership of Literary Titles," *Studies in English* 31 (1952): 125–35.

4. Ben Grant, letter to HHR, 6 August 1950 (CAH). Grant, later executive vice president of *U.S. News and World Report*, had served with Ransom in Orlando and Washington.

5. Patricia Billfaldt, letter to author, 27 May 1990.

6. HHR, letter to A. P. Brogan, 18 July 1951 (CAH).

7. Barnes, interview. Reflecting back, Robert J. Barnes thought that he might have been the one who first coined the term "being Ransomized."

8. Marshall, letter.

9. Amy Jo Long, interview by author, Austin, 8 July 1990.

10. "Dr. Ransom Is Luncheon Speaker for Standard Club," newspaper article, undated (CAH).

11. "Report of the Memorial Resolution Committee," 2 September 1977.

12. "Dr. Harry Ransom to Talk at DRT [Daughters of the Republic of Texas] 'Historical Evening,'" *Austin American-Statesman*, 13 May 1955; "Report of the Memorial Resolution Committee."

13. "Social Workers to Hear Ransom," *Austin American-Statesman*, 9 April 1954.

14. "Ransom Says Grades Vital," *Daily Texan*, 8 November 1955.

15. "Language Arts and the Teacher," University of Texas News Service, 9 August 1955.

16. Hazel Ransom, interview, 17 January 1990.

17. William S. Livingston, interview by author, Austin, 3 October 2004.

18. Ralph B. Long, letter to HHR, 15 July 1955 (CAH).

19. Winifred Vigness, telephone interview by author, Lubbock, 2 October 1992.

20. Peter T. Flawn, interview by author, Austin, 5 October 2004.

21. Kenneth Ashworth, interview by author, Austin, 5 October 2004.

22. Winfred P. Lehmann, interview by author, Austin, 3 October 2004.

23. Billfaldt, letter.

24. HHR, speeches in Clarence Cline, comp., "Bibliography of Harry Huntt Ransom," University of Texas at Austin, 1971.

25. HHR, *The First Copyright Statute: An Essay on an Act for the Encouragement of Learning, 1710* (Austin: University of Texas Press, 1956).

26. Langford, interview.

27. HHR, letter to C. P. Boner, 26 January 1956, 3–4 (CAH).

28. HHR, letter to Allen Hazen, 11 January 1954 (CAH).

29. "Ransom Elected to Board Position," *Daily Texan,* 9 January 1955 (CAH).

30. Press release, UT News Service, 8 December 1955 (CAH).

31. HHR, memorandum to "Dr. Wilson and Dr. Boner," August 1956, 10 (CAH).

32. HHR, "UT Gets a New Kind of Foundation," *Alcalde,* April 1956, 187.

33. Carl Howard, "Program Stimulates Literary Criticism," *Daily Texan,* 19 December 1957.

34. Henri Peyre, letter to HHR, 25 December 1957 (CAH). Peyre's topic was "Contemporary Literary Criticism in France."

35. HHR, letter to Robert W. Coonrod, 30 January 1961 (CAH). This was a letter of recommendation for Handy to the dean of Montana State University, Missoula.

36. Roger Shattuck, letter to author, 15 June 1992.

37. William S. Livingston, interview by author, Austin, 3 October 2004.

38. William Burford, letter to HHR, 23 September 1958 (CAH).

39. Henrietta Jacobsen, interview by author, Austin, 6 October 2004.

40. John Silber, Boston, telephone interview by author, 3 October 2004.

41. HHR, memorandum to C. P. Boner, undated (CAH).

42. Almetris Marsh Duren and Louise Iscoe, *Overcoming: A History of Black Integration at the University of Texas* (Austin: University of Texas at Austin, 1979), 5.

43. John Silber, Boston, telephone interview by author, 3 October 2004.

44. James Pinckey Hart had served as chancellor of the UT System from 1950 until 1953; in 1954, the chancellorship was abolished.

45. Graves Landrum, interview by author, Austin, 7 March 1991.

46. Landrum, interview by author, Austin, 16 February 1990.

47. J. C. Dolley, "Report on Progress in Fiscal and Building Matters," in Ed C. Gullion, letter and enclosures to HHR, 21 December 1959, 3 (CAH).

48. Siva Vaidhyanathan, "Ex-UT President, Logan Wilson, Dies," *Austin American-Statesman,* 8 November 1990, B1–4.

49. W. Gordon Whaley, letter to HHR, 5 August 1957 (CAH).

50. HHR, letter to W. Gordon Whaley, 8 August 1957 (CAH).

51. Joe B. Frantz, letter to HHR, 22 July 1957 (CAH).

52. HHR, "A Sense of Mission," speech delivered to Committee of 75 and guests

on 6–7 September 1957. Copies of the speech were included in W. D. Blunk, letter and enclosures to members of Committee of 75, 7 October 1957 (CAH).

53. HHR, "Great Expectations," press release, UT News and Information Service, 10 January 1958.

54. Richard M. Morehead, "UT Observes Anniversary," *Dallas News,* 11 January 1958.

55. Logan Wilson, "Roads to Realization," in Ed C. Gullion, memorandum.

56. T. R. Fehrenbach, *Lone Star: A History of Texas and the Texans* (New York: Collier Books, 1968), 667.

57. Martin Waldron, "Books Rival Athletics at the U. of Texas," *New York Times,* 2 January 1973 (HRHRC).

58. Thomas H. Law, telephone interview by Irene Wong, Austin, 28 September 1989.

59. HHR, letter to Thomas Murray Kryger, 11 February 1960 (CAH).

60. Gerhard J. Fonken, interview by author, Austin, 9 February 1990.

61. Press release, UT News and Information Service, 6 August and 22 October 1959; Otis A. Singletary, memorandum, 30 June 1959 (CAH).

62. HHR, "The Superior Student," *Texas Quarterly,* Summer 1949, vi.

63. Press release, UT News & Information Service, 6 August 1959.

64. "Arts and Sciences," The University of Texas, Fall 1959, 6–7 (CAH).

65. Frances Hudspeth, letter to F. Warren Roberts, 2 May 1958 (CAH).

CHAPTER SEVEN

1. "Texas Historians Sell 200 Books," *Daily Texan,* 18 May 1949 (CAH). For a version of the speech, see HHR, "Swante Palm: 1815–1899," in HHR, *The Other Texas Frontier* (Austin: University of Texas Press, 1984), 59–72.

2. HHR, letter to A. W. Yeats, 21 May 1956 (CAH).

3. HHR, letter to Henry Goodard Leech, 18 September 1956 (CAH).

4. Program in HRHRC.

5. "Women Pioneers in Texas Libraries," Texas Library History Colloquium, Austin, 27 April 1990. The conference featured presentations by Clara L. Sitter and Margaret A. Cox documenting Fannie Ratchford's contributions to the University of Texas.

6. Clara Loewen Sitter, "The History and Development of the Rare Books Collections of the University of Texas Based on Recollections of Miss Fannie Ratchford," M.L.S. thesis, University of Texas at Austin (1966): 38.

7. Clara L. Sitter, interview by author, Austin, 27 April 1990. According to Sitter, this gracious gesture also assuaged Ratchford's concerns about security for the rare materials in her charge—there would be less movement by the patrons and staff, and no losses of books.

8. Margaret A. Cox, interview by author, Austin, 27 April 1990.

9. Cox, interview.

10. Hazel Ransom, interview by author, Austin, 11 April 1991.

11. Harold Billings, "The Woman Who Ran Ransom's University," in *The Texas Book,* ed. Richard A. Holland (Austin: University of Texas Press, 2006), 25. Billings testified that Ratchford obligingly allowed him to "wander as I wished" (letter to author, 28 July 2007).

12. Fannie Ratchford, *The Brontës' Web of Childhood* (New York: Columbia University Press; London: Oxford University Press, 1941).

13. "Littlefield Bought Wrenn Collection," newspaper article, 6 April 1956 (CAH). Accounts have varied through the years about the actual number of books in the Aiken Library. For instance, Sitter's 1966 thesis says 5,000 (38); Ratchford had alluded to 6,000 ("Growth of the Rare Book Collections," 1947, CAH).

14. John Carter and Graham Pollard, *An Enquiry into the Nature of Certain Nineteenth-Century Pamphlets* (New York: Charles Scribner's Sons, 1934).

15. See John Collins, *The Two Forgers: A Biography of Harry Buxton Forman and Thomas James Wise* (New Castle, Delaware: Oak Knoll Books, 1992), 253–67.

16. Among other accounts, Richard D. Altick, *The Scholar Adventurers* (New York: Free Press, 1950), 40.

17. For example, *Between the Lines: Letters and Memoranda Interchanged by H. Buxton Forman and Thomas J. Wise,* ed. Fannie Ratchford. Intro. by Carl Pforzheimer (Austin: University of Texas Press, 1945). Altick praised Ratchford's work and relied on her accounts in retelling the stories of Charlotte Brontë's juvenilia and Wise's forgeries in his landmark study, *The Scholar Adventurers* (1950).

18. Sitter, "The History," 43.

19. Sitter, "The History," 69.

20. Sitter, "The History," 52.

21. Fannie Ratchford, letter to Dudley K. Woodward, 9 May 1949 (HRHRC).

22. HHR, letter to C. P. Boner, 7 December 1955 (CAH).

23. Fannie Ratchford, "Growth of the Rare Book Collections," 1947 (CAH). Three similar drafts of this document exist.

24. D. T. Starnes, Leo Hughes, and Harry Ransom, "A Recommendation of the Committee on Rare Book Collections," 10 February 1948 (CAH). Ransom took it upon himself to write to President T. S. Painter as "an individual teacher" on 10 March 1949, recommending "a change that benefited the director of the RBC" and a reorganization of the RBC "that recognized its true purpose" (HRHRC).

25. "Memorandum for Administration of the RBC," 28 July 1953 (HRHRC).

26. Richmond Bond, letter to HHR, 19 May 1957 (CAH).

27. According to John B. Thomas III, Ratchford took the precaution of paying for these refreshments herself (*Collecting the Imagination: The First Fifty Years of the Ransom Center,* ed. Megan Barnard. Intro. by Thomas F. Staley [Austin: University of Texas Press, 2007], 12).

28. F. Warren Roberts, unpublished memoir, 1996, TS, 8–9.

29. Fannie Ratchford, unsigned typescript copy of letter to T. S. Painter, 22 April 1948 (retired campus file: 1948, HRHRC). John Chalmers, librarian at the HRHRC, located this letter for the author. No reply from President Painter was found.

30. Logan Wilson, letter to R. H. Griffith, 27 January 1954 (HRHRC).

31. Fannie Ratchford, letter to Logan Wilson, 18 May 1954 (HRHRC).

32. HHR, memorandum to "Dean Boner," 31 May 1954 (CAH).

33. Fannie Ratchford, letter to HHR, 7 December 1956 (HRHRC).

34. Lewis Hanke, memorandum to A. P. Brogan, 19 June 1956 (HRHRC).

35. HHR, letter to A. P. Brogan, 22 June 1956 (HRHRC).

36. HHR, letter to Logan Wilson, 23 October 1956 (HRHRC).

37. Ann Bowden, interview by author, Austin, 26 January 1997.

38. The entirety of the Pforzheimer Library did not go to UT. In 1987 the Pforzheimer Foundation donated the Shelley and Romantics materials to the New York Public Library, and certain other collections were sold or dispersed elsewhere.

39. Press release, UT News and Information Service, 8 December 1956.

40. "Library Research Center Proposal," *Austin American-Statesman,* 9 December 1956 (CAH).

CHAPTER EIGHT

1. *Texas Quarterly* 1 (Spring 1958).

2. Albert J. Griffith, "Good Words from Texas," *Austin American-Statesman,* 9 March 1958 (CAH).

3. "The Texas Quarterly," *UT Record,* Winter 1957–1958. The UT News and Information Service issued this quarterly publication.

4. HHR, memorandum, "The Texas Quarterly," 1 September 1958 (CAH).

5. HHR, letter to Roger Shattuck (CAH).

6. By 1960 these two women had been promoted on the masthead to positions as Assistant to the Editor and Research Associate, respectively.

7. Edwin T. Bowden, interview by author, Austin, 27 September 1989.

8. HHR, letter to Dr. E. M. Clark, 11 February 1960 (CAH).

9. Griffith, "Good Words."

10. "The Texas Quarterly," *Dallas News,* 11 March 1958.

CHAPTER NINE

1. Fannie Ratchford, letter to David F. Foxon, 14 June 1957 (HRHRC).

2. HHR, letter to Henry Allen Moe, 6 November 1956 (CAH).

3. HHR, letter to Henry Allen Moe, 21 November 1956 (CAH).

4. HHR, letter to A. Moffit, University Librarian, 21 June 1957 (CAH).

5. HHR, letter to William ("Bill") Friday, 28 January 1957 (CAH).

6. HHR, letter to William ("Bill") Friday, 8 February 1957 (CAH).

7. HHR, letter to Rosalie Oakes, 20 May 1957 (CAH).

8. Richmond Bond, letter to HHR, 3 March 1957 (CAH).

9. HHR, letter to Will Clayton, 8 April 1958 (CAH). Gifts from Mr. and Mrs. Will Clayton of Houston, Mr. and Mrs. St. John Garwood of Austin, and the M. D. Anderson Foundation of Houston made possible this enormous acquisition.

10. HHR, letter to Ellen Garwood, 12 February 1957 (CAH).

11. William S. Livingston, note to author, 20 September 2005.

12. Anita Brewer, "UT Launching Drive to Save Vital Papers," *Austin American-Statesman,* 3 March 1957, C-1.

13. HHR, letter to Will Clayton, 10 September 1957 (CAH).

14. HHR, memorandum to Logan Wilson, 18 April 1957 (CAH).

15. W. O. S. Sutherland, interview by author, Austin, 29 September 1989.

16. HHR, "Rare Books in Texas," 1957 (CAH).

17. Bud Mims, "Ransom Views Changes," *Daily Texan,* 4 October 1957 (CAH).

18. HHR, letter to Fannie Ratchford, 2 January 1958 (CAH). This is the first of two letters that Ransom wrote to Ratchford the same day.

19. Fannie Ratchford, letter to HHR, 9 January 1958 (CAH).

20. HHR, letter to Fannie Ratchford, 14 January 1958 (CAH).

21. HHR, letter to Jack Stillinger, 2 December 1957 (CAH).

22. HHR, letter to William B. Todd, 10 December 1957 (CAH).

23. William B. Todd, interview by author, Austin, 26 October 1989.

24. Ann Bowden, interview by author, Austin, 26 October 1989. Ransom had previously met Alfred and Blanche Knopf in New York City.

25. Winfred P. Lehmann, interview by author, Austin, 3 October 2004.

26. Harold Billings, "The Woman Who Ran Ransom's University," 22.

27. F. Warren Roberts, telephone interview by author, Austin, 26 January 1997.

28. Frances Hudspeth, memorandum to HHR, 4 March 1970. Hudspeth listed the expenditures for 1969–1973, including "Humanities Research Center Outstanding Obligations as of 31 August 1970" (HRHRC).

29. Typed memorandum, "Payable in 1972–73," 17 July 1972, accompanied by a three-page list of acquisitions from the House of El Dieff (HRHRC).

30. HHR, letter to Lew David Feldman, 10 December 1957 (CAH).

31. HHR, letter to Lew David Feldman, 15 March 1958 (CAH).

32. Lew David Feldman, letter to HHR, 15 October 1958 (CAH).

33. Lew David Feldman, letter to HHR, 24 March 1958 (CAH).

34. HHR, letter to Lew David Feldman, 19 March 1959 (CAH).

35. HHR, letter to Lew David Feldman, 20 August 1962 (CAH).

36. Charles Hamilton, *Auction Madness: An Uncensored Look Behind the Velvet Drapes of the Great Auction Houses* (New York: Everest House, 1981), 20–21.

37. Roberts, interview.

38. Nicholas A. Basbanes, *A Gentle Madness: Bibliophiles, Bibliomanes, and the Eternal Passion for Books* (New York: Henry Holt and Company, 1995). Subsequently Bas-

banes would marvel at the fact that the HRHRC "owns twenty-seven of the exceedingly scarce first editions of James Joyce's *Ulysses*, published in 1922." Many of these were inscribed by Joyce to various recipients. These volumes, together with proof sheets and correspondence in the extensive Joyce holdings in the HRHRC, enable scholars to "study the work through every stage of the creative process" (*A Splendor of Letters: The Permanence of Books in an Impermanent World* (New York: HarperCollins, 1993), 249–50.

39. HHR, letter to Robert Barnes, 21 March 1961 (CAH).

40. Anthony Rota, interview by author, Houston, 3 November 1989. Rota's *Books in the Blood: Memoirs of a Fourth-Generation Bookseller* (New Castle: Private Libraries Association/Oak Knoll Press, 2002) would mention Ransom and praise his amazing memory, which enabled him to resume in mid-paragraph a year-old conversation (105–7).

41. Reported by Dr. Miguel Gonzalez-Gerth, interview by the author, Austin, 7 October 2004.

42. HHR, "Announcing the Offer to Texas of the Ellery Queen Law Enforcement Collection," 18 November 1957 (HRHRC).

43. HHR, untitled draft about the Ellery Queen collection (HRHRC).

44. Notes in Box 3U362 (13) in CAH.

45. HHR, letter to Mrs. Frederic Dannay, 17 July 1958 (CAH). Ransom did succeed in procuring Dannay a one-semester Professorial Lectureship in Writing, and wrote to inform the Dannays that "the later months of autumn and winter in Austin are, almost without exception, really beautiful."

46. Quoted by Cathy Henderson, "The Birth of an Institution: The Humanities Research, 1956–1971," in *Collecting the Imagination*, 30.

47. Richard W. Oram, "'Going Toward a Great Library at Texas': Harry Ransom's Acquisition of the T. E. Hanley Collection, in *The Texas Book: Profiles, History, and Reminiscences of the University*, ed. Richard A. Holland (Austin: University of Texas Press, 2006), 158, 153.

48. Roberts, interview.

49. F. Warren Roberts, unpublished memoir, 1996, TS, 13.

50. HHR, letter to Dr. Merton M. Minter, 2 June 1959 (CAH).

51. David A. Randall, letter to HHR, 25 September 1958 (CAH).

52. HHR, letter to David A. Randall, 2 October 1958 (CAH).

53. HHR wrote the introduction to the catalogue that celebrated the opening of "An Exhibition of the Occasion of the Opening of the T. E. Hanley Library," 17 November 1958.

54. HHR, letter to William J. Burke, 24 July 1958 (CAH).

55. "Alcalde Explains Academic Center," *Daily Texan*, 1 July 1958 (CAH).

56. HHR, "Comments on the Undergraduate Academic Center," unpublished notes, March 1958? (CAH).

57. HHR, letter to E. G. Fletcher, 11 November 1958 (CAH).

58. Graves Landrum, letter to Logan Wilson, 19 December 1960 (CAH).

59. HHR, memorandum to Olen Clements, *Houston Chronicle*, 21 January 1960 (CAH).

60. Frances H. Hudspeth, letter to Stark Young, 8 February 1960 (CAH).

61. Richard M. Morehead, "New UT Center Helps Attract World-Famed Library Gift," *Dallas News,* 10 July 1960 (CAH).

62. HHR, memorandum to Clements.

63. HHR, letter to J. Frank Dobie, 31 December 1957 (CAH).

64. J. Frank Dobie, letter to HHR, 5 January 1958 (CAH).

65. HHR, letter to J. Frank Dobie, 12 May 1960 (CAH).

66. J. Frank Dobie, letter to HHR, 8 December 1960 (CAH).

67. "Design Summary for Academic Center," a fourteen-page booklet with floor plans in CAH.

68. Margaret C. Berry, *Brick by Golden Brick: A History of Campus Buildings at The University of Texas at Austin, 1883–1993* (Austin: LBCo Publishing, 1993), 96. The Academic Center was later renamed the Peter T. Flawn Academic Center.

69. J. Frank Dobie, letter to HHR, 7 November 1958 (CAH).

CHAPTER TEN

1. HHR, letter to Logan Wilson, 12 June 1958 (CAH).

2. Regents' minutes, 20 September 1958 (CAH).

3. HHR, letter to Winfred P. Lehmann, 7 August 1958 (CAH).

4. HHR, letter to Joe C. Thompson, 31 July 1958 (CAH).

5. HHR, letter to Giles E. Dawson, 8 September 1958 (CAH).

6. HHR, letter to Thompson.

7. HHR, letter to Lawrence Clark Powell, 26 September 1958 (CAH).

8. Lawrence Clark Powell, *Return to the Heartland: Reminiscences of Texas Books and Book People* (Dallas: DeGolyer Library, 1987), 2.

9. HHR, letter to Logan Wilson, 22 August 1958 (HRHRC).

10. HHR, "Proposed Organization of the Humanities Research Center, Main University, 1958–59" (HRHRC).

11. HHR, letter to Donald Gallup, 29 August 1958 (CAH).

12. Harold Billings, "The Woman Who Ran Ransom's University," 26.

13. HHR, letter to James Meriwether, 19 August 1959 (CAH).

14. HHR, "Annual Report, 1958–1959," 24 November 1959 (CAH).

15. "The Masses at UT," *Dallas News,* 3 December 1959 (CAH).

16. *Texas Quarterly* 2 (Summer 1959): ix.

17. "Ransom Reveals Junior Fellows," *Daily Texan,* 12 April 1959 (CAH).

18. Shirley Bird Perry, interview by author, Austin, 5 October 2004.

19. "SDX to Hear Harry Ransom," *Austin American-Statesman,* 18 January 1959 (CAH).

20. "University Group to Hear Speech by Dr. Ransom," *Dallas News,* 2 March 1959 (CAH).

21. "University Chief to Address Exes," *Big Spring [Texas] Herald,* 24 February 1960 (CAH).

22. Press release, UT News and Information Service, 12 October 1959 (CAH).

23. Press release, UT News and Information Service, 20 November 1959 (CAH).

24. "Future Goals of University up to Texans," *Daily Texan,* 13 December 1959 (CAH).

25. "Ransom Outlines Four 'Stress Areas,'" *Daily Texan,* 15 February 1959 (CAH).

26. HHR, memorandum to Logan Wilson for the Academic Affairs Committee, 12 June 1959 (CAH).

27. "Junior College Role Cited by Ransom," *Daily Texan,* 10 February 1960 (CAH).

28. Robb Burlage, "Investigate Potential Power of Students, Ransom Urges," *Daily Texan,* 10 December 1958 (CAH).

29. Burns, *Awkward Embrace,* 62.

30. "Estimation of Construction Periods and Cash Requirements, 1959–1960" (CAH, 3U364 [13]).

31. HHR, letter to Leonard Broom, 16 February 1959 (CAH).

32. W. A. ("Bill") Cunningham, letter to HHR, 24 August 1959 (CAH).

33. HHR, letter to W. A. Cunningham, 31 August 1959 (CAH).

34. Helen Hargrave, letter to HHR, 20 February 1959 (CAH).

35. HHR, letter to Helen Hargrave, 27 February 1959 (CAH).

36. HHR, letter to Duane Howard, 23 February 1959 (CAH).

37. HHR, letter to Winfred P. Lehmann, 18 October 1960 (CAH).

38. List attached to a letter from HHR to Dr. D. W. Bronk, 25 May 1959 (CAH).

39. HHR, letter to Price Daniel, 2 March 1959 (CAH).

40. HHR, letter to Richmond Bond, 19 March 1959 (CAH).

41. HHR, letter to Richmond Bond, 1 June 1959 (CAH).

42. HHR, letter to R. J. Lewallen, 1 February 1960 (CAH).

43. HHR, letter to Jim T. Booth, 23 August 1960 (CAH).

44. HHR, letter to Edwin W. Gaston, Jr., 23 September 1960 (CAH).

45. Information in 3U372 (22), CAH.

46. Information in 3U360 (1), CAH.

CHAPTER ELEVEN

1. "Science, Industry, and the University's Overview," *Texas Quarterly,* 3 (Spring 1960). Also reprinted in *Austin American-Statesman,* 17 April 1960.

2. Anita Brewer, "University's 'Ivory Tower' Is No More, Ransom Says," *Austin American-Statesman,* 26 October 1960 (CAH).

3. DeWitt C. Reddick, letter to HHR, 26 October 1960 (CAH).

4. William C. Gardiner (1933–2000), interview by author, Austin, 16 November 1990.

5. Gardiner, interview.

6. HHR, letter to William Friday, 14 July 1960 (CAH).

7. Hamilton A. Mathes, letter to HHR, 1 December 1960 (CAH).

8. HHR, note to Frances Hudspeth, undated (CAH).

9. Ernestine Wheelock, "President Calm Despite Busy Schedule," *Austin American-Statesman,* 23 October 1960 (CAH). Wheelock would later become editor of *Alcalde,* the magazine of the UT Ex-Students' Association.

10. Bob Sherrill, "Ransom Says UT's No 'Rabbit Warren,'" *Austin American-Statesman,* 31 August 1960 (CAH).

11. Conoly Cullum, "Trend Indicts Education, New UT President Says," *Dallas Herald,* 18 May 1960 (CAH).

12. "UT's Admission Policy Liberal, Ransom Claims," *Dallas Herald,* 5 October 1960 (CAH).

13. Press release, UT News and Information Service, 12 September 1960 (CAH).

14. Press release, UT News and Information Service, 1 October 1960 (CAH).

15. Winfred P. Lehmann, letter to HHR, 9 September 1960 (CAH).

16. HHR, letter to Winfred P. Lehmann, 19 September 1960 (CAH).

17. Jack R. Maguire, "Resolution of the Ex-Students' Association," 8 November 1960 (CAH).

18. Helen Hargrave, letter to HHR, 1 October 1960 (CAH).

19. R. Henderson Shuffler (1908–1975), letter to HHR, 2 December 1960 (CAH).

20. HHR, letter to W. W. ("Bill") Heath, 26 May 1960 (CAH).

21. *UT Record,* 6, no. 1 (Winter 1960), in CAH.

22. HHR, memorandum to Logan Wilson, 7 December 1960 (CAH).

23. J. C. ("Jodie") Thompson, letter to HHR, 26 September 1960 (CAH).

24. HHR, letter to "Jodie," 28 September 1960 (CAH).

25. Quoted by Jack Maguire, "Harry Ransom: The Liveliest Experimenter of All," *Alcalde,* March 1961, 6; reprinted in Burns, *Awkward Embrace,* 61.

26. HHR, letter to John Fielden, 29 April 1960 (CAH).

27. George W. Hoffman, letter to HHR, 29 November 1960 (CAH).

28. HHR, letter to George W. Hoffman, 5 December 1960 (CAH).

29. Jim G. Ashburne, letter to HHR, 30 November 1960 (CAH).

30. HHR, letter to Jim G. Ashburne, 1 December 1960 (CAH).

31. Frank Land, "Tuition, etc., Ransom Topic," *Daily Texan,* 29 November 1960 (CAH).

32. *New York Times* book review, 20 November 1960, reprinted in "Circular Letter," American Association of Land-Grant Colleges and State Universities, 15 December 1960 (CAH).

33. Raymond Brooks, "UT's Wilson Quits; Ransom Gets Post," *Austin American-Statesman,* 11 December 1960 (CAH).

34. "Dr. Ransom to Assume New Position on April 1," unidentified newspaper clipping (CAH). Columbia University–educated Dr. Joseph R. Smiley had been con-

firmed as Ransom's successor as vice president and provost at the regents' meeting on September 5, 1960.

35. File 3U378 (1) in CAH. It should perhaps be noted that at UT, in contrast with some other universities, the office of president is under that of chancellor.

36. Graves Landrum, interview; Lincoln memento in HRHRC.

37. William S. Livingston, interview by author, Austin, 3 October 2004.

38. Richmond Bond, letter to HHR, 12 December 1960 (CAH).

39. HHR, letter to Richmond Bond, 21 December 1960 (CAH).

40. "Those Who Write the News Honor Those Who Make It," *Austin American-Statesman,* 1 January 1961, 9 (CAH).

41. HHR, letter to F. Warren Roberts, 6 February 1958 (CAH).

42. *Time* allowed the *Austin American-Statesman* to run an advance summary, "Two at UT Are Praised," undated newspaper clipping (CAH).

43. Ronnie Dugger, letter to HHR, 23 September 1960 (CAH). Clark Kerr and the University of California would be featured on the magazine cover. The article highlighted the California Master Plan that assigned students to three levels of schools according to their abilities.

44. HHR, letter to Ronnie Dugger, 4 November 1960 (CAH).

45. Ronnie Dugger, letter to HHR, 13 November 1960 (CAH).

CHAPTER TWELVE

1. Subsequent chancellors, beginning with Charles A. LeMaistre in 1971, would reside in Bauer House, an elegant West Austin property on three acres at 1909 Hill Oaks Court, purchased by UT Regent William H. Bauer and his wife, Louise, and originally intended for occupancy by the Ransoms, although as things turned out they never lived there.

2. Hoyt Purvis, "Dr. Ransom Satisfied by Remaining Busy," *Daily Texan,* 15 December 1960, 1–2 (CAH).

3. Jack Maguire, "Harry Ransom: The Liveliest Experimenter of All," *Alcalde* 49 (March 1961): 6–8.

4. The source of the quotation was Art Department Chairman Donald Goodall (Bob Sherrill, "Ransom: Room at the Top," *Texas Observer,* 23 December 1960).

5. Kathleen G. Hjerter, who would become curator of the Harry Ransom Humanities Research Center, quoted by Nicholas A. Basbanes, *A Gentle Madness: Bibliophiles, Bibliomanes, and the Eternal Passion for Books,* 328.

6. Sherrill noted that "artificial light bothers his eyes. To avoid grading papers and preparing his lessons by lamplight, he used to show up at his office in the tower at the first break of day, to work by natural light—and, coincidentally, build a reputation for early-rising industry" (Sherrill, "Ransom").

7. Margaret Berry, interview by author, Austin, 13 November 1989.

8. Edwin T. Bowden, interview by author, Austin, 27 November 1989.

9. John Silber, Boston, telephone interview by author, 3 October 2004.

10. Norman Hackerman, interview by author, Austin, 3 October 2004.

11. Henrietta Jacobsen, interview by author, Austin, 6 October 2004.

12. Hackerman interview.

13. William S. Livingston, interview by author, Austin, 3 October 2004.

14. Harold Billings, interview by author, Austin, 19 August 1991.

15. Hackerman interview.

16. Pat Roberts, interview by author, Austin, 4 October 2004.

17. Billings, interview.

18. Billings, "The Woman Who Ran Ransom's University," 31.

19. Billings, interview.

20. Press release, UT News and Information Service, 19 January 1961 (CAH).

21. Elconan H. Saulson, letter to D. M. "Buck" McCullough, 9 February 1961 (CAH).

22. HHR, "Speech by Dr. Harry Ransom—January 30, [1961]," TS (CAH).

23. Stephen E. Clabaugh, letter to D. M. "Buck" McCullough, 13 February 1961 (CAH).

24. Leonard Broom, letter to HHR, 10 February 1961 (CAH).

25. HHR, letter to Leonard Broom, 15 February 1961 (CAH).

26. D. M. "Buck" McCullough, memorandum to "All Staff and Faculty Members," 17 February 1961 (CAH).

27. Trueman O'Quinn, letter to HHR, 18 February 1961 (CAH).

28. Leonard Broom, letter to HHR, 17 February 1961 (CAH).

29. HHR, letter to Forty Acres Club, 7 March 1961 (CAH).

30. Record of membership (CAH). Taylor Branch's *Pillar of Fire: America in the King Years, 1963–65* (New York: Simon & Schuster, 1998), a book about the dramas behind the civil-rights movement, gives credit to Lyndon B. Johnson for finally breaking down the Forty Acres Club color barrier by escorting an African American White House secretary to a New Year's Eve reception there in 1963 (199–200).

31. Correspondence, 18 January 1961 to 4 February 1961 (CAH).

32. "Last Chance to Be Great Seen for UT," *Dallas News,* 31 August 1962 (CAH).

33. "Ransom Talks on Problems" (full text of speech), *Daily Texan,* 30 November 1962, 8; Carlos Conde, "UT Leader Appeals to South's Schools," *Dallas News,* 29 November 1962 (CAH). Despite Ransom's views expressed in these types of remarks, Dwonna Goldstone takes a condemnatory view of Ransom as well as the UT Regents in *Integrating the Forty Acres: The 50-Year Struggle for Racial Equality at the University of Texas* (Athens: University of Georgia Press, 2006).

34. "Ransom Lauds Bank Chairman," *Daily Texan,* 16 March 1962 (CAH).

35. "Technology Is Sweeping U.S., Executives Told," *Port Arthur [Texas] News,* 22 March 1962 (CAH).

36. HHR, memorandum to Logan Wilson, 7 December 1960 (CAH).

37. Press release, UT News and Information Service, 10 March 1961.

38. "Educational Requirements for the Nuclear-Space Age," 28 August 1962, type-script copy; "Regimenting of Mind Hit by Chancellor Ransom," *Austin American-Statesman,* 29 August 1962; "UT Chancellor Urges Hard-Work Education," *Houston Post,* 29 August 1962 (CAH).

39. Graves W. Landrum, autograph notes to author, 21 December 1989.

40. Thornton Hardie, letter to HHR, 8 August 1962 (CAH).

41. "Dr. Ransom Named to Rhodes Post," *Dallas News,* 7 December 1961 (CAH).

42. "UT Chancellor Heads SACS Unit," *Dallas Morning News,* 1 December 1962 (CAH).

43. HHR, "Education During the Scientific Revolution," *Texas Quarterly* 5, no. 3 (Autumn 1962): 6, 8–9; condensed by Olen Clements, "Education Has Cut Loose," *Houston Chronicle,* 16 December 1962; excerpted in *Chronicles of Opinion on Higher Education: 1955–1975,* ed. Hazel Ransom (Austin: University of Texas at Austin, 1990), 86–87.

44. HHR, "Educational Resources in Texas," collected in *Chronicles of Opinion,* 37, 41, 42–43. Also see *The Conscience of the University,* 24–25.

45. "Valuable Volume of 'Alice,'" *National Observer,* 10 December 1962 (CAH).

46. The Earl of Crawford, letter to "Dear Sir," 31 December 1961; *Book Collector* 8 (Spring 1959): 11–12.

47. HHR, letter to the Earl of Crawford, 9 February 1962 (HRHRC).

48. HHR, letter to William B. Todd, 13 March 1962 (HRHRC).

49. Bertram Rota, letter to HHR, 11 April 1962 (HRHRC). These materials did make their way to the HRC.

50. Anthony B. Rota, letter to F. Warren Roberts, 8 May 1962 (HRHRC).

51. Bertram Rota, letter to HHR, 26 November 1962 (HRHRC).

52. James H. Drake, letter to HHR, 10 May 1962 (HRHRC).

53. Barbara Schmidt, "A Strange Case of the Disputed Millets," *The Twainian* (January–February 2003): 1–4; reprinted http://www.twainquotes.com/disputedmillets .html, 11/18/2005.

54. Larry Carver, "Topolski at the Ransom Center," British Studies Seminar presentation, 2 February 2001, Harry Ransom Humanities Research Center, http://www. felikstopolski.com/HRC.html.

55. HHR, letter to Elvin M. Smith, 16 January 1961 (CAH).

56. Richard West, "Ransom Emphasizes Financial Problems," *Daily Texan,* 21 October 1962 (CAH).

57. Press release, UT News and Information Service, 1 March 1962.

58. John McKetta, interview by author, Austin, 10 November 1989; Graves W. Landrum, interview by author, Austin, 22 February 1990.

59. Graves W. Landrum, "Conversation Notes with Mr. W. W. Heath, 9:45 AM–12:45 PM," 22 February 1962 (CAH).

60. Thornton Hardie, letter to HHR, 24 October 1961 (CAH).

61. HHR, letter to Thornton Hardie, 24 April 1961 (CAH).

62. Henrietta Jacobsen, interview by author, Austin, 6 October 2004.

63. "Daily Aide: The Silent Secretary/1961," memorandum book (CAH).

64. Frances Hudspeth, letter to Jack Maguire, 29 March 1961: "Dr. Ransom has your note reminding him to discuss the housing of the 'Lyndon Johnson Papers' permanently at the University of Texas. . . . He will certainly bring the matter up when he talks with Mr. Johnson in April" (CAH).

65. HHR, letter to John B. Connally, 16 January 1961 (CAH).

66. "Dr. Ransom Says Move Talk Untrue," *Austin American,* 28 January 1961 (USouth).

CHAPTER THIRTEEN

1. Harry and Hazel Ransom, telegram to Frank C. Erwin, Jr., 22 March 1963 (CAH). Erwin was tapped after W. St. John Garwood's appointment was not ratified by the Texas Senate because of his reputed political liberalism (Norman Hackerman, interview by author, Austin, 12 September 1990; William S. Livingston, note to author, 20 September 2005).

2. HHR, "Statement to the Committee on Budget and Personnel Policy," 1 May 1963 (CAH).

3. Graves W. Landrum, interview by author, Austin, 22 February 1990.

4. The capable Dr. Hackerman had been a member of the Manhattan Project that created a nuclear weapon, had developed equipment to homogenize milk, was becoming a recognized expert on metal corrosion, and would chair the National Science Board.

5. HHR, "Annual Report of the Chancellor to the General Faculty" (revised version), 29 October 1963 (CAH).

6. "Faculty Can OK Politico, Ransom Says," *Daily Texan,* 16 December 1963 (CAH).

7. Willie Morris, "Renaissance at the University of Texas," *Harper's* magazine, June 1963, 76–86.

8. "He Believed in a Dream, and Made It a Reality," *Houston Chronicle,* 18 August 1963.

9. Ransom first delivered this speech at the Sigma Delta Chi Awards Banquet in Dallas on May 11, 1963; reprinted in *Texas Quarterly* 6 (Summer 1963).

10. "Dr. Ransom Hits Proposal to Curb Fund Soliciting," *Daily Texan,* 28 March 1963. The *Daily Texan* used the *Dallas Morning News* as its source for this article.

11. Richard M. Morehead, "Dr. Ransom Foresees," *Dallas News,* 2 June 1963 (CAH).

12. HHR, "Education? Talk Isn't Enough," *Houston Chronicle,* 27 January 1963 (CAH).

13. *Houston Chronicle,* 8 September 1963 (CAH).

14. HHR, "Universities Shouldn't Waste Money, Mustn't Waste Minds," *Daily Texan,* 3 October 1963 (reprinted from *Houston Chronicle*) (CAH).

15. HHR, "The Frontier Stereotype Is Pretty Phony History," *Houston Chronicle,* 13 October 1963.

16. John McKetta, interview by author, Austin, 8 October 2004.

17. Press release, UT News and Information Service, 8 July 1963 (CAH).

18. "Chancellor Named to Special Group," *Daily Texan,* 10 December 1963 (CAH). Other members of that committee included Mayor Lester Palmer, Dan Crowley, chairman of the Chamber of Commerce, and representatives from Bergstrom Air Force Base, the local newspaper, television and radio stations, public relations firms, and the state legislature.

19. "Chancellor Ransom Presides at Ground-Breaking Services," *Daily Texan,* 27 September 1963 (CAH).

20. "Ransom Stresses Importance of Generation's Engineers," *Daily Texan,* 4 December 1963 (CAH).

21. Darrell Royal, telephone interview by author, Austin, 16 October 1990. Ransom took on the critics of Royal's academic status in "Prof Royal Is Defended," *Austin American-Statesman,* 17 March 1964.

22. Dave Oliphant, interview by author, Austin, 12 September 1989. A quarter of a century later Oliphant would write for the *Texas Observer* (14 July 1989, 20) an appreciative assessment of Ransom's pronouncements, linking him with other native-born Texans such as Walter Prescott Webb, Eugene C. Barker, and J. Frank Dobie. "Harry Ransom has willed to the state the most far-reaching intellectual inheritance of them all," Oliphant would declare.

23. "Ransom Now Chairman," *Daily Texan,* 4 January 1963 (CAH).

24. Honorary certificate in CAH.

25. "TCU Graduates to Hear Ransom," *Dallas Morning News,* 26 May 1963 (CAH).

26. Lon Tinkle, "Amory's Quotable Notables," *Dallas News,* 1 December 1963 (CAH). Tinkle, a personal friend of Ransom, was reviewing *Celebrity Register,* ed. Cleveland Amory and Earl Blackwell (New York: Harper & Row, 1963).

27. Norman Hackerman, vice chancellor for academic affairs, compiled a detailed list of "non-monetary gifts received" from various HRC donors in 1963 (CAH).

28. "Conrad Manuscript Bought for $21,000," *New York Times,* 9 May 1963 (CAH).

29. HHR, letter to Ezra Pound, 7 October 1964 (HRHRC).

30. Ann Holmes, "A Texas Brag for the Books," *Zest Magazine* in *Houston Chronicle,* 15 September 1963 (CAH).

31. HHR, "Introduction to the Chancellor's Presentation of the University of Texas System Budget Requests," 12 February 1963 (CAH).

32. "General Statement," The University of Texas, Main University, 1964 (CAH).

33. HHR, "Report of the Chancellor," press release, UT News and Information Service, 2 November 1964 (CAH).

34. Julius Glickman, letter to author, 30 October 1989.

35. Charles Ward, "'Academic Progress' Is Given Added Meaning by Ransom," *Daily Texan,* 3 April 1964 (CAH).

36. "UT To Get Oil Portrait of Ransom," *Austin American-Statesman,* 30 March 1964 (CAH).

37. E. G. Morrison, "Presentation of Ransom Portrait," TS, 4 April 1964, 2 (CAH).

38. W. W. Heath, "Acceptance of Ransom Portrait," TS, 4 April 1964, 2 (CAH).

39. "Remarks Selected from Panel Discussion," press release, UT News and Information Service, 15 October 1964.

40. Royal, interview.

41. "Rumors Say Ransom to Quit at UT," *Houston Chronicle,* December 1963 (USouth).

42. Decherd Turner, interview by author, Austin, 27 July 1991.

43. Graves W. Landrum, interview by author, Austin.

44. HHR, "Memorandum to the Executive Committee," 17 August 1964 (HRHRC).

45. "Statement by Chairman Heath," press release, UT News and Information Service, 16 May 1964 (CAH).

46. It would later be pointed out that Cora Eiland Hicks had been hired earlier as a teaching assistant in English, making her technically the first black person who taught in a UT classroom.

47. "Ransom Favors Rice Integration," *Daily Texan,* 14 February 1964 (CAH).

48. W. W. Heath, letter to HHR, 9 June 1964 (CAH).

49. W. W. Heath, letter to HHR, 6 August 1964 (CAH).

50. HHR, letter to W. W. Heath ("Bill"), 10 August 1964 (CAH).

51. "Dr. Ransom Joins Local Bank Board," *Daily Texan,* 12 February 1964 (CAH).

52. "Harry Ransom Named to Panel," *Austin American-Statesman,* 10 April 1964 (CAH).

53. "LBJ Forms Student 'Fellows,'" *Daily Texan,* 4 October 1964 (CAH).

54. "Dr. Ransom to Chair Panel at White House," *Austin American-Statesman,* 12 August 1964 (CAH).

55. "President Honored," *Charleston [South Carolina] News and Courier,* 1 June 1964 (USouth).

56. John De La Garza, "Mrs. Johnson Pays Surprise Visit to UT," *Houston Chronicle,* undated (USouth).

57. "Two College Presidents: An Exchange of Views," *One of a Kind* [series], 1 March 1964, CBS television network.

58. David Boroff, "Cambridge on the Range," *Saturday Review,* 20 June 1964, 48–65.

59. Regents minutes, 7 November 1964 (CAH).

CHAPTER FOURTEEN

1. Sam Keach, "'UT in Transition'—Ransom," *Daily Texan,* 17 March 1965 (CAH). The text of this speech was issued in a press release from the UT News and Information Service and reprinted in *Alcalde,* May 1965, 10–13.

2. Shirley Bird Perry, interview by author, Austin, 9 February 1990.

3. Glen Castlebury, "Ransom Asks Aid of Texas Editors," *Austin American-Statesman*, 24 January 1965 (CAH).

4. Press release, UT News and Information Service, 20 February 1965 (CAH).

5. HHR, letter to Thornton Hardie, 10 March 1965 (CAH).

6. HHR, notes for Bo Byers, 4 January 1965 (CAH).

7. TS, notes of a testimonial for Heath, 13 July 1964 (CAH).

8. Kenneth Ashworth, interview by author, Austin, 5 October 2004.

9. "UT Chancellor Denies Rumor He May Resign," *Austin Statesman*, 17 March 1965 (CAH).

10. "Heath Says, 'Ransom Staying With UT,'" *Austin Statesman*, 20 March 1965 (CAH).

11. Ronnie Dugger, *Our Invaded Universities: Form, Reform, and New Starts* (New York: W. W. Norton & Company, 1974), 98–99. Ransom had apologized to Johnson after the presidential election of 1960 for "not being able to become active in a cause of first consequence to American education"—the Kennedy-Johnson campaign—owing to "present University regulations." He assured Johnson it was "a matter about which I cared and still care a great deal, both personally and professionally" (HHR, letter to Lyndon B. Johnson, 21 December 1960 [CAH]).

12. William S. Livingston, interview by author, Austin, 17 January 1990.

13. W. W. Heath, letter to HHR, 11 May 1965. Included "Letter of Intent" (CAH).

14. Mrs. Lyndon B. Johnson ("Lady Bird"), letter to W. W. Heath ("Bill"), 5 February 1966 (CAH).

15. Frank C. Erwin, Jr., letter to William S. Livingston, 12 September 1966 (CAH). Dr. Otis Singletary (1921–2003), a historian specializing in the Mexican-American War, was destined to become the eighth president of the University of Kentucky, a post he would hold for eighteen years (1969–1987).

16. Press release, UT News and Information Service, 23 January 1965. Conservative Democrat Preston Smith would succeed Governor Connally.

17. In April 1967, for instance, the Coordinating Board recommended to the governor and the legislature that the University of Texas be allowed to open a dental school in Dallas and a medical school in Houston. Harry Ransom and Frank C. Erwin, Jr., issuing a joint news release, registered their gratification at receiving this permission (Press release, UT News and Information Service, 3 April 1967).

18. "The Law and the Citizen," press release, UT News and Information Service, 30 April 1965 (CAH).

19. "Relevant Earlier Actions of the Board Concerning Unified Administration," 19 May 1965 (CAH).

20. HHR, "Memorandum for the Organization Committee," 1965 (CAH).

21. Sixty of these orange books would be discovered in 2003 and deposited in the Center for American History (interview with Arthur H. Dilly, Austin, 7 October 2004).

22. HHR, letter to W. W. Heath ("Bill"), 21 June 1965 (CAH).

23. HHR, letter to Virginia Dabney, 11 August 1964 (CAH).

24. Gayle McNutt, "UT Raids Treasure Trove," *Houston Post,* 6 February 1966.

25. M. S. Handler, "Manuscript of 'In His Steps,' Pastor's Best Seller, Auctioned," *New York Times,* 26 January 1966.

26. "Herrick Book is Auctioned for $95,200," *Austin Statesman,* 29 June 1965 (CAH).

27. "Harry H. Ransom Finally Confronts Harry H. Ransom," *Daily Texan,* 8 April 1964 (PH in CAH).

28. "Power of the Prairies," *Time* magazine, 2 July 1965, 82.

29. Howard Mumford Jones, letter to HHR, 21 September 1965 (CAH).

30. "New UT Library to House LBJ Papers," *Fort Worth Star-Telegram,* 10 August 1965. The General Services Administration, a federal agency, operated presidential libraries after their establishment.

31. Press release, UT News and Information Service, 8 September 1965 (CAH).

32. "Chancellor's Reception," *Daily Texan,* 18 February 1966 (CAH).

33. Frances Hudspeth, letter to Leo Perper, 8 November 1965 (CAH).

34. Amy Jo Long, interview by author, Austin, 8 September 1990.

35. HHR, "Report to the General Faculty," 15 November 1965 (CAH).

36. "Ransom Urges Technology Use," *Daily Texan,* 18 February 1966 (CAH).

37. "Speakers Told: Texas Today and Tomorrow," *Daily Texan,* 1 March 1966 (CAH).

38. *The Rag* 1, no. 8 (28 November 1966): 20.

39. Graves W. Landrum, interview by author, Austin, 22 February 1990.

40. Graves W. Landrum, interview by author, Austin, 19 February 1990.

41. *Houston Post,* 15 March 1966 (CAH).

42. Gary W. Chason, letter to W. W. Heath, 30 March 1966 (CAH).

43. Glenn A. Welsch, letter to HHR, 16 March 1966 (CAH).

44. Samuel P. Ellison, Jr., letter to HHR, 16 March 1966 (CAH).

45. Irwin Spear and Robert Montgomery, press conference, 16 March 1966 (CAH).

46. H. J. "Doc" Blanchard, letter to HHR, n.d. (CAH).

47. W. W. Heath, press release, 1 April 1966 (CAH).

48. "Ransom Sets Date for 'Speech' Panel," *Daily Texan,* 18 March 1966 (CAH).

49. Judy Zaffirini and Kay Canter, "Chancellor Ransom Testifies to Importance of Libraries," *Daily Texan,* 24 March 1966 (CAH).

50. Stephen Neuville, "Engineers' Role Vital," *Daily Texan,* 1 April 1966 (CAH).

51. John J. McKetta, interview by author, Austin, 10 November 1989.

52. "Dr. Ransom to Address College Seniors," *Dallas News,* 20 May 1966. Honorary certificate in HRHRC.

53. Graves W. Landrum, interview by author, Austin, 10 November 1989.

54. Long, interview.

55. George Kuemple, *Daily Texan,* 2 August 1966. Reprinted as "Sniper's Terror Ends with 15 Dead," *Daily Texan,* 1 August 1991.

56. Over the years, however, the Tower attracted visitors with suicidal intentions; when nine individuals had leaped at intervals from the deck, the UT administration closed it again on October 28, 1974, reopening it thereafter for special authorized tours (Laura Leman, "25 Years Later, Witnesses Reflect on Tower Massacre," *Daily Texan*, 1 August 1991, 12, 15).

57. Robin Wilson, "Officials of Universities That Have Been Targets of Past Killers View U. of Florida Tragedies with Horror and Concern," *Chronicle of Higher Education*, 12 September 1990, A33.

58. "Ransom Cited for Work in UT Development," *Houston Chronicle*, 18 December 1966 (CAH).

59. Cigarette boxes and commendation certificate in HRHRC.

60. W. W. Heath, "Statement," 5 November 1966 (CAH).

61. HHR, letter to W. W. Heath ("Bill"), 23 November 1966 (CAH).

62. Frank C. Erwin, Jr., letter to members of the Board of Regents, 7 December 1966 (CAH). Erwin promptly showed his concern about the faculty's welfare by asking Ransom to "pay immediate and urgent attention" to the lack of office telephones for UT professors. "If I were a professor . . . , that would be the first fringe benefit that I would demand," Erwin wrote. Most faculty members still had to make and receive their "Centrex System" calls in cramped hallway booths (Frank C. Erwin, Jr., letter to HHR, 27 March 1967 [CAH]).

CHAPTER FIFTEEN

1. William Burford, "The Chancellor," in William Burford, *A Beginning* (New York: W. W. Norton, 1966).

2. Olivia Dwight, *Close His Eyes* (New York: Harper, 1961).

3. Joe Neal, interview by author, Austin, 5 April 1991. Ransom relied on Dr. Neal for special assignments.

4. HHR, letter to "Professor Adams," 25 September 1958 (CAH). HHR wrote, "I do not think that any man should be persuaded to stay among surroundings he dislikes to carry on work in which he finds no satisfaction." Adams would subsequently become a prominent professor of critical theory at the University of Washington after being an administrator at the University of California at Irvine.

5. Hazard Adams, *The Horses of Instruction* (New York: Harcourt, Brace & World, 1968). Adams eventually wrote two other academic novels with different settings as well as a revealing critique of the world of higher education.

6. Margaret Mayer, "Is Texas Gauche? Washington Thinks So," *Dallas Times Herald*, 17 October 1971, 10-B.

7. Horace Busby, "Memorandum for John Macy," 16 December 1964 (Lyndon Baines Johnson Library). Hereafter LBJ Library. Busby (1924–2000) had edited the *Daily Texan* and worked as a reporter in Austin before joining Johnson's staff.

8. Graves W. Landrum, interview, 22 February 1990.

9. Burns, *Awkward Embrace,* 63.

10. Dugger, *Invaded Universities,* 114.

11. "The University of Texas," December 1966 report, TS (CAH).

12. David Nevin, "Texas—What a State!" *Life* magazine, 1 July 1966. An excerpt was reprinted in "Research Facilities for Humanities Match Laboratories for Sciences," *Development Newsletter,* August 1966.

13. Carolyn Bengston, "She Entertains Beautifully . . . and Is Pretty, Too," *Austin American-Statesman,* 22 January 1967 (CAH).

14. "A Letter to President Johnson," *Austin American-Statesman,* 5 March 1967, A7.

15. Carmichael adopted the name Kwame Ture after he emigrated to Guinea in 1968.

16. Press release, UT News and Information Service, 22 April 1967 (CAH).

17. James L. Grantham, letter to HHR, 25 April 1967 (CAH).

18. Robert S. Strauss, letter to the *Daily Texan,* 26 April 1967 (CAH).

19. Wales Madden, Jr., letter to HHR, 27 April 1967 (CAH).

20. Jack Holland, dean of students during this period of unrest, was a person on whom Ransom depended for many things. He later took Holland with him into the System office.

21. Press release, UT News and Information Service, 1 May 1967.

22. "Statement of Chancellor Harry Ransom," UT News and Information Service, 3 May 1967.

23. "Notes for Dr. Ransom on Discussions in Regents' May 1967 Meeting" (CAH).

24. "Notes for Dr. Ransom on Discussions in Regents' May 1967 Meeting" (CAH). The final act of the drama surrounding the Students for a Democratic Society rally against Hubert Humphrey's visit transpired on January 26, 1968, when the Texas System Board of Regents affirmed the penalty assessed by the Faculty Committee on Discipline against six UT students charged with violating the chancellor's order by speaking at the unauthorized meeting on April 23, 1967. The six students were placed on disciplinary probation until June 1968, but were allowed to attend classes provided that they did not engage in "any similar violations of University regulations." This decision was approved by newly appointed President Norman Hackerman and Chancellor Harry Ransom. (SDS had already been reinstated as an approved student organization in November 1967.) The students had argued that they believed the chancellor's order violated their Constitutional right of free speech and expression, and that they therefore did not feel obligated to obey it. Frank C. Erwin, Jr., Board chairman, wrote a statement to accompany the university's opinion. "We have all too frequently heard this argument that each citizen has a right to make a subjective judgment about the legal and/or moral rightness of every rule or regulation. . . . Fortunately, there is no legal support for any such course of conduct. The fact is that when any citizen violates a rule or regulation duly promulgated by appropriate authority, he does so at his peril." Since the students had appealed their probation to the regents, this opinion effectually exhausted their ability to seek relief within the UT System.

25. HHR, "The State University as Book Collector," speech to Pittsburgh Biblio-philes, 18 May 1967 (HRHRC).

26. "Maugham Items Sold in London," *New York Times*, 22 November 1967.

27. Certificate in HRHRC.

28. Burns, *Awkward Embrace*, 66–67.

29. John Silber, letter to HHR, 14 June 1967 (CAH).

30. HHR, letter to Frank C. Erwin, Jr., 21 June 1967 (CAH). Ransom's letter may have been a hint to Erwin to temper his public remarks after Ransom received a copy of a letter from Erwin to Norman Hackerman, Vice Chancellor for Academic Affairs, regarding Erwin's refusal to submit any rules and regulations of the Board of Regents to "the Faculty Council, the Austin Chapter of the AAUP, [or] the Faculty Committee of Counsel on Academic Freedom" for their "approval or disapproval."

31. Among other accounts, Richard A. Holland, "Thirteen Ways of Looking at Chairman Frank," *The Texas Book*, 68.

32. Hackerman, interview.

33. John R. Silber, letter to HHR, 4 January 1965 (CAH).

34. "Regents' Unit OK's Position," *Daily Texan*, 8 October 1967.

35. Wilson, interview.

36. Perry, interview.

37. "Ransom Tells Procedures for Recommending Officer," *Austin American*, 10 October 1967 (CAH). See also "Committee to Advise Regents on President," *Daily Texan*, 10 October 1967.

38. "Panel of 10 to Help Select UT at Austin President," *Fort Worth Star-Telegram*, 10 October 1967. Shirley Bird Perry sensed that Frank C. Erwin, Jr., "deliberately be-came the lightning-rod for issues like [the reports of] decreased faculty workloads in order to protect Ransom and his University. Ninety percent of the faculty were within the guidelines, anyway—only Arrowsmith and a few others had special prerogatives. Legislators thanked Erwin for 'cleaning that place up.' And Harry got to keep his *mys-tique*." Perry, interview.

39. "Chancellor Harry Ransom's Report to the General Faculty," press release, UT News and Information Service, 19 October 1967. Also reported in "Growth Heart of UT System, says Ransom to Faculty," *Daily Texan*, 20 October 1967 (CAH).

40. Ann Watson, "Ransom Quits Presidency of UT Without Any Pomp," *Dallas Times Herald*, 22 October 1967 (CAH).

41. *Alcalde*, July/August 1990, 12.

42. HHR, "For Discussion with N. H.," 1 November 1967 (CAH).

43. Press release, UT News and Information Service, 10 May 1968.

CHAPTER SIXTEEN

1. HHR, *The Song of Things Begun: A Selection of Verse*, ed. Hazel Ransom (Austin: The University of Texas at Austin, 1988), 7.

2. Hazel Ransom, too, had a privately expressive side. In 1995, Professor Miguel Gonzalez-Gerth, sorting her papers, came upon a collection of short stories with modernistic, daring themes that she had written and never published out of loyalty to her husband's public image.

3. Hazel Ransom, interview, 17 January 1990.

4. HHR, *The Song of Things Begun,* 11, 27, 58, 59.

5. Hazel Ransom reproduced examples of Ransom's artful doodles in *The Song of Things Begun.*

6. Amy Jo Long, memorandum to HHR, 1 March 1968.

7. Frank C. Erwin, Jr., letter to HHR, 29 March 1968. A copy of the telegram from Scoggins was attached (CAH).

8. HHR, "The Next Decade in Higher Education," *Texas Times,* February 1968 (CAH).

9. HHR, letter to Ima Hogg, 12 March 1968 (CAH).

10. Will Clifford Hogg, son of Texas Governor James S. Hogg and late brother of Ima Hogg, had served on the Board of Regents from August 1912 to January 1917. He had endowed the Hogg Foundation for Mental Health, established in 1939.

11. Press release, UT News and Information Service, 15 January 1968.

12. Press release, UT News and Information Service, 8 November 1968.

13. "Ransom Named," *Daily Texan,* 19 December 1968.

14. TS list of HHR's honors for 1968–69 (CAH).

15. Press release, UT News and Information Service, 28 March 1968. Includes HHR's text of "Overview."

16. Press release, UT News and Information Service, 10 May 1968. In this case it appears that Ransom wrote his own press release and submitted it to the UT News and Information Service.

17. A. Phillips Brooks, "Sharp Criticizes UT System Renovation Cost," *Austin American-Statesman,* 21 July 1991. More than three million dollars, however, were immediately required to renovate and refurbish the buildings. The System administrative offices would move to Claudia Taylor Johnson Hall in 1970, and after 1971 the chancellor's office would be housed in O. Henry Hall.

18. Graves Landrum, interview with author, Austin, 5 January 1990.

19. Press release, UT News and Information Service, 21 June 1968.

20. HHR, memorandum to Norman Hackerman, 8 July 1968 (CAH). Lincoln Gordon (b. 1913) of Massachusetts had served as U.S. Ambassador to Brazil (1961–1966) and Assistant Secretary of State for Inter-American Affairs (1966–1967), and had recently (1967) been named president of Johns Hopkins University, a post he would hold until 1971.

21. *Vogue* magazine, April 1968, 223.

22. HHR, "Academic Anniversary as Educational Prospect," *Texas Times,* December 1968 (CAH).

CHAPTER SEVENTEEN

1. HHR, letter to Ben Barnes, 8 February 1969 (CAH).

2. Frank C. Erwin, Jr., letter to HHR, 1 April 1969 (CAH).

3. HHR, letter to James Lawrie ("Jim"), 17 March 1969 (CAH).

4. "Harry Ransom: Chancellor," *Texas Times,* March 1969 (CAH).

5. HHR, letter to Allen Hazen, 29 July 1969 (CAH).

6. "Summary of Decennial Report on the Humanities Research Center," July 1969 (CAH).

7. Press release, UT News and Information Service, 12 November 1970.

8. John Lehmann, "John Lehmann on a Visit to the Humanities Research Centre, University of Texas," *Times Literary Supplement,* 10 July 1969. Lehmann's comments possessed a special élan inasmuch as an American edition of his autobiography, *In My Own Time: Memoirs of a Literary Life,* had just appeared. A *New York Times Book Review* notice of *In My Own Time* called it "easily the most important account of British life from the thirties to the fifties" and mentioned that Lehmann "has known virtually everyone from T. S. Eliot . . . to Gore Vidal" (Julian Mitchell, "Born with a Silver Pencil in His Hand," *New York Times,* 27 July 1969).

9. Lon Tinkle, "Arbiter Horgan; Austin Treasures," *Dallas News,* 20 July 1969.

10. Anthony Hobson, letter to HHR, 28 October 1969 (CAH).

11. Graves Landrum, interview.

12. C. L. Cline, letter to Frank Erwin, 29 October 1969 (CAH).

13. Ernest Stromberger, "UT Faces the 1970s," *Dallas Times Herald,* 21 December 1969 (CAH).

14. Leslie Taylor, "UT Faces 1970 with Size Problems," *Austin American-Statesman,* 7 January 1970 (CAH).

15. Clifton M. Grubbs, Jr., letter to HHR, 17 January 1970 (CAH).

CHAPTER EIGHTEEN

1. HHR, letter to John Groth, 12 January 1970 (CAH).

2. "TU Chancellor Lists Top Student Qualities," *Houston Post,* 29 January 1970 (CAH).

3. James A. Hall, M.D., letter to HHR, 2 April 1970 (CAH); HHR letter to James A. Hall, M.D., 3 April 1970 (CAH).

4. "Spotlight on Ransom's Role," *Daily Texan,* 7 May 1970 (CAH). At Rice, Dr. Hackerman would bring that university out of a deficit and establish several new schools. In 1985 President Peter T. Flawn would persuade Dr. Hackerman to return to UT Austin to teach, offering him an office and a chemistry laboratory.

5. Graves W. Landrum, interview by author, Austin, 5 January 1990.

6. *Daily Texan,* 9 May 1970. This was a special Saturday edition.

7. Norman Hackerman, interview by author, Austin, 3 October 2004.

8. Graves W. Landrum, interview.

9. John Silber, letter to HHR, 24 May 1970 (CAH).

10. "Ransom Resigns as UT Chancellor," *Dallas Morning News,* 30 May 1970 (CAH).

11. Norman Hackerman, interview by author, Austin, 3 October 2004.

12. Kenneth Ashworth, interview by author, Austin, 5 October 2004.

13. "Dr. Ransom Quits as UT Chancellor," *Austin American-Statesman,* 30 May 1970 (CAH).

14. "Ransom Resigns as UT Chancellor," *Dallas Morning News,* 30 May 1970 (CAH).

15. Kenneth Ashworth, interview.

16. "Ransom Resignation Said His Own Idea," *Dallas Morning News,* 4 June 1970 (CAH).

17. Landrum, interview.

18. Arthur H. Dilly, interview by author, Austin, 29 April 1991.

19. Jenkins Garrett, interview by author, Houston, 2 November 1989.

20. Clarence Cline, letter to author, 4 September 1996.

21. This is the version Blunk himself gave Cline.

22. Merton M. Minter, M.D., letter to "Hazel and Harry," 31 May 1970 (CAH).

23. Mrs. Charles Devall ("Lyde"), letter to "Hazie and Hal," 31 May 1970 (CAH).

24. "Chancellor Emeritus Ransom," *Houston Chronicle,* 7 June 1970 (CAH).

25. Certificate in HRHRC.

26. Mrs. Theophilus S. Painter, letter to "Harry & Hazel," 15 June 1970 (CAH).

27. John B. Connally, letter to HHR, 16 June 1970 (CAH).

28. Lyndon Baines Johnson (LBJ), letter to HHR, 22 June 1970 (CAH).

29. J. J. Pickle, letter to HHR, 15 July 1970 (CAH).

30. Preston Smith, letter to HHR, 1 September 1970 (CAH); Allan Shivers, letter to HHR, 1 September 1970 (CAH).

31. Bertha Dobie, letter to HHR, 15 July 1970 (CAH).

32. HHR, letter to Mrs. Lyndon Baines Johnson, 18 June 1970 (CAH).

33. HHR, letter to "Morris," 22 June 1970 (CAH).

34. Dr. Miguel Gonzalez-Gerth, interview by author, Austin, 7 October 2004.

35. John W. Meaney, letter to HHR, 11 June 1970 (CAH).

36. HHR, letter to John W. Meaney, 19 June 1970 (CAH).

37. William S. Livingston, note to author, 20 September 2005.

38. John McKetta, interview by author, Austin, 8 October 2004.

39. William S. Livingston, note to author, 20 September 2005.

40. "Hackerman Says Erwin Interferes with Management," *Jacksonville (Texas) Journal,* 29 June 1970 (CAH).

41. "Departing Prexy Gives UT Regents Food for Thought," *Abilene Reporter-News,* 5 July 1970 (CAH).

42. Jack Josey, "Statement," 12 September 1970 (CAH).

43. "UT Loses a Good Man," *Houston Post,* 18 September 1970 (CAH).

44. HHR, letter to Jack Josey, 14 September 1970 (CAH).

45. John Silber, telephone interview by author, Boston, 3 October 2004. A variant version of this encounter and its aftermath appears in Deborah L. Bay's "The Influence of Frank Erwin on Texas Higher Education," 345–56.

46. Erwin placed a letter drafted three days previously in front of President ad interim Jordan and said: "Sign that letter. You just fired John Silber." The letter charged Silber with continuing insubordination. Five other people were present at that moment in the chancellor's office (Kenneth Ashworth, interview by author, Austin, 5 October 2004).

47. Quoted in *Scene* magazine, *Dallas Morning News,* 11 December 1977.

48. Edwin Gale, letter to C. B. Smith, 17 December 1970 (CAH). Arrowsmith would go on to prove himself a stern and perpetual critic of English departments, university administrators, classicists, and other targets as he moved restlessly around the country—teaching at Boston University, Princeton University, MIT, Yale University, Johns Hopkins University, New York University, and Emory University until his death in 1992. It was Arrowsmith who had characteristically mocked the décor of the new UT Faculty Club as "dubious Danish and whorehouse provincial" (John Silber, interview). But Arrowsmith's intellectual intensity, exciting classroom performances, brilliant translations, incisive criticism of T. S. Eliot, and co-founding of the *Hudson Review* made his departure seem like a huge loss for Texas, especially when compounded by that of his friends Roger Shattuck and John Silber.

49. Shattuck wrote *The Banquet Years: The Arts in France, 1885–1918* (1958) and *Proust's Binoculars: A Study of Memory, Time, and Recognition* (1963). Eventually, in 1988, he joined John Silber's faculty at Boston University.

50. Vartan Gregorian, letter to author, 31 July 2007. Also recounted in Vartan Gregorian, *The Road to Home: My Life and Times* (New York: Simon & Schuster, 2003), 201–13.

51. John Silber, letter to HHR, 14 September 1970 (CAH).

52. Silber, interview.

53. Hackerman, interview. Ronnie Dugger would analyze the showdown similarly, observing that "Dr. Ransom's apparent distaste for or disinclination concerning frontal personal conflicts rendered him at most a minor factor in the outcome of that struggle. He was too gentlemanly, restrained, and private to tell much in that controversy" (Ronnie Dugger, Somerville, Massachusetts, e-mail to author, 13 June 2007).

54. William S. Livingston, interview by author, Austin, 3 October 2004.

55. Silber, interview.

56. Avrel Seale, "John Silber Gets the Last Word," *Alcalde* 95, no. 6 (July/August 2007): 32–33. Seale's article, the most discerning piece ever written about the background and consequences of Silber's firing, ponders whether Erwin was "a cynical, power-drunk profiteer and Silber a martyr for academic excellence," or whether Erwin was "a visionary and Silber simply a contrarian with a martyr complex" (30).

57. Norman Hackerman, interview by author, Austin, 3 October 2004.

58. Kenneth Ashworth, interview by author, Austin, 5 October 2004. Ashworth

would later serve as the UT vice chancellor for academic affairs (1971–1973) and then move to the new UT San Antonio campus where he became executive vice president.

59. Silber, interview.

60. Ashworth, interview.

61. HHR, letter to Dr. Volterra, 13 July 1970 (HRHRC).

62. Vartan Gregorian, telephone interview by author, New York City, 12 April 2006. See also Gregorian, *The Road to Home: My Life and Times,* 207.

63. Frank C. Erwin, Jr., letter to members of the Board of Regents, 10 August 1970 (CAH).

64. Editor's Notes, *Daily Texan,* 23 September 1970 (CAH).

65. HHR, "The Case for the Large College," *Family Weekly,* 13 September 1970, 10, 20. The deadline for this article came so quickly amid the rush of other events that Ransom prevailed on librarian Harold Billings to carry the manuscript to New York City for him. "An absolute kindness on his part," Billings would term that flight. "First class Braniff, the Algonquin, the dinky office of the *Family Weekly* in a long hall on an upper floor of a Manhattan office building, then trips to the New York Public Library and other libraries" (Billings, letter to author, 30 July 2007). Billings also recounts details about this "generous learning opportunity" in "The Woman Who Ran Ransom's University," *The Texas Book,* 32.

66. HHR, letter to Bryce Jordan, 24 September 1970 (CAH).

67. Leroy Jeffers, letter to HHR, 30 December 1970 (CAH).

68. Tom Sealy, letter to HHR, 30 December 1970 (CAH).

69. John S. Redditt, letter to HHR, 30 December 1970 (CAH).

70. HHR, "Chancellor's Council Comments," *Texas Times,* 15 December 1970, 8 (CAH).

71. Clarence L. Cline, "Harry Ransom: Some Personal Reminiscences," *Texas Times,* 15 December 1970, 6 (CAH).

72. Debby Bay, "Departure Marks End of Era," *Daily Texan,* 13 December 1970 (CAH).

CHAPTER NINETEEN

1. "UT Chancellor Ransom Dons 'Emeritus' Robes," *Austin American-Statesman,* 31 January 1971 (CAH).

2. Arthur Dilly, interview by author, Austin, 29 April 1991. Dilly eventually inherited this portrait.

3. Kathleen Gee, interview by author, Austin, 20 March 1990.

4. Hazel Ransom, interview, 17 January 1990.

5. Anthony Hobson, *Great Libraries* (New York: G. P. Putnam's Sons, 1970).

6. Press release, UT News and Information Service, 8 January 1971.

7. Gordon N. Ray, "The Humanities Research Center of the University of Texas," 26 January 1971 (HRHRC).

8. HHR, letter to Harold E. Mertz, 5 February 1971 (HRHRC).

9. "They Knew Each Other When," *Houston Chronicle,* 21 March 1971 (USouth).

10. Elaine Shelton, letter to author, 13 November 1989.

11. Honorary certificate in HRHRC.

12. "UT Chancellor Emeritus Receives Santa Rita Award," *Austin American-Statesman,* 28 May 1971 (CAH).

13. *AB Bookman's Weekly,* 19–26 July 1971.

14. HHR, "Development of Research Collections at the University of Texas in Recent Years," press release, UT News and Information Service, 18 June 1971.

15. John Silber, letter to "Harry," 30 July 1971 (CAH).

16. HHR, letter to John Silber ("Mr. President"), 11 January 1971 (CAH).

17. Umlauf's "Torch Bearers [of Knowledge]" graced the entrance to the new Academic Center in 1963. Umlauf would retire as an emeritus professor in 1981 after 40 years of teaching. In 1991 he was honored by having 250 sculpture pieces displayed near Barton Creek in a garden ("Staring into the Heavens," *Daily Texan,* 12 June 1991, 5). Subsequently the Umlauf Sculpture Garden was established.

18. Gee, interview.

19. Gee, interview.

20. Gee, interview. Kathleen Gee, an HRC research associate who had been initially hired by Ransom as a secretary in 1970 after returning to Texas from Connecticut, remembered thinking of Mrs. Hudspeth as Ransom's prime minister yet also the person who even planned his meals.

21. Press release, UT News and Information Service, 31 January 1972.

22. Harold Billings, "The Woman Who Ran Ransom's University," *The Texas Book,* 33.

23. C. Fred Folmer, University Librarian, memorandum to faculty, staff, and graduate students, 4 February 1972.

24. Press release, UT News and Information Service, 30 August 1972.

25. Maria X. Z. Wells, interview by author, Austin, 27 September 1989.

26. Honorary certificate in HRHRC.

27. Herbert H. Reynolds, letter to HHR, 22 August 1972 (CAH).

28. HHR, letter to Herbert H. Reynolds, 29 August 1972 (CAH).

29. Martin Waldron, "Books Rival Athletics at the U of Texas," *New York Times,* 12 January 1973.

30. Press release, UT News and Information Service, 19 June 1973.

31. Stephen Spurr, interview by author, Austin, 28 September 1989. Werbow, a professor of Germanic languages, would hold the deanship until an expanded College of Liberal Arts came into being in 1979.

32. William S. Livingston, interview by author, Austin, 3 October 2004.

33. Esther R. Moore, interview by author, Austin, 5 January 1990.

34. Ralph Elder, interview by author, Austin, 19 July 1989.

35. Dugger, *Our Invaded Universities,* 76–77.

36. Decades later, Dugger would recall Ransom as "a civilized and liberal man"

and agree that "certainly the Ransom Center is a permanent addition to the scholarly resources of the country and his role in it secures his place in the record" (Ronnie Dugger, Somerville, Massachusetts, e-mail message to author, 13 June 2007).

37. Margaret Berry, interview by author, Austin, 3 October 2004.

38. Spurr would later allege that Erwin, in his eleventh year as a regent, often acted as a *de facto* chancellor by coming onto the campus to oversee various operations (*Daily Texan*, 2 December 1981). Spurr was allowed to return to teaching forest ecology (he had founded and edited *Forest Science* and co-founded the Organization for Tropical Studies, Inc.) in the Department of Botany and the Lyndon B. Johnson School of Public Affairs. Until his death in 1990, Spurr would thereafter be engaged in a heroic struggle with Parkinson's disease (*Alcalde*, September/October 1990: 91).

39. Arthur H. Dilly, interview by author, Austin, 7 October 2004.

40. Richard Fly, "Spurr Inquiry Will Explore HRC Squabble," *Daily Texan*, 22 October 1974, 1.

41. The historian Hanna Gray would serve as acting president at Yale University in 1977 and then begin a fifteen-year tenure as president of the University of Chicago in 1978.

42. Finally, toward the end of the academic year, the Faculty Senate decided to recommend the resumption of faculty participation in university affairs, and so William S. Livington, the Faculty Senate chairman, issued a summons to another General Faculty meeting. There was a large turnout for this meeting. On the Faculty Senate's recommendation, the General Faculty voted to rescind the actions it had taken in the fall after the appointment of Lorene Rogers (William S. Livingston, notes to author, 20 September 2005).

43. "Harry Ransom Center," *On Campus*, 11 November 1974 (CAH).

44. "UT Stops Paying Library's Bills," *Fort Worth Star-Telegram*, 19 January 1975; Holly Hudlow, "Cutbacks Put HRC in Debt," *Austin American-Statesman*, 19 January 1975; "Power Play Seen in Halt of UT Library Bill Payments," *Dallas Times Herald*, 19 January 1975; "Library Hassle Feeds UT Fires," *San Antonio Express*, 19 January 1975.

45. "UT—Austin Head Blocks Paying Bills of Ransom Center," *Houston Post*, 19 January 1975.

46. Holly Hudlow, "Confusion Caused Part of HRC Debt," *Austin American-Statesman*, 21 January 1975.

47. W. Rea Keast, telephone interview by author, Lebanon, New Hampshire, 13 November 1989.

48. "Artists Affected by Law on Tax Reform," *Houston Post*, 12 May 1975. Any owner *except* the creator could still take a deduction by giving it as a gift to a non-profit institution.

49. "Ransom to Receive Distinguished Alumnus Prize," *Daily Texan*, 24 October 1975 (CAH).

50. Burns, *Awkward Embrace*, 82.

51. May Ellen MacNamara, interview by author, Austin, 8 April 1990.

52. "He stopped smoking long before he died," according to Miguel Gonzalez-Gerth, interview by author, Austin, 7 October 2004.

53. Hazel Ransom, interview.

54. "Heart Attack Fatal to Ransom," *Austin American-Statesman,* 19 April 1976 (CAH); "Ex-Chancellor Ransom Dies, *Austin American-Statesman,* 20 April 1976 (CAH).

55. Press release, UT News and Information Service, 19 April 1976.

56. "Chancellor Emeritus Ransom Dies Unexpectedly," *On Campus,* May 1976 (CAH).

57. "Heart Attack Fatal," *Austin American-Statesman.*

58. "Chancellor Emeritus Ransom Dies at 67," *Daily Texan,* 20 April 1976 (CAH).

59. Brenda Bell, "Ransom Remembered For Human Frailties . . . And His Magic," *Austin American-Statesman,* 5 May 1976 (CAH).

60. Morris Kaplan, "Harry Huntt Ransom, 67, Dies; Texas Educator and Bibliophile," *New York Times,* 20 April 1976.

61. Bell, "Ransom Remembered."

62. Bell, "Ransom Remembered."

63. "Chancellor Emeritus Harry Ransom Dies," *UT Development Newsletter,* Spring 1976, no. 38 (HRHRC).

CHAPTER TWENTY

1. Lon Tinkle, "A Moveable Feast of Art and Literature," *Dallas Morning News,* 6 June 1976, F1–2.

2. "Ransom Memorial," *On Campus,* June 1976 (HRHRC).

3. "Minutes of the Board of Regents," 30 November 1976, 3.

4. Joe B. Frantz, interview by author, 6 November 1989.

5. Margaret Berry, interview by author, 13 November 1989.

6. Berry, interview.

7. Margaret C. Berry, *The University of Texas: A Pictorial Account of Its First Century.* Foreword by Peter T. Flawn (Austin and London: University of Texas Press, 1980). Even though out of print, this volume with its nearly 1,100 photographs nevertheless stands as the most reliable and comprehensive survey of the university's history to date.

8. Joe B. Frantz, *The Forty-Acre Follies* (Austin: Texas Monthly Press, 1983), ix–xi. Complaining about the disappearance of beloved landmarks, for example, Frantz declared that "the University of Texas campus has all the warmth of the Pentagon, and as much concern for tradition" (126).

9. James E. Bauerle, D.D.S., letter to Hazel Ransom, 21 April 1976 (Hazel Ransom Collection).

10. Betty Boatright, letter to Hazel Ransom, 20 April 1976 (Hazel Ransom Collection).

11. Matthew M. Gouger, letter to Hazel Ransom, 18 April 1976 (Hazel Ransom Collection).

12. Hazel Ransom, list provided to Alan Gribben, 9 July 1990.

13. Miguel Gonzalez-Gerth, note to author, August 2005.

14. Harry and Hazel Ransom, *Snow in Austin: A Collection of Photographs from 1895 to 1985* (Austin: Clearstream Press, 1986). Their 77-page book listed the occasional snowfall accumulations and portrayed the resulting white cityscapes and wind-sculpted university campus. Hazel Ransom explained in an introductory sketch that before his death Ransom had set aside pictures for "a small volume of snow scenes."

15. HHR, *Chronicles of Opinion on Higher Education, 1955–1975*, ed. Hazel Ransom. Foreword by Hans Mark (Austin: University of Texas at Austin, 1990).

16. Hazel Ransom, interview, 17 January 1990.

17. Hazel Ransom, notes to Mme. Elizabeth Shoumatoff, 27 August 1977 (HRHRC).

18. "Report of the Memorial Resolution Committee for Harry Ransom," Documents and Minutes of the General Faculty, 2 September 1977.

19. Although done from life, the bust had its detractors; some found the likeness too thin, too angular, too remote-looking. Hazel Ransom felt that the image failed at reproducing Harry's more delicate features, but she respected Umlauf's goal of injecting the face with an aura of inner strength. She regretted that Umlauf kept trying to elevate Ransom's brow and make his forehead craggy-looking (Hazel Ransom, interview by author, Austin, 11 April 1991). A duplicate of the bust would be obtained by the DuPont Library of the University of the South at Sewanee and displayed in its Special Collections gallery.

20. Ann Atterberry, "Buy a Bible? Isn't That Nice?" *Dallas Morning News,* 3 December 1978; Paul Rosenfield, "How Texas Got the Gutenberg Bible," *Dallas Times Herald,* 7 January 1979; Paul Rosenfield, "How to Buy a Gutenberg Bible," *Saturday Evening Post,* April 1979, 58–62.

21. Shirley Bird Perry, interview by author, Austin, 5 October 2004.

22. Robert Reinhold, "The Education of the University of Texas," *New York Times* magazine, 4 December 1983, 64.

23. Pete Szilagyi, "Tough Erwin Overwhelmed UT 'Enemies,'" *Austin American-Statesman,* 5 October 1980.

24. "Top 10 Influential People in UT History," *Texas Alcalde,* March–April 1995, 13.

25. Kenneth Ashworth, interview by author, Austin, 5 October 2004. Ashworth served as Commissioner of the Texas Higher Education Coordinating Board from 1976 until 1997.

26. Harold W. Billings, letter to author, 31 July 2007.

27. Donald L. Weismann, *Follow the Bus with the Greek License Plates* (Ardmore, Pennsylvania: Dorrance & Co., 1981), 24–25, 29.

28. HHR, *The Conscience of the University and Other Essays,* ed. Hazel Ransom (Austin: University of Texas Press, 1982); Press release, UT News and Information Service, 21 December 1982.

29. Although she deeply appreciated the gesture, Hazel Ransom felt that the necessarily posthumous process handicapped the artist and resulted in a flawed final product; the eyes in the painting were too beady and squinting and the face too heavily browed, Hazel maintained privately (Hazel Ransom, interview, 17 January 1990).

30. Dave Oliphant discussed the change in "Collections at Texas," *The Library Chronicle,* no. 27 (1984), 7. The building itself had been known as the Harry Ransom Center since 1974, when the regents renamed it.

31. Miguel Gonzalez-Gerth, interview by author, Austin, 7 October 2004.

32. Decherd Turner, interview by author, 27 July 1991.

33. HHR, *The Other Texas Frontier,* ed. Hazel H. Ransom. Foreword by John Graves (Austin: University of Texas Press, 1984). Reviewed by Shelley Emling, "'Frontier' Presents Forgotten Heroes," *Daily Texan,* 1 February 1985.

34. Lawrence Gibson, "Sewanee Dinner Honors Harry Huntt Ransom," *Sewanee News,* June 1988, 23.

35. HHR, *The Song of Things Begun: A Selection of Verse,* ed. Hazel H. Ransom (Austin: University of Texas Press, 1988).

36. Notes taken by author on 1 May 1989 at the reading in the Knopf Room of the Flawn Academic Center. See also "Ransom's Poetry Due for Reading," *On Campus,* 1–7 May 1989.

37. Jules Loh, "UT Library Amassing Treasures," *Dallas Morning News,* 8 December 1991, 43A, 46A–48A.

38. The aesthetically satisfying transformation of the building and the public programs that the new galleries made possible are described in detail by Megan Barnard, "The Expanding Mission: The Harry Ransom Humanities Research Center, 1988–Present," in *Collecting the Imagination,* 98–104.

39. James Michener, interview by author, Austin, 30 October 1989. See also "Ransom Center Receives Michener Papers," *Harry Ransom Humanities Research Center Bulletin,* no. 29 (Summer 1992), 1, and Nicholas A. Basbanes, *A Gentle Madness: Bibliophiles, Bibliomanes, and the Eternal Passion for Books* (New York: Henry Holt and Co., 1995), 347.

40. "Hazel Ransom, Author, Widow of UT Leader, Dies," *Austin American-Statesman,* 29 August 1993, B3.

41. "Hazel Ransom, Author, Widow of UT Leader, Dies at Age 73," *On Campus,* 7 September 1993; "Hazel Harrod Ransom Remembered," *Harry Ransom Humanities Research Center* 1 (Fall–Winter 1993), 3.

42. "The Estate of Hazel Ransom," *Harry Ransom Humanities Research Center* 4 (Fall–Winter 1996). Additional details from interview with Miguel Gonzalez-Gerth, Austin, 7 October 2004.

43. D. T. Max, "Final Destination: Why Do the Archives of So Many Great Writers End Up in Texas?" *New Yorker* 83, no. 16 (11 & 18 June 2007), 54–71, delivers a glowing tribute to the "mercurial and hard-driving" Staley and his success in adding to the million-plus books, thirty-six million manuscript pages, five million photographs, and ten thousand objects in the Harry Ransom Humanities Research Center.

44. Richard W. Oram, "Years of Consolidation: The Harry Ransom Humanities Research Center, 1972–1988," in *Collecting the Imagination,* 86.

45. "Top 10 Influential People in UT History," *Texas Alcalde,* 14.

46. Robert D. King, interview by author, Austin, 30 September 1989.

47. Earnest F. Gloyna, interview by author, Austin, 8 November 1989.

48. Fonken, interview.

49. Clark Kerr, telephone interview by author, Berkeley, California, 13 August 1990.

INDEX

Brooks, Raymond, 310n33
Broom, Leonard, 156–158
Brown University, 250
Brown v. Topeka Board of Education,
82, *84*
Brown, Ronald M., 264
Browning, Elizabeth Barrett, 53, 94, 122,
262, 280
Browning, Robert, 40–43, 47–48, 53,
262, 280
Bryan, J. P., 109
Bryan, William Jennings, 21
Bull, A. C., 181
Bunyan, John, 33, 41
Burbank, Dr. Reginald, 166
Burdine Hall, *254*
Burdine, John Alton, 85, 216
Burford, William, 81–82, 105–106, 206
Burns, Joan Simpson, 65, 209; *The Awk-
ward Embrace,* 271
Burns, Robert, 40
Busby, Horace, 208, 319n7
Business Administration-Economics
Building, 132
Butler, Roy, 147
Byron, Lord George Gordon, 34, 41, 94–95

Cabeza de Vaca, Álvar Núñez: docu-
ments of, 95
Cakes and Ale (Maugham), 174
California, 42, 170, 172, 227
Calloway, Morgan, Jr., 33, 36
Cambodian bombing, 234, *238,* 240
Cambridge, MA, 27, 114, 139
Cambridge High School, MD, 12–13, 23
Campbell, Killis, 33
Canzoni (Pound), 121
Cap and Gown, 21
Capitular Library, Verona, 233
Carleton, Don, 283
Carlota, Empress, 263
Carlson, Margarette, 104
Carlyle, Thomas, 20, 26–27, 48

Carmichael, Stokely, 210, 213–214, 320n15
Carnegie Corporation of New York, 89,
250
Carnegie Foundation for the Advance-
ment of Teaching, 167, 172, 225, 256
Carne-Ross, Donald S., 81, 215, 249
Caroline, Lawrence, 223, 251
Carpenter, Liz, 272
Carter, John, 94
Carver, Larry, 64, 164
Carysfort, Earl of, 281
Caskey, John, Reverend, 300n58
Catalogue of Horace Walpole's Library
(Hazen), 232
Catholic Student Center, 173
Catto, Mrs. Henry E., Jr., 229
Caxton, William, 77
CBS television network, 183, 203
Celebrity Register (Amory), 174, 315n26
Centennial (Michener), 286
Centennial Observance, University of
Texas, 282
Center for American History, UT Aus-
tin, 265, 283. *See also* Barker History
Center.
Center for American Studies, San Anto-
nio, 181
Chamber of Commerce, Austin, 134, 172
Chancellor's Council, 229, 244, 253–254,
282, 287; founding of, 209; honors
HHR, 292
Channel 7-TV, Austin, 146
Chaucer, Geoffrey, 34, 44
Chicago, IL, 8, 44, 99, 199, 234
Chicago School of literary criticism, 79
*Chronicles of Opinion on Higher Educa-
tion* (Ransom), 280
Churchill, Winston, 60, 256
Civil Rights Act, 192
Civil War, American, 1–2, 171
Clabaugh, S. E., 156
Clark, Edward, 267
Clark, George, 166